ROMANTICISM AND CHILDHOOD

How and why childhood became so important to such a wide range of Romantic writers has long been one of the central questions of literary historical studies. Ann Wierda Rowland discovers new answers to this question in the rise of a vernacular literary tradition. In the Romantic period the child came fully into its own as the object of increasing social concern and cultural investment; at the same time, modern literary culture consolidated itself along vernacular, national lines. *Romanticism and Childhood* is the first study to examine the intersections of these historical developments and the first study to demonstrate that a rhetoric of infancy and childhood – the metaphors, images, figures and phrases repeatedly used to represent and conceptualize childhood – enabled Romantic writers to construct a national literary history and culture capable of embracing a wider range of literary forms.

ANN WIERDA ROWLAND is an Associate Professor of English Literature at the University of Kansas. She has published articles on William Wordsworth, Walter Scott, the Romantic ballad revival, the Romantic novel and sentimental fiction.

D1547226

CAMBRIDGE STUDIES IN ROMANTICISM

This series aims to foster the best new work in one of the most challenging fields within English literary studies. From the early 1780s to the early 1830s a formidable array of talented men and women took to literary composition, not just in poetry, which some of them famously transformed, but in many modes of writing. The expansion of publishing created new opportunities for writers, and the political stakes of what they wrote were raised again by what Wordsworth called those "great national events" that were "almost daily taking place": the French Revolution, the Napoleonic and American wars, urbanization, industrialization, religious revival, an expanded empire abroad and the reform movement at home. This was an enormous ambition, even when it pretended otherwise. The relations between science, philosophy, religion and literature were reworked in texts such as *Frankenstein* and *Biographia Literaria*; gender relations in *A Vindication of the Rights of Woman* and *Don Juan*; journalism by Cobbett and Hazlitt; poetic form, content and style by the Lake School and the Cockney School. Outside Shakespeare studies, probably no body of writing has produced such a wealth of comment or done so much to shape the responses of modern criticism. This indeed is the period that saw the emergence of those notions of "literature" and of literary history, especially national literary history, on which modern scholarship in English has been founded.

The categories produced by Romanticism have also been challenged by recent historicist arguments. The task of the series is to engage both with a challenging corpus of Romantic writings and with the changing field of criticism they have helped to shape. As with other literary series published by Cambridge, this one will represent the work of both younger and more established scholars, on either side of the Atlantic and elsewhere.

For a complete list of titles published see end of book.

ROMANTICISM AND CHILDHOOD

The Infantilization of British Literary Culture

ANN WIERDA ROWLAND

CAMBRIDGE UNIVERSITY PRESS

CAMBRIDGE
UNIVERSITY PRESS

University Printing House, Cambridge CB2 8BS, United Kingdom

Cambridge University Press is part of the University of Cambridge.

It furthers the University's mission by disseminating knowledge in the pursuit of
education, learning and research at the highest international levels of excellence.

www.cambridge.org
Information on this title: www.cambridge.org/9781107479678

© Ann Wierda Rowland 2012

First published 2012
First paperback edition 2014

A catalogue record for this publication is available from the British Library

Library of Congress Cataloguing in Publication data
Wierda Rowland, Ann, 1966–
Romanticism and childhood : the infantilization of British literary
culture / Ann Wierda Rowland.
p.   cm. – (Cambridge studies in romanticism)
Includes bibliographical references and index.
ISBN 978-0-521-76814-6 (Hardback)
1. English literature–19th century–History and criticism.   2. Romanticism–Great Britain.
3. Children in literature.   I. Title.
PR468.C5W54 2012
820.9′007–dc23
2011039517

ISBN 978-0-521-76814-6 Hardback
ISBN 978-1-107-47967-8 Paperback

Contents

Acknowledgments

It is a humbling experience to finish a book and take stock of all the people, occasions, places, ideas and influences that have shaped its course, not in the least because of my acute sense that I cannot possibly remember and reckon all my many debts. My first thanks goes to Ian Duncan whose encouraging and insightful readings of my work from graduate school to the present day, and whose unflagging efforts to promote a magnanimous and spirited exchange of ideas in the field as a whole, have had the most significant impact on my intellectual and professional life. My second thanks goes to Sonia Hofkosh, a terrifically shrewd reader and interlocutor who is also wise in the ways of the academic world and a wonderfully loyal friend. I consider myself tremendously lucky to have been mentored, supported and befriended by two such generous intellectuals and genuine individuals.

While I would have to search hard for any remnants of my Yale dissertation in this volume, the influence of my graduate advisor, Paul Fry, is evident to me on every page. It is to him that I owe my most sustained and satisfying literary project, my study of Wordsworth's poetry. Karen Swann, Katie Trumpener and Penny Fielding wrote thrilling essays and books that changed my intellectual horizons, in addition to offering conversation, support and friendship at critical moments. At one such critical moment, Janet Sorensen, Leith Davis and Ian Duncan gave me an opportunity to write an article for their volume, *Scotland and the Borders of Romanticism*; that article, parts of which can be found in Chapters 4 and 5, is the origin of this present study. I am also grateful for the invigorating work and conversation of Yoon Sun Lee, Mary Favret, Susan Manning and Deidre Lynch.

This book took shape while I was teaching at Harvard and I am particularly indebted to the people I met, taught, worked with and learned from while living in Cambridge. I am especially grateful for the camaraderie of Maureen McLane and her ever ready, always stimulating exchange of work, wit and ideas. For conversation both encouraging and challenging, thanks are also due to Lynn Festa, Eric Eisner, Larry Buell, Sharmila Sen, Jim Engell, Anna Henchman, Marge Garber, Oren Izenberg, the late Barbara Johnson, Robert Koelzer, John Picker, Phil Fisher, Debra Gettelman, Leah Price, Helen Vendler and Eric Idsvoog. I am also grateful for the visiting scholars and regular participants of the Romantic Literature and Culture seminar at the Harvard Humanities Center which I had the privilege of co-chairing with Sonia Hofkosh during my Harvard tenure.

The final stages of this book owe much to the guidance and advocacy of James Chandler. I am grateful to have my work published in the Cambridge Studies in Romanticism series under the editorship of a scholar whose work has had such a profound influence on my own. I am also grateful to Dorice Elliott and my other wonderful colleagues at the University of Kansas for their belief that this project was worth rewarding. The early stages were supported by a fellowship from the AAUW, and a NFGRF award from the University of Kansas allowed me the time to do final revisions.

Friends and family members have shown a steadfast interest in this project, have helped with kids and meals and, perhaps more importantly, given me other things to do and think about when needed. I am particularly thankful for the support and friendship of Geraldine Higgins, Charlotte Iselin, Lisa Egger, Allison Suttle, Sarah Wierda and Liza Townsend. Sarah and Landon Rowland provided incalculable material and intellectual support, and my parents, Daryl and Mary Wierda, provided the ground on which everything becomes possible. In ways I can never reckon, Joshua Rowland made the writing of this book possible, and our children, Alice and Wil, have never let the topic of childhood remain purely academic. This book is for them, for the prattle and trifles of our family life.

Introduction: The infantilization of British literary culture

An anonymous and, frankly, forgettable essay in the September 1807 issue of *Monthly Literary Recreations* takes up the ponderous yet predictable question of "Whether the Present Age Can, or Cannot be Reckoned Among the Ages of Poetical Excellence." Beginning with a restatement of what he describes as the generally held opinion that the present age is characterized by a "mediocrity of talents" in all branches of the arts and sciences, the writer equivocates and ultimately, while claiming to disagree, agrees. "We have not one whose transcendency of genius is capable of electrifying and astonishing the public mind," he admits, but then the public has become so accustomed to excellence that "their minds are no longer capable of being astonished at any thing"; we have no Milton or Shakespeare, he insists, but we do have many who are "far above mediocrity in their writings."[1] Damning with faint praise at the outset, the rest of the short piece is, itself, an exercise in mediocrity as the writer composes his list of above average poets, first apologizing for the omission of "many whom I have either not met with, or at the present moment not recollected," then turning fussy and refusing a few names that did apparently come to mind, but whose inclusion may have "brought [the] list into disrepute."[2]

Only two recent tendencies in contemporary poetry disturb this critic's bland approval and come in for criticism: the "effeminately poetical junto" of the Della Cruscans, on the one hand, and the "over affected simplicity [that] has usurped its place and crept into the works of some of our really otherwise excellent authors" on the other. While the Della Cruscans' "monotonous" harmonies, "affected sensibility" and "glitter of imagery" threaten the "energy of thought and diction, manly feelings and even sense" of present-day poetry, the "simplicity" of poets such as Southey and Wordsworth has also failed to restore manly vigor to the poetry of the age. Indeed, when such poets "descend to what they call their beautifully simple style," they simply remind this critic of the "namby pamby songs of the nursery." It is this identification of "simplicity" as a significant and new feature of recent poetry and, even more interesting for our purposes here, the comparison of this new poetry to nursery rhymes that makes this essay noteworthy.

Noteworthy, however, only as evidence that these rhetorical evocations of the nursery were common currency in literary discussions, for, like the poets he describes, this critic is neither singular nor original in his comparison of contemporary poetry to nursery songs and children's literature. He himself cites a recent review of Wordsworth's poetry by Lord Byron as also criticizing the poet for his nursery sensibility. In that review, which appeared the previous month in *Monthly Literary Recreations* and which Thomas Moore cites as his first, Byron praises some of the pieces in Wordsworth's *Poems in Two Volumes* for their "native elegance" and their "natural and unaffected" sensibility, but he also objects strenuously to many of the poems, especially the series entitled "Moods of my own Mind."[3] These, Byron complains, are written in "language not simple, but puerile" and are "neither more nor less than an imitation of such minstrelsy as soothed our cries in the cradle, with the shrill ditty of 'Hey de diddle, the cat and the fiddle.'" "What will any reader or auditor, out of the nursery, say to such namby-pamby," Byron asks, concluding with the regret that Wordsworth "confines his muse to such trifling subjects."[4]

Criticism of Wordsworth's trivial subjects continued, as did the complaint that his overly simplistic language and trifling subject-matter were products of the nursery or of a childish or infantile sensibility. When Francis Jeffrey's review of *Poems in Two Volumes* appeared the very next month in the *Edinburgh Review*, he also sounds this keynote and develops its theme still further. For Jeffrey, Wordsworth's latest volume continues the "alarming innovation" first evidenced in *Lyrical Ballads* of mixing "originality" and "natural feeling" with "vulgarity," "silliness" and "childishness."[5] It is Wordsworth's diction that is most objectionable to Jeffrey, and he warns that "no poetry can be long or generally acceptable, the language of which is coarse, inelegant or infantine." Jeffrey compares Wordsworth's poems to the "ditties of our common song writers," dismissing them as "namby-pamby," as "babyish absurdity," and as "childish verses" that are the "very paragon of silliness and affectation." When he does praise a piece, such as "The Character of the Happy Warrior" or "Song, at the Feast of Brougham Castle," he points to its "manly lines" and wishes that Wordsworth would "throw aside his own babyish incidents" more often. Jeffrey has praise for Wordsworth's sonnets and admits that there are "occasional little traits of delicate feeling and original fancy" in the two volumes, although they are "quite lost and obscured in the mass of childishness and insipidity." "Resolution and Independence" is singled out for particularly severe censure, but Jeffrey seems to be rendered almost speechless by those poems that unite a childish subject with a child-like style. He simply lists and quotes with almost no commentary what he calls the "ineffable compositions" of "Moods of my own Mind," introducing "My Heart Leaps up When I Behold" – the short piece that contains Wordsworth's most famous line on childhood, "The Child is Father of the Man" – with simply "This is the whole of another," as if the poem manifestly condemns itself in its brevity and triviality. Of the "Ode" that concludes the volume – the poem that will become Wordsworth's most popular in the nineteenth century and the period's manifesto of childhood – Jeffrey can only say: "This is, beyond all doubt, the most illegible and unintelligible part of the publication. We can pretend to give no analysis or explanation of it; – our readers must make what they can of the following extracts."

In the language and images of these reviews, the shape of the larger literary culture – its shared discourse, points of contestation and habits of self-presentation – comes into view. The persistent rhetoric of infancy and childhood we find here is not simply a strategy for a particularly belittling critique of Wordsworth alone, but is, we will see, a central feature of how the Romantics understood, described and evaluated the literature of their day. That more is at stake in his review than Wordsworth's *Poems in Two Volumes*, Jeffrey makes very clear. Indeed, he defends the severity of his criticism of both *Lyrical Ballads* and the present volume (the infamous review of *The Excursion* is yet to come) with the claim that the growing influence of this "new school of poetry" necessitates the very strongest words. The *Lyrical Ballads*, Jeffrey admits, were "unquestionably popular," even, he grants, "deservedly popular"; they have been "quoted and imitated" and have helped to establish a poetic "system" which has "excited a good deal of attention." Condemning Wordsworth and his "brotherhood of poets," Jeffrey suggests that he sets himself against the dominant poetic movement of the day: what the poets call a turn toward natural expression and a simplicity of language and subject matter, and what Jeffrey, and Byron before him, call childishness and triviality.

Jeffrey's essay thus also makes clear the extent to which the increasingly vernacular quality of the poetry of the day was associated with and described as a return to the nursery, to the songs and rhymes of childhood. Wordsworth gives us the most famous declaration of a vernacular poetics in the "Preface" to the *Lyrical Ballads* when he states his intention to "chuse incidents and situations from common life" and to relate them "in a selection of language really used by men."[6] But he also insists that his turn to the "real language of men" entails a rejection of the "gaudiness and inane phraseology of many modern artists" and that he thus cuts himself off from the "phrases and figures of speech which from father to son have long been regarded as the common inheritance of Poets." Jeffrey will have none of Wordsworth's claim to originality and voluntary disinheritance, insisting that "Wordsworth and his friends" are "as much mannerists, too, as the poetasters who ring changes on the common-places of magazine versification." These "new poets are just as great borrowers as the old," Jeffrey comments, "only that, instead of borrowing from the more popular passages of their illustrious predecessors, they have preferred furnishing themselves from vulgar ballads and plebian nurseries." By turning to native, vernacular and popular literature – Jeffrey mentions ballads and immediately associates them with nursery lore – the new poets have threatened the "manly" strength of English literature and the elite status of its verse.

In short, the new poets have infantilized the literature and literary taste of the present day: they have introduced trivial and insignificant subjects, diminished the strength, refinement and high seriousness of style, and returned literature to an earlier, more primitive state. For Romantic scholars, such attacks on the Lakers' low subject matter, vulgar or common language, and affected primitivism are familiar and much discussed, and yet the fact that these charges are delivered in a rhetoric of infancy and thus associated with childhood and childish things has not been sufficiently addressed.[7] This study will take seriously this charge of infantilization, but will expand our understanding of what it means to say that the literature of the period we now call Romantic was characterized as infantile and childish. A condemnation of contemporary poetry in the hands of Byron, Jeffrey or, later, Thomas Love Peacock, the evocation of infancy and childhood also supports an account of the origins of poetry according to Johann Gottfried Herder and Percy Bysshe Shelley, justifies the preservation of traditional ballads according to Walter Scott and other popular antiquarians, offers a model for how adults read and respond to literary texts according to Thomas Reid and Anna Letitia Barbauld, and enables a developmental account of literary history according to Thomas Blackwell and Hugh Blair, to name only a few of the ideas about literature articulated in and through a rhetoric of infancy and childhood. Thus, although this study begins and ends with Wordsworth's poetry, in the pages between it tracks a rhetoric of infancy and childhood – the images, phrases, metaphors and figures of children and childhood – through a wide range of Enlightenment and Romantic writing: philosophical treatises on the origin of language and human understanding, conjectural histories, literary histories, defenses of poetry, defenses of popular poetry, children's reading primers, ballad collections, folklore collections, educational treatises, lyric poems, autobiographical writings and historical novels.

What emerges from this survey of Romantic-era writing is evidence of a broad discursive shift in the understanding and evaluation of literature, a shift that I am calling "the infantilization of literary culture." While "infantilization" does labor under a cloud of pejorative associations (fully deployed in Jeffrey's review, as we have seen), the term can also bring the period's significant engagement with childhood, children and childish things into focus in ways that have not been sufficiently clear nor adequately examined. How and why childhood and the figure of the child became so important to such a wide range of Romantic writers has long been one of the central questions of literary historical studies. We will find new answers to this question in the period's concomitant rise of a vernacular literary tradition. In the Romantic period the child was "discovered," as we will discuss below, coming fully into its own as the object of increasing social concern and cultural investment; at the same time, modern literary culture consolidated itself along vernacular, national lines. By examining the intersections of these social and historical developments, this study will examine how a rhetoric of infancy and childhood enabled Romantic writers to construct a national literary culture capable of embracing a wider range of literary forms. New theories about infancy, mental development, early language and childhood memory gave this period innovative ways to value and include the most trivial and popular literary forms within a native culture and national history. In turn, the newly expanded sense of national and popular literature that emerged in these years brought children and childhood into the arena of cultural production and reproduction.

While some of the values associated with infancy (depreciatory or otherwise) are very much the concern of this study – the attempt to bring the unvoiced, gestural and non-semantic elements of language into literary culture, to incorporate nursery rhymes and popular ballads into a national literary tradition, to preserve innocence within the field of cultural production, to create a poetry of the trivial and insignificant – my aim is not solely to describe an ascendancy of the values typically associated with infancy and childhood within Romantic literary culture. I am equally interested in the ways in which the figure of the child and notions of infancy and childhood served as rhetorical and conceptual tools in the long process of re-thinking human history, language, development and literature that we call the Enlightenment. The first half of this study, therefore, moves through a variety of Enlightenment and Romantic texts in order to demonstrate the centrality of an idea of infancy and a rhetoric of childhood to the new accounts of language, literature and history that emerged in these years. The second half of this study then turns to popular antiquarianism to track how new ideas of the child's mind and memory enabled new ways of accommodating popular literature within a national literary tradition.

THE DISCOVERY OF CHILDHOOD

Historical studies of childhood – whether social, visual or literary, such as this one – understand and discuss childhood as something that was "discovered" at a particular historical moment, by which they mean that there was a period in which a set of social factors and cultural practices cohered to bring children and childhood into greater focus and import-ance in the larger culture than previously seen. To speak of this process as "the discovery of childhood" is meant to defamiliarize and estrange what can easily be seen as a universal and ever-present fact of human life. Childhood becomes not something that we all have and, therefore, that all humans have always had, but something more like a new planet that floated into view on a particular night or a new species arduously tracked and meticulously described by an intrepid explorer. Another frequently used and related phrase, "the invention of childhood," pushes the element of estrangement still further, as if childhood had not even been there to be found, but rather was something made, made up, or constructed to fill a need, explain a phenomenon, or fool a crowd.

Such rhetoric of discovery and invention reveals some key assumptions about the historiography of childhood that this study shares. First and fundamental is the notion that, in Steven Mintz's words, "childhood is not an unchanging biological stage of life but is, rather, a social and cultural construct that has changed radically over time,"[8] an idea that sets the historical study of childhood apart from the biological.[9] "Biology" in such a statement is, to put it rather more crudely, another way of saying "body," and thus the historical study of childhood insists that the physical factors of human development do not, in themselves, add up to "childhood" and should certainly not be taken as evidence of a universal experience of childhood. Histories of childhood go further, in fact, claiming not only that cultural, economic and social factors play an equally important role as the biological, neurological and psychological in shaping what childhood is, but also that they determine just how we perceive, describe and manage the biological or bodily "facts" of children and childhood. The need to defamiliarize childhood, to separate it from its physical state and to insist on its susceptibility to change, remains an important charge and defining principle of historical studies of childhood.

The second critical assumption underlying the historiography of children and revealed by its rhetoric of discovery is that the history of children and the history of childhood are two different things. Thus Hugh Cunningham distinguishes between "children as human beings and childhood as a shifting set of ideas," and James Christen Steward insists on a distinction between "a social history of *children* and a cultural history of *childhood*."[10] Historians who are interested in documenting the lived experience of children in a particular place and time, Cunningham notes, must always "tease out the relationship between ideas about childhood and the experience of being a child."[11] They must, in other words, always mind the gap between adult notions of children and childhood – whether articulated in parenting manuals, autobiographies, social policy or literary texts – and the children being described or the experience of being a child. Histories of childhood that focus primarily on conceptions and representations of children and childhood are thus more accurately described as histories of adult ideas about childhood, and that is one reason why we can posit a "discovery" or "invention" of childhood even though children have always existed.

Rhetorical elaborations of "the discovery of childhood" are, in fact, as old as the historiography of childhood itself, and the phrase should be seen as the founding conceptual metaphor of the discipline.[12] "The discovery of childhood" not only entails the emergence of the idea that childhood is an important stage of life, but also the idea that childhood is its *own* stage of life, a time separate from adulthood with its own unique qualities and experiences. Thus the gap between adults and children – by which I mean both the difference between adult ideas of childhood and the lived experience of children, as well as the assumption that childhood is a distinct time of life to be held and studied apart from that of adulthood – is another fundamental tenet of childhood studies, an idea that emerged at a particular historical moment and has been subsequently reinforced by the rhetoric and disciplinary boundaries of the field.

In crafting his account of "the discovery of childhood" in *Centuries of Childhood*, the 1962 study unanimously acknowledged as the seminal text of the field, Philippe Ariès describes the emergence of a "sentiment de l'enfance," an ambiguous phrase, as Colin Heywood points out, "which conveyed both an awareness of childhood and a feeling for it."[13] Ariès took what has subsequently been called the "sentiments approach" (as opposed to the "demographic approach" or the "household economics approach"), one often criticized for being more speculative than factual, for focusing on adult ideas of childhood rather than the experience of actual children, and, given the affective investments that childhood so readily inspires, for being overly influenced by emotion and fantasy.[14]

Adult feelings for children and ideas about childhood are without doubt tricky and ambiguous objects of study. Dating the emergence of a new "sentiment de l'enfance" is even more precarious and controversial. Historians have dated "the discovery of childhood" across many years and even centuries. Ariès notoriously declared that there was no idea of childhood in medieval society; he and other early scholars, such as Lloyd de Mause and Lawrence Stone, argued that attitudes toward children changed fundamentally over the course of the seventeenth and eighteenth centuries.[15] Later historians sharply criticized their accounts of childhood in the medieval period, arguing for a robust and relatively stable interest in children from the medieval to the modern period.[16] Yet in a convergence of opinion significant for our purposes, the period most frequently cited as that in which childhood was "discovered," that in which ideas of childhood and the experience of being a child changed most dramatically, is the eighteenth century. "Framed by the writings of John Locke at its beginning and of the Romantic poets at its end, and with the strident figure of Rousseau at centre stage," writes Hugh Cunningham, "for most historians the eighteenth century holds pride of place."[17]

What is striking about this privileging of the eighteenth century is that, despite the acknowledged importance of Locke and the significant social and economic changes that were already in place to make a mid-century text such as Rousseau's *Emile* possible and popular, the child that is "discovered" or "invented" in the eighteenth century is most often referred to as the "Romantic child." For scholars of Romantic literature, this nomenclature appropriately reflects their sense that the writers of this period dramatically transformed the representation of childhood and the figure of the child in literature. Thus Peter Coveney begins his study with the claim that "until the last decades of the eighteenth century the child did not exist as an important and continuous theme in English literature."[18] Art historians make similar claims, crediting the paintings of Sir Joshua Reynolds, Thomas Gainsborough, Sir Thomas Lawrence and Sir Henry Raeburn with the invention of a new image of childhood that they, too, commonly label "the Romantic child."[19] Perhaps the new child of the eighteenth century is named for the last decades of the period because it was not until these later years that the demographic and social changes affecting childhood and children were given full cultural and artistic expression. That the artists and writers of what we call the Romantic period created images of children that powerfully condensed and encapsulated the new ideas of childhood that had been circulating and gaining pace over the course of the century is indeed a generally accepted feature of Romantic literature and culture.

But the idea of the "Romantic child" does more than refer back to and embody ideas of childhood developed over the course of the eighteenth century; it also gestures ahead to the ideas of childhood that will dominate Western culture well into the twentieth century. Thus the "Romantic child" is also often called the "modern child" and studies of the "discovery of childhood" in the latter half of the eighteenth century also claim to trace the "origins of modern childhood." Steven Mintz's history of childhood in America points to the early years of the nineteenth century as the moment when modern, middle-class childhood was invented, one supported by new mandatory school attendance laws, restrictions on child labor, a sharp reduction in birthrate and a host of institutions devoted to children's health and education, but one that he also labels "Romantic," using the images and rhetoric of Wordsworth, Rousseau and Bronson Alcott to describe the ideas and ideology underpinning this new middle-class version of childhood.[20] Anne Higonnet's study of the Romantic child often conflates the modern with the Romantic, pointing to a "modern Romantic child" that emerged in elite art forms in the latter decades of the eighteenth century and then tracking its diffusion into popular, commercial culture over the course of the nineteenth and twentieth centuries.[21] For these scholars and many others, the "Romantic child" earns its sobriquet because it is essentially an idealized, nostalgic, sentimental figure of childhood, one characterized by innocence, imagination, nature and primitivism, qualities associated with Romanticism that survive today in very few cultural figures, the child being one of the most enduring. Thus perhaps the child that emerges in the eighteenth century is called "Romantic" to signal our sense of its modernity, our recognition that in the images of childhood from these years we see our own assumptions about children and childhood first taking shape.

Ariès gestures toward the modernity of the Romantic child in his discussion of one characteristic that will be particularly important to this study: the child as a figure of the primitive. The child's association with primitivism appears in Rousseau's writings, Ariès writes, but it is an idea that really "belongs to twentieth-century history." Writing in 1960, he adds that "it is only very recently that it passed from the theories of psychologist, pedagogues, psychiatrists and psycho-analysts into public opinion."[22] George Boas' contemporaneous study, *The Cult of Childhood*, also treats the idea of the primitive child as a largely twentieth-century phenomenon. While Rousseau, according to Boas, suggests that childhood is "something inherently different from manhood" and something "midway between animality and humanity," it is not until the nineteenth and twentieth centuries that these primitive associations with childhood develop into the full-blown theories of cultural and historical recapitulation so central to early anthropology, psychology, sociology and paidology.[23] The belief that the child represents the childhood of the race as a whole, that the life of the individual reproduces the history of the race, has social and psychological applications that shape academic and popular ideas of human history and culture well into the twentieth century.[24]

What is important about the history of the idea of childhood as Boas tells it is the extent to which he traces its influence on larger ideas of history and culture. Indeed, Boas' interest in childhood came out of work undertaken with A. O. Lovejoy on the history of primitivism; his study is unabashedly a history of childhood, as opposed to children, and his topic is the role that ideas of childhood have played in how twentieth-century American society explains the world as a whole. What his study makes evident is something that many more recent and more specialized histories of childhood have forgotten: that the images and ideas of childhood first articulated or "discovered" in the eighteenth century have radiated outward, shaping subsequent ideas of history, psychology, subjectivity, human culture and artistic endeavor. Thus the "Romantic child" can seem uncannily familiar to us not simply because it embodies ideas of childhood that we somehow still believe, or because this ideal child has remained somehow magically "fixed" and unchanged into the modern day, but because the ideas associated with childhood that emerged in the Romantic period, and the rhetoric and images that gave them shape, became foundational to the dominant cultural and historical paradigms of the nineteenth and twentieth centuries and thus to how, for a significant period of time, we have explained the world.

Exactly how these new ideas of childhood made possible new ways of thinking about language, literature, history and culture is the major task of this study. Taking up the "discovery of childhood" in eighteenth-century and Romantic period writing, I have necessarily undertaken a history of childhood, as opposed to a history of children, but because this is a literary history, I pay particular attention not only to ideas of childhood, but to the representation of those ideas, to the images, metaphors, figures and phrases that express and embody those ideas. To that extent this study is more accurately described as a rhetorical history of childhood, one interested in tracking the figure of the child through a variety of literary texts, as well as in describing the strategic and conceptual power of this figure, how it is used and what other ideas it makes possible. At the risk of being old-fashioned or, in other words, too general in my historical periodization and claims, I have followed the ideas and images of childhood from Enlightenment and Romantic writing into fields of inquiry and writings that are not, seemingly, directly engaged with the topic of children and childhood – the origin and history of language; the philosophical framework of conjectural history and stadial theory; popular antiquarianism – in addition to those that are – education, children's literature, parenting manuals, autobiographical writings. I have also followed the ideas and images of childhood that emerge in the Romantic period into later nineteenth- and twentieth-century texts, tracing lines of continuity and evaluating how, where and to what effect a Romantic rhetoric of childhood shapes later ideas of literary culture and cultural history.

A book about childhood in Romantic literature labors under the contradictory burden of being labeled both grandiose and trivial. An interest in childhood – whether in childhood memories, the child's natural or privileged existence, childhood education or child literacy – is so pervasive and fundamental to the literature of the period that the topic can seem coterminous with the whole and thus to fail in offering any selection and focus. On the other hand, the academic study of childhood in whatever field always suffers from what Brian Sutton-Smith has called the "triviality barrier," the assumption that childhood and children – their play, literature, development, education and representation – are not weighty academic topics or, at least, not nearly as significant as others. This study has tried to embrace both sides of this double bind, arguing on the one hand that a rhetoric of infancy and childhood is fundamental to new ideas of history and literature, particularly to new ways of thinking about vernacular and popular literature, and thus fundamental to the emergence of Romantic literary culture. The figure of the child we will discover in the pages that follow carries historical associations and cultural charges and is, thus, very far from the figure of autonomy, nature and idealized innocence so often presented as the "Romantic child." The emergence of infancy as a new cultural paradigm and the recurring figuration of children and childhood in new theories of history and new descriptions of literary culture is the major topic of the first half of this study, "History of an analogy." On the other hand, the triviality of childish things is also a major concern of this study and, I argue, a central element of Romantic popular literary culture. How Romantic writers grappled with their own triviality barrier, how they gave value to the "trifles" of popular literature and brought the "prattle" and insignificant things of childhood into their national literary culture through the discourse of antiquarianism is the main subject of the second half of this study, "Prattle and trifles."

HISTORY OF AN ANALOGY: "FOR THE SAVAGE IS TO AGES WHAT THE CHILD IS TO YEARS"

At an early point in *A Defence of Poetry* (1821), Percy Bysshe Shelley makes a remarkably casual comment of truly staggering implications. In discussing the primitive origins of poetry and language, Shelley compares a child to a savage, and he justifies that comparison with a parenthetical aside: "(for the savage is to ages what the child is to years)."[25] What Shelley assumes in this statement is that the human individual in its early stages of infancy and childhood can be compared to the human race in its early stages of primitive or "savage" existence. By offering the comparison in this particular form of an analogy, however, Shelley moves the relationship of child and savage beyond simple comparison to the logic of an equation in which each term necessarily offers descriptive analysis of the other. As any teenager studying for a standardized test can tell you, analogies must be able to work in reverse. For Shelley's analogy this means that the child describes the savage *and* that the savage describes the child; that the years offer a pattern for the ages *and* the ages for the years.

Shelley's analogy signals a major transformation of what is, of course, an age-old rhetorical tradition: that of using the life span of the individual to describe the grander sweeps of human history. This historical metaphor is so longstanding and persistent, indeed so dangerously familiar, that bringing its cultural significance for a particular period into focus can be difficult. But in fact, the long Romantic period – or roughly the seventy years prior to Shelley's *Defence* – witnessed an explosion of interest in the historical metaphor of the individual life, most particularly in the comparisons it began to make possible between child and savage. Enlightenment and Romantic philosophers, historians, antiquarians, poets and novelists transformed this hoary metaphor into a new and vigorous conceptual tool that enabled innovative ways of narrating history, comparing cultures, describing the human organism and, what is the particular concern of this study, valuing and understanding language and literary arts.

Indeed, the Romantics remade the ancient historical metaphor of the individual life into what would become the dominant cultural paradigm of the nineteenth century. The idea that the life of the individual and the course of history follow parallel and recapitulating patterns – whether that history is political, national, cultural or evolutionary – shaped every scholarly discipline that emerged in the Victorian period, including anthropology, folklore, sociology, history, psychology and biology. As one intellectual historian notes generally: "by far the most pervasive paradigm in the nineteenth century is the parallel between the life of the individual and life-cycle of the civilizations"; historians of the individual Victorian sciences and social sciences all make similar claims in their separate studies.[26] Comparisons between the beginning life of the human organism and man's primitive social state, or analogies such as Shelley's which equate children and savages, not only abound in these years, they anchor the conceptual frameworks and discursive fields of nineteenth-century intellectual and cultural endeavor.

Thus in 1895, for example, an early and influential psychologist in the new field of child studies can state with confidence: "As we all know, the lowest races of mankind stand in close proximity to the animal world. The same is true of the infants of civilized races."[27] The emerging biological sciences were particularly fascinated with recapitulation theory – Ernst Haeckel's "biogenetic law" or the theory that "ontogeny recapitulates phylogeny" – and despite repeated criticism and evidence to the contrary, popular biology texts at the end of the century continued to advance the fantasy of recapitulation: "Evolution tells us that each animal has a pedigree in the past. Embryology reveals to us this ancestry, because every animal in its own development repeats its history, climbs up its own genealogical tree."[28]

Victorian historiography and the emerging fields of anthropology and folklore also relied heavily on this paradigm. The popular historian and novelist Charles Kingsley used the cultural dogma that "races, like individuals ... may have their childhood, their youth, their manhood, their old age, and natural death" to describe the Teutonic peoples who destroyed Rome in what qualified as serious analytical and classificatory categories in his day: as "great boys; very noble boys; very often very naughty boys – as boys with the strength of men might be."[29] Sir J. G. Frazer, whose *Golden Bough* is a foundational text of modern cultural anthropology, justified his work and discipline in language that gathers together the biological, cultural and historical strands of the individual life as metaphor: "For by comparison with civilized man the savage represents an arrested or rather retarded stage of social development, and an examination of his customs and beliefs accordingly supplies the same sort of evidence of the evolution of the human mind that an examination of the embryo supplies of the evolution of the human body."[30] This rhetoric continues to exert its analytical influence as late as 1959 in what remains one of the most important texts in the field of children's folklore, *The Lore and Language of Schoolchildren*, where Iona and Peter Opie caution their readers: "It must, after all, be borne in mind that the children here under observation are only at the stage of mental development sometimes ascribed to a savage tribe, whom anthropologists are not at all surprised to find dominated by superstition."[31]

In comments such as these we see the pervasive influence of a cultural metaphor that uses the life of the individual to describe a course of history and a version of history to narrate the development of the individual. We also glimpse the disturbing and, indeed, staggering implications of a cultural discourse that enables comparisons between children and savages. Such comparisons were foundational to the intellectual fields and disciplines that emerged in the nineteenth century and that largely continue to organize intellectual pursuits today. This cultural paradigm is arguably still very much with us, present if not in serious academic theory, then in rhetorical habits, conceptual clichés and other residual cultural forms: present, for example, when adults refer to children as "little savages," or when the best-intentioned National Public Radio affiliate organizes a package tour to Kenya and invites its members to "travel back in time."

Before such comparisons between children and savages formed the theoretical framework of Victorian sciences and social sciences, however, they animated Enlightenment and Romantic discussions of history, language and literature. The first half of this study will thus excavate and specify the various associations between child and savage that were in place and made Shelley's metaphor both possible and powerful in 1821. I aim to provide a rhetorical history of a major cultural analogy – "for the savage is to ages what the child is to years" – and to investigate what theories of literary history and culture became possible when the child and savage were understood as comparable figures. To that extent, this study turns to that "family of privileged epistemological subjects" which Locke gives to the eighteenth century – "*Children, Ideots, Savages*, and the grossly *Illiterate*" – to focus on the child and the savage and the specific charges the relationship between them is made to bear.[32] Locke's philosophy of mind presents all these figures as examples of early or primitive "understanding," but his theory of mental development enables new ways of describing history and culture that we find particularly articulated in the rhetorical analogy between child and savage. Enlightenment and Romantic philosophers writing about history, language, society and culture use the parallel between child and savage to construct a notion of the "primitive" that could be located simultaneously in the historical past, in the far reaches of the globe and in the nurseries of Britain. The "primitive" thus takes on portability as well as analytical weight in these years, becoming a cultural category that makes it possible to draw connections between radically different places and times. The "primitivism" of Enlightenment and Romantic culture should thus be understood and studied as an important aspect of the period's emerging historical and social theory, as much as an aesthetic value or nostalgic posture.

This study goes still further in its favoritism when it comes to Locke's epistemological family, privileging the child as the period's most important "primitive." The historical parallel articulated in Shelley's analogy between the child's years and humanity's ages involves a major re-imagining of how the individual life can serve as a metaphor for history. Over the course of the eighteenth century, that individual life was more and more often embodied in the figure of a child (as opposed to the "single man who persists forever") and was increasingly understood as a life that began in and developed out of infancy and childhood. The history represented by this figure of the child was also increasingly understood as both developmental and progressive. But "development" in the eighteenth century was not yet the inevitable, natural, biological or physiological phenomenon that it became in the nineteenth century. To this extent, when we track the rhetoric of childhood through the major historical narratives and methodologies that emerged in these years – the inquiry of origins, conjectural history, stadial theory – we are forced to reexamine our understanding of "history" and "development" and to reevaluate what was at stake for the Romantics when they used these two different temporal narratives to represent and explain each other.

Eighteenth-century conjectural histories of the Scottish and European Enlightenment increasingly articulated the relationship between the individual life and the course of human history as a parallel and mutually enhancing progress, one which they represented through comparisons between child and savage, between the individual's infancy and society's primitive state. These writers use the analogy between child and savage not only to theorize the stages of history, but also to describe the state and growth of the child, its mental capacities, its relationship to language, its education and development. The interest in what we might describe as the reverse work of Shelley's analogy – the ways in which the figure of the "savage" and primitive history might shed light on the child and individual development – increasingly characterizes nineteenth-century elaborations of this historical discourse. The child becomes newly interesting in the long Romantic period and, by the end of the nineteenth century, is the privileged object of study in a host of emerging sciences and disciplines, from developmental psychology and Freudian psychoanalysis, to evolutionary biology, anthropology and folklore. The notion that the development of the individual life or organism follows or repeats the history of the race or species is foundational doctrine to these new disciplines. This paradigm and its cultural prominence, I will argue, places new emphasis on the child who is increasingly understood through the framework of history as a figure of cultural recapitulation and reiteration, and who, in turn, enables new ways of understanding British national culture and history: new ways of valuing its range of literary forms, new ways of narrating national continuity and progress, and new ways of making the past perpetually available to the present.[33]

PRATTLE AND TRIFLES

Anna Letitia Barbauld's poem "Washing-Day" begins by calling on the Muses to "sing the dreaded Washing-Day," an invocation that suggests simultaneously a humbling of the classical Muses and the elevation of women's domestic work. It is this contradictory tension between high poetic conventions and low subject matter that gives any mock epic, and this one in particular, its interpretive complexity and pleasure. Barbauld alternately seems to champion the ordinary and everyday tasks of the home and, like Jeffrey almost a decade later, ridicule their presence in poetry:

The Muses are turned gossips; they have lost
The buskin'd step, and clear high-sounding phrase,
Language of gods. Come, then, domestic Muse,
In slip-shod measure loosely prattling on
Of farm or orchard, pleasant curds and cream,
Or drowning flies, or shoe lost in the mire
By little whimpering boy, with rueful face.[34]

Describing poetry's fall in language – from "clear high-sounding phrase, /
Language of gods" to "slip-shod measure loosely prattling on" – and in
subject matter – from the "buskin'd step" of tragedy to "shoe lost in the
mire / By little whimpering boy" – Barbauld's lines position themselves
on the same fault-line of contemporary poetry that will later cause Byron
and Jeffrey such anxiety: the shift from a classical to a vernacular literature
and the extent to which such a shift brings domestic or trivial matters into
elite literary forms. In his review of Wordsworth's *Poems in Two Volumes*,
Jeffrey uses Barbauld's poem as evidence of how the new poetry of the
day courts ridicule: "All the world laughs at Elegiac stanzas to a sucking-
pig – a Hymn on Washing-day – Sonnets to one's grandmother – or
Pindarics on gooseberry-pye."[35] Much of "Washing-Day" seems to ridicule such poems of domestic matters as well, and it is not until the poem
turns its mocking gaze on the male head of the household – "thou / Who
call'st thyself perchance the master there" – and gathers strong words to
represent the physical labor of laundry – "All hands employed to wash, to
rinse, to wring, / To fold, and starch, and clap, and iron, and plait" – that
it may be said to participate sincerely in the overthrow of the social and
literary hierarchies that Jeffrey so staunchly defends.

Significantly, Barbauld's "domestic Muse" sings of both women and
children, evoking both the labor of women and the language and concerns
of children. In representing the turn to ordinary and everyday subject
matter as a turn to childish things, Barbauld again creates an allusive
fabric of contradiction and tension. The "prattle" of children, as we will
see, will become a common, although not unproblematic, image of poetic
inspiration and linguistic innocence in these years. Yet Barbauld's epigraph from *As You Like It* – "and their voice, / Turning again towards
childish treble, pipes / And whistles in its sound" – evokes not childhood,
but the "second childhood" of old age, an image that will also recur in
criticisms of contemporary literature as a complaint about poetry's
affected and inauthentic return to childhood. As we will find Thomas
Love Peacock protesting, the poetry of the day has become the "gewgaws
and rattles for the grown babies of the age," and poetry's claim to a

natural, original state through the inclusion of childish things is nothing more than a symptom of its senility and infirmity.

Images of childhood and infancy are central rhetorical figures in both Romantic poetry and critical reviews, and Barbauld's poem, while usually discussed as a poem about women's work, is equally invested in representing childhood. The poem takes a formal and situational turn, away from the contradictions and ironies of mock epic to a lyric of childhood memory, and away from the work of women to a child's perception of that work: "I well remember, when a child, the awe / This day struck into me." Here the poem offers a variation of a phrase, "remembered from childhood," that, as we will see, is a significant refrain in a variety of Romantic texts, from lyric poems and historical romances, to antiquarian ballad collections and educational treatises. Indeed, what the first-person speaker who emerges in the final section of "Washing-Day" remembers from childhood is another iconographic scene of Romantic writing: the figure of woman and child by the hearth:

> so I went
> And shelter'd me beside the parlour fire:
> There my dear grandmother, eldest of forms,
> Tended the little ones, and watched from harm.

Whether mother, nurse or old matron, the figure of the woman singing to a child, reading to a child, or teaching a child to read, is a central figure of the vernacular literary culture that takes shape in these years. The "mother's mouth" and the maternal figure, as Friedrich A. Kittler has argued, embodies an important Romantic myth of language and culture: a pure orality that makes the voiced origins of language ever present and gives the denatured process of acculturation – learning to speak, learning the alphabet, learning to read – a natural locus.[36]

It can be difficult to separate the mother and child in such a figure; women and children tend to be taken together, and the child, often mute or *infans* and thus more inaccessible, is easily overlooked in our focus on the important gender dynamics at work in this image. It is the contention of this study, however, that Romantic writers and readers were as interested in the figure of the child in this pairing as in the figure of the woman, and that the child, who can seem a rather passive object of acculturation is, in fact, a particularly charged figure of cultural significance with a rather complex role and agency in cultural production and reproduction. "Washing-Day" makes evident, for example, that the image of the mother's mouth always leads to images of the child's ear and the child's mouth, to the question of what and how the child hears, remembers and later repeats or reproduces. Unable to coax "butter'd toast" or a "thrilling tale / Of ghost, or witch, or murder" from the busy maids, retiring to the parlour fire with her grandmother who is an "indulgent" but silent caretaker, Barbauld's child recalls that "at intervals my mother's voice was heard / Urging dispatch, briskly the work went on." While the poem thus evokes a common notion of vernacular literature as a "cultural bequest passed from one female generation to the next," it is important that the child is at least temporarily denied these stories and kept at a remove from the mother's voice.[37] "Washing-Day" presents a child's perspective on the scene, emphasizing how the child perceives and relates to the mother's distanced voice and making this less a scene of maternal presence than of childish reflection: "Then would I sit me down, and ponder much / Why washings were."

In other words, Barbauld inserts some temporal and spatial distance into the image of mother and child, and that slight distance allows the poem to portray, and the reader to perceive, the child's aural, emotional and reflective experience and activity. The final lines of the poem thus focus on children's play:

> Sometimes thro' hollow bole
> Of pipe amused we blew, and sent aloft
> The floating bubbles, little dreaming then
> To see, Mongolfier, thy silken ball
> Ride buoyant thro' the clouds – so near approach
> The sports of children and the toils of men.
> Earth, air, and sky, and ocean, hath its bubbles,
> And verse is one of them – this most of all.

As the child makes bubbles out of the laundry soap, she transforms women's domestic labor into child's play. A close affinity between childish games and the work of men is also asserted, but the relationship between them is significantly different. Where the child's play takes the material conditions of domestic work and turns them into play, much like Barbauld's poem does, Mongolfier's balloon is, itself, a toy or game, a bubble of beauty and pleasure and buoyancy. The "sports of children and the toils of men" are alike here in that they are both an effervescence, a flight of fancy, and even an insignificance, that which floats above and free from the daily, material world and its ordinary labors but is also tied to, made possible by such work and the sheltered spaces it creates. Barbauld's poem thus uses the category of childhood to cut across the hierarchies of gender and literature and to challenge the very terms of the debate about poetry's ordinary and insignificant subjects. The poem, itself, is a trifle, a bubble of insignificance like the games of children.

The second half of this study examines how Romantic writers used a rhetoric of childhood to grapple with the problem of insignificant or trivial literature. One major class of trivial literature in the Romantic period was "popular literature" or "popular poetry," the traditional oral ballads and stories that were voraciously rediscovered, transcribed, edited, printed and imitated in these years. This study thus turns to the collections of popular antiquarianism and the later nineteenth- and twentieth-century folklore collections that developed out of Romantic antiquarianism and identifies a surprisingly strong rhetorical engagement with childhood in these "dry-as-dust" scholarly volumes, one that builds on the new historical ideas of infancy and primitive origins and extends the notion of a developmental and recapitulative literary culture. Indeed, in Romantic antiquarianism, "so near approach the sports of children and the toils of men" that we will see the antiquarian collector repeatedly evoke and conflate his own personal childhood with the "infancy of poetry" as a way of justifying his attention to the "trivial" and "vulgar" verses of his childhood.

Antiquarian writings, however, go beyond a nostalgic sociology of childhood, constructing an understanding of the child's mind and memory as particularly and exactly retentive, as remembering and repro-ducing cultural forms yet doing so as innocent and unknowing play. Thus in the figure of the old woman and child which recurs in antiquarian writings, they are particularly invested in what the child remembers and later recites, giving the child a role in the preservation and transmission of literary forms that we have failed to notice because of our exclusive attention to maternal agency. A shift in focus from mother to child will also shift our understanding of how the Romantics understood and represented language and literary culture; where the mother's voice has been used to suggest a preoccupation with speech and embodied presence, the child's mind and memory is often figured as a textual site, overwritten and impressed by exterior forms, thereby exposing another aspect of how Romantic writers understood the relationship between the individual and the larger structures of language, culture and history. The figure of the child that we will discover in antiquarian discourse is one used to explore the relationship of the individual to culture and history, rather than to embody an idea of self-sufficiency or autonomy outside the cultural field.

This is not to deny the values of innocence and artlessness with which Romantic writers layered the figure of the child. The child's cultural innocence, however, is a more complex construct than we might expect. The "prattle" of children, for example, is a recurring image not only for original language – the inarticulate, expressive sounds of the child at play that Shelley, following Enlightenment tradition, claims are the origins of poetry – but also for the child's ability to turn significant language back into insignificant noise, to break the meanings of words apart from their sounds and to transform the most overly determined and knowing literary forms into innocent, affective noise. The cultural significance of the child who repeats or recites poems, songs and ballads she does not fully understand is debated in a variety of Romantic texts, from educational discussions of rote memorization to antiquarian discussions of childhood memory. In this figure Romantic writers confront the shaping influence language and history have on the individual at the same time as they imagine a way to slip free of their determinative force.

Antiquarians imagine both the child and the literary text as capable of slipping free of history even as they understand literature and childhood within an historicist framework. In their collections of old ballads, nursery rhymes and popular folklore, we will trace an "antiquarian formalism" that elides the content of these literary forms – content that is all too often scandalous, vulgar or trivial – and instead emphasizes their form as a vehicle for cultural and national continuity. The "trifles" of popular literature become the "relics" of a national literary culture, and childhood becomes the place where past literary forms are preserved. It is my contention, however, that the methods and strategies developed largely in antiquarian discourse for giving value to the trifles of literary culture were important to the wider Romantic engagement with the ordinary and insignificant. When Elizabeth Inchbald in *Nature and Art* (1796) remarks that "trifles" are often "more grateful to the sensible mind than efforts of high importance" and asserts that it is by the trifle that "the artist in the human heart will accurately trace a passion, wholly concealed from the dull eye of the unskilled observer," she articulates an artistic and affective creed of insignificance that we recognize as central to Romantic writing.[38] William Wordsworth will embrace this creed when he proclaims that "the human mind is capable of excitement without the application of gross and violent stimulants" and that "one being is elevated above another in proportion as he possesses this capability."[39] In writing poems that reject extraordinary incident, ballads that tell no tales, Wordsworth, as we have seen, also defends himself against charges of "triviality and meanness both of thought and language," of subjects that are "too low" and expressions that are "too familiar."[40] The *Lyrical Ballads* is wholly involved in a discourse of the trivial and insignificant, adapting antiquarian strategies for historicizing and psychologizing the scandal and sensation of popular literary forms. It is in Wordsworth's major autobiographical poem, *The Prelude*, however, that the poet fully exploits an antiquarian understanding of childhood to develop a poetics of the trifle. Wordsworth makes childhood memory into a literary genre – the "spot of time" – lyrics embedded within the longer autobiographical narrative which repeatedly stage the interior life of the child as impressed upon and inhabited by exterior, material forms. The significant forms of these memories persist and acquire a permanence in the adult mind, but the emotions and significance attached to them are often left unstated, considered trivial, or acknowledged as transitory and changeable. Wordsworth thus uses the formalism of Romantic antiquarianism to claim these trivial or meaningless memories of childhood for poetry and to prove both autobiographical and anthropological continuities.

PART I

History of an analogy
"for the savage is to ages what the child is to years"

CHAPTER I

The child is father of the man

It should not be surprising that, at the beginning of our history of Shelley's analogy – "(for the savage is to ages what the child is to years)" – we would land immediately on an epigram that stands as one of the best-known phrases of Romantic writing. Indeed, the title of this first chapter is perhaps the most familiar, commonly quoted and widely circulating line of poetry written by William Wordsworth, a line that one is as likely to find in a psychology textbook, business manual or local newspaper story as in a discussion of Romantic literature.[1] This is particularly the case, of course, whenever childhood, development, education or child-rearing is the topic of conversation. Here this line circulates as a proverb of modern childhood, containing in its short gnomic expression all we hold true about the importance of childhood to the development of the individual. Placed back in its historical context – whether that be a history of childhood or a history of literary culture – this epigram functions more like an epitaph, summarizing and laying to rest the "Romantic Child," that figure of ideal innocence who must be nourished, protected and set apart because of its guiding influence on later, adult life. Histories of childhood regularly describe the new middle-class childhood of the nineteenth century and the figure of the Romantic Child, the Ideal Child, the Quintessential Child that embodies its ideals.[2] Here one routinely finds Wordsworth's line, "The Child is Father of the Man," used as shorthand, saying all one needs to know (and only what one already knows) about an understanding of childhood that emerged around 1800 and remains culturally compelling to this day.

For scholars interested in the cultural and literary history of the Romantic period, the figure of the "Romantic Child" has often been seen as central to the delineation of what has been called the "Romantic self," that private, interior and natural version of subjectivity, identity and individual growth considered the ideological invention of the major Romantic writers. The "Romantic discourse of essential childhood," as described by Judith Plotz, establishes the mind of the child as a "sanctuary or bank vault of valuable but socially endangered psychological powers: idealism, holism, vision, animism, faith, and isolated self-sufficiency."[3] This is a process of creating the ideal child as a version of the ideal self, attributing to a figure who cannot speak for or represent itself everything the adult self wishes for itself. In these acts of self-fashioning, the figure of the child is particularly appealing to the Romantics because of its claims to a "natural" state and its capacity to evoke an interior, remembered existence. Adults inevitably see children and childhood through memories of their own childhood: representing the ideal self in and through the figure of the child is thus an act of privileging the interior life of feeling and memory as what constitute the self.[4]

This version of self as child risks omitting the connecting father figure in the Wordsworthian formula: in this representational economy, the child is the ideal of man rather than the father of the man. This is an elision of parenting that Plotz, for example, finds everywhere in Wordsworth's representations of child and self and one that she connects to Romanticism's larger suppression of history and historical contingency. "*Childhood*," Plotz asserts, "operates along with *imagination* and *nature* within romantic discourse as the third autonomous power immune to the pressures of history."[5] Childhood's intrinsic susceptibility to temporality and transience, when it is acknowledged at all, is described as a by-product of "growth" or "development," narrative discourses understood to preserve a continuity of self, to naturalize change, or otherwise deny the vicissitudes of "history." In this account of Romanticism and history, Wordsworth's epigram is again a major refrain. Thus Clifford Siskin describes lyric autobiography as working "in concert with 'development' ('The Child is Father of the Man'), which ... is a contemporaneous formal strategy for naturalizing social and literary change."[6] The parentheses around Wordsworth's line, like those around Shelley's analogy, signal just how dangerously familiar – and, even, clichéd or diminished in the range and resonance of its meanings – the phrase has become.

More recent scholarship has challenged this representation of Romantic subjectivity and, even more aggressively, the idea of Romanticism's monolithic hostility toward history and refusal of historical explanation. James Chandler's attention to the historicist sensibility of the Scottish Enlightenment, its influence on Romantic literary culture and, indeed, on present-day historical practice, has re-drawn the map of British Romanticism into that of a "self-consciously historicist literary culture."[7] Chandler's account, along with the work of Ian Duncan, Katie

Trumpener, Ina Ferris and others, places Walter Scott and the historical romance at the center of this new British Romanticism, and a range of historically engaged genres and writers has been added to this literary terrain, from national tales to antiquarian ballad collections to Gothic romances.[8]

This well-placed focus on other Romantic writers and genres, however, has left the rhetorical family of the Romantic child, its version of "development," and its relationship to "history," largely unchallenged and unchanged. "The Child is Father of the Man" thus continues to be produced and reproduced as a psychological commonplace or Romantic cliché, and the utter strangeness of these words that Gerard Manley Hopkins once exclaimed upon is no longer in currency. "The words are wild," Hopkins wrote, issuing a challenge: "Suck any sense from that who can: / 'The child is father to the man.'"[9] One task of this chapter is, in fact, to accept Hopkins' challenge: to recover the strangeness of these words – "the child is father to the man" – and, in so doing, to uncover the particular associations and significances animating the rhetoric of infancy and childhood that enabled Wordsworth's epigram and Shelley's later analogy.

The larger task of this first chapter is, thus, to demonstrate the extent to which images of infancy and childhood emerge as a pervasive *historical* rhetoric in British Enlightenment and Romantic writing. Our focus in this first chapter will be on Enlightenment historical writing and theory. Here we will track the transformation of the oldest historical metaphor, that of using the life span of the individual to describe the larger course of human history, from an image of static parts – youth, maturity and old age – to an image of development and, indeed, one that helps to establish development as the dominant way of describing change over time in the increasingly historicist culture that emerges over the course of the eighteenth century. Trying to recreate how Enlightenment writers thought about development in both the individual and the species – how, for example, they related the development of the mind to the history of the species – demands that we rethink what they meant by, and what we mean by, the terms "development" and "history." Rather than using the discourse of natural development to suppress the contingencies of history, and rather than writing from within an historicist framework remarkably similar to our own (two accounts of Romantic literary culture that have significantly shaped current literary scholarship in the last thirty years[10]), Enlightenment and Romantic writers, I will argue, used new ideas of development to articulate a compelling and new historical paradigm: one that emphasizes origins, attempts to explain change as occurring in relatively uniform or stable patterns, grapples with different temporal scales and rates and, significantly, uses analogy to relate the individual to larger historical sweeps and vice versa.

Increasingly, as we will see, the interest in the individual life as an analogy for history comes to fall on infancy and childhood. Infancy thus becomes an important way of understanding and representing *origins*, a central preoccupation of Enlightenment historicism that must, in fact, be understood as a major methodology of their inquiry. Indeed, the name used by Enlightenment and Romantic writers to describe and locate the obscure origins of human nature or human understanding is "infancy," a term they use to refer to the beginnings of the individual human life as well as to the primitive stages of human history and, to the extent that the same term names both, to reinforce the analogical connection between the two. Both child and savage can be "infants" in this discourse, as Shelley's analogy makes evident. While twenty-first century usage of the term "infancy" privileges the earliest period of the individual human life, the condition of the human infant or baby, figuratively, infancy can describe the "earliest period in the history of anything capable of development" or the "initial and rudimentary stage in any process of growth."[11] Here the *Oxford English Dictionary* lays bare the established connection between "infancy" and "development" – to have an infancy is to be capable of growth and development – as well as our persistent metaphorical habits of transferring the attributes of an individual human life to the histories of other entities.

In the case of Wordsworth's phrase, we will discover a network of historical images and issues that tie the phrase back into the paradoxical and charged terrain of Enlightenment historicism. "The Child is Father of the Man" must be seen as an historical as much as a psychological metaphor, one that, like Shelley's later analogy, neatly condenses the theories and images of history circulating in Enlightenment and Romantic culture. The phrase works like Shelley's analogy to construct explanatory comparisons between individual, mental development, on the one hand, and cultural, historical change, on the other, between psychology and history, between "man" and "Man." Indeed, these analogies are so central to Enlightenment historicism that *analogy* must also take its place as another major methodology of the period. "The Child is Father of the Man" thus articulates the idea of development out of childhood origins as a description of the individual life, as well as an account of human history and human culture that understands "primitive man" as both the "child" and the "father" of modern man. Wordsworth's epigram works not as a hermetically sealed and circular account of individual psychology which is itself enclosed and self-sufficient. Rather it works as an historical and developmental puzzle, a condensation of contemporary debates about history, progress and the relationship of the individual life to larger historical and cultural forces.

WE ARE THE ANCIENTS; THEY ARE THE INFANTS

In *Social Science and the Ignoble Savage*, Ronald Meek made a strong case for what he called the "French and Scottish pioneers of the 1750s" and the importance of Enlightenment human sciences, particularly stadial or "four-stages" theory, to the "subsequent development of economics, sociology, anthropology and historiography, right down to our own time."[12] While more recent intellectual and literary historians continue to credit the far-reaching influence of the Scottish philosophers in particular, the importance of their ideas was also well understood and proclaimed by their Enlightenment and Romantic contemporaries. Meek quotes one Semyon Efimovich Desnitsky, a Russian who made a pilgrimage to Scotland in the 1760s to study with Adam Smith and John Millar and who, in a later lecture delivered in Moscow, pays tribute to his Scottish professors as the "newest and most assiduous explorers of human nature." Touching on three characteristic and guiding notions of Scottish Enlightenment historiography – an interest in primitive beginnings or origins, an understanding of human history as a progress out of these primitive origins, and an emphasis on material conditions as determinative of human history – Desnitsky describes how these "explorers" have "discovered incomparably better means for studying nations in their various successes according to the circumstances and conditions through which those peoples, starting from their primordial society with wild animals, rose to the highest degree of greatness and enlightenment."[13] Desnitsky details the four stages through which the human race progresses according to Scottish Enlightenment historical theory – hunter/gatherer, pastoral, agricultural and commercial – concluding that from these successive "conditions of peoples" one can "deduce their history, government, laws, and customs and measure their various successes in sciences and arts."

What I find most interesting about Denitsky's account of Scottish Enlightenment historical theory is his sense of how the new historical ideas coming out of Glasgow relate to older historical habits and methods,

in particular his declaration that Scottish historiography achieves a significant break with past practice when it comes to the familiar convention
of assigning history the various stages of an individual life. "We cannot,"
he insists, "measure the various successes of the human race, its risings and
falling, on the basis of its imputed childhood, youth, maturity, and old
age."[14] Over and against this historical convention – prominent enough to
single out at the beginning of his lecture – Desnitsky measures the
innovation of the Scottish school, claiming that it has been rendered
obsolete by their new theories and methods.

What Desnitsky learned from Smith and Millar does indeed involve a
significant re-evaluation of this old historical metaphor, but it would
more accurately be described as a renovation rather than a wholesale
rejection. As we shall see, Scottish Enlightenment thinkers remade this
metaphor into the cultural paradigm of parallel development between the
individual life-cycle and human history, one that remained compelling
throughout the nineteenth and well into the twentieth centuries, and one
that was crucial to how exactly stadial theory dominated the emerging
social sciences of these later centuries. We can track the transformation of
this old historical metaphor into an ontogenetic analogy with reinvigor-
ated conceptual and methodological power in a variety of debates on
history and culture leading up to and throughout the eighteenth century.

For example, in what often count as documents in the early history of the
idea of progress, the seventeenth-century debate about the relative value of
ancient and modern literature – the so-called "battle of the ancients and the
moderns" joined by writers in both France and England – offers a sustained
reflection on and reworking of the historical metaphor of the individual
life.[15] It is Francis Bacon in his *Novum Organum* who, in arguing against
undue admiration of "antiquity," influentially articulates an idea of
progress in human history by manipulating images of youth and age:

The opinion which men cherish of antiquity is altogether idle, and scarcely
accords with the term. For the old age and increasing years of the world should
in reality be considered as antiquity, and this is rather the character of our own
times than of the less advanced age of the world in those of the ancients; for the
latter, with respect to ourselves, are ancient and elder, with respect to the world
modern and younger. And as we expect a greater knowledge of human affairs,
and more mature judgment from an old man than from a youth ... so we have
reason to expect much greater things of our own age ... than from antiquity ...
Reverence for antiquity has been a retarding force in science.[16]

The life of the single man as a metaphor for history, certainly not new,
becomes newly interesting in the subsequent debate about who should be

considered "ancient." As René Descartes quips, "C'est nous qui sommes les anciens," a phrase that recurs in all the major documents of this literary debate.[17]

Blaise Pascal, for example, uses man's ability to retain and transmit knowledge from generation to generation to argue that "the same thing happens in the succession of men in general as in the different ages of a single individual man." The history of mankind and modern man's relationship to the ancients should thus be seen through the metaphor of a single life:

So that the whole succession of men, throughout the course of so many centuries, should be envisaged as the life of a single man who persists forever and learns continually: whence we see how unjustly we respect antiquity in our philosophers; for, seeing that old age is the age which is farthest from childhood, who does not see that the old age of this universal man should be looked for, not in the times nearest his birth, but in those most remote therefrom? Those whom we term ancients were in reality new in everything and constituted properly the infancy of mankind; and since we have added to their knowledge the experience of the centuries which have followed them, it is in ourselves that that antiquity is to be found which we reverence in them.[18]

Not only are we the ancients, but they are the children, Pascal insists, having earlier commented that "men are to-day in a sense in the same condition in which those ancient philosophers would have found themselves could they have survived to the present day." Knowledge is a factor of experience here, and Pascal uses the image of the "single man who persists forever" to figure history as a sustained and unified experience.

The debate about how much reverence and admiration the ancient authors deserve was thus typically expressed as a question of where to locate the "infancy" and "old age" of human history. In the dialogic *Parallele des Anciens et des Modernes* (1692), Perrault's *Chevalier* asks: "Is not the duration of the world ordinarily conceived as that of a man's life, as having had its childhood, its youth, and its prime, and as having now reached old age? ... Granted that this is so, must we not look upon our forefathers as the children and ourselves as the old men and true ancients?" To this, the *Abbé* replies:

That is a very just conception, but custom has given us a different version. With regard to the prejudice, almost universally held, that those whom we term ancients are more capable than their successors, it comes from the fact that the children, seeing ordinarily that their fathers and their grandfathers are wiser than they, and imagining that their great-grandfathers were much wiser still, have unconsciously associated with age an idea of sufficiency and capacity which they conceive to be the greater in proportion to the antiquity of past ages.[19]

Cultural reverence for antiquity is based on a child's respect for the wisdom of his father and grandfather. The *Abbé*'s metaphor for cultural history is not the course and maturation of the individual life but the relationship between parent and child, and filial appreciation of what the child learns and inherits from the parent. The moderns maintain their advantage over the ancients, however, and the *Abbé* quickly places his rhetorical images at their service: "the latest arrivals have, as it were, inherited the estate of their predecessors." Moderns have more accumulated experience and knowledge than their fathers and grandfathers, not because they are "ancient" but because they are "children" who have learned and inherited more.[20]

These two conceptions of cultural history locate the "childhood" of the species at different ends and involve two very different ideas of the child. In one historical narrative, the figure of the child embodies the earliest stages of inexperience and is located in the distant past, at the beginning of a process of maturation. In the other historical narrative, the child is an object of education, inheritance and cultural transmission and is located in the present and future and at the receiving end of a process of acculturation and accumulation. The two figures of the child and the historical narratives they inspire and support are, of course, intimately related to and involved in each other even as they oppose each other. They will only become more entangled over the course of the eighteenth century. Together they will produce the figure of a child who is simultaneously ancestor and progeny, past and future, an embodiment of both wisdom and ignorance. The figure of the child who contains these contradictions – Wordsworth's "The Child is Father of the Man" – we have long recognized as powerfully and centrally important to British Romantic culture, although these historical and cultural associations animating the phrase have been lately obscured.

What is at stake in these historical metaphors and the idea of childhood they employ is, in fact, a notion of historical and cultural progress, of how it happens and even, perhaps, of whether or not parents or children deserve the greater credit for its course. We can turn to one more influential essay from *"la querelle des anciens et des modernes"* to find anticipations of how the conjectural historians of the eighteenth century will deploy ontogenetic historical metaphors. "Nothing," argues Fontenelle in his *Digression sur les anciens et les modernes* (1688), "is such an impediment to progress, nothing hinders mental development so much, as excessive admiration of the ancients."[21] Fontenelle makes clear that what is emerging from this debate on modern culture's relationship to the

classical age is a concept of historical progress that is based on an analogy
to mental development:

> The comparison which we have just drawn between the men of all ages and a
> single man is applicable to our whole problem of the ancients and moderns.
> A good cultivated mind contains, so to speak, all the minds of preceding
> centuries; it is but a single identical mind which has been developing and
> improving itself all this time. Thus this man, who has lived since the beginning
> of the world up to the present, had his infancy, when he occupied himself merely
> with the most pressing needs of existence; his youth, when he was fairly successful
> in imaginative pursuits, such as poetry and eloquence, and when he even began
> to reason a little, though with less soundness than fire. He is now in his prime,
> when he reasons more forcefully and has greater intelligence than ever before; but
> he would be much farther advanced than he is had not the passion for war long
> occupied him and caused him to despise those sciences to which he has finally
> returned.[22]

Acknowledging the role of education and the transmission of knowledge
from one generation to the next in his notion that a "good cultivated
mind contains . . . all the minds of preceding centuries," Fontenelle also
offers the image of human history as that of a "single identical mind
which has been developing and improving itself all this time." In his
language of "mental development" and his outline of human history as
defined by mental stages and linguistic styles – from the imaginative
pursuits of poetry and eloquence, to greater reason and intelligence –
Fontenelle comes closest to anticipating the stadial theory of manners in
later philosophical histories. A century later the language of mental
development will be even sharper, and the ages of the life (infancy,
childhood, youth and maturity) will become the stages of ontogenetic
development.

The writers who debated the relative value of the "ancients" and
"moderns" over the course of the seventeenth century used the
metaphor of the individual life to articulate new narratives of history as
a progress. Of particular importance to our later period is their transformation of the "ancients" into "infants" or "children" and the ancient period
into a period of "infancy" or "childhood." Antiquity is no longer a
cultural or social ideal lost to a modern world; it is, instead, an original
state, a place of primitive origins, out of which humankind is presumed to
have steadily and continuously progressed. When we move ahead to the
histories of the Scottish Enlightenment, we will see how they have
extended this understanding of the "infancy" of ancient history into an
understanding of the globe. Rather than wonder if and when modern man

has fully returned to and repeated the glorious achievements of ancient man – an historical paradigm that leads to comparisons between "moderns" and "ancients" – the question increasingly becomes how man has progressed out of "rude origins" into a highly advanced modern state.[23]

The historical metaphor that Desnitsky declares displaced by the new Scottish theory is, we will see, everywhere in Scottish Enlightenment writing, actively reflected upon, revised and employed. While the historical metaphor of the individual life can take the form of the "single man who persists forever," increasingly it takes the form of the developing child. By the end of the eighteenth century, the representation of human history as a stable and reiterated sequence of stages depends to an ever-greater extent on the figure of the child and a rhetoric of infancy. "We are the ancients" increasingly becomes "we all begin in infancy." Infancy emerges as the dominant rhetorical strategy for figuring origins.

TRACING ORIGINS IN ENLIGHTENMENT INQUIRY

Fascination with and attention to "origins" in the eighteenth century is fundamental to Enlightenment inquiry generally. In his 1812 memoir of Adam Smith, Dugald Stewart looks back on the central questions of the Scottish Enlightenment and describes its questions and methods in these terms:

When, in such a period of society as that in which we live, we compare our intellectual acquirements, our opinions, manners and institutions, with those which prevail among rude tribes, it cannot fail to occur to us as an interesting question, by what gradual steps the transition has been made from the first simple efforts of uncultivated nature, to a state of things so wonderfully artificial and complicated. Whence has arisen that systematical beauty which we admire in the structure of a cultivated language; that analogy which runs through the mixture of languages spoken by the most remote and unconnected nations; and those peculiarities by which they are all distinguished from each other? Whence the origin of the different sciences and of the different arts; and by what chain has the mind been led from their first rudiments to their last and most refined improvements?[24]

Stewart presents the period's interest in origins as part of its penchant for cultural comparison. The comparison of the "opinions, manners, and institutions" of the society "in which we live" to those of "rude tribes" leads to questions of causation and progress – "by what gradual steps" and "by what chain" – as well as to questions of beginnings – "whence has arisen" and "whence the origin." "Origins" and "progress" are key terms of historical, philosophical and scientific inquiry of these years, a fact that can be seen simply by looking at various volume titles covering a range of topics: John Millar's *Origin of the Distinction of Ranks,* Jean-Jacques Rousseau's *Discourse upon the Origin and Foundation of Inequality,* Antoine-Yves Goguet's *The Origin of Laws, Arts and Sciences, and their Progress among the Most Ancient Nations,* Samuel Farr's *A Philosophical Enquiry into the Nature, Origin, and Extent of Animal Motion,* Charles Davy's *Conjectural Observations on the Origin and Progress of Alphabetic Writing,* Richard Eastcott's *Sketches of the Origin, Progress and Effects of Music,* Benjamin Barton's *New Views of the Origin of the Tribes and Nations of America,* James Tytler's *A Dissertation on the Origin and Antiquity of the Scottish Nation,* John Whitaker's *The Real Origin of Government.* A volume such as Lord Kames' *Sketches of the History of Man* includes chapters such as "Origins and progress of commerce," "Origin and progress of arts," "Origin and progress of American nations," "Progress of manners."

Origins in Stewart's passage are the "first simple efforts of uncultivated nature" and "first rudiments." They are early, elemental efforts of social organization and human culture. But his last question – "by what chain has the mind been led from their first rudiments to their last and most refined improvements?" – suggests a link between human nature and human history that is also characteristic of the intellectual tradition he describes here. Philosophical investigations into the workings of the human mind and social historical speculation were not distinct or fully separate fields of inquiry in Enlightenment writing. Accustomed as we now can be to pitting psychology against history, neuroscience against social science, it can be difficult to grasp how thoroughly integrated these concerns were to eighteenth-century thinkers. The new ways of thinking about and relating human development and history that emerged in the late eighteenth century relied on new ways of understanding and using origins as a major methodological and narrative tool. Here Condillac's *Essay on the Origin of Human Knowledge* is particularly instructive; indeed, because of its dialogue with Locke and its significant influence on the British debate on the origins of language, it is an important example to consider more fully. Condillac is instrumental in establishing the analogous relationship between the individual's acquisition of language and developing reason, on the one hand, and a nation's invention of language and advancement of literary arts on the other. The analogy between individual development and human history that he uses to conceptualize

the origins of language becomes important for philosophical and historical inquiries into origins more generally.

Condillac is often credited with extending Locke's *Essay Concerning
Human Understanding* by offering a fuller account of language and its
importance to mental constructions.[25] Condillac indeed shares the basic
tenets of Locke's empirical and sensationalist psychology: he rejects the
possibility of innate ideas and understands sense perceptions as providing
the first thoughts and materials of the mind. Answering the question of
how the mind advances from being, in Locke's famous phrase, an "empty
cabinet," to registering and making use of the most basic sense
impressions, to formulating increasingly complex and abstract ideas, is
Condillac's main object in the *Essay*. Like Locke, he is interested in the
developing mind. But while he follows Locke to a certain degree – indeed
the subtitle of the 1756 English translation of Condillac's *Essay* was
"A supplement to Mr. Locke's Essay on the Human Understanding" –
Condillac also faults Locke's *Essay* on two related counts. Locke, he
asserts, assumes that "as soon as the soul receives ideas by sense, it can
at will repeat, compose, and unite them together with infinite variety and
make all sorts of complex notions of them."[26] To counter this assumption
Condillac reminds us how "it is well established that in infancy we had
sensations long before knowing how to turn them into ideas," an evocation of the significance, silence and mysteries of infancy which resonates
in this period, as we shall see. Locke has passed too lightly over the very
earliest mental processes, and "in order to give a better explanation of the
origin of our knowledge," Condillac gives himself the necessary task of
showing "how it [the soul] acquires that exercise [of uniting ideas], and
what progress it makes in it." In other words, more attention must be paid
to the beginnings – to the "origins of knowledge" – and the earliest
processes of mental development and progress, to how exactly the mind
first forms ideas out of early sense impressions.

Here is where Locke's second major shortcoming becomes relevant: his
insufficient attention to words.[27] Words, and language more generally,
must "occupy a large part of my work," Condillac insists, chiefly because
he is convinced that "the use of signs is the principle that develops the seed
of all our ideas." Indeed his theory that ideas connect to signs which in
turn enable ideas to connect to each other is the "single principle"
announced in the *Essay*'s original subtitle as the fulcrum of Locke's work
on human understanding: "A work in which all that concerns the human
understanding is reduced to a single principle." Mental signs, the earliest
elements of language, make memory, reason and reflection possible, and

Condillac asserts that "the progress of the human mind depends entirely on the skill we bring to the use of language."[28] Condillac's essay thus plays a central role in establishing the study of language in the eighteenth century as the study of mental development or, in other words, "the natural history of understanding, of thought, of mind."[29]

Condillac does indeed devote a large part of his work to a discussion of language, particularly to the role it plays in the "progress of the human mind." But a glance at the organization of the *Essay* – how he divides its parts, the headings and titles of the various sections – still raises questions (for most twenty-first-century readers, at least) about how exactly he understands and pursues the origins and progress of the human mind and the significance of signs and language. Part I, entitled "The materials of our knowledge and especially the operations of the soul," is comprised of sections and subsections carrying such headings as: "Perception, consciousness, attention, and reminiscence," "How the connection of ideas, formed by attention, brings forth imagination, contemplation, and memory," "The use of signs is the true cause of the progress of imagination, contemplation, and memory," "Simple and complex ideas," and "The operation by which we give signs to our ideas." The bulk of Part II, entitled "Language and method," is devoted to Section 1, "The origin and progress of language," and here the headings seem to have a more historical, even literary, reach or orientation: "The language of action and that of articulated sounds, considered from their point of origin," "The prosody of the first languages," "Progress of the art of gesture among the ancients," "The origin of poetry," "Words," "Writing," and "Origin of the fable, the parable, and the enigma, with some details about the use of figures and metaphors."

How, we must ask, did Condillac understand and represent the relationship between Part I and Part II of his *Essay*? Why exactly does his theory that signs play a critical role in the development of the mind's capacity for reasoning and abstract thinking (Part I), either require, become, or make use of, a history of poetry, prosody, parables, music and other art forms (Part II)? Condillac speaks directly to these questions when he describes his project as one that requires him to trace the "operations of the soul in all their advances" but also to "explore how we have acquired the habit of using signs of all kinds."[30] Once again both advances and origins must be considered, as well as how we get from a point of origin to a more advanced state. Condillac continues:

In order to fulfill this double task, I have traced things as far as I could. On the one hand I have taken a new look at perception, because it is the first operation of the soul that we notice, and I have shown how and in what order it produces all the operations we gain the power to exercise. On the other hand I have begun with the language of action. It will be shown how it has produced all the arts that pertain to the expression of our thoughts: the art of gesture, dance, speech, declamation, the art of recording it, the art of pantomime, of music, of poetry, eloquence, writing, and the different characters of languages. This history of language will show the circumstances in which signs are imagined; will reveal their true meaning and show how to prevent their abuse; and it will not, I believe, leave any doubt about the origin of our ideas.[31]

Condillac's exploration of "how we have acquired the habit of using signs" involves both an examination of perception, the "first operation of the soul," as well as a history of language which begins with what he calls the "language of action": the gestures, facial expressions and vocal exclamations or "cries of passion" that are the human body's first, natural language. These are not the same tasks, and he keeps the doubled quality of his project before us in this passage: his "double task" involves, "on the one hand," a developmental narrative of the human mind and, "on the other hand," a speculative, quasi-historical narrative of language, literature and related art forms. These two inquiries are thus presented as paralleling each other: "perception" and the "language of action" occupy similar or parallel positions of origin in their respective narratives of progress.

Condillac thus presents the relationship between the development of the mind and the historical development of language and literary forms as analogous. His theories of how understanding first arises in the mind and how the first words of the first language were formed emerge together as complementary and mutually dependent narratives, each offering evidence to support and prove the other. For example, when Condillac is describing how the use of arbitrary signs is necessary for the development and operation of "reflection," he runs into a significant impasse: "It seems that one would not know how to make use of instituted signs if one was not already capable of sufficient reflection to choose them and attach ideas to them: how then, so goes the objection, is it that the exercise of reflection can only be acquired by the use of signs?" To this question of what comes first, the sign or the capacity to reflect and establish a sign, Condillac responds: "I answer that I shall meet this difficulty when I treat the history of language. Here it is enough for me to say that the difficulty has not escaped me."[32]

Condillac here refers his readers to his subsequent discussion on "The language of action and that of articulated sounds considered from their point of origin." There he imagines and narrates what will become a classic scene of Enlightenment history: "two children, one of either sex, sometime after the deluge, had gotten lost in the desert before they would have known the use of any sign." Perhaps, he continues, "some nation owes its origin only to such an event?" The question, then, is "to know how this budding nation made a language for itself?"[33] Condillac proceeds to narrate a hypothetical history of how these two children, by repeatedly observing in each other the gestures and facial expressions naturally attached to certain feelings of pain or desire, would gradually begin to call these natural signs to mind with the conscious exercise of their memory and imagination, thereby "doing by reflection what they had formerly done only by instinct."[34] The slow and gradual transition from observing involuntary natural signs to the voluntary use of arbitrary and conventional signs is Condillac's account of the invention of language. But he offers it chiefly as evidence within an account of how language makes thought possible, suggesting that each child in learning language repeats or re-enacts the scene of language's invention. The process of inventing or learning new signs enables the mental operations of memory, imagination and reflection to increase and improve, or to develop, and Condillac presents that "progress of mind" as occurring in both the individual and the species.

Condillac's *Essay* relies on a framework that becomes central to linguistic theory in the eighteenth century and that one can subsequently find in the writing of all the major thinkers in this field, including Jean-Jacques Rousseau, Adam Smith, Lord Monboddo and Johann Gottfried Herder: the practice of understanding how the mind develops through a hypothetical history of language and literature and of understanding the history of language and literature through a speculative narrative of mental philosophy or developmental psychology. Condillac's scene of children inventing language thus serves as an original scene for both the history of the species and the history of the individual. He moves between these histories, between Part I and Part II of his essay, always with a sense of his "double task," understanding the history of how a nation invented language for itself and the process by which the mind gradually begins to understand and make use of the arbitrary signs of language not only as complementary and parallel, but as analogous and thus offering critical support and key explanatory evidence for each other. Indeed, the development of the mind and the history of language and literature are perhaps best described as rhetorical re-presentations of each other in this philosophical tradition. Condillac plays a major role in establishing the logical and rhetorical structure of analogy that relates the history of individual language acquisition to the history of language's first invention, the same analogical framework that Shelley will later assume when, with deliberate casualness, he asserts the relationship of child and savage.

What makes Condillac's analogy possible is his understanding of "origins," and with this concern we can move our discussion out from Condillac's *Essay* into the broader context of the historicism and cultural theory that emerges in Scottish and Continental Enlightenment writing. Condillac's phrase, "I have traced things as far as I could," implies that he has traced things as far *back* as he could and is a repeated and common refrain in the writing of this period. Nevertheless, we must recognize Enlightenment interest in tracing things back to their point of origin as more of an analytical method than an historical inquiry. This is what Hans Aarsleff calls the "capital point" to be made about the period's understanding and use of origins: "the search for origins concerned the present state of man, not the establishment of some 'historical' fact or 'explanation' of how things actually were at some point in the past."[35] "Origins" in Enlightenment historical discourse are temporal and historical only to an extremely limited degree: they are first and foremost the basic principles of "human nature" which become, in this period, the privileged point of reference for philosophical explanation. Hence David Hume's famous declaration for the age that "Human Nature is the only science of man" and that all philosophical inquiry – from history and politics, to morality and mathematics – must begin from "the principles of human nature."[36] "To trace the origins" is precisely to identify and describe those "principles of human nature," a genetic methodology often traced to Locke's influence. "Origins" in Enlightenment and Romantic discourse are thus both beginnings and ongoing principles, the first, but also the "natural" or basic elements of the human being. The blending of these temporal and constitutive categories – or the movement between them – is fundamental to the intellectual inquiry of these years and one reason why answers to such questions as the origin of language always unfold as both history and philosophy of mind. It is precisely the ability to conceive of the early, elemental historical past as something that can still be found in present, persistent principles of human nature that the idea and notion of the "origin" enables in this period.

Of course this turn to the origins or basics of human nature as the central explanatory tool of philosophy and natural history is accompanied by a valorization of the "natural" and the "primitive" in wider Sentimental and Romantic culture. What is "natural" is opposed to what is "artificial," "social" and highly refined or advanced, "nature" and "art" being a central dichotomy of both Sentimentalism and Romanticism. "Origins," it is assumed, are more clearly evident in a primitive state, and are obscured or perverted by social advancement. The turn to origins usually entails a rejection of civil refinements. But as Stewart reminds his readers in his memoir of Adam Smith, relying on "natural causes" for an account of the origins of language is also a significant rejection of divine origins and explanations: "if we can show, from the known principles of human nature, how all [language's] various parts might gradually have arisen . . . a check is given to that indolent philosophy, which refers to a miracle, whatever appearances . . . it is unable to explain."[37] One of the recurring points of debate on the question of the origin of language in the eighteenth century was, in fact, the discussion of what knowledge can be gained by *not* assuming that language was a divine gift, but instead attempting to explain how early man might have first invented or discovered language using his own "natural" abilities. Thus Condillac takes up "two children . . . sometime after the deluge" and precisely *not* Adam and Eve who, coming from the hands of God, "did not owe the exercise of the operations of their soul to experience."[38] Rejecting both divine explanations and innate ideas – tantamount to the same thing in this period – Enlightenment thinkers turned instead to what they called the "origins" of human history and human nature, both its beginnings and its basic uniform principles, as the "best mode of explanation and analysis they knew."[39]

NEW HISTORICAL METHODS

We need to take this understanding of origins as a genetic methodology rather than an object of historical inquiry into our recovery and understanding of Enlightenment and Romantic historicism. In describing the period's interest in origins and progress, Dugald Stewart outlines a "species of philosophical investigation" which, significantly, both is and is not historical. There is, he insists, very little "direct evidence," very few "facts," pertaining to the origins of language or to the origins of any other social institution: "on most of these subjects very little information is to be expected from history." This is, of course, because these origins and earliest stages precede formal history: "for long before that stage of society when men begin to think of recording their transactions, many of the most important steps of their progress have been made."[40] Where history is silent, contemporary "travels and voyages" may offer some "detached facts." The philosopher, according to Stewart, can gather a "few insulated facts" from the "casual observations of travellers," who have "viewed the arrangements of rude nations." Even these curious sources, however, ultimately cannot provide anything that approaches a "regular and connected detail of human improvement." One must turn to theoretical speculation or conjecture:

In this want of direct evidence, we are under a necessity of supplying the place of fact by conjecture; and when we are unable to ascertain how men have actually conducted themselves upon particular occasions, of considering in what manner they are likely to have proceeded, from the principles of their nature, and the circumstances of their external situations.[41]

Stewart's memoir of Adam Smith becomes, in these paragraphs at least, a memoir of the Scottish Enlightenment and a defense of one of its central analytical tools, that of conjecture. Stewart presents conjecture as a philosophical and historical methodology and then names it as such: "to this species of philosophical investigation, which has no appropriated name in our language, I shall take the liberty of giving the title of *Theoretical* or *Conjectural History*," a practice, he suggests, that closely coincides "with that of *Natural History*, as employed by Mr. Hume" or with "what some French writers have called *Histoire Raisonnée*."[42]

Conjectural history thus becomes necessary when history otherwise fails to offer evidence and explanation about man's earliest origins. Stewart is describing a strategy for what to do when the trail of history goes cold. "When we cannot trace the process by which an event *has been* produced," he writes, it becomes important to speculate: "to show how it *may have been* produced by natural causes," working from the "known principles of human nature." Here again we find the period's interest in historical origins re-described as and re-directed toward "the known principles of human nature" which are, in turn, understood as uniform and stable throughout the varieties of history, geography, climate and culture. Origins and conjecture must thus be understood as two central and mutually supporting methodologies which together produce a major genre of Enlightenment historical writing, that of conjectural or philosophical history.[43] Faced with unknown historical origins – the question of how language was first invented, for example – conjecture becomes a legitimate analytical tool precisely because it assumes and relies on the uniform origins of human understanding – how the mind first makes use of language. The circularity here is central to and symptomatic of how this discourse works by constantly redirecting historical inquiry into philosophical psychology and vice versa, and by always assuming their reciprocal relationship. This relationship between history and mental development thus also assumes and depends upon a relationship between past and present: answers to the mysteries of the past can thus be sought in minds still present, particularly, as we shall see, in the minds of present-day children and savages.

To these new Enlightenment methodologies of origin and conjecture, we must add that of stadial theory, the "four-stages" theory that we have seen Meek identify as the central innovation of Enlightenment human sciences. Significantly Stewart points to the anecdotes of contemporary travelers as another legitimate resource in the effort to reconstruct the primitive past. Turning to travel for answers to the questions of history is an important characteristic of the new anthropological and historiographical practice that emerges out of the Scottish Enlightenment. The inventive framework that enables and makes sense of these geographical and temporal entanglements is stadial theory, which understood human societies to move through a series of "stages" or "states" in an order or pattern that was relatively uniform and stable. A four-stage sequence that progresses from a barbaric or savage state, through a pastoral, agricultural, and finally to a commercial state is the basic framework and most common elaboration of Enlightenment stadial theory.[44] This historical approach emphasizes both the autonomy and stability of the sequence – the idea that every nation or culture has or will move through this basic sequence of social development – as well as the unevenness or the differences between various social groups at a given time – the idea that different nations will be at different stages in the sequence and might proceed through these stages at different rates. Understood in its most general sense as a stable and reiterating sequence of stages, stadial theory can be seen as the master narrative or theoretical framework that guided the speculations and accounts offered in the wide range of Enlightenment conjectural histories.

Stadial theory thus gave Enlightenment historians another way of approaching the question of "origins" by suggesting that the historical past can be encountered and observed in the far reaches and "rude tribes" of the present-day globe. The figures of "savages" populating eighteenth-century travel literature are routinely compared to the primitive men of ancient history and understood as occupying the same stage of social development. Of particular importance here are the "savages" of North America who were taken as a living model of primitive social organization. Once again, Locke's influence is critical: it was he who promoted the idea that "in the beginning all the World was *America*."[45] Travel texts such as Joseph François Lafiteau's influential and widely quoted *Customs of the American Indians Compared with the Customs of Primitive Times* approached their exotic subjects looking for "traces of the most remote antiquity."[46] One can see how such comparisons frame an understanding of history in John Millar's description of stadial theory in his 1771, *Origin of the Distinction of Ranks*:

When we survey the present state of the globe, we find that, in many parts of it, the inhabitants are so destitute of culture, as to appear little above the condition of brute animals; and even when we peruse the remote history of polished nations, we have seldom any difficulty in tracing them to a state of the same rudeness and barbarism. There is, however, in man a disposition and capacity for improving his condition, by the exertion of which, he is carried on from one degree of advancement to another; and the similarity of his wants, as well as of the faculties by which those wants are supplied, has every where produced a remarkable uniformity in the several steps of his progression. . . . There is thus, in human society, a natural progress from ignorance to knowledge, and from rude to civilized manners, the several stages of which are usually accompanied with peculiar laws and customs.[47]

One of the most significant features of this passage is that Millar considers himself, from the vantage point of eighteenth-century Glasgow, able to survey both "the present state of the globe" and "the remote history of polished nations." In both globe and history he finds "the same rudeness and barbarism," a primitive state understood as the "origin" of his own advanced and highly differentiated society.[48]

Millar's articulation of stadial theory thus brings into focus a central fantasy enlivening the conjectural history that emerges in the eighteenth century, making it a vital part of Britain's increasingly colonial culture: the idea that access to the far reaches of the world makes the far reaches of history equally accessible. As Joseph-Marie Degérando famously proclaims in his *Observation of Savage Peoples*, "The philosophical traveller, sailing to the ends of the earth, is in fact travelling in time; he is exploring the past; every step he makes is the passage of an age."[49] In a letter to William Robertson upon the 1777 publication of his *History of America*, Edmund Burke famously praises the "very great advantages towards the knowledge of human nature" possessed by the British, particularly with the opening of the "New World." Those advantages, according to Burke, are that "we need no longer go to history to trace [human nature] in all stages and periods . . . now the great map of mankind is unrolled at once, and there is no state or gradation of barbarism, and no mode of refinement which we have not at the same moment under our view."[50]

Arguing that "human nature" should no longer be studied through history, Burke, in fact, celebrates a more omniscient historicism and charges the remote areas of the world with historical significance. His "great map of mankind" turns the globe into an historical pageant viewed all "at the same moment"; the "New World" is also the ancient past, its frontier the place where man's future and origin exist together. In an earlier, seminal lecture on philosophical history and stadial theory, Jacques Turgot also celebrates the "single glance" of global and historical vision:

through these infinitely varied inequalities [between various nations], the existing state of the universe, in presenting at once on the earth every shade of barbarism and refinement, shows us in a manner at a single glance the monuments, the vestiges, of every step taken by the human mind, the likeness of every stage through which it has passed, the history of all the ages.[51]

To explore the world is to view the course of human history; to travel to the far reaches of the planet is to go back in time.

In the confident imperialism of Turgot's "single glance" or Burke's "great map of mankind" we see an historical and anthropological practice emerging that encodes geography as history, history as geography, to produce a theory of culture and a schematic of cultural gradation, a framework in which different societies or cultures can be compared, measured and situated in relation to each other and to the state of the world as a whole. That this cultural scheme is both a geographical map and an historical time line is critical to how it works. In pointing to Enlightenment discourse as the beginnings of modern anthropology, Johannes Fabian pinpoints this strategy of *spatializing Time* as foundational to anthropology's emergence as an academic discipline in the nineteenth century and to its dominant methodologies throughout the twentieth century. In this discourse, cultural difference is consistently and systematically read as historical distance.[52] James Chandler describes this conceptual framework as the product of an analogy between historiography – ways of describing difference through time – and anthropology – ways of describing difference across space. Stadial theory – an account of "uneven development," in Chandler's terms – is thus a coding system that articulates how the relationships and identifications of this historiographic and anthropological analogy work, a grid that enables, for example, the North American Indians to be compared to the Scottish Highlanders or

the ancient Scythians. History becomes a cultural, geographical and
temporal calibration or, in Chandler's words: "a periodical coding of
relationships among unevenly developing national narratives and
temporalities."[53]

What risks being left out of recent accounts of Scottish Enlightenment
historicism, however, is the extent to which these historical theories that
we have been outlining rely on the analogy between individual
development and human history and a rhetoric of infancy and
childhood. Take, for example, William Robertson, whose writings have
been credited with transforming the practice of Western historiography.
Robertson's project in his *History of America* (which went through
approximately twenty editions in the forty years between 1777 and 1817)
is, in fact, "to complete the history of the human mind."[54] The project
requires that he "follow [man] in his progress through the different stages
of society, as he gradually advances from the infant state of civil life
towards its maturity and decline." For Robertson, the discovery of infant
America is so valuable precisely because it allows the philosopher historian
to "examine the sentiments and actions of human beings in the infancy of
social life."[55] In addressing the issue of the remarkable similarities between
the Americans of the "New World" and the ancient people of the "Old
World," Robertson dismisses the idea that these commonalities are proof
of genetic descent or racial affinity. Correspondences of culture and
manners, he insists, are the result of like climate and situation: two tribes
"in the most remote regions of the globe" yet living in a similar climate
and at the same stage of social "improvement," will "feel the same wants
and exert the same endeavours to supply them."[56]

Significantly, Robertson emphasizes the extent to which basic economic and social organization determines human behavior in history:
"the disposition and manners of men are formed by their situation, and
arise from the state of society in which they live." But his emphasis on
climate and situation is enabled by a belief in the uniformity of an
embodied human nature and articulated through a rhetoric of similarity:
"the same objects will allure, the same passions will animate them, and the
same ideas and sentiments will arise in their minds."[57] Robertson's stress
on situation, subsistence and social organization thus leads him to this
conclusion: "in every part of the earth, the progress of man hath been
nearly the same; and we can trace him in his career from the rude
simplicity of savage life, until he attains the industry, the arts, and the
elegance of polished society."[58] This "progress of man" is the "history of
the human mind," a history that, Robertson insists, must be traced

through all the diverse conditions in which man has been placed. Variety and diversity are thus brought into and made part of a singular history, and this emphasis on material conditions and their many varieties is put at the service of a larger, unified narrative.

In Robertson's explication of the historical premises underlying stadial theory, and in his argument for the importance of America in writing the history of the human mind, we see the extent to which the idea of environment and material situation as determinative of human behavior and history relies on a prior notion of the uniformity of human nature and rhetorically offers itself as a narrative of mental development. These two notions – historical and cultural determinism, on the one hand, and the uniformity of human nature, on the other – ideas which increasingly came to oppose each other over the course of the twentieth century, are essential to each other in the larger intellectual culture in which Robertson writes. Cornelius de Pauw's 1768 *Recherches Philosophiques sur les Américains* makes this connection even more explicit in his discussion of similarities between Americans and the ancient Scythians, between the Canadians and the Siberian Tunguses:

I return here to that great principle of which I have already made use, and say that it is not only natural but also necessary that there should be, as between savages located in such similar climates, as many resemblances as there possibly are between the Tunguses and the Canadians. Equally barbarous, equally living by hunting and fishing in countries which are cold, infertile, and covered with forests, what disproportion between them would one expect? Where people feel the same needs, where the means of satisfying them are the same, where the atmospheric influences are so similar, can the manners be contradictory, and can the ideas vary?[59]

The environmentalist and materialist emphasis of Enlightenment stadial theory assumes that when people "feel the same needs" and face the same basic material conditions, they will respond in the same way. While this theory offers an innovative way of describing, comparing and calibrating cultural *difference*, it displays equally strong interests in the uniformity, similarity and reiteration of human nature and in human progress. This, of course, enables Robertson and other Enlightenment historians to conceive of their histories of America and other "rude nations" as the "history of man" or the "history of the human mind": "man" and "mind" thus signaling an individual who can be generalized as well as a general derived from what can be known about the individual.

I have been belaboring the basics of Enlightenment discourse in the hope that we might see anew the rhetorical strategies of metaphor and analogy, and the philosophical assumptions of human uniformity, connecting specific to general, singular to multiple, individual to species, in the historical writing of these years. James Chandler has productively argued that the Scottish Enlightenment developmental framework must be differentiated from the notion of a universal progress of spirit articulated by Hegel and German Romantic historicism. The Scottish Enlightenment developmental sequence, Chandler notes, stresses "measurement, comparison, and explanation: rates of historical change are measurable by comparing the progress of different societies with one another and are to some degree explicable by relating the state of society with the 'state of the world' at that same moment."[60] This important distinction is misleading only if, in stressing its non-universalizing sensibilities, we forget that this method is not simply interested in the wide range of human culture and diversity of materials suddenly made available to historical study, but is instead invested in what Chandler elsewhere describes as the "measurable forms of dislocation," invested, that is, in placing human difference and diversity into a geographical historical grid that allows it to be measured, located and compared. Mark Salber Phillips describes this historical method in these terms:

But although the speculative historians drew heavily on the materials of the history of manners, they were not content simply to represent common life in all its diversity of appearance. In their commitment to create a history that would be more systematic and farseeing, they built on a philosophical psychology of the human mind, as well as a comparative study of manners and customs. The reciprocities between these two methods of understanding provided the principal basis for a grand-narrative whose purpose was to represent the vast, undocumented history of human experience at every stage of social progress.[61]

The grand-narrative of Scottish Enlightenment conjectural history is not that of the universal spirit, but there is a grand-narrative, nevertheless, and it relies on some fundamental and unifying principles. Perhaps the most important of these is what de Pauw above refers to as "that great principle" and what Hans Aarsleff over 200 years later will describe as "one of the great commonplaces of the eighteenth century": the "doctrine of uniformity of human nature in all ages and climes."[62]

This philosophical assumption of human uniformity and the grand-narrative of stadial theory allowed Enlightenment historians to construct the peoples of North America, Africa or the Caribbean as, in Alan Bewell's words, "observable or empirical figures of human origins." The exotic and foreign "savage" thus serves as an uncanny figure of the European self, a "means of self-reflection, a way of recovering aspects of the self that could no longer be easily recognized."[63] Such identifications are possible, however, only in a philosophical and representational system in which individual development and human history are understood as analogous, in which "the savage is to ages what the child is to years." These figures of human origins were thus perceived and represented through the rhetorical and conceptual lens of infancy and childhood.

FERGUSON'S COLONY OF CHILDREN

Adam Ferguson's 1767 *Essay on the History of Civil Society* offers some of the most vivid and important examples of just exactly how Scottish historical writing deployed and depended upon ontogenetic analogies and a rhetoric of infancy. One of the best-known conjectural histories in the Scottish Enlightenment tradition, the *Essay on the History of Civil Society* is part of a larger literary tradition that uses the image of the child, or the narrative of individual development out of infancy, to evoke larger historical narratives and the possibilities of historical and cultural recapitulation. Ferguson's discussions of history turn on the paradoxical images of infant and ancestor, child and father, while also offering a "colony of children" as a major new metaphor for history. In these images we discover the rhetorical antecedents to Wordsworth's epigram, "The Child is Father of the Man."

Like so many philosophic and natural historians of his day who viewed North America as a laboratory of primitive culture, Ferguson trumpets the importance of America, not only in completing our knowledge of "man" in all ages and stages, but, particularly and paradoxically, in writing the history of Europe. In a rather remarkable elaboration of just what stadial theory means for historical knowledge and writing, Ferguson suggests that the history of a nation is not found in its own past, but in the present-day of a more primitive neighbor or in the travel narratives of foreign observers:

Thucydides, notwithstanding the prejudice of his country against the name of *Barbarian*, understood that it was in the customs of barbarous nations he was to study the more ancient manners of Greece. The Romans might have found an image of their own ancestors, in the representations they have given of ours; and if an Arab clan shall become a civilized nation, or any American tribe escape the poison which is administered by our traders of Europe, it may be from the relations of the present times, and the descriptions which are now given by travellers,[64] that such a people, in after ages, may best collect the accounts of their origin.

History here becomes a complex process of shifting temporality and geography in order to discover one's own past in another's present. James Chandler has described how anachronism (things out of time) and anatopism (things out of place) become inverted mirrors of each other in the historical method of the Scottish Enlightenment. Here the "customs of barbarous nations" can be understood as the "more ancient manners of Greece," and "the relations of the present times, and the descriptions which are now given by travellers" are the future history of an "Arab clan" or "American tribe" when they attain the state of "a civilized nation." By reading the present as past or future, by looking for one's own history in the present-day of another, this historical method uses the forms and strategies of dislocation to situate or locate a culture in its anthro-historical framework.[65]

This chiastic figure relating time and space, history and geography, informs the particular importance of America to Europe for Ferguson:

It is in their present condition that we are to behold, as in a mirror, the features of our own progenitors; and from thence we are to draw our conclusions with respect to the influence of situations, in which we have reason to believe that our fathers were placed. What should distinguish a German or a Briton, in the habits of his mind or his body, in the manners or apprehensions, from an American, who, like him, with his bow and his dart, is left to traverse the forest; and in a like severe or variable climate, is obliged to subsist by the chase?[66]

The inverted mirror that structures the relationship between things in and out of time and things in and out of place here structures the relationship between Europe and America. On the one hand, this mirror enables Ferguson to remake the world into an earlier, less advanced and presumably inferior version of Europe, a place where human "origins" can be clearly seen. In this reading, we might see Europe as always, solidly in its own place and time, providing the standard against which the anachronisms and anatopisms of other cultures can be measured. But the mirror and the metaphor reflect in both directions, devices that also work to throw Europe out of a solid sense of place and time. Ferguson's mirror of history shows him an image of savage America as well as savage Europe. His imagined figure who traverses the forest with his bow and dart is simultaneously German, Briton and American.

Embedded in Ferguson's rhetorical question – "What should distinguish a German or a Briton . . . from an American" – are some of the key assumptions of stadial theory, conjectural history and the inquiry of origins that we have identified. Ferguson's question assumes that given a similar climate – "a like severe or variable climate" – and a similar mode of subsistence – "obliged to subsist by the chase" – nothing will distinguish the German, Briton or American in the "habits of his mind or his body." His emphasis on material and environmental conditions as shaping human behavior and characterizing the different stages of human history is precisely what makes Scottish Enlightenment historiography important to twentieth-century commentators who have found in this theory early articulations of their own historical practice. Here, however, is another instance where we need to take seriously Phillips' caution against using stadial theory to support a presentist historical agenda, either by overemphasizing the materialism of four-stages theory or by losing sight of how its analysis of the determinative force of material conditions is based on a prior notion of the uniformity of human nature. German, Briton and American in Ferguson's passage do not differ in habits of mind and body, and *that is how and why they can be compared.*[67] This idea of a uniform human nature is not, however, the simplistic idea that humans are always and everywhere the same, that human nature is static and unchanging. Ferguson and other key Scottish Enlightenment theorists of stadial theory have an understanding of the human mind and human nature as developing, as changing, as becoming capable of greater complexity of thought and refinement in behavior. For these philosophical historians, the uniformity of human nature becomes something more like a uniformity of human development, one that they trace at both the individual and the societal level and, even more critically, one that they understand and describe by way of the analogy between individual and societal growth. The comparison between Europe and America that views present America as past Europe is thus predicated on that prior comparison or analogy between history and individual development.

Ferguson's passage on the importance of America to Europe continues, and in the lines that follow we see the extent to which these geographical/anthropological and temporal/historical mirror games rely on a rhetoric of infancy:

If, in advanced years, we would form a just notion of our progress from the cradle, we must have recourse to the nursery; and from the example of those who are still in the period of life we mean to describe, take our representations of past manners, that cannot, in any other way, be recalled.[68]

Here is Wordsworth's epigram – "The Child is Father of the Man" – anticipated in the form of historical theory and methodology. For Ferguson, present-day Americans allow Europe "to behold, as in a mirror, the features of our own progenitors" and to understand the "influence of situations, in which we have reason to believe that our fathers were placed." At the same time, America is Europe's "nursery," providing Ferguson and his fellow Europeans with the evidence needed to "form a just notion of our progress from the cradle." Americans are both fathers and infants, ancestors seen as children and children seen as ancestors. These contradictory images – later captured by Wordsworth in such a condensed and powerful form – come directly out of an historical discourse that enables present-day cultures to be situated in the past and understood as "ancient," and that uses the metaphor of the individual life to describe "primitive" populations as both "ancestors" and "infants."

The mixed metaphors in Ferguson's historical theory thus signal the contradictions and tensions in the notions of culture and historical progress embedded within conjectural history and stadial theory. He begins his *History of Civil Society* with a conventional, but newly important statement of what makes human development and progress unique. Significantly, his understanding of human development is neither physiological nor biological; organic and natural models of growth and development are useful but not fully adequate in representing human progress. "Natural productions are generally formed by degrees," he notes, adding that "vegetables grow from tender shoot, and animals from an infant state." These images of natural development and organic growth can be applied to animal life, but are not sufficient for describing the progress of humankind. While all animals "exhibit a progress in what they perform, as well as in the faculties they acquire," human progress has an added dimension: "This progress in the case of man is continued to a greater extent than in that of any other animal. Not only the individual advances from infancy to manhood, but the species itself from rudeness to civilization."[69] Here we can see how the analogy between the progress of the individual from infancy to manhood and that of the species from rudeness to civilization working in a number of ways. Not only are the progresses of individual and species implied to be parallel and comparable, but they are also understood as reinforcing and extending each other. The progress of the species affects and augments the progress of the individuals within that species, and the progress made by individuals, in turn, adds to and is retained by that of the larger species.

Importantly this sense of parallel and mutually enhancing progresses becomes, for Ferguson, as well as other Enlightenment and Romantic writers, humankind's distinguishing characteristic: "In other classes of animals, the individual advances from infancy to age or maturity; and he attains, in the compass of a single life, to all the perfection his nature can reach: but, in the human kind, the species has a progress as well as the individual."[70] In his prize-winning and influential *Treatise on the Origin of Language*, J. G. von Herder likewise insists that it is precisely because humans have an extended, relatively helpless childhood that they also make progress as a species. Contrasting the human infant, who has "no obscure, innate drive which pulls him into his element and into his circle of efficacy, to his means of subsistence and to his work,"[71] to the bird, who "brings the skill of building nests with it from its egg," Herder declares that the human infant is abandoned by nature and natural instincts, is excessively weak and helpless, and remains that way for so long precisely in order that he "may enjoy an *upbringing*":

Nature consequently bonded together the human being [with other human beings] through necessity and a caring parental drive for which the Greeks had the word *storgê*, and in this way "a bond of *instruction* and *upbringing*" became essential to him. In this case parents had not collected the circle of their ideas *for themselves*; at the same time it was there in order to be *communicated*, and the son has the advantage of already inheriting the wealth of their spirit early, as though in epitome. The former pay off nature's debt by teaching; the latter fill up the idea-less need of their own nature by learning, just as they will later in turn pay off their natural debt of increasing this wealth with their own contribution and transferring it again to others.[72]

The bird that brings "the skill of building nests with it from its egg" also "takes it with it, without transferring it to others, into its grave." With other animals, according to Herder, "everything remains individual, the immediate work of nature, and so there arises '*no progression of the soul of the species*.'" With the human species it is otherwise: "no individual human being exists *for himself*; 'he is *inserted into the whole of the species, he is only one for the continuing series*.'"[73]

The human animal thus distinguishes itself from all other animals because it has an extended childhood and because it has a history, and these two characteristics are fundamentally related: in other words, humans have a unique capacity to have history because they alone have a childhood. This is Herder's key insight: humans are historical because they are children. Again Herder makes these points by drawing the contrast between the human and other creatures. "The bee," he explains, "builds in its childhood as it does in advanced age, and will build the same way at the end of the world as in the beginning of creation."[74] Here Herder gives the bee a "childhood" and an "advanced age" in order to claim, in fact, that it has neither. The bee's life is one state of being, eternal for the short time it lasts, because the bee never changes: "the bee was a bee when it built its first cell."[75] In contrast, human beings "are always growing out of a childhood, however old we may be, are ever in motion, restless, unsatisfied." "The essential feature of our life," Herder comments, "is never enjoyment but always progression, and we have never been human beings until we – have lived out our lives."[76]

Both Herder's and Ferguson's discussions of human history and development reveal the extent to which notions of progress and development are inextricably tied to notions of infancy and childhood. Significantly, neither Herder's nor Ferguson's analogy between the individual life-cycle and the history of the species makes any mention of old age and decline. Later in the *History of Civil Society*, Ferguson reflects on the tradition of applying the "images of youth, and of old age" to nations. "Communities," he notes, "like single men, are supposed to have a period of life." These images of history's "youth" and "old age" are both "apposite" and "familiar." But Ferguson insists that "the case of nations, and that of individuals, is very different":

The human frame has a general course; it has in every individual a frail contexture and limited duration; it is worn by exercise, and exhausted by a repetition of its functions: But in a society, whose constituent members are renewed in every generation, where the race seems to enjoy perpetual youth, and accumulating advantages, we cannot, by any parity of reason, expect to find imbecilities connected with mere age and length of days.[77]

Pascal's "single man who persists forever" is here granted "perpetual youth," much like Herder's collective humanity that is "always growing out of a childhood, however old we may be."

Indeed Ferguson's preferred historical image is neither that of the single man, nor that of natural, vegetable growth, but rather that of a "colony of children." He turns to this historical image as part of his initial, extended attack on Rousseau's representation of man in his original "state of nature" as a solitary and isolated brute without language or social relationships. Imagining an isolated man in the wilds of a primitive world as an example of "natural man," or using the discovery of a "wild man" who has "always lived apart from his species" as a "specimen of any general character" is a flawed methodology in Ferguson's view. If the question must be asked, "What the mind of man could perform when left to itself, and without the aid of any foreign direction?" then Ferguson insists that the answer must be found not in the spectacular cases of "wild children" or in imaginary figures of solitary men, but in "the history of mankind."

He reminds us furthermore that, "mankind are to be taken in groupes, as they have always subsisted." As we know, Ferguson is as interested as any of his peers in primitive states and the histories of "rude nations," but he insists that every historical "experiment" should be made "with entire societies, not with single men":

We have every reason, however, to believe, that in the case of such an experiment made, we shall suppose, with a colony of children transplanted from the nursery, and left to form a society apart, untaught, and undisciplined, we should only have the same things repeated, which in so many different parts of the earth, have been transacted already. The members of our little society would feed and sleep, would herd together and play, would have a language of their own, would quarrel and divide, would be to one another the most important objects of the scene, and, in the ardour of their friendships and competitions, would overlook their personal danger, and suspend the care of their self-preservation. Has not the human race been planted like the colony in question? who has directed their course? whose instructions have they heard? or whose example have they followed?[78]

This passage reveals how imagining an historical experiment – "a colony of children transplanted from the nursery, and left to form a society apart" – is also an act of constructing an historical metaphor – "Has not the human race been planted like the colony in question?" Here human history itself becomes a grand experiment undertaken without guidance and instruction. The "single man who lives forever" and the "single identical mind which has been developing and improving itself all this time" as figures for representing human history as an individual life are replaced by the figure of a child and, significantly, a group of children "left to form a society apart."

In offering a "colony of children" as a major metaphor for human history, Ferguson's immediate motivation is the desire to break down an exaggerated sense of the difference between man's natural state and his artificial and social state. Left to himself, "apart, untaught," man would still be the social, inventive and self-improving animal he has always been. "We speak of art as distinguished from nature," Ferguson comments later, "but art itself is natural to man."[79] Thus, where his fellow philosophic historians typically point to the "savages" of America when answering the question "where is the state of nature to be found," Ferguson's answer is a resounding: "It is here; and it matters not whether we are understood to speak in the island of Great Britain, at the Cape of Good Hope, or the Straits of Magellan."[80] History is not simply a progress or fall out of an original natural state. Much like Herder's idea that man's "essential feature" is that of progression or continual development, man's "natural state" according to Ferguson is precisely his capacity for self-improvement and invention and is thus carried forward and made part of the most refined societies. The "primitive" and "natural" are not simply or exclusively located elsewhere in time or space; "it is here ... in the island of Great Britain."

In this context, the image of the "colony of children" does important work for Ferguson. First of all, it suggests that history unfolds much like children develop and grow. Importantly, here again, the development of the child is not described in the natural, biological rhetoric that will dominate later in the nineteenth century. It is rather a function of the child's social life and interaction with other children. Thus where other Enlightenment philosophers see this parallel only in the singular cases of "wild children," Ferguson insists on the normative and social qualities of this analogy; his "little society" of children "feed and sleep," "herd together and play," invent "a language of their own," and experience both "friendships and competitions" much like any group of children might and do. Significantly, Ferguson's portrait of childhood has all the major elements of stadial theory or a conjectural history: attention to means of subsistence, social organization, the development of language, and even a hint of property, conflict and war. The image of the child growing up provides history with a developmental narrative, but the child's development is more stadial than physiological or biological.

The image of children growing up also provides history with a narrative of predictable and familiar *reiteration*. Indeed, what is important in Ferguson's image is not only that history unfolds like children grow up, but that we "have the same things repeated, which in so many different parts of the earth, have been transacted already." In this way, Ferguson's "colony of children" probably refers back to Locke's use of the same image in the *Essay Concerning Human Understanding*. Arguing against innate principles, and particularly against an innate idea of God, Locke insists that we cannot assume that the universal belief in some God found "in all the tribes of mankind" is proof of an innate idea of God. If that were so, then we would equally have to posit an innate idea of fire, since "there is not a person in the world who has a notion of a God, who has not also the idea of fire." These ideas, however, are present generally in "men grown to maturity in all countries," and they are "extended no further than that." In other words, they are not present in children, as Locke illustrates:

I doubt not but if a colony of young children should be placed in an island where no fire was, they would certainly neither have any notion of such a thing, nor name for it, how generally soever it were received and known in all the world besides; and perhaps too their apprehension would be as far removed from any name, or notion, of a God, till some one amongst them had employed his thoughts to inquire into the constitution and causes of things, which would easily lead him to the notion of a God; which having once taught to others, reason, and the natural propensity of their own thoughts, would afterwards propagate, and continue amongst them.[81]

Locke's "colony of young children" is also an image of developmental and reiterative history. The children have no knowledge of God, but they will come to it through their own inquiry, reason and social interaction, thereby repeating the steps followed by "all the tribes of mankind." This is an idea of children teaching themselves through experience that will subsequently be championed by Rousseau in outlining his course of "negative education" in *Emile*. The child left on an island arguably remains a guiding image for Rousseau; significantly, *Robinson Crusoe* is the only book Emile will be allowed to read.[82]

HISTORY AS REITERATION; HISTORY AS RECAPITULATION

The image of the colony of children, an image of developmental and reiterative history, is thus intimately bound up in the changing conceptions of historical time that emerge over the course of the eighteenth century. One common way of describing the shift in historical thought from the seventeenth to the eighteenth century is to note how classical, cyclical or sacred models of historical time give way to linear and progressive notions of historical time. In his influential discussion of nationalism, for example, Benedict Anderson describes these changes in the representation of temporality and history as the shift from a sacred temporality in which "'the here and now is ... simultaneously something which has always been, and will be fulfilled in the future'" to an idea of "'homogeneous, empty time'" through which an imagined community moves, constituting itself in the present through relations marked by "calendrical coincidence" and articulated in the temporal gesture of "meanwhile."[83] For Anderson, this new way of thinking about simultaneity allows "horizontal-secular, transverse-time" communities, such as the nation, to become possible, and he understands them as constituting themselves largely in an imagined present. For Walter Benjamin, from whom Anderson borrows the phrase, "homogeneous, empty time" is a form of temporality that is intimately tied to and makes possible the notion of progressive history: "the concept of the historical progress of mankind cannot be sundered from the concept of its progression through a homogeneous, empty time."[84] Time undifferentiated except by the devices of clock and calendar and thus emptied of significance and difference *in itself*, becomes the medium in which historical progress unfolds.

Of course, historical progress can unfold in different places at different rates and different times; empty, homogenous time thus also allows for the calibrations and comparisons across time and geography that we have seen stadial theory develop to understand and organize a world of "uneven development." Thus to Benjamin's and Anderson's discussions of modern temporality we need to add an awareness of how this emerging idea of progressive history is increasingly figured as developmental (or stadial) and reiterative. Indeed, another way to describe the shift in thinking about and representing historical time that happens over the course of the eighteenth century might be to note its new ways of conceptualizing repetition in history: the *repetitions* of cyclical time are replaced by the *reiterations* of developmental, progressive time.

The difference I want to draw attention to is between repetition as *return* and repetition as *another instance of.* If cyclical or sacred historical narratives understand repetition as a return of what has come before and will come again, or as the fulfillment of what has been foreseen and awaited, repetition carries historical significance in itself. Reiteration seems to empty repetition of its significance: it is again and again, and one instance is not the fulfillment of the previous nor a prophecy of the next, but simply another iteration of. Here is where the stadial theory of Enlightenment historicism becomes a new framework for understanding repetition in history and making reiteration both meaningful and measurable. As different social groups are understood to move through the stages of development at different rates and times, history becomes a set of reiterations held in relationship to each other. The fact that the stages of social and historical development are compared to the development of the individual and, in fact, conceptualized through an analogy between individual and social development, adds a further dimension to this scheme of historical reiteration. History's reiterations can unfold in the development of an individual or in the progress of a nation. Reiteration promises meaning by leaving open the possibility of *recapitulation*; the individual or the social entity's movement through time is charged with the significance of repeating a larger pattern in the particular, or recapitulating an intimate relationship on a grand scale.

Ferguson's colony of children, offered as a developmental or stadial metaphor and historical experiment, is imagined and staged repeatedly in fictional texts of sentimental and Romantic literary culture. Bernardin de Saint Pierre's *Paul and Virginia*, Eliza Fenwick's *Secresy*, Elizabeth Inchbald's *Nature and Art*, Thomas Campbell's *Gertrude of Wyoming*, Walter Scott's *Guy Mannering*, William Wordsworth's *Prelude* are only a few examples of the many different sorts of texts that place child figures in various degrees of solitude and wilderness. These texts exploit what Paul de Man called the "Babes in the Wood" topos, referring to the traditional ballad of child abandonment that became a recurring example of native poetry and the natural charms of simple, traditional verse in the ballad revival of the latter eighteenth century.[85] The centrality of this topos in the articulation and consolidation of Britain's native, national literature is no accident. The image of children left to themselves on islands, in woods or amidst other wilds is not simply a depiction of natural virtue or a staging of sentimental simplicity. The scene also carries historical charges, suggesting that national and individual history might begin and unfold together. Telling the story of how the children live, learn and grow becomes an act of national historical narrative.

The "Babes in the Wood" or "colony of children" topos – whether in fictional or philosophical texts – thus offers a fantasy of recapitulation that becomes increasingly important to how Romantic historical and anthropological discourse represents the parallel between individual development and human history, as well as the relationship between individual and history or culture.[86] It is an image that becomes important again in the twentieth century when stadial theory and the comparative methods of anthropology and child studies begin to be questioned. Texts such as J. M. Barrie's *Peter and Wendy*, Richard Hughes' *A High Wind in Jamaica* and William Golding's *Lord of the Flies* all return to the idea of a children's colony precisely in order to revisit and revise the notions of cultural and historical progress that the historical metaphors of the Scottish Enlightenment first articulated. This tradition of novels – one that might be traced from *Paul and Virginia* to *Lord of the Flies*, for example – offers a very different type of national temporality than that identified and located in the novel by Benedict Anderson. These narratives are less interested in a temporality of coincidence and "meanwhile" than they are in a temporality of shifting scales (from adult world, to child's world, from the time and history of the individual, to the time and history of the nation) and the temporal devices of analogy and recapitulation that bring these different scales into meaningful relationship. They imagine the nation not as a community constituted in a present-moment of meanwhile and moving steadily through empty, homogeneous time, but as something formed in and through the relationship of analogy and the promise of recapitulation: that the past of the nation can be found in the present of the child, that the growth and education of the individual can repeat the stages of a cultural history. Time is not empty; it is rich with the possibility of meaningful alignment, with the possibility that the grand-narratives of history and nation might be repeated and experienced on a smaller, local or individual level. The novel thus assumes its place in constructing and imagining the nation simply by taking up its role as a vehicle of reiteration.[87]

The image of a "colony of children transplanted from the nursery, and left to form a society apart" provides the Romantic period with new ways of conceptualizing history, shaping historical time into something that can be reiterated or recapitulated at the level of individual, nation and species. The promise is that the child might repeat and experience in his own lifetime the full course of human history. The fact that Ferguson insists on viewing the child not simply as an isolated individual but as part of a "colony" or "society" underscores the extent to which this image also represents the individual's relationship to culture, society and history, staging what Herder called the "bond of instruction and upbringing" that, of necessity, binds human beings into social groups. History does not unfold in the child naturally and inevitably like a plant grows; its repetitions are relatively stable, measurable and predictable, but they involve social sentiments and formations between people and must account for how these social relationships impinge on and impress the individual.

NO LONGER NEEDING HISTORY IN THE SCOTTISH ENLIGHTENMENT

In tracing the transformation of the historical metaphor of the individual life from that of the "single man who persists forever" into that of a developing child or "colony of children," we have necessarily revisited a number of Enlightenment maxims and methodologies: origins, conjecture, stadial theory, the idea of uniform human nature, and the analogy between individual mental development and human history. My hope is that the work of looking again at these familiar doctrines of Enlightenment thought will significantly alter our sense of just how familiar the "history" from this period is; thus, in many ways, this chapter has offered the simple reminder that the historicism of the British Enlightenment and Romantic period is *not* our own. But this work of de-familiarization should also alert us to the uncertain status of "history" within Enlightenment historicism. For example, Turgot's "single glance" and Burke's "great map of mankind" as figures of historical vision and knowledge differ significantly in tone and emphasis from Stewart's description of conjectural or philosophical history. Where Turgot and Burke both stress the new and comprehensive visibility of history – the "single glance" that can encompass all of history – Stewart emphasizes the blind spots and silences of history, the moments when what cannot be known necessarily leads to speculation and conjecture. Without making too much of what are, no doubt, differences of context and rhetorical stance, I want to highlight the questions raised in these years about whether or not what can be known about the history of man is, in fact, *historical* knowledge. Even Burke's triumphant embrace of Robertson's *History of America* describes the omniscient historicism of imperial Britain as a turn *away* from history. If one "need no longer go to history to trace [human nature] in all stages and periods," then exactly what and where is the "history" in the emerging historicism of the Scottish Enlightenment?

This question has been debated – and should continue to be – from the heyday of conjecture in the years of the Scottish Enlightenment up to our own present interest in recuperating the historical discourse of British Romantic writing. Aarsleff, whose "capital point" about Enlightenment philosophical inquiry is that its investigation of origins was never meant to establish historical facts or to describe "how things actually were in the past," makes the point so forcefully because it is at the center of how Enlightenment discourse was *misunderstood* in the following century:

The eighteenth century did not fool itself that it was establishing facts about the primitive state of mankind; it sought reasoned plausibilities with the chief intent of separating man's natural endowments from his artificial accomplishments ... It is one of the curious quirks of history that the nineteenth century became so compulsively historical in the factual sense that it misinterpreted the eighteenth century on this important point.[88]

The questions raised about just how the eighteenth century understood "history" and its own historical methodologies were not, however, asked only by those in the nineteenth century suffering from being "compulsively historical in the factual sense." Aarsleff's insistence that the eighteenth century never fooled itself about the historical and factual status of its hypothetical histories overlooks the debate that accompanied these conjectural narratives from the beginning.

In fact, uneasiness about the fictional and imaginative elements of Enlightenment conjectural histories, as Alan Bewell reminds us, is expressed by their own authors in the very act of penning their "special and complex fusion of fact and fiction, textual speculation and observation."[89] In the opening pages of his *Essay on the History of Civil Society*, Ferguson cautions his readers about current popular depictions of man's primitive origins:

The progress of mankind from a supposed state of animal sensibility, to the attainment of reason, to the use of language, and to the habit of society, has been accordingly painted with a force of imagination, and its steps have been marked with a boldness of invention, that would tempt us to admit, among the materials of history, the suggestions of fancy, and to receive, perhaps, as the model of our nature in its original state, some of the animals whose shape has the greatest resemblance to ours.[90]

Ferguson is specifically taking issue with Rousseau's *Discourse on the Origins of Inequality* in this criticism of the fictions that are being admitted into the "materials of history." In introducing that influential and imaginatively gripping account of man's state of nature, Rousseau, in fact, insists that his researches "must not be taken as historical truths, but merely as hypothetical and conditional reasonings, designed more properly to throw light on the nature of things rather than showing their actual origin."[91] But a little more than a decade later, Ferguson clearly feels that Rousseau's caution has not been heeded.

Conjectural history may be conjecture presented in the form of history rather than an account of "how things actually were in the past," but it has always been read or misread as history, and our current recovery of Enlightenment and Romantic historical discourse risks being the latest version of misreading. We are bumping up against not only the seductive powers of imaginative narratives but, as well, the capacity of rhetoric to shape conceptual work and determine knowledge. In fact, in the speculative historical writing of this period, "history" is always closely tied to a theory of the human mind and an understanding of human nature as uniform in its development across cultures and time; indeed it is often a theory of the human mind represented in and through a narrative of history. Thus what makes "conjectural history" different from "history" is not simply its use of non-factual, even fictional scenes and narratives, but, more specifically and significantly, its way of conceptualizing history as a theory of human nature and closely tied to a narrative of what we would now call "individual development."

Thus the close analogical connections between mental development and social history must be taken more fully into account when we talk about "Enlightenment historicism" and the historicism of the British Romantic period. Indeed the analogy between the course of individual development and the course of human history influenced how these writers were able to understand and conceptualize history *as* development, as progress. This, in turn, has particular implications for how we understand those acts of translation between cultures and across geographical and historical scales that give this period its particular historical character – those moments of spatializing time (or temporalizing space) when an eighteenth-century North American can be called a "savage" and compared to or placed in the same stage as an "ancient Briton." Such comparisons are predicated on a prior analogy between individual and human history and enabled by acts of translation between the life of the individual and the history of the species, nation or culture.

If Enlightenment and Romantic historicism is not exactly our own, neither is their understanding and elaboration of the idea of development. We tend to understand development and, more significantly, understand the relationship between history and development, through a Victorian lens, applying later ideas back to this earlier period. Development is undoubtedly a central feature of Victorian discourse, as George Henry Lewes' account of mid-century intellectual culture makes evident. It is "worthy of remark," he writes:

> that the study of Development is quite a modern study. Formerly men were content with the full-statured animal – the perfected art, the completed society. The phases of development were disregarded, or touched on in a vague, uncertain manner. A change has come over the spirit of inquiry ... we are now all bent on tracing the phases of development. To understand the *grown* we try to follow the *growth*.[92]

An interest in development – whether of an animal, an art form or a society – means an interest in growth, an interest in the process and phases of change and, consequently, an interest in the young animal, in earliest stages or primitive origins. When the individual life is understood as a process of growth or development, the childhood where one begins and out of which one grows becomes newly important and interesting.

By the mid-nineteenth century, growth and development were predominantly understood as physiological phenomena. As cellular theory developed over the course of the century and as biological and evolutionary ideas took hold, organic accounts of life and growth moved inward to the level of the cell and outward to the level of the species. Analogy remained a central strategy for explaining and relating the growth of different entities and different scales. Thus Lewes could write that "the growth and decay of an organ is like the growth and decay of a nation or a tree," analogies that leave as much unanswered as they explain.[93] As Carolyn Steedman makes clear, the idea of "growth" becomes the dominant explanatory paradigm at the same time that it remains a central mystery: growth was "both the bottom line – the factor beyond which explanation could not reach – and, at the same time, a mystery."[94] Physiologists thus used the growth of social entities or plant organisms to explain newly discovered and harder to perceive processes of growth and development, such as cellular growth or evolutionary change. In so doing, they imputed a physiological, organic and natural growth to things that were neither organic nor natural: nations, races, histories.

"History," according to John Draper in the seventh edition of *Human Physiology*, "is in truth only a branch of Physiology." In his 1860 lecture to the Oxford meeting of the British Association for the Advancement of Science, Draper claims that:

The procession of nations does not move forward like a dream, without reason or order, but there is a predetermined, a solemn march, in which all must join, ever moving, ever restlessly advancing . . . individual life and its advancement through successive stages is the model of social life and its secular variations.[95]

The idea that "social advancement is as completely under the control of natural law as is bodily growth" exemplifies the Victorian elaboration of the historical metaphor of the individual life. History is firmly considered a course of progress, and the development of the individual is understood as an organic and natural process of "bodily growth."

Draper's rhetoric describing a nation or society as having, like the life of an individual, an infancy, childhood, youth and maturity has strong and obvious appeals. Large, grand, impersonal history is personified, made manageable, familiar and predictable, as well as given a narrative of continuity, progress and natural, organic growth. The multiplicity of the world is seemingly re-made into uniformity, its diverse and random events re-described as following a stable and singular course. Clifford Siskin diagnosed such historical rhetoric as a "strategy for naturalizing social and literary change," and an entire generation of literary critics understood the relationship between history and development in these terms. Thus in identifying the importance of the idea of development to Romantic articulations of progressive history, Siskin writes: "the model for all histories of progress is the tale of individual development. Because the latter is understood to be biologically inevitable, all examples of the former are taken to be naturally appropriate."[96]

While Siskin insists on a plurality of "histories," however, he understands the "tale of individual development" as singular and as always asserting a biological inevitability. As we have seen, however, there are many different and competing tales of individual development – children nurtured and taught by parents; solitary wild children abandoned and never fully developing; colonies of children left to form societies apart; children recapitulating the course of history in their individual development – and each of these figures also tells a story, or stages a theory, of social and cultural history. The tale of individual development that is biologically and organically inevitable does not, in fact, cohere and dominate notions of the individual life until much later in the nineteenth century. Indeed, it is the earlier terrain of historical anachronism and cultural paradox that Wordsworth captures in his epigram: "The Child is Father of the Man."

What I have hoped to show in this first chapter is that the analogy between the individual life and the course of history at work in Enlightenment and Romantic writings is instrumental in first articulating an idea of development which is not yet biological nor yet inevitable, but is instead both historical and individual, both natural and social. More particularly, I have hoped to demonstrate how writers in this period use a notion of childhood and development to articulate new notions of history. Far from being the discursive field that shuts down historical explanation, the discourse of development enables the emergence of historical thinking in this earlier period. The individual's development from childhood to old age is no more natural or inevitable than a society moving from the pastoral to an agricultural stage: both are "developmental" and "historical" narratives at a period when those terms were not yet oppositional nor firmly located in different epistemological fields. If their understanding of "development" is less organic and natural than it subsequently came to be understood, their understanding of "history" is also more uniform, systematic and philosophical than it subsequently came to be understood.

The developmental and historical discourses of Enlightenment and Romantic writers use the figure of the child to embody history and evoke historical process. The images and rhetoric of children and childhood that recur in the histories of this period are central to their new ways of thinking about historical time – its stages, reiterations and recapitulations. By the end of the nineteenth century, new fields of comparative anthropology and child studies will rely on the figure of the child as offering historical evidence of the development or evolution of the human species.[97] But that historical figure of the child – the comparisons it makes possible between nations and cultures, the promises of recapitulation it holds – emerges first in the conjectural histories of the Enlightenment and Romantic periods. We will see that child figure as critical to how writers in these years thought about language and literary culture in the pages to follow.

CHAPTER 2

Infancy, poetry and the origins of language

One way of judging the scale of the claim P. B. Shelley makes for poetry in *A Defence of Poetry* is to note that an essay which ends with the famous declaration, "Poets are the unacknowledged legislators of the World," begins with the image of the poet as a child. "A child at play by itself will express its delight by its voice and motions," Shelley writes, and "these expressions are, what Poetry is to higher objects."[1] Written in response to Thomas Love Peacock's now nearly forgotten "The Four Ages of Poetry," an essay that proclaims the redundancy of poetry to the modern age, Shelley's *Defence of Poetry* begins with a story of origins and ends with the "gigantic shadows which futurity casts upon the present."[2] "Poetry, in a general sense," Shelley writes, "may be defined to be 'the expression of the Imagination,'" and it is poetry in the most general sense that Shelley describes and defends.[3] He finds it at work in the best elements of human nature and civil society, from the inarticulate sounds and gestures of the solitary infant at play, to the prophetic and socially transformative language of the political adult, two examples of human existence intended to evoke past and future, beginnings and ends, the individual mind as well as man's social and historical condition.

Shelley's story of origins begins with the image of an Aeolian lyre. "Poetry is connate with the origin of man," he writes, and man is first an "instrument over which a series of external and internal impressions are driven, like the alternations of an ever-changing wind over an Aeolian lyre, which move it by their motion to ever-changing melody."[4] Physically designed for sonority and motion, the human body manifests sensation in gesture and tone. Unlike the lyre, however, the human being (and, significantly, all "sentient beings") can adjust the "sounds or motions thus excited," tuning or accommodating them to the "impressions which excite them." Each cry or gesture proportions or "tunes" itself to reflect or represent the impression that inspires it, and at this point of what he calls "determined proportion," Shelley locates the origins of poetry.

In this image of the human lyre, Shelley describes original poetry as embodied expression that is prior to the articulate, meaningful sounds of language. What Shelley calls poetry in these first paragraphs of the *Defence* is not verbal art, but the capacity of the human mind and body to match a sensual impression with a corresponding or "reflected image" in sound or gesture. While this redefines poetry's relationship to what we traditionally consider human language, it also redefines the boundaries of language, since Shelley suggests that the inflexions of tone and gesture, the various sounds and actions that the human body can make are, themselves, a sort of language or original mode of expression. Poetry thus precedes its medium in verbal language and is, for Shelley, the animating force propelling language's perpetual development and change, rather than, as we might expect, the other way around. Poetry is the origin of language.

This developmental narrative is not yet fully explicit in Shelley's image of the Aeolian lyre. For in this description of man as a physical instrument, origins are largely essences; in other words, Shelley suggests that human beings are fundamentally and always creatures of bodily sensation and expression. To this image of the lyre, however, Shelley immediately adds two figures that embody this original condition of poetry making. In these figures, the developmental and historical assumptions underlying his rhetoric of origins become clearer. Here we find Shelley's analogy – "(for the savage is to ages what the child is to years)" – in its full context:

A child at play by itself will express its delight by its voice and motions; and every inflexion of tone and every gesture will bear exact relation to a corresponding antitype in the pleasurable impressions which awakened it; it will be the reflected image of that impression; and as the lyre trembles and sounds after the wind has died away, so the child seeks, by prolonging in its voice and motions the duration of the effect, to prolong also a consciousness of the cause. In relation to the objects which delight a child, these expressions are, what Poetry is to higher objects. The savage (for the savage is to ages what the child is to years) expresses the emotions produced in him by surrounding objects in a similar manner; and language and gesture, together with plastic or pictorial imitation, become the image of the combined effect of those objects and of his apprehension of them.[5]

For Shelley, the child and the savage speak or, more accurately, body forth language in its original form. Like the tones of the lyre, the sounds and movements of both the child and the savage are not articulated in words. Voice and gesture are physical and natural movements, not conventional signs, their meanings expressive of emotion rather than significant of meaning. But in Shelley's description of the child prolonging "consciousness of the cause," and in his suggestion that the savage's language and gesture will become an "image" along with other plastic and pictorial arts, we are also given a brief suggestion of how embodied expression will develop into more elaborate and abstract systems of language and representation.

Shelley's deployment of the analogy between individual mental development and human history, between child and savage, signals his debts to Enlightenment historical thinking. The fact that Shelley's analogy occurs in a discussion about the origins of language is thus no coincidence. Intellectual culture of the eighteenth century pursued the question of the origin of language with particularly intense interest. "It is safe to say that no other century has debated that question with greater zeal, frequency, consistency, and depth of insight," Hans Aarsleff has commented.[6] And indeed, the list of the philosophers who wrote significant essays on the origin of language reads as a roll call of the century's major intellectual figures: Etienne Bonnot de Condillac, Jean-Jacques Rousseau, Adam Smith, Johann Gottfried Herder, Joseph Priestley. The Scottish Enlightenment produced a particularly impressive tradition of debate and speculation on the origin of language: in addition to Adam Smith, Thomas Blackwell, Thomas Reid, Hugh Blair, Lord Kames, Lord Monboddo, James Beattie, Dugald Stewart, Alexander Murray and Robert Chambers all made significant contributions.

Nowhere is the analogy between individual development and human history featured more explicitly than in philosophical histories of the origin of language where it is repeatedly articulated in comparisons between child and savage. In the *Defence*, the figures of lyre, child and savage all suggest that the origins of language and poetry are found in embodied acts of perception, sensation and expression, a notion that informs the essay as a whole. For Shelley, poetry is clearly not, as we tend to think of it today, a stylized subset of language and literature, a specialized or boutique literary offering. "Connate with the origin of man," poetry, according to Shelley, is where language begins, how it develops and what it makes possible. In later sections of the essay Shelley will indeed take up the subject of poetry in its "more restricted sense," that is, as "arrangements of language."[7] But never will he limit himself to metrical language or commit the "vulgar error" of making distinctions between "poets and prose writers": Plato, Bacon, "all the authors of revolutions in opinion" and "all the great historians" are poets in Shelley's "restricted sense," judged to be so based on the "truth and splendour of [their] imagery and the melody of [their] language."[8] Even when Shelley eventually turns to poetry in language, his focus remains on the perceptual and formative capacities of language itself, the ways in which language makes new thinking possible. Thus Shelley emphasizes the "vitally metaphorical" power of language which "marks the before unapprehended relations of things, and perpetuates their apprehension."[9] Metaphor in this famous formulation, as John Wright and William Keach have each observed, is a "specific form of relational apprehension," "a way of thinking" and "not merely a vehicle for expressing or articulating thoughts."[10]

   With its attention to origins, to the different "classes of mental action," and to the principles underlying the work of "reason" versus that of "imagination," Shelley's essay situates itself within an Enlightenment tradition of discourse on "human understanding," the "origins of human knowledge" and the "faculties of the human mind." Shelley, however, understands the vital metaphoric powers of poetry and language not only as a category of mental activity, but as an equally crucial force in the social and political relations of history. The passage in its entirety, although perhaps familiar, is worth quoting at greater length:

Their [poets'] language is vitally metaphorical; that is, it marks the before unapprehended relations of things, and perpetuates their apprehension, until the words which represent them, become through time signs for portions or classes of thoughts instead of pictures of integral thoughts; and then if no new poets should arise to create afresh the associations which have been thus disorganized, language will be dead to all the nobler purposes of human intercourse.[11]

How words mean changes over time; fresh insights and new relations become generalized or institutional "signs," clichéd and dead in their meanings and associations. This is an inevitable historical process, fundamental to language's temporal condition. William Keach detects an emotional shift in this passage from confidence to anxiety; it accompanies Shelley's shift in emphasis from an "ideal perspective in which linguistic categories are essentially mental" to one which "acknowledges the necessarily external, temporal and systematic dimension of language."[12] But Shelley's keen sense of the historical condition of language, acknowledged here with no small degree of ambivalence, is also what enables him to fashion a social and political poet and to proclaim his scope of influence with all the enthusiasm and confidence used to announce the shaping powers of metaphoric apprehension: "But Poets, or those who imagine and express this indestructible order, are not only the authors of language and of music, of the dance and architecture and statuary and painting: they are the institutors of laws and the founders of civil society and the inventors of the arts of life."[13]

One may read such rhetoric as another example of Shelley's ambition for poetry. And indeed it is: this essay defining and defending poetry begins as nothing less than an account of the human mind as well as an account of human history, one that sees poetry and language as the origin and developmental engine of both.[14] The fact that he understands the development of the individual mind and the history of the human species as analogous is not coincidental but rather foundational to his defense of poetry. Shelley's analogy – "(for the savage is to ages what the child is to years)" – despite its parenthetical status, is not simply a casual aside, but rather the condensed articulation of a historical paradigm that Shelley inherits from Enlightenment thinkers and assumes his readers understand. In the first chapter we saw how this paradigm of parallel development in the individual and the species worked to create new ways of thinking about history. In this chapter we will focus exclusively on Enlightenment and Romantic accounts of the origin of language to specify how the analogy between individual development and human history works in literary discourse. When poetry and language are described through a rhetoric of infancy and development, sound, gesture, metaphor and music all become critical components of the linguistic and literary field. The idea of poetry as the origin of language entails a naturalistic and developmental history of language and literary form, one in which infants and children figure prominently.

FIRST IN THE WOODS AND WILD, AND AFTERWARDS IN THE NURSERY

The central scene of conjectural histories of language – by which I mean both where they begin, as well as how they stage the dominant assumptions of their theory and narrative – is that of two primitive beings encountering each other and trying to communicate.[15] Although these primitives are usually referred to as "savages," this scene must also be understood as participating in the "colony of children" or "Babes in the Wood" topoi, serving as an original scene of language in particular, and of human history more generally. While the "savages" of these scenes were, of course, rhetorical or imagined figures (and quickly became "stock characters" in origin of language texts), their capacities and characteristics were, as we have seen, often drawn from and compared to the figures of "savages" populating the travel literature of the day. Condillac's influential version of this scene exemplifies the "Babes in the Wood" topos: "I am assuming that two children, one of either sex, sometime after the deluge, had gotten lost in the desert before they would have known the use of any sign."[16] His account is, in fact, unusual in so far as he refers to his two figures as two "children" rather than two "savages," but typical in that he places these children in a wild, post-deluvian or savage scene. As he reminds his readers, his narrative of language invention has implications for other sorts of histories: it opens both inward – as a representation of mental development – and outward – as a representation of a national history. "Who can tell whether some nation owes its origin only to such an event?" Condillac asks, evoking an historical fantasy of national and individual recapitulation. Other writers influenced by Condillac will call this isolated pair of primitives "savages" in order to suggest the complete absence of larger human society, their lack of language, an existence of bare subsistence, and their position at the "origins" of history.

Here, for example, is Adam Smith's version of the same scene: "Two savages, who had never been taught to speak, but had been bred up remote from the societies of men, would naturally begin to form that language by which they would endeavour to make their mutual wants intelligible to each other, by uttering certain sounds, whenever they meant to denote certain objects."[17] What I find most interesting about Smith's discussion, however, is how readily it turns to very different scenes and figures. Pointing out how particular or proper names are often applied to general categories in the early stages of language, Smith next offers this example:

And thus, those words, which were originally the proper names of individuals, would each of them insensibly become the common name of a multitude. A child that is just learning to speak, calls every person who comes to the house its papa or its mama; and thus bestows upon the whole species those names which it had been taught to apply to two individuals.[18]

In Smith's easy juxtapositions of disparate figures and in his assumption of an analogous relationship, we see the characteristic way that children and savages are brought into relationship in conjectural accounts of original language. For Smith, both the savage "bred up remote from the societies of men" and the child learning language in the emotional nexus of the domestic realm are examples of an early and original relationship to language and expression.

Significantly both child and savage move from the particular to the more general, following a developmental pattern that will come to dominate naturalistic accounts of language. Smith's savages give names first to the objects most familiar to them – the "particular cave," "particular tree," and "particular fountain" – names which will later come to refer to larger classes of things "when the more enlarged experience of these savages had led them to observe" more widely. They begin with the particulars of their limited world, applying proper names more generally, as the child first "calls every person who comes to the house its papa or its mama"; or mistaking general terms for proper names, as a "clown" who knows the river which runs by his house simply as "the river." From his ignorance of its proper name, Smith concludes that the rustic's "experience, it seems, had not led him to observe any other river."[19] This last example raises objections from Alexander Murray in his *History of the European Languages* where he argues that Smith has been misled by the "unqualified assertions of philosophers" into supposing that "savages form few abstract ideas, and that their notions and their names of objects are all individuals." In arguing that children, savages and peasants do, in fact, engage in a limited degree of abstract reasoning, Murray nevertheless remains within the terms of a tradition that allows these figures to be equated. "Children, or persons in a low state of society," he writes, "draw their notions from particular sensations and perceptions."[20] In the same vein, J. G. von Herder observes that "names are the vocabulary of a child," by which he means particular "nouns" and "verbs," adding that "likewise in language," nouns and verbs emerge first. Still now, he continues, "the languages of the Hurons, the Iroquois, and other original nations consist mostly of verbs."[21] This is just another example, Herder proclaims, in which "the parallel between children and a newly born people runs still more exactly."

Conjectural accounts of the origin and history of language thus move fluidly between descriptions of savage manners and of infant minds, between accounts of primitive language and the first words of a child, as both are understood to follow the same developmental pattern. Murray Cohen notes that the emerging notion of language as having a history of human origin, development and change meant that the eighteenth century's "newly emphasized methods of linguistic analysis include studying the language of children and 'primitives.'"[22] The child is "'discovered' linguistically" in this period, and the child joins the savage as figures of man's original *infans*, or unspeaking, condition. Paired with the savage, the child facilitates some purely practical matters for the philosopher interested in studying the origins of language and man's natural state. As one enthusiast, Thomas Gunter Browne, advises his like-minded readers: "It is to the nursery you must go at last, to learn the rudiments of speech; for it is not safe, or possible, to go far in the wilds of Africa or America."[23]

Indeed the child learning to talk provides a ready-to-hand example of how language might gradually have come into use. Writers repeatedly note, as Anselm Bayly does in his *Introduction to Languages, Literary and Philosophical,* that children "arrive at Language and Maturity of Reason" only with "Difficulty and Length of Time," and from this evidence they argue that the invention of language would have been a long, arduous process."[24] "If language was invented," Lord Monboddo theorizes in his important *Of the Origin and Progress of Language,* "it was of very difficult invention: For if, even after it is discovered, it be learned, as we have seen, with so much pains and labour, it must have been invented with infinitely more."[25] Gregory Sharpe introduces his dissertations on the origin of language with the same analogy – "We may form some notion of the slow progress men would make in this discovery, from the time and trouble necessarily employed in acquiring languages now they are made" – and he follows the implications of this analogy with the declaration that the "first man" must have been, no matter his size, an infant: "Infants learn not to prattle the imperfect language of the nursery, under several years, and whenever the first man was formed, and of whatever stature he might be, he must in every other respect, strength *perhaps* excepted, have been as much an infant as is the newborn babe."[26] Indeed, one can find this figure of the child learning language as a model for how primitive man invented language well into the texts of the nineteenth century. In his *Vestiges of the Natural History of Creation,* for example, Robert Chambers addresses the question of how men in an "untutored and barbarous" state could have taught themselves language and, with the same example, reaches opposite conclusions: "language itself seems to be amongst the things least difficult to be acquired, if we can form any judgment from what we see in children, most of whom have, by three years of age, while their information and judgment are still as nothing, mastered and familiarized themselves with a quantity of words."[27]

Whatever individual conclusions about the difficulty or ease of inventing language are reached, the figures of child and savage – whether inhabiting a similar primitive scene, or enabling a move between that scene and a modern, European, domestic tableau – are the organizing comparison and animating figures of almost every major Enlightenment treatise on the origins of language. For Monboddo, both the infant and the savage embody "the natural state of man when he first appears upon this stage." Although Monboddo generally disagrees with the materialism and naturalism of Locke's and Condillac's account of mind and language, he nevertheless adopts some elements of their genetic approach, especially in his declaration that to know what is common to all men, one must study what is characteristic of original man, "beginning with the infants of our own species" and then turning to consider "the state of savage and barbarous nations" (as well as, more famously, the "Orang Outangs" who form, according to Monboddo, a "whole nation" of "savages").[28]

Monboddo is also acutely interested in anecdotes of deaf–mute children whose "infancy of mind" lasts longer than ordinary children, as well as in the various cases of "wild children" who were particularly vivid examples of how childhood and savagery were mutually and naturally related states.[29] Wild children such as Peter of Hanover, Marie-Angélique Leblanc and Victor de l'Aveyron were understood (as we have seen Adam Ferguson complain) as examples of man in his natural state and thus often appear as exhibits in discussions of original language. *Mere Nature Delineated: or a Body without a Soul*, a 1726 account of Peter (discovered in Germany in 1724) attributed to Defoe and written upon the boy's arrival in England to be a "guest" of the Royal house of Hanover and studied by Dr. John Arbuthnot, describes him as "the very creature" which the "learned World" has awaited: "*viz.*, one that being kept entirely from human Society, so as never to have heard any one speak, must therefore either not speak at all, or, if he did form any Speech to himself, then they should know what Language Nature would first form for Mankind."[30] In this account, Peter stands as an eighteenth-century equivalent of Psammetichus' experiment as reported by Herodotus: the Egyptian pharaoh ordered two children to be brought up in isolation, hearing no language, in order to find out what language they would speak if left to themselves and, thus, what language was "original." (The first word the children spoke sounded like the Phrygian word for "bread," thus proving, to the Egyptian king's disappointment, that Phrygian was the original language and the Phrygians the oldest nation.)

That children, particularly those left to themselves, might contain within them the secrets of original language is a long-standing notion; indeed it is one still circulating rhetorically in current discussions about the innate grammatical machinery of the brain.[31] This notion gathered new energy in the eighteenth century around these figures of the "wild child," *enfant sauvage* or "feral man." For Monboddo, who visited both Peter and Marie-Angélique (discovered in France in 1731), Peter represented the infantine state of both the individual life-cycle and the species, an "eternal childhood," in Julia Douthwaite's words. In *Epître II sur l'homme*, Louis Racine presents the figure of Marie-Angélique

Leblanc as child, savage and ancestor, focusing on her incapacity to speak words:

> And what were then our savage forefathers,
> A girl in our day reveals to the eye,
> It was not words her mouth articulated:
> Only one sound came out, a piercing, wild cry.[32]

Leblanc eventually learned to speak French, while Peter only ever mastered a few words and Victor remained mostly mute. As Douthwaite's study of these "wild children" makes clear, their relationship to language was studied as part of a larger debate on whether language could be taken as the defining characteristic of humanity.

I am primarily interested here, however, not in the singular cases of wild children, but in the connections readily made between the every-day, ordinary "child" easily observed in any philosopher's back garden and the "savage" at a distance of either time or space apparently easily imagined by the same philosopher. That these connections were routinely made and yet also the subject of intellectual scrutiny and debate is evident from Wordsworth's reaction to Richard Payne Knight's *Analytical Inquiry into the Principles of Taste*. Knight quotes Hugh Blair on the inversions of savage speech: "Fruit give me" is Blair's example of how a savage would talk, a bit of dialogue that fits both Condillac's and Smith's scene of original language. Wordsworth lodges this protest in the margins of Knight's text:

What means all this parade about the Savage when the deduction as far as just may be made at our own firesides, from the sounds words gesticulations looks &c which a child makes use of when learning to talk. But a Scotch Professor cannot write three minutes together upon the Nature of Man, but he must be dabbling with his savage state, with his agricultural state, his Hunter state &c &c.[33]

Wordsworth's complaint that Scottish Enlightenment writers on original language too often imagine savages when they might easily observe children reveals his own domestic sensibility, or what Bewell aptly terms his "domestic anthropology."[34] At the same time, Wordsworth suggests that the Enlightenment's parade of savages might be a masquerade of ordinary little children learning their first words. Indeed, the number of times these "Scotch Professors" shift between examples of savage and child suggests that some speculative history of their domestic life – beginning with the question of where the study was in relation to the nursery – might provide some insight into how they imagined the savage and the invention of language.

We might read Wordworth's objection to all the savages and stages of Scottish philosophy as an attempt to shore up England's "own firesides" by shutting out its exotic marginal figures and denying their relevance to language and the "Nature of Man." But Wordsworth replaces the savage with the child by way of the analogy between them given to him by the same philosophical tradition. It is an analogy that enables and works much like Adam Ferguson's proclamation about where to find the state of nature: "It is here; and it matters not whether we are understood to speak in the island of Great Britain, at the Cape of Good Hope, or the Straits of Magellan."[35] The notion of the "primitive" that emerges in Scottish Enlightenment writing on history and language and subsequently becomes so important to Wordsworth's own poetic project and Romantic literary culture more widely, takes shape through the analogy between child and savage. The "primitive" is thus a flexible, moveable construct, one that can be located at the far margins of empire, the far reaches of the historical past, and, crucially, at one's "own fireside" in the heart of the British home, in the figure of the child.

The connections readily made between the British child and the exotic "savage," the traffic between domestic hearth and foreign wilderness, and the portability of the "primitive": these rhetorical exchanges are critical to how these histories of language build and unfold their developmental narratives. Before conceding the dangers and distances of Africa or America and advising his readers to stick to the nursery, for example, Thomas Gunter Browne announces that theories of language must be tested and proved "first in the woods and wild, and afterwards in the nursery."[36] The "woods and wild" and the "nursery" are comparable spaces of experimentation where early, even original, language can be observed.

IDEAS OF INFANCY

The empirical basis for the study of language is usually traced back to Locke whose philosophy of mind influentially establishes the child and savage as comparable objects of study in eighteenth-century discourse of human origins. In arguing against the possibility of innate principles in human understanding in *An Essay Concerning Human Understanding*, Locke describes "children, idiots, savages, and illiterate people" as sharing the same pre-rational and pre-linguistic mind. "The senses," Locke insists, "let in particular ideas, and furnish the yet empty cabinet" of the mind with perceptions that are gradually retained and named in the memory, and eventually become the "ideas and language" which will allow the mind "to exercise its discursive faculty."[37] Locke's empiricism, in short, can imagine the mind of the child and the mind of the savage at the same level of inexperience:

> But alas, amongst children, idiots, savages, and the grossly illiterate, what general maxims are to be found? what universal principles of knowledge? Their notions are few and narrow, borrowed only from those objects they have had most to do with, and which have made upon their senses the frequentest and strongest impressions. A child knows his nurse and his cradle, and by degrees the play-things of a little more advanced age; and a young savage has, perhaps, his head filled with love and hunting, according to the fashion of his tribe. But he that from a child untaught, or a wild inhabitant of the woods, will expect these abstract maxims and reputed principles of science, will, I fear, find himself mistaken.[38]

In this and similar passages, Locke designates a "family of privileged epistemological subjects" for eighteenth-century inquiry into human origins and human conditions.[39] His description of the inexperienced mind as furnished with only a few ideas taken from the immediate material world and formed from the most forceful and frequent of sense impressions, places both child and savage, as well as "idiots" and "the grossly illiterate," in a similar physical or sensual state. "Immersed in matter, and *imbruted*" is how Monboddo later describes this primitive state of both infant and savage.[40]

    In describing the gradual progress of the mind toward greater powers of thinking, Locke refers repeatedly to children and their acquirement of language, as well as to the progress of language toward greater complexity: "When children have, by repeated sensations, got ideas fixed in their memories, they begin by degrees to learn the use of signs. And when they have got the skill to apply the organs of speech to the framing of articulate sounds, they begin to make *use of words* to signify their *ideas* to others."[41] For Locke, and for Condillac after him, language is necessary for thinking to advance in complexity, and, in Hans Aarsleff's description of this tradition, the "key question about the beginnings of the exercise of the understanding has been converted into a question about the origin of language."[42] The child and savage first learn only words and names for the particular "external things . . . which make the most frequent impressions on their senses"; as we see in the passage from Locke above, the child knows his nurse and cradle, the savage knows love and hunting.[43] In following "our notions and names from their beginning, and observ[ing] by what degrees we proceed, and by what steps we enlarge our ideas from our first infancy," Locke thus posits a progression from immediate sense impressions, to particular ideas and names, to greater abstraction and general notions.[44] This becomes the basic developmental narrative that dominates both histories of literature and theories of literary culture by the end of the eighteenth century.

This movement out of infancy evidenced in the child's increasingly complex ideas and use of language might also be traced in the development of a language whose words carry within them the history of progression from particular to general, from sensible to abstract. Locke speculates:

It may also lead us a little towards the original of all our notions and knowledge, if we remark how great a dependence our words have on common sensible ideas; and how those which are made use of to stand for actions and notions quite removed from sense, have their rise from thence, and from obvious sensible ideas are transferred to more abstruse significations, and made to stand for ideas that come not under the cognizance of our senses . . . and I doubt not but, if we could trace them to their sources, we should find, in all languages, the names which stand for things that fall not under our senses to have had their first rise from sensible ideas.[45]

Thus we might gain, Locke hopes, "some kind of guess what kind of notions they were, and whence derived, which filled their minds who were the first beginners of languages."[46] This is an important statement of how languages progress from words naming "common sensible ideas" to words with more abstract or "abstruse significations." Condillac, who quotes this passage in his *Essay on the Origin of Human Knowledge*, concludes from it and his own work, that the "first beginners of languages" were "happy to find some relation between a mental and a physical action in order to give the same name to both." In other words, "names" from the physical world are applied to mental ideas and actions based on a perceived similarity and relationship. This leads Condillac to maintain that "all these names had a figurative origin," an important assertion of language's metaphoric origins to which we will necessarily return.[47]

Hans Aarsleff points to this passage in Locke and its reappearance in Condillac as responsible for the eighteenth century's major methodological shift in the philosophy of mind and study of language: "the individual's introspection into the operations of his own mind and growth could now, so it seemed, be replaced by the philosopher's study of the origin and progress of language, of etymology, both in regard to words and grammar."[48] One could now understand the history of language, its various parts and forms, as a history of both mental development and human culture. Jacques Turgot, Charles de Brosses and, later, John Horne Tooke all subsequently and enthusiastically embraced the study of etymology and language as central to their philosophical inquiries into the mind and the history of man. Other writers – Rousseau, Smith, Blair, Monboddo, Herder and, of course, Shelley, to name a few – heartily embraced the notion of metaphor at the origins of language which in turn affected how they value and historicize poetry and other literary forms. The important point for our purposes is that language became an historical document over the course of the eighteenth century in two distinct but interconnected ways: it documented the natural history of the mind as reiterated in the development of each individual, and it documented the history of society and culture, representing and testifying to the social condition or historical stage of its speakers in a particular period.

What emerges from this philosophy of mind and language is a discourse and theory of *infancy* as the origin of human development both ontogenetically and phylogenetically conceived. Infancy not only refers to the unspeaking or *infans* condition of both child and savage, but also the state out of which speech and language will arise. Thus infancy signifies not only a lack of language, but also a mind confined to material, sense impressions, capable of knowing and attending to only the particular objects of its immediate, external world and its physical, bodily existence. Infancy attends and responds to the things of the immediate world, most of which are strange and new, provoking wonder and amazement, if not fear. Knowledge of that world comes directly from physical sensations registered on and by the body. Indeed, infancy is an embodied state to the extent that even its mental operations are imagined and described as a function of physical force and pressure. "Impression" is the term commonly used by philosophers in these years to describe how perceptions act on the developing mind. Impressions are frequent, repeated, often striking or entering the mind, in Hume's words, with "force and violence."[49] Infancy is understood as the most "impressionistic" of states, the most susceptible to the sudden, violent and forceful pressings of the world on the body and mind.[50]

Speculating on how sense impressions and attention to physical objects might lead to simple ideas and signs, Condillac and other philosophers of mind and language will locate the building blocks of language in the physical, sensual state of infancy, in the expressions of the face, the gestures of the body, the sounds and cries of passion that characterize the infant state. Whether or not, and exactly how, the history of language begins with embodied sounds and gestures and advances to articulate signs or words, whether or not the history of language is an exclusively human history or includes non-human animals, all these will become key points of debate throughout the Enlightenment and Romantic periods. Conjectural and speculative inquiries into the origin of language, in other words, cohere into a developmental narrative that begins in infancy, a narrative that increasingly takes on historical status. The *infans* of infancy is thus re-imagined as an original state out of which language develops, and a theory of language coheres that is deeply invested in what is *not* articulate speech.

Important to this notion of infancy is its capacity to describe both the origins of individual development and the origins and early stages of language and culture. Just as Locke extends the condition of infancy beyond children to "idiots, savages, and illiterate people," later Enlightenment writers will use "infancy" to suggest primitive social and cultural stages: the "infancy of society," the "childhood of the race," the "infancy of the art of poetry" or the "infancy of religion." Such cultural categories imply a range of "natural" values. As Locke describes his privileged group of primitives:

children, idiots, savages, and illiterate people, being of all others the least corrupted by custom, or borrowed opinions; learning and education having not cast their native thoughts into new moulds; nor by superinducing foreign and studied doctrines, confounded those fair characters nature had written there.[51]

Infancy here takes on "native" and "natural" qualities over and against the corruptions, borrowings and foreign impressions of more acculturated and educated states. We can see signs of how the "singular" and "particular" qualities of early language and the child's mind inform the presumed "localism" and "insularity" of primitive culture.

The majority of writers in the wake of Locke embrace a theory of infancy and development that allows them to compare child and savage, the individual life and the course of history, and repeatedly to describe primitive man as, in short, a big baby. Gregory Sharpe, who introduces his study of the origin of language with the assertion that the "first man" must have been "as much an infant as is the newborn babe," gives this account of his inexperienced state:

What ideas or images could he have for the employment of his mind, when the senses, which are the inlets for conveying these images or impressions to be perceived by the mind, were but newly created, and when the repository for all sensible objects was but just opened to the several organs of sense? Man, therefore, must, in such a state, have been so entirely destitute of knowledge, that he could not have directed himself to the performance of such things as might be necessary even for the support of his life; and, for want of habit and experience, he must have been ignorant of the consequences of his actions, and could therefore have done nothing with any view to any end.[52]

"Nothing," Sharpe concludes, "can be conceived more helpless and insufficient than man in his infancy." And nothing, perhaps, can be conceived more incongruous than the full-grown figures of infancy that populate eighteenth-century conjectural histories. Sharpe's infant-man is not the only hybrid creature in a tradition invested in seeing primitive man through a rhetoric and theory of infancy. Rousseau, after declaring that "we are born capable of learning but able to do nothing, knowing nothing," illustrates the helplessness of infancy by imagining a full-grown baby:

Let us suppose that a child had at his birth the stature and the strength of a grown man, that he emerged, so to speak, fully armed from his mother's womb as did Pallas from the brain of Jupiter. This man-child would be a perfect imbecile, an automaton, an immobile and almost insensible statue. He would see nothing, hear nothing, know no one, would not be able to turn his eyes toward what he needed to see.[53]

Both Sharpe's infant-man and Rousseau's man-child begin by learning to make use of their senses: "everything is learning for animate and sensitive beings," Rousseau insists, and "the education of man begins at his birth."[54] This "man formed all of a sudden" thus combines the physicality of an adult with the inexperience of an infant. Rousseau suggests such a creature would not be able to stand or walk, in no small part because he would not know to make the attempt, and he asks us to imagine "this big body, strong and robust, staying in place like a stone, or crawling and dragging himself along like a newborn puppy."[55]

These awkward, even monstrous figures of infant men – Mary Shelley's creature in *Frankenstein* is their direct heir – embody the fictional extremities of a tradition invested in seeing and representing "primitive" men through a rhetoric of infancy.[56] Rousseau's "man-child" must be seen in a continuum with his "nascent man," "infant man" or "savage man," the more familiar figure from his *Discourse on the Origins of Inequality* and *Essay on the Origin of Languages*. Such phrases as "infant man," "the infancy of states" or "the infancy of societies" are common in Enlightenment and Romantic histories and essays, so clichéd and familiar that pressure on them may seem misguided. But, in fact, they do important conceptual work in this period: naming and characterizing an original state that is both psychological and historical, and providing a way to describe mental development and the history of language and culture as parallel and recapitulating progresses.

INFANCY AND THE HISTORY OF LANGUAGE

Indeed a strong consensus about the characteristics and history of infant language and literary forms emerges in these years and its basic features are told and re-told in a range of texts by writers who often otherwise disagree. Man's original "mute" condition; the infant's cry; the range of sounds, tones, noises, gestures and facial expressions which constitute such a significant part of human communication; and the proximity of language to music are all discussed and debated as elements of early language and its developmental history. What follows is an overview and discussion of the dominant, naturalist history of language that emerges in the eighteenth century.

Natural language and mute man

Interest in a language, or those parts of a language, that works without words is articulated within a larger Enlightenment discourse opposing "nature" to "art," the "natural" to the "artificial." Most Enlightenment writers agreed that the "cultivated languages" of modern Europe were the products of human invention and art, and thus, in Dugald Stewart's words, "wonderfully artificial and complicated" in their eighteenth-century state.[57] Some of the most basic units of language were also increasingly described as products of "art" and "artifice." Locke began his discussion of "Words" in Book Three of the *Essay Concerning Human Understanding* by insisting that there is no "natural connexion" between "particular articulate sounds and certain ideas," thereby signaling an important shift in the understanding of words at the center of eighteenth-century linguistics. No longer understood as the "natural" signifiers of *things*, words were understood rather as signs of *ideas*, and the relationship between the sign and the idea it signified was increasingly understood as "artificial," "arbitrary" or "conventional."[58]

Locke describes man as having "by nature his organs so fashioned, as to be fit to frame articulate sounds which we call words."[59] But the question of whether or not language is thus "natural" to man, or what basic elements of language might be considered "natural," remained an important topic of debate throughout the eighteenth century, particularly as the interest grows in charting the "gradual steps" of progress from "uncultivated nature" to that "state of things so wonderfully artificial and complicated."[60] After noting that man is naturally "fit to frame articulate sounds," for example, Locke immediately adds that parrots and several other birds also seem to be so fit and fashioned, and yet they are "not capable of language." The articulation of words or the formation of articulate sounds is one way to define language, as well as to claim it for human beings alone. "Speech distinguishes man from the animals," Rousseau writes: "Language distinguishes nations from each other."[61] Monboddo defines language in *The Origin and Progress of Language* as "the expression of the conceptions of the mind by articulate sounds," and insists that it is never found in the "natural" state of human beings. Words and articulation are "altogether the work of art" or the product of "habit acquired by custom and exercise," Monboddo claims, adding that "we are truly by nature the *mutum pecus* Horace makes us to be."[62]

Many eighteenth-century writers, Rousseau and Monboddo the most prominent of them, thus imagine primitive man as existing for extended periods without language in a prolonged "infancy of mind." Monboddo's central example is, notoriously, that of the nation of "Orang Outangs" whom he classed as "human":

They are exactly of the human form; walking erect, not upon all-four, like the savages that have been found in Europe; they use sticks for weapons; they live in society; they make huts of branches of trees, and they carry off negroe girls, of whom they make slaves, and use them both for work and pleasure. These facts are related of them by Mons. Buffon in his natural history. And I was further told, by a gentleman who had been in Angola, that there were some of them seven feet high, and that the negroes were extremely afraid of them; for, when they did any mischief to the Orang Outangs, they were sure to be heartily cudgeled when they were caught.[63]

For Monboddo, the Orang Outangs are important because they have "made some progress in the arts of life," progress which seems to include everything from using tools and building shelters, to making war, taking slaves and intimidating their neighbors. (This appears to be progress and society along a European model.) All this they do without language. As Monboddo continues: "they have not advanced so far as to invent a language; and accordingly none of them that have been brought to Europe could speak, and, what seems strange, never learned to speak."

Rousseau's more solitary savages wander the forests "without industry, without speech, without domicile, without war and without liaisons, with no need of his fellows, likewise with no desire to harm them." Rousseau's "savage man" is famously "self-sufficient": "he felt only his true needs, saw only what he believed he had an interest to see; and his intelligence made no more progress than his vanity." Indeed, there is neither "education nor progress" in the life of this savage. As in Monboddo's discussion, this is an extended period of infancy or childhood. "Centuries passed in all the crudeness of the first ages," Rousseau concludes: "the species was already old, and man remained ever a child."[64]

Infant cries

Reading Monboddo's description of Orang Outang society or this particular description of Rousseau's solitary savage wandering the forest is a bit like watching a film clip without the soundtrack. Not only is there no articulate language; there are no sounds, no cries, no voices or noise, human or otherwise. Elsewhere, particularly in his *Essay on the Origin of Languages*, Rousseau is more interested in the "first voices" of humanity: "nature dictates accents, cries, complaints."[65] Pronunciation and the use of words is a later development: the "modifications of the tongue and palate that produce articulation require attention, practice," Rousseau notes: "all children need to learn them and some do not easily succeed in doing so." But "simple sounds issue naturally from the throat" and "cries and groans are simple voices."[66] "Man's first language," Rousseau proclaims, "and the only language he needed before it was necessary to persuade assembled men, is the cry of Nature."[67] In *Emile*, Rousseau analogically extends his sense of "man's first language." "All our languages are works of art," Rousseau writes in rhetoric that should now be familiar to us:

Whether there was a language natural and common to all men has long been a subject of research. Doubtless there is such a language, and it is the one children speak before knowing how to speak. This language is not articulate, but it is accented, sonorous, intelligible.[68]

We have forgotten this first language, Rousseau laments, urging us to "study children" and learn it again from "Nurses" who are "our masters in this language" of sound, tone and accent.

In pointing to the "cry of Nature" as "man's first language," Rousseau echoes a major strain of eighteenth-century linguistic thought, and we can

see the extent to which the question of where human language begins –
with articulate words? expressions of the mind? sounds and gestures? –
involves contested and constantly shifting terrain. Condillac influentially
focused conversation about the origin of language on the cries, gestures
and movements of the human body. The human body, he argued,
expresses passion and perceptions naturally, instinctually, even involuntarily, in sound and gesture; such corporeal movements are "natural signs"
and make up what Condillac calls a "language of action."[69] In Condillac's
account, this spontaneous expression of emotion is inherently tied to
man's natural sociability and sympathy: "by instinct alone," the two
children in his scene of original language, "asked for help and gave it,"
each "eager to ease the other's pain."[70]

Herder also begins his *Treatise on the Origin of Language* with the
"cries," "sounds" and "wild, unarticulated noises" of human beings that
constitute what he calls a "language of sensation."[71] But Herder insists
that the human being, like any animal, will produce these sounds even if
no one else is present to hear and sympathize: "a suffering animal, as
much as the hero Philoctetes, when overcome with pain, will whine!, will
groan!, even if it were abandoned, on a desolate island, without the sight,
the trace, or the hope of a helpful fellow creature." In images that
anticipate Shelley's lyre, Herder insists that the body is an expressive
instrument: "the struck string performs its natural duty: it sounds!" For
Herder this is a "law of nature": "'*Here is a sensitive being which can enclose
none of its lively sensations within itself, which in the first moment of surprise,
even without volition and intention, has to express each of them in sound.*'"[72]
Feelings sound forth; sensations resound. Ultimately, Herder suggests, the
body cannot contain and must express its sensations so that they will be
perceived and understood sympathetically by others; indeed, every
sounding forth is directed "at an expression to other creatures" even when
none is present or there is no conscious desire to communicate. But in
that figure which expresses its feelings even "on a desolate island," Herder
suggests *sounds* and *soundings* that are prior to social communication and
interaction. This is an idea of original language that we will repeatedly see
embodied in the figure of the child who talks and sings to itself, prattles
and plays oblivious to others.

Sound, noise, gesture

Condillac's "language of action" and Herder's "language of sensation"
challenge the notion of man as a mute animal with no natural language or

cry of his own. For Condillac, this first language of sound and gesture makes subsequent language possible. Men slowly create and invent a new language – a "language of articulated sounds" that makes use of "arbitrary signs" – but it is "the natural cries" which serve "as a model for them to make a new language."[73] His developmental account thus gives language a natural and embodied origin, and this naturalistic tradition, which dominates conjectural histories of language in the eighteenth century, expands what is considered and called "language" to include inarticulate sounds and bodily gesture.

Thus in the *Inquiry into the Human Mind*, Thomas Reid defines language as "all those signs which mankind use in order to communicate to others their thoughts and intentions, their purposes and desires." He divides these signs into the "natural" – those that "have a meaning which every man understands by the principles of his nature" and are expressed by "modulations of the voice, gestures, and features" – and the "artificial" – those that "have no meaning, but what is affixed to them by compact or agreement among those who use them."[74] Reid then follows the developmental logic set forth by Condillac in insisting that "if mankind had not a natural language, they could never have invented an artificial one by their reason and ingenuity." For Reid, the existence of this "natural language of mankind" challenges the common notion that language is "purely an invention of men, who by nature are no less mute than the brutes."[75]

Writers often disagreed about whether or not the sounds and movements of the human body should be called "language" and understood as the origin out of which artificial language naturally develops, but they all describe and rehearse the importance of gestures, expressions and sounds to an early language with a limited stock of words. Condillac describes his "two children" slowly and gradually building a new language through a process of articulating new sounds, repeating them "to the accompaniment of some gesture that indicated the objects to which they wished to draw attention," and thereby becoming "accustomed to giving names to things."[76] This is a state of infancy when the mind first attends only to particular objects in the immediate world and the impressions they make on the senses. Thus the first words of a language, like the first words of a child, are names for things. Drawing on William Warburton's account of how Hebrew and other ancient languages were supplemented by dance and gesture, Condillac extends this idea of how articulate sounds and gestures might be used together into an important early stage of language when discourse is a "mixture of words and actions."[77]

The idea of language as moving through a stage where natural and artificial signs are used together becomes a common one in Enlightenment histories of language. Alexander Murray describes the "imperfect system of communication" formed by "children and the deaf, in civilized nations" which remains "the principal one still in use among savages." Voice, body and countenance all participate and, over time, the use of articulate sounds and words increases "as the convenience of them began to be felt."[78] A gradual awakening to the convenience of words is, in fact, a central feature of this mixed stage of language. Monboddo, in describing an African nation whose language was "so rude and imperfect" that its speakers were "obliged to supply the defects of it by signs and gestures" reports with all seriousness that these people "could not understand one another in the dark."[79]

An emphasis on the accented and sonorous qualities of early language is another common strain in Enlightenment and Romantic histories of language. If early language was accompanied by "more gesticulation," it was also expressed with "more and greater inflexions of voice, than what we now use." In short, according to Hugh Blair: "there was more action in it; and it was more upon a crying or singing tone."[80] Condillac theorized the sounds of speech as a transitional symptom of language's move from gesture to words: "When speech succeeded the language of action, it preserved the character of its predecessor ... to take the place of the violent bodily movements, the voice was raised and lowered by strongly marked intervals."[81] Coarseness of speech organs in early man; the difficulty of forming new words; the comparative ease of changing the tone or accent of an established sound; the formation of words out of imitative sounds (Rousseau writes that "onomatopoeia would constantly make itself felt" in primitive language[82]) – all these are offered as theories for why early language would be more inflected and full of sound. The exclamations, interjections and accents of languages from around the globe and throughout history became evidence of their age and proximity to origins. Herder describes the guttural letters, unpronounceable accents, half-articulated sounds and "unwriteable" words of the Hurons, Peruvians, Siamese, Amazonians, ancient Hebrews and Greeks, arguing that the "living noise" of these languages proves the "animal origin," as opposed to the "divine origin," of language itself.[83]

Music

The proximity of primitive speech to music is thus repeatedly assumed and asserted. Rousseau's inclination to discuss language alongside music – the full title of his essay on language is, of course, "Essay on the Origin of Languages in which Melody and Musical Imitation are Treated" – is not only a function of his life-long interest in music and extensive writings on music theory. Eighteenth-century aesthetic theory typically compared and ranked the "sister arts" of poetry, music and painting. When discussions turned historical, as they increasingly did, language and music were understood to share the same origin. Condillac presents the strongly accentuated and inflected speech of the first human beings in a chapter entitled "The prosody of the first languages." While he reserves the label of "chant" for later Greek and Roman declamation, he describes the manner of articulation "at the origin of languages" as allowing for "inflections of voice that were so distinct that a musician would have been able to record it with all but small adjustments" and as thus partaking "of the quality of chant."[84] Early language would make the most use of "voices, sounds, accent, and number, which are from nature," Rousseau writes, leaving "little to be done by articulations, which are conventional." Thus "one would sing it rather than speak it."[85] According to Rousseau, this is a language completely lost to the modern French: we have "no idea of a sonorous and harmonious language that speaks as much by its sounds as by its words."[86]

Not everyone agreed with Rousseau that the music and harmonies of language were completely lost, however. Adam Smith defends the "musicall ear in the English nation" and describes how the guttural sounds of the English language have been largely dropped in favor of the "melody of sound."[87] It is the "harmonious and sonorous pronunciation peculiar to the English nation," Smith adds, that has the greatest effect on the sound of the language: "there is a certain ringing in their manner of speaking which foreigners can never attain. Hence it is that this language which when spoke by the natives is allowed to be very melodious and agreeable."[88] In his own *Lectures on Rhetoric and Belles Lettres*, Blair also pays considerable attention to the "harmony of sentences" and the "beauty of musical construction in prose." Language, according to Blair, "can be rendered capable of [the] power of music," a power which is primarily to "prompt and facilitate certain emotions."[89]

EVERY NEW OBJECT FINDS THEM UNPREPARED

Naturalist and developmental accounts of language thus begin in infancy with the signs of the body: the sounds, gestures and expressions that are "natural signs" and that lead to the "artificial signs" of articulate language.

First words are names for particular things or sense impressions, and the earliest language is a mixture of gesture, accent and primitive words. Another important characteristic of early language, one closely connected to the notion of infancy that frames this developmental history, is its metaphorical quality. That early language was both closely tied to physical existence and, at the same time, highly figurative and imaginative is a significant linguistic paradox that one finds repeatedly discussed and described in Enlightenment and Romantic histories of language. Condillac, we recall, takes Locke's notion of how languages begin with words for "common sensible ideas" and only later develop words with "abstruse significations," and thereby suggests that most early words "had a figurative origin."[90] To explain this theory, Condillac speculates that primitive men would gradually move beyond needs "related only to the body" and become capable of "distinguishing mind from body." The more they reflected on the operations of the mind, the more they would feel the need for new words and terms to describe them. They would not, Condillac insists, "imagine new terms, for that would not have been the readiest way to be understood." Instead, they "extended the signification" of terms they already had; and thus "a sign which initially was limited to an action of the body, became the name of an operation of mind."[91] Condillac's example is the term "I see" which names both a sense perception and, metaphorically, a mental action.

In Condillac's discussion, the "figurative origins" of language, in fact, assume a prior physical and natural origin; words are figurative to the extent that they can be traced back to an earlier term for a physical and bodily action, object or impression. Metaphors are a matter of efficiency and economy, a way of coping with a lack of terms. Hugh Blair offers an account of the origin of figures and tropes that employs a similar narrative of primitive resourcefulness and frugality. Men begin, according to Blair, with few ideas and a "narrow nomenclature," and as their ideas multiply, so too will their "stock of names and words."[92] But "no language is so copious, as to have a separate word for every separate idea," and men "naturally sought to abridge this labour of multiplying words *in infinitum.*" They thus "made one word, which they had already appropriated to a certain idea or object, stand also for some other idea or object; between which and the primary one, they found, or fancied, some relation."[93] Tropes, Blair concludes, abound in all languages in their early stages and are "plainly owing to the want of proper words."[94]

The basic economy of making one word do the work of two is an important theory of the metaphoric nature of early language circulating in these years, but certainly not originating here. Blair quotes Cicero's *De Oratore* on the extensive use of figurative language resulting from a "paucity of words, and barrenness of Language."[95] The eighteenth-century understanding of early, metaphoric language, however, places more emphasis on the developmental progression from "sensible objects" and "sensible ideas," to "mental objects" and "obscure conceptions." Blair's economy of nomenclature, like Condillac's, works in one direction: terms are always borrowed from the sensible, physical world and applied to "operations of the mind and affections."[96]

This is not the only account of language's metaphoric origins circulating in these years, however. Indeed, this developmental account that grounds metaphor in the physical, natural world seems contradicted completely by another important explanation of language's figurative basis. Blair, for example, insists that the "want of words" is not the only reason for the rise of figurative language, nor even the principal one: "tropes have arisen more frequently, and spread themselves wider, from the influence which Imagination possesses over all language."[97] In turning to imagination as a source of metaphoric language and as a significant influence on language as a whole, Blair thus brings in another important strain of eighteenth-century linguistic theory.

The work of the imagination is a mental function closely associated with the ignorance and inexperience of infancy. Condillac, for example, describes the process by which the mind connects ideas to signs as the work of the imagination – which "presents signs to the mind as yet ignorant of their use" – and of attention – which "links them to ideas."[98] Primitive man, it follows, having fewer words and fewer ideas, is faced with more unknown sights and signs, and the imaginative work of grappling with the unknown would occur under the pressure of the emotions caused by his ignorance. Thomas Blackwell's influential account of primitive man in *An Inquiry into the Life and Writings of Homer*, an account that one finds referenced throughout the eighteenth century in theories and histories of language, is a critical text in the project of re-making the "ancients" into "infants," as well as in establishing the imaginative and emotional pressures on early language:

'Tis certain, that in the Infancy of States . . . [men] are ignorant and undesigning, governed by Fear, and Superstition its Companion: There is a vast Void in their Minds; they know not what will happen, nor according to what Tenour things will take their Course; Every new Object finds them unprepared; they gaze and stare, like Infants taking in their first Ideas of Light: Their Words express these Feelings; And as there is a mighty Distance from this Starting-place of *Ignorance* and *Wonder*, to the Condition of a wise experience'd Man, whom few things surprize; who is acquainted with the Fates of Nations, and the Laws and Limits of *our* Situation, the *Language* is tinctured in proportion, and bears the Marks of the intermediate Stages.[99]

This passage reads a state of "infancy" into the figure of a primitive man, imagining, once again, a fully-grown adult figure as an infant newly arrived in the world. These infant men are "governed by Fear" and their words "express these Feelings"; the language they speak bears the marks of the developmental stage in which it is formed. Thus according to Blackwell, language in this infant stage "must be full of Metaphor; and that Metaphor of the boldest, daring, and most natural kind," for their words are all "invented under some Passion."[100]

Blackwell's description of primitive man is both psychological and social, an account of early mental operations as well as a picture of primitive existence. Their lives are dominated by "Terror, Rage or Want," emotions incident to "Creatures living wild and defenceless," and their language is consequently "broken, unequal and boisterous," a mixture of "rude accidental Sounds," and rough and fiery metaphors. Herder takes this description of primitive man and language directly from Blackwell and describes the growth of language at this early stage not as organic, orderly or progressive, but as a wild and chaotic encounter with the unknown:

New subject matters, new objects, conditions, circumstances, yielded new names ... In this way language became full of crazy and untamed word trans-formations, full of irregularity and stubborn idiosyncrasy. Images were intro-duced as images as far as possible, and in this way there arose a stock of metaphors, of idioms, of sensuous names. Rough strength in passions and deeds, in virtues and vices, was the stamp of the age – and inevitably of the language as well, which with each people in a thousand contingent circumstances was just as good and as bad as it had to be in order to be a language *of the sensuous people.*[101]

Early language, according to Herder, is metaphoric, full of images and idiom, because of the "crazy and untamed word transformations" that occur in the irregular, passionate minds and lives of infant man. In his insistence that early language is sensuous and metaphoric to the extent that it privileges *images*, Herder also articulates an idea important to many discussions of primitive language in these years: the idea of infancy as a state which records and reproduces the images and forms which make a striking impression on the mind – "images were introduced as images as far as possible." The images of infant language – as Herder suggests here, and as we will see Rousseau, Wordsworth and a range of antiquarian writers repeat – function not as mimetic supplements (trying to recreate or approximate an original experience) but as repetitions or reassertions of the image or form itself as it strikes or impresses the infant mind. Infant language is thus material and sensual: full of "sensuous names," stocked with the images and forms of the world as they have pressed upon and been felt by the bodies and minds of a primitive people.

In Blackwell's and Herder's accounts of the emotional life of primitive men, fear and horror, as well as wonder, astonishment and amazement, are the dominant passions and those that produce and shape infant language. These ideas also animate Rousseau's well-known account of the figurative origins of language as an encounter between two savage men who mistake each other for giants:

> Upon meeting others, a savage man will initially be frightened. His fear will make him see them as bigger and stronger than himself; he will give them the name *giants*. After many experiences, he will recognize that these supposed giants are neither bigger nor stronger than he, and that their stature did not correspond to the idea that he had originally attached to the word *giant*. Therefore, he will invent another name common to them and to himself, such as, for example the name *man*, and will leave *giant* for the fictitious object that had impressed him during his illusion. This is how the figurative word is born before the literal word, when passion enchants our eyes, and how the first idea it offers us is not the truth.[102]

Stressing inexperience, fear and the ways in which passion affects perception and "enchants our eyes," Rousseau participates in the tradition of representing primitive men as infants who reproduce their physical and emotional impressions. Indeed, he gives his "savage man" the eyes of a child who sees an unknown other as "bigger and stronger than himself" and does not yet know himself as a "man."

Hugh Blair's primitive man is a similar creature: "for the savage tribes of men are always much given to wonder and astonishment. Every new object surprises, terrifies, and makes a strong impression on their mind; they are governed by imagination and passion, more than by reason; and, of course, their speech must be deeply tinctured by their genius." Blair also offers a brief description of mental operations to demonstrate just how language might take the color of the emotions it is made to express. Every object that "makes any impression on the human mind," Blair writes, is always "accompanied" by other circumstances that "strike us at the same time." Likewise, every idea "carries in its train some other ideas" which are its "accessories." These accessories, Blair continues, "often strike the imagination more than the principal idea itself," being perhaps more agreeable, more familiar, or more resonant with other memories, and the imagination will rest on and make use of the name of the "accessory" or "correspondent" idea over that of the principal."[103] In Blair's account, the mental operations that produce figurative language work by accidental association and contingency, and the replacement of the "principal idea" with an "accessory" seems an operation as much metonymic as metaphoric. The pressure of emotion, rather than any relationship of similarity, causes ideas to link up to signs.

These discussions about primitive figurative language are thus part of the larger Enlightenment interest in sentiment and passion and how they shape language and social interaction. One issue at stake in these accounts of the emotional and imaginative elements of language is the question of just how openly and immediately feelings are expressed, communicated and circulated in society. In the developmental scheme of Scottish Enlightenment history, primitive man is assumed to be more subject to strong passions, but also to express those passions more directly. In his "Critical Dissertation on the Poems of Ossian," for example, Blair repeats the familiar description of men "in the infancy of societies" regularly faced with unknown and strange objects, whose fear and wonder are continuously excited: "their passions are raised to the utmost." He continues with this account of their language: "their passions have nothing to restrain them: their imagination has nothing to check it. They display themselves to one another without disguise: and converse and act in the uncovered simplicity of nature."[104] Here Blair employs a standard opposition of sentimental culture – the simplicity of nature, the duplicity of art and artifice – in order to imagine the language of primitive man as the unchecked and uncovered expression of their emotion. In contrast, modern man has learned to "subdue or disguise their passions; they form their exterior manners upon one uniform standard of politeness and civility."[105] Romanticists will, of course, recognize this rhetoric from Wordsworth's explanation for why he has chosen the language and situations of "low and rustic life" for his *Lyrical Ballads*: "because in that situation the essential passions of the heart find a better soil in which they can attain their maturity, are less under restraint, and speak a plainer and more emphatic language." In this situation, he continues, "our elementary feelings exist in a state of simplicity and consequently may be more accurately contemplated and more forcibly communicated."[106]

Alan Richardson points to the apparent contradiction in Wordsworth's poetics between this call for a "plainer and more emphatic language" in the 1800 "Preface" to the *Lyrical Ballads*, and his turn to the "original figurative language of passion" as used by the "earliest poets of all nations" in his 1802 "Appendix" on poetic diction.[107] There is a similar tension running through these Enlightenment accounts of the figurative origins of language between a language developing out of physical sensations and thus figurative as its words transform in an orderly manner from sensible impressions to abstract ideas, and a language whose figurative origins are a function of "crazy and untamed word transformations" and the enchantments of passion. Richardson points to Rousseau and Herder and their view of primitive language as simultaneously "more sensuously concrete and more metaphorical and emotive" as influencing Wordsworth's seemingly paradoxical ideas about figurative, original language and poetry.[108] But we also need to see the extent to which all these eighteenth-century thinkers, Wordsworth included, relied on a notion of infancy to imagine a "natural" or "original" language that is both tied to the material world and formed by the irregular and idiosyncratic work of passion and the imagination.

Original language is understood as expressing the imagination and sentiment of a mind and body reacting to, attending to, or desiring the unnamed and often unfamiliar objects, images and forms of the world. The term repeatedly given to that mental and developmental stage which is passionately and imaginatively impressed or struck by the unknown objects of the world is "infancy." It is the infant mind that confronts an unknown world, that is shaped by the violent and sudden impressions of that external world striking upon its senses, and that grapples with these sense impressions through the work of the imagination and under the influence of strong emotion. It is the mental and social state of infancy that produces a language both physical and emotional, concrete and imaginative, sensuous and metaphorical. Thus the origins of language can be both natural and metaphorical because they are located not in forms of the natural world, but in the "infant" body perceiving and responding to that world. Infancy thus represents an embodied imaginative state, a state that uses language sensually, gesturally and metaphorically, a state whose language is poetry.

AT FIRST ONLY POETRY WAS SPOKEN

The writers participating in this discussion about the origins of language were well aware that by insisting on the metaphoric origins of language they were re-animating the classical notion that poetry was the first language and literary form. As Blackwell concludes: "hence came the ancient Opinion, 'That Poetry was before Prose.'"[109] They were also quite conscious that this notion of poetry's primacy was counter-intuitive and easily misunderstood by a modern eighteenth-century reader. "It has been often said," Blair comments, "and the concurring voice of all antiquity affirms, that Poetry is older than Prose. But in what sense this seemingly strange paradox holds true, has not always been well understood."[110] Smith lays out more explicitly the cultural values and hierarchies animating this "strange paradox": "It will no doubt seem at first sight very surprising that a species of writing so vastly more difficult should be in all countries prior to that in which men naturally express themselves . . . This indeed may appear very unnatural that what is most difficult should be that in which the Barbarous least civilized nations most excell in."[111] Emphasizing the seeming strange, unnatural and paradoxical quality of poetry's priority to other forms of writing, Smith's and Blair's discussions seem to delight in comparing the "most difficult" and "refined" form of writing to the productions of the "Barbarous least civilized nations."

Their animation on this paradox is, perhaps, a function of how easily they then claim to explain it away. "It will not be very difficult to account for it," Smith insists, although the explanation he offers rejects what Rousseau rather famously claimed: that "at first only poetry was spoken."[112] The idea that primitive man first "spoke in poetry" is, according to Smith, part of the misunderstanding surrounding the idea of poetry as the first language and literary form. As Blair elaborates: "There never, certainly, was any period of society, in which men conversed together in Poetical Numbers. It was in very humble and scanty Prose, as we may easily believe, that the first tribes carried on intercourse among themselves, relating to the wants and necessities of life."[113] Both Blair's and Smith's understanding of that "humble and scanty Prose" first spoken, however, is one characterized by inversion and metaphor, shaped by imagination and passion. As we have seen, early or humble language, if not metrical, is highly figurative, thus "figures" are not exclusive to refined modern poetry. As Smith comments: "there is nowhere more use made of figures than in the lowest and most vulgar conversation."[114] The poetical qualities of language are thus moved out into the domain of everyday common language, preparing the way for Wordsworth's representative counter-movement of taking that common language back into the domain of poetry.

In explaining how it might be that the "most barbarous and rude nations" excel in poetry before any other form of literary arts, these

Enlightenment writers develop a proto-anthropological account of social or stadial history, one that connects social and material conditions – means of subsistence – to manners, customs and styles of expression. Blair's primitive men converse in scanty prose about the necessities of life, but "from the very beginning of Society, there were occasions on which they met together for feasts, sacrifices and Public Assemblies; and on all such occasions, it is well known, that music, song and dance, made their principal entertainment."[115] Blair echoes Smith's description of how "the Savage nations on the coast of Africa, after they have sheltered themselves thro the whole day in caves and grottos from the scorching heat of the Sun come out in the evening and dance and sing together." "Poetry," Smith continues:

> is a necessary attendant on musick, especially on vocall musick the most naturall and simple of any. They naturally express some thoughts along with their musick and these must of consequence be formed into verse to suit with the music. Thus it is that Poetry is cultivated in the most Rude and Barbarous nations, often to a considerable perfection, whereas they make no attempts towards the improvement of Prose.[116]

In these scenes of primitive feasts and assemblies, the connections between language (poetry), gesture (dance) and sound (song) so important to the natural, developmental history of language are staged as the close relationship between original art forms in primitive society.

The most poetic of "rude nations" in Scottish Enlightenment writing was, once again, America. "It is chiefly in America, that we have had the opportunity of being made acquainted with men in their savage state," Blair writes, and "we learn from the particular and concurring accounts of Travellers, that, among all the nations of that vast continent, especially among the North Tribes, with whom we have had most intercourse, music and song are, at all their meetings, carried on with an incredible degree of enthusiasm."[117] Adam Ferguson, always interested in the nursery of America, returns there to defend the idea that "man is a poet by nature." He particularly cites North American oratory: "'We have planted the tree of peace,' says an American orator; 'we have buried the axe under its roots: we henceforth repose under its shade; we will join to brighten the chain that binds our nations together.'" "Such are the collections of metaphor," Ferguson proclaims, "which those nations employ in their public harangues."[118] But what these writers see in America stands as evidence of the customs of all "rude nations," and once again the paradoxical comparison between the barbarous and the refined animates this anthropological–historical discourse. Thus Ferguson concludes his description of North American oratory:

> If we are required to explain, how men could be poets, or orators, before they were aided by the learning of the scholar and the critic? we may inquire, in our turn, how bodies could fall by their weight, before the laws of gravitation were recorded in books? Mind, as well as body, has laws, which are exemplified in the practice of men.... Occasioned, probably, by the physical connection we have mentioned, between the emotions of a heated imagination, and the impressions received from music and pathetic sounds, every tale among rude nations is repeated in verse, and is made to take the form of a song. The early history of all nations is uniform in this particular.[119]

Ferguson's comparison of a man reciting poetry in advance of the "learning of the scholar and the critic" to a body falling before the "laws of gravitation" were "recorded in books" leads immediately into a characteristically embodied understanding of early language and literary forms. Emotions and impressions combine to produce verse and song. Ferguson suggests that there is a "physical connection," a psychological and physiological "law" leading to the development of, and animating the pleasures of, poetry.

These anthropological and historical stagings of primitive poetry thus take the natural characteristics and developmental accounts of early language and transpose them into scenes of social and stadial history. With poetry (closely tied to dance and music) established as the original literary form, writers in this tradition develop a fairly uniform narrative of literary history that becomes an important subset of stadial theory and conjectural histories. Adam Smith's economic history has an accompanying literary history in which literary forms or genres are products of a society's economic and social stage. "It is always late before prose and its beauties come to be cultivated," Smith writes: "'tis the Introduction of Commerce or at least of opulence which is commonly the attendent of Commerce which first brings on the improvement of Prose." This is a matter of pragmatics as well as of style: "Prose is naturally the language of business; as Poetry is of pleasure and amusement. Prose is the Stile in which all the common affairs of Life all Business and Agreements are made." Different economic needs and stages take different literary styles: as Smith quips, "No one ever made a Bargain in verse."[120]

But Smith also describes a literary history tied to mental capacities and emotional habits. "The Poets were the first Historians of any," he writes, and "they recorded those accounts that were most apt to surprise and strike the imagination such as the mythological history and adventures of their Deities." The style, in addition to the content, of these early poetic narratives is representative of the manners of the people and designed to please them:

The first Historians as well as the first Poets chose the marvellous for their Subject as that which was most likely to please a Rude and Ignorant People. Wonder is the passion which in such a people will be most easily excited. Their Ignorance renders them Credulous and easily imposed on, and this Credulity makes them delighted with Fables that would not be relished by a people of more knowledge.[121]

Smith uses a rhetoric of infancy in his descriptions of "first Poets" and "first Historians" who record those things that will "strike the imagination" and excite the "Wonder" of an people "easily imposed on." Social advancement is matched by literary advancement, as genres emerge to reflect the manners and sensibility of the culture: "thus it was that tragedy succeeded the Fabulous accounts of Heroes and centaurs and different monsters, the subject of the first Romances; and thus also, Novells which unfold the tender emotions or more violent passions in the characters they bring before us succeeded the Wild and extravagant Romances which were the first performances of our ancestors in Europe."[122]

This is literary history that is both developmental and historical. Indeed it is *historicist* in the way we currently use that term to the extent that it assumes literature is a product of and must be evaluated within its historical and cultural context. Smith's stadial account of literary genres echoes Blackwell's influential discussion of the historical basis of literature and language. "If there is then an inviolable and necessary Connexion between the Dispositions of a Nation and their Speech," Blackwell wrote at the beginning of the century, "we must believe that there will be an *Alloy* of Simplicity and Wonder in the Beginnings of every Language; and likewise that the Dialect will improve with the Affairs and Genius of the People."[123] Like Smith later in the century, Blackwell understands historical and material change to be reflected in changes of language, style, mental disposition and custom, changes in what he calls "manners" and what we might call "culture": "There is, *My Lord*, a thing, which, tho' it has happened in all Ages and Nations, is yet very hard to describe ... It may be called a *Progression of Manners*; and depends for the most part upon our Fortunes: As they flourish or decline, so we live and are affected; and the greatest Revolutions in them produce the most conspicuous Alterations in the other."[124]

Hugh Blair effectively summarizes Blackwell and Smith (as well as Rousseau and others) to give the Romantic and Victorian periods their dominant version of stadial literary history. Poetry comes first, as we have seen, because "the style of all Language must have been originally poetical; strongly tinctured with that enthusiasm, and that descriptive, metaphorical expression, which distinguishes Poetry." The rise of prose he describes in terms that are social, psychological and stylistic:

As Language, in its progress, began to grow more copious, it gradually lost that figurative style, which was its early character. When men were furnished with proper and familiar names for every object, both sensible and moral, they were not obliged to use so many circumlocutions. Style became more precise, and, of course, more simple. Imagination too, in proportion as Society advanced, had less influence over mankind. The vehement manner of speaking by tones and gestures, became not so universal. The understanding was more exercised; the fancy, less. Intercourse among mankind becoming more extensive and frequent, clearness of style, in signifying their meaning to each other, was the chief object of attention. In place of Poets, Philosophers became the instructors of men; and, in their reasonings on all different subjects, introduced that plainer and simpler style of composition, which we now call Prose.[125]

In describing this progress from figurative language to precision, from imagination to reason, from vehemence of tone and gesture to a "plainer and simpler style of composition," Blair does something that is even more important for our understanding of how this literary history worked and was understood in these years: he relates this historical progress to the development of the individual from childhood to adulthood. Here is his restatement of literary history with the analogy to individual development made explicit:

It appears, that, in all the successive changes which Language has undergone, as the world advanced, the understanding has gained ground on the fancy and imagination. The Progress of Language, in this respect, resembles the progress of age in man. The imagination is most vigorous and predominant in youth; with advancing years, the imagination cools, and the understanding ripens. Thus Language, proceeding from sterility to copiousness, hath, at the same time, proceeded from vivacity to accuracy; from fire and enthusiasm, to coolness and precision. Those characters of early Language, descriptive sound, vehement tones and gestures, figurative styles and inverted arrangement, all hang together, have a mutual influence on each other; and have all gradually given place, to arbitrary sounds, calm pronunciation, simple style, plain arrangement. Language is become, in modern times, more correct, indeed, and accurate; but, however, less striking and animated: in its antient state, more favourable to poetry and oratory; in its present, to reason and philosophy.[126]

The cultural paradigm supporting Blair's literary history and, indeed, the dominant literary history of the period, is the analogy between individual development and social history, between child and savage. It is this analogy, and the developmental narrative of language and literary style it supports, that will lead a writer such as Thomas Love Peacock to declare poetry's irrelevancy for his own "modern times." In responding to these charges, Shelley's *Defence of Poetry* relies on the same cultural paradigm but uses this developmental narrative against itself, remaking poetry into the very origin and engine of language's development and change, rather than a particular style of primitive art and expression. Clearly the history of language and literature circulating in these years – one that located poetry at the point of origins and understood those origins through a rhetoric of infancy – fueled a vigorous debate about the value and qualities of poetry in the present day. What exactly did the idea of infancy mean for poetry in these years? What idea of poetry does a rhetoric of infancy support and promote?

OLDEST WRITERS, YOUNGEST TALKERS: HOMER'S CHILDHOOD

Perhaps we can begin to answer these questions by reversing their terms: what does this account of poetry mean for infancy and childhood? The narratives of linguistic and literary history that we have been reading provide a proto-anthropological account of early childhood and the sounds of the nursery, one that, in turn, plays a new part in literary culture. In his discussion of original language, for example, Alexander Murray compares the infant's "habitual reference in their minds of new perceptions to those already known" to the savage's tendency to combine and apply known words to new objects: "a savage calls brandy 'fire-water'; cannon 'the white man's thunder'; a ship, 'a water-wigwam,' &c."[127] Thus Herder takes the prattle or babble of infants as proof that poetry is older than prose. He returns to his foundational analogy – "for of course the human species in its childhood formed for itself precisely the language which a child-without-any-say stammers" – to locate the origins of language in the sounds of the nursery: "it is the babbling vocabulary of the wet-nurse's quarters." Herder then asks, "where does that [original language] remain in the mouths of adults?" It remains, he concludes, in poetry: "for what was this first language but a collection of elements of poetry," elements that include "sounds ... images of action, of passion and of living effect."[128] Herder, in effect, moves the babbling vocabulary of infants into the adult world and calls it "poetry"; the nursery becomes a part of the literary cultural field.

In this chapter we have been tracing the contours of what we might call an infantile account of poetry, one that makes the state of infancy the historical and genetic origin of language and literature. This understanding of language and literature supports some critical and characteristic new features of poetry in the Romantic period; perhaps most obviously, it helps redefine poetry as, in Blair's influential terms, "the language of passion, or of enlivened imagination, formed, most commonly, into regular numbers."[129] Although he nods to metre in his definition here, Blair participates in the larger Romantic trend of downplaying the importance of versification as the defining characteristic of poetry. Metre is increasingly seen as an "artificial" or "mechanical" embellishment, one not essential to poetry.[130] When it is discussed and defended, it is situated within the dominant anthropological historical account of primitive culture. Versification, it is often stated, has its origins in oral songs and "national Ballads," products, again, of infancy that linger on in the nursery. Thus Blair writes that "before Writing was invented, Songs only could last, and be remembered. The ear gave assistance to the memory, by the help of Numbers; fathers repeated and sung them to their children."[131] Metre is also described as adding to the "pleasure" of poetry, and pleasure, along with passion and imagination, are seen as poetry's special purview: "The Historian, the Orator, the Philosopher, address themselves, for the most part, primarily to the understanding: their direct aim is to inform, to persuade, or to instruct. But the primary aim of a Poet is to please, and to move; and, therefore, it is to the Imagination, and the Passions, that he speaks."[132]

The work of imagination and passion in the writing, reading, reciting and hearing of poetry returns us to the importance of sound, gesture, tone and image in this primitive poetics. Discussions of early language as a mixed mode of sound and words complement an emerging emphasis on embodied expression and a growing interest in the extra-semantic elements of language, as we will explore further in the next chapter. Poetic images are valued not for their refinement and wit, but for their capacity to repeat a striking impression. The craft and conventions of poetry, as in the case of metre, are demoted in favor of the bodily emotion and sensuous experience that poetry now hopes to repeat and communicate.

A definition of poetry as "the language of passion, or of enlivened imagination," however, also has the potential to re-imagine the most artificial and conventional elements of modern poetry as original and vital. Blair, who insists that early language would be characterized by inversions and "bold figures of speech," thus extends his discussion to poetic devices more generally:

Under the influence too of any strong emotion, objects do not appear to us such as they really are, but such as passion makes us see them. We magnify and exaggerate; we seek to interest all others in what causes our emotion; we compare the least things to the greatest; we call upon the absent as well as the present, and even address ourselves to things inanimate. Hence, in congruity with those various movements of the mind, arise those turns of expression, which we now distinguish by the learned names of Hyperbole, Prosopopoeia, Simile, &c. but which are no other than the native original language of Poetry, among the most barbarous nations.[133]

What in modern times become "artificial ornaments" and evidence of imitated passion on the part of authors who "affect what they did not feel," are, in this early moment, the "native original language of Poetry."

But native, original poetry is not merely a poetry of powerful feelings and figures, nor simply one of sincere expression and true experience: it is a poetry that has a privileged relationship to its historical and cultural context. It records the "striking" events and strong "impressions" of the day in a style similarly strong and forceful. Here again the notion of infancy as the most "impressionistic" state plays a crucial role in formulating these literary values. And here again Blackwell's account of Homer was an important theoretical and rhetorical model for the century to follow. To the question of how Homer could be unequalled as an epic poet in the 2,000 years before and after he composed, Blackwell insists that the answer lies in Homer's fortuitous relationship to history, by which he means both his relationship to the subject matter of his poetry as well as to the manners or style of his day. This was "Homer's first Happiness," according to Blackwell:

He took his plain natural Images from *Life*: He saw *Warriors*, and *Shepherds*, and *Peasants*, such as he drew; and was daily conversant among such People as he intended to represent: The Manners used in the *Trojan* Times were not disused in his own: The same way of living in private, and the same Pursuits in publick were still prevalent, and gave him a Model for his Design. . . . For so unaffected and simple were the Manners of those Times, that the Folds and Windings of the human Breast lay open to the Eye; nor were People ashamed to avow Passions and Inclinations, which were entirely void of Art and Design.[134]

We have already discussed this idea of primitive manners as a state in which the "human Breast lay open to the Eye," in which man's sentiments and desires are expressed so simply, naturally and directly as to make interior "Folds and Windings" completely transparent, exterior and fully present to others. This is also a poetics of personal experience, one which participates, as Janet Sorensen makes clear, in the "metaphysics of presence" – with its privileging of immediacy and "self-presence" – that Jacques Derrida uncovers in Rousseau as symptomatic of this period.[135] Thus Blackwell will conclude: "In short, it may be said of *Homer*, and of every *Poet* who has wrote well, That *what* he felt and saw, *that* he described."[136]

But this rhetoric of embodied presence again depends on key historical and historicist assumptions that we cannot overlook. The fact that Homer could take his "plain natural Images from *Life*" is not simply a factor of writing about what he witnessed around him, although the fact that he *saw* the warriors, shepherds and peasants he represented and "was daily conversant among such People" is indeed important to Blackwell. Homer had the good luck to be born at a time when he might be a "Spectator of all the various Situations of the human Race; might observe them in great Calamities, and in high Felicity." But Blackwell also speculates that Homer's must have been the "first or second Generation, after the Transplantation or rather the final Settlement of this Colony" and that, while he witnessed the violence and distresses of wars, Homer's age was largely one of prosperity and growing stability, one in which cities were "increasing in Wealth and Discipline." Thus Homer's felicity lies as much, if not more, in the manners of his age than in the subject matter it presented:

Homer had the good fortune to see and learn the *Grecian* Manners, at their true Pitch and happiest Temper for Verse: Had he been born much sooner, he would have seen nothing but Nakedness and Barbarity: Had he come much later, he had fallen in the times either of wide Policy and Peace, or of General Wars, when private Passions are buried in the common Order, and established Discipline.[137]

Homer's relationship to his subject matter, the Trojan War, thus becomes one of a carefully calibrated historical and cultural distance: at a sufficient remove so that it can be reflected upon and narrated in a mature style, and yet not so far away that its manners, customs, ways of living and styles of expression were lost or unfamiliar: "The Manners used in the *Trojan* Times were not disused in his own: The same way of living in private, and the same Pursuits in publick were still prevalent." The poetics of presence seemingly embedded in that key phrase "That *what* he felt and saw, *that* he described," involves, in fact, a more complex historical cultural formula that balances the right degree of historical distance with a clear continuity of manners.

Thus Adam Ferguson describes a "simple poet" as having "impressions that more than compensate the defects of his skill." Such a primitive poet can be "simple and vehement in his conceptions and feelings," according to Ferguson, because he is "not engaged in recalling, like Virgil or Tasso, the sentiments or scenery of an age remote from his own: he needs not be told by the critic to recollect what another would have thought, or in what manner another would have expressed his conception."[138] Robert Burns will echo this notion and rhetoric almost exactly in announcing his own poetic debut in the preface to his *Poems, Chiefly in the Scottish Dialect*: "the following trifles are not the productions of the Poet, who with all the advantages of learned art, and perhaps amid the elegancies and idleness of upper life, looks down for a rural theme, with an eye of Theocrites or Virgil." Burns lays claim to a strong, "rustic" poetry by advertising his unfamiliarity with the "necessary requisites for commencing Poet by rule" and proclaiming that he instead "sings the sentiments and manners he felt and saw in himself and his rustic compeers around him, in his and their native language."[139] The complexity of Burns' rhetoric here, however, cannot be over-stated; disavowing the advantages of learning and the position of a "Theocrites or Virgil" even as he proves his knowledge of them, Burns claims no naïve authenticity of expression or language, but rather an emotional and perceptual proximity to his "rural theme" that is highly aware of all the ways cultural, linguistic, historical and national differences affect the poet's "song."

Propping up these historicist assumptions about the relationship of the poet and his poem to the events and manners of his period are additional developmental assumptions. What becomes clear, for example, in Blackwell's discussion of Homer's fortuitous mix of distance and proximity to his heroic subject matter is the importance of his childhood in shaping that distance and fashioning his poetic style. "*Young Minds*," Blackwell insists, "are apt to receive such strong Impressions from the Circumstances of the Country where they are born and bred, that they contract a mutual kind of Likeness to those Circumstances, and bear the Marks of the Course of Life thro' which they have passed."[140] Our "Thoughts and Manners" are "influenced by the Strain of our Lives," Blackwell asserts, but they are particularly influenced in childhood, and the impressions made upon "young minds" will continue through life. The "*State of the Country* where a Person is born and bred" will "make us *what we are*," he claims, stressing the importance of manners, both public – the "ordinary way[s] of living" – and private – the "particular way of Life" and education that one is given. Blackwell's historical cultural account of

Homer's genius requires, in fact, a developmental understanding of his childhood and an emphasis on the "striking impressions" made on the infant mind. It is on and through the infant mind that the events of history and the manners of society influence the poet and the poetry. This is not just an understanding of how childhood plays a particularly important role in shaping individual identity; it is also an understanding of how history plays a particularly important role in shaping individual identity and cultural production through the impressions made in infancy and childhood.

Blackwell's account of Homer's ideal relationship to his historical age thus stresses the importance of the poet's childhood: *when* Homer was a child shapes *what* poetry he writes as a man. The strong and continuous connection to the great events of history, or the significant events of one's own life, that becomes the standard for poetry in this period is increasingly imagined as made in the period of infancy and childhood. Savage, bard, ploughman and baby are all poets in this psycho-social history of language and literature that must be proved "first in the woods and wild, and afterward in the nursery." We thus return to Thomas Gunter Browne's discussion of the metaphoric origins of language to find the savage and the child paired as poets in a complex cultural framework that can also account for the representative "ancient" poet, Homer. Browne details the metaphoric and associative powers of what he calls the "first talkers"; these are, as we might expect, the savage and the child who, grappling with the lack of words characterizing the "infancy of speech," rely on metaphoric associations to make one word serve as noun, verb and adjective:

I believe that there may be tribes of men *now* living, whose art of speech is so *young*, that they may talk without any distinction (as we make it) of *adjective* and *substantive*, and without any distinction of *verb* and *noun*; i.e. whose words are all substantives. And I suppose there may be tribes, who have no words to express time *past*, or the time to come; whatever they may *feel* internally – for thus we hear our own children talk. – And I apprehend mere savages and children have very faint ideas of things are not *immediately* pressing upon them. – And I conceive that no word was at first necessary, or wanted, to express present time.[141]

This is an account of the "infancy of language" now familiar to us, particularly in the way it brings children and savages together, as it was increasingly familiar and established in Browne's time. "This is the way children speak, and this is the way whole nations are found to talk," Browne concludes, with full confidence that the evidence of the nursery proves the state of things in the wilds and vice versa.[142]

This is also a way of talking that is conducive to poetry. Thus Browne echoes Blackwell's question about how to account for Homer's genius in these terms:

How comes it that the oldest writers (such as Homer and Isaiah) were the happiest poets? I answer – Because they were the youngest talkers – Their art of speech was in an earlier state than our's. – They seized the boldest metaphors. – Every noun, every verb, every adjective, every particle, is or may be used as a *metaphor*. – Every compound word is a poem; thus every child, or savage, may be called a poet – [143]

Again these are ideas and images about the "happiest poets" that were familiar and well-established when Browne repeated them here. But his deployment of that dominant analogy between child and savage mutates into something related but significantly different: a transformation of the "oldest writers" into the "youngest talkers" and a comparison between the "Greek poet" and the "infant Briton."

Browne insists that the "*simplicity* of the Greek (usually called its grandeur) resembles the early conversation of children in the English nursery." Let other "proud Grecians" compare the "supposed mistakes of his little boy" with all the "various dialects and phraseology of his favorite poets and orators," Browne proclaims. He, himself, has often thought his "little master of rhetoric, in the nursery, was talking elegant Greek, when, in fact, he was only giving me a lecture in pure Saxon."[144] The frisson of paradox animating Smith's and Blair's accounts of primitive poetry in which the "Barbarous least civilized nations" excel in the most "difficult" and "refined" of literary forms here results in strange figurative confusions of classical and vernacular, ancient and infant, foreign and native. "The infant Briton often speaks whole sentences without a verb," Browne comments: "he speaks, in many respects, in a classical Greek style; till his barbarous English tutors have quite corrupted his grand *Helenistic* vein." Indeed, the "British boy" of three years of age, "may truly be said to speak the Attic, the Aeolic, the Doric, the Ionic and the Poetic dialects of the Saxon tongue." Every poetic and metaphoric figure can be heard at the nursery table: "There is not a figure of speech, nor a trope, nor a metaphor, in the Greek or Latin grammar, that I have not heard my learned little master use; when seated at table in his high chair, he was longing to be engaged with the plum-pudding."[145]

The rhetorical flourishes in which "savage man," "infant Briton" and "Greek poet" are comparable figures for original poetry enact a cultural and historical theory that is critical for the emergence of a vernacular, native and national literary tradition in Britain in the Romantic period. Browne's deliberately incongruous images – the infant in his high chair speaking in "classical Greek style"; the accomplishments of the "oldest writers" re-described as the felicities of the "youngest talkers" – bestow value on the earliest and crudest linguistic expressions and provide a framework for relating them to the most learned literary forms. Giving poetry infant origins insists on vital connections between infantile and masculine expression, between the child and the man.

CHAPTER 3

Becoming human

Animal, infant and developmental literary culture in the Romantic period

Johann Gottfried Herder begins his influential *Treatise on the Origin of Language* with the statement, *"Already as an animal, the human being has language,"* a sentence that exemplifies the tendency of Enlightenment and Romantic writings on the origin of language to assume affinity and close kinship between man and animal.[1] The natural and developmental history of language and literature that we have traced thus far assumes man's animal origins and asserts significant continuities, rather than categorical distinctions, between animals and humans. Sounds, cries and gestures are forms of communication that humans share with other animals. To call these sounds and gestures a "language" is thus to credit animals with having a language as well.[2] Clearly what is at stake in these conjectural histories of the origin of language is not only what constitutes language but what constitutes the human.

Thus a significant stream of thought running through these developmental narratives of language is one that breaks down fundamental distinctions between man and animal. Keith Thomas describes the eighteenth century as a period in which "popular and learned notions about animals combined to weaken the orthodox doctrine of man's uniqueness," and this was particularly the case in discussions of language where the traditional idea of speech as what separates human beings from the rest of the animal world eroded significantly over the course of the century.[3] As Herder comments about Condillac and Rousseau and their theories of original language – and his comment, as we shall soon see, is a criticism – "the former made animals into human beings, and the latter made human beings into animals."[4]

Monboddo, whose *Origin and Progress of Language* was widely read and discussed in Britain and Europe, begins by listing the resemblances between savages, infants and animals, asking "Does not this plainly indicate, that there is no natural difference betwixt our minds and [the mind of the brute], and that the superiority we have over them is *adventitious*, and from *acquired habit*?"[5] Acquiring the habits of the human becomes, in Monboddo's account, a process of development:

Thus is man formed, not however at once, but by degrees, and in succession: For he appears at first to be little more than a mere vegetable, hardly deserving the name of a *Zoöphyte*; then he gets sense, but sense only, so that he is yet little better than a muscle; then he becomes an animal of a more complete kind; then a rational creature; and finally a man of intellect and science, which is the summit and completion of our nature.[6]

Man is not born human; he becomes human. Monboddo traces this developmental process on both the ontogenetic and phylogenetic level. Indeed, Monboddo's conception of human development has strong recapitulative elements, suggesting that the human being moves through every stage of vegetable and animal existence on its path to becoming fully human.[7]

Language thus becomes not what distinguishes human from animal, but rather a critical stage in the process of becoming human and even that which propels the course of human development. Along with this, infancy becomes something of a border state and the infant becomes a "betwixt and between" (as J. M. Barrie would have it some years later), a human-becoming animal or an animal with hidden human resources. Infant language acquisition thus becomes newly interesting, along with infant education more generally, not only as a way to observe and influence an important phase in the formation of the human, but also as the place to monitor the differences and similarities between the human and the animal. To this end, scenes of children learning to read also become newly significant as enacting another crucial step in the process of becoming human; as animals are credited with language, it is not the ability to speak, but the ability to read and write that becomes an important distinguishing characteristic of human beings. Literature thus takes its place as a critical category in the development and distinction of the human.[8]

I have been suggesting that "infancy" and "childhood" become important terms in Enlightenment writings, not just for naming the early stages of the individual life, but for naming and evaluating cultural and historical stages, and for enabling the stages of an individual life to be mapped on to those of a cultural history and vice versa. When history and culture are understood to develop, they are understood to develop out of an "infancy," to retain key elements and impressions of a "childhood." This leads, as we will see, to a particular way of understanding and describing literary history and of organizing and evaluating literary culture. We are tracking how literature becomes a developmental construct or category and literary art comes to be understood as a function of human development.

Indeed, the history of language and literature that emerges over the course of the eighteenth century shapes a developmental framework through which contemporary literary culture is understood, one that explains how different literary genres relate to each other, how they should be experienced, in what order and at what age. By the end of the nineteenth century, the forms and activities of literature are firmly placed on a developmental map that assigns each time of life its proper literary style and genre, at the same time that it organizes literature into psychological hierarchies and mental stages. This chapter will trace the contours of the developmental literary culture that emerges in the Romantic period as a consequence of new historical understandings of language and literature. We will begin with two meditations on the silences and mysteries of human infancy: J. G. von Herder's evocation of the hidden powers of infancy in his theory of the origin of language, and Samuel Taylor Coleridge's meditations on infants and other inarticulate beings in his lyrics "Frost at Midnight" and "The Nightingale." Both writers understand the inaccessible state of infancy as the origin of human language and culture. We will then turn to accounts of the animal origins of language and the close connections between children and animals as depicted in a variety of Romantic texts, from philosophical essays, to ballads and reading primers. We will see how notions of recapitulation, revival and return – concepts that we have seen as crucial to the historical and developmental ideas of language and culture – shape how the Romantics understood their own literary moment and its varieties of literary experiences. Placing conjectural histories of the origin of language into the larger context of sentimental and Romantic culture will also disclose the historicist assumptions underpinning Romantic interest in sympathy, sentiment and the expressive qualities of language.

"BORN DUMB," BUT ...

We have observed how the developmental discourse of Enlightenment historicism uses the idea of infancy as a way of figuring origins and does so to the extent that the conceptual paradigms of infancy and development necessitate each other. To have an infancy is to be capable of further development, and to develop is to emerge out of infant origins. When it comes to language, infancy comes to mean not just a speechless state or a lack of language (*infans*), but the state out of which speech and language will arise. Thus we have seen writer after writer speculate on the origins of language by trying to describe the state of infancy, reflecting not only on the particular qualities of infancy, but also about how these qualities might give rise to language, to speech and, eventually, to the multiple forms and genres of literature. In his *Treatise on the Origins of Language*, Herder uses the rhetorical figure of aposiopesis to signal the infant's future proficiency in the midst of apparent deficiency, to suggest the unknown yet infinite potential of the human infant: "*Born dumb*, but . . ."⁹

The infant mind thus comes to represent the ultimate mystery of human origins. Thomas Reid, for example, begins his *Inquiry into the Human Mind* bemoaning his lack of access to the "simple and original principles" of human mental faculties and the subsequent impediments his inquiry faces. He embodies the obscurities of origins and the mysteries of the human mind in two figures: the primitive "savage" – a "two-legged animal" who nevertheless has within him "the seeds of the logician, the man of taste and breeding, the orator, the statesman, the man of virtue, and the saint"¹⁰ – and the child. Just as the full capabilities of man "lay hid in the savage state," so does the child's mind become an inaccessible but invaluable hiding place. "Could we obtain a distinct and full history of all that hath passed in the mind of a child from the beginning of life and sensation, till it grows up to the use of reason," Reid writes, "this would be a treasure of natural history, which would probably give more light into the human faculties, than all the systems of philosophers about them since the beginning of the world." But, Reid laments, "it is vain to wish for what nature has not put within the reach of our power. Reflection . . . comes too late."¹¹ The mind is a hiding place of buried and unarticulated secrets in the opening pages of Reid's *Inquiry* and is represented as such in descriptions of both the "savage state" and the "mind of a child."

For Herder the drama of infancy lies in the juxtaposition of the infant's circumscribed state to the "large sphere" which it is ultimately destined to inhabit. As "the most orphaned child of nature . . . . naked and bare, weak and needy, timid and unarmed," the human infant, according to Herder, has only a "dispersed, weakened sensuality" and "divided and weakened drives." The child is "destined for a large sphere – and yet so orphaned and abandoned that it does not even enjoy the gift of a language with which to express its shortcomings."¹² That man who is capable of so much would be born capable of so little – without language, without a strong instinct to do any particular thing – is a "contradiction" in the natural order of things that ultimately Herder cannot believe. To resolve this conundrum Herder resorts to the image of the infant mind as a hiding place: "There must, instead of instincts be other hidden powers sleeping in the human child!"[13]

It is Herder's sense of these powers sleeping in the infant that enables his important break with Condillac, Rousseau and their naturalist accounts of the origins of language. Herder's philosophical stance on the animal or natural origins of language can seem contradictory. As we have seen, the first sentence of his important *Treatise on the Origin of Language* is, significantly: "*Already as an animal, the human being has language.*" Man and beast share a language of sensation, but Herder explicitly rejects Condillac's developmental narrative and the idea that the "cry of the sensations" could ever be the "origin of human language." Criticizing Condillac and Rousseau for turning animals into humans, humans into animals, Herder insists that this animal language of sound and gesture, is *not* the origin of human language: "Children utter noises of sensation like the animals, but is not the language that they learn from human beings a quite different language?"[14] Indeed, Herder's account of the origin of language ultimately argues against the developmental narrative connecting animals and humans that otherwise characterizes natural histories of language. If we were to identify those "hidden powers sleeping in the human child," Herder writes, if we were to find "in the hollow of that great bereftness of drives to art, the *germ of a substitute*," some trait that compensated for the lack of instinctual drive, we would find the "*human being's distinctive feature*" and demonstrate that "the human species does not stand above the animals in *levels* of more or less, but in *kind*."[15] As we shall see, Herder identifies and describes the human being's "distinctive feature" by revisiting and revising the scene of the child imitating the sounds of animals. He thereby makes the mystery of how the infant without language comes to language – "*Born dumb*, but . . ." – the mystery of what makes humans human.

This does not mean, however, that Herder makes language or speech the distinguishing characteristic of the human. What Herder ultimately identifies as the distinctive feature of human beings is something like the capacity for self-consciousness. Not only is the human being a creature who "cognizes, wills and effects," he is also one who "know[s] that it cognizes wills, and effects."[16] Herder calls this disposition of human nature "awareness," a capacity to reflect and also to be conscious of that act of reflection, and he is particularly interested in the act of paying attention that such moments of reflection entail:

The human being demonstrates reflection when the force of his soul operates so freely that in the whole ocean of sensations which floods the soul through all the senses it can, so to speak, separate off, stop, and pay attention to a single wave, and be conscious of its own attentiveness. The human being demonstrates reflection when, out of the whole hovering dream of images which proceed before his senses, he can collect himself into a moment of alertness, freely dwell on a single image, pay it clear, more leisurely heed, and separate off the characteristic marks for the fact that this is that object and no other.[17]

This basic act of reflection – of collecting oneself into a "moment of alertness" and paying heed to a single "image" – is one, Herder insists, that the infant is able to perform. "The infant thinks with awareness," he argues, and, more significantly, the infant can identify and acknowledge to himself the "characteristic marks" which separate one image or object from another.[18] That moment not just of paying attention, but of distinguishing and acknowledging a "characteristic mark" by which an object will be known is, for Herder, the beginning of language. In his words: "A characteristic mark which he had to separate off and which as a characteristic mark of taking-awareness fell distinctly within him. . . . This *first characteristic mark of taking-awareness was a word of the soul! With it human language is invented.*"[19]

Here, then, is Herder's version of the scene of the invention of language in which a child sees and, significantly, hears a lamb:

Let that lamb pass before his eye as an image – [something that happens] to him as to no other animal. Not as to the hungry, scenting wolf!, not as to the blood-licking lion – they already scent and savor in their minds! sensuality has overcome them! instinct impels them to attack it! . . . Not so to the human being! As soon as he develops a need to become acquainted with the sheep, no instinct disturbs him, no sense tears him too close to the sheep or away from it; it stands there exactly as it expresses itself to his senses. White, soft, woolly – his soul, operating with awareness, seeks a characteristic mark – *the sheep bleats!* – his soul has found a characteristic mark. The inner sense takes effect. This bleating, which makes the strongest impression on the soul, which tore itself away from all the other properties of viewing and feeling, jumped forth, penetrated most deeply, remains for the soul. The sheep comes again. White, soft, woolly – the soul sees, feels, takes awareness, seeks a characteristic mark – it bleats, and now the soul recognizes it again! "Aha! You are the bleating one!" the soul feels inwardly. The soul has recognized it in a human way, for it recognizes and names it distinctly, that is, with a characteristic mark.[20]

Here Herder elevates a typical childhood scene – that of the child learning and imitating the sounds of the animals, one we will see depicted, for example, in children's reading primers – into the primal scene of the invention of language. In so doing, he transforms a scene of imitation into a scene of attention and reflection, suggesting that the invention of language may indeed arise out of the imitated sounds of animals, but what appears to be imitation is more properly understood as recognition. Herder's "learning child-without-any-say [*Unmündige*]" hears the bleat and thinks, "Now I will know you again. You bleat! The turtle-dove coos! The dog barks!"[21] Thus an infant vocabulary of imitated sounds is rewritten into acts of acknowledgment: "Aha! You are the bleating one!" In an interesting, infantile version of Adamic language, the child hears the sound that nature offers up and acknowledges that sound as the animal's name. Thus in Herder's account of the invention of human language, to imitate an animal sound is to pay attention to, to hear and be impressed by a sound, and to acknowledge that sound as the characteristic mark or name of a non-human creature. It is not just to make a sound, but to think a word. Human imitation of animal sounds is therefore of an entirely different order than animal imitation of human sounds. "Parrot and starling have learned enough human sounds," Herder admits, "but have they also thought a human word?"[22]

With Herder's emphasis on reflection and self-consciousness, the dramatic scene of the invention of language moves inward and becomes less an encounter between two primitive men or between man and animal than a dialogue of the self with itself. "Even if the human being never reached the situation of conveying this idea to another creature," Herder continues, "still his soul has, so to speak, bleated internally when it chose this sound as a sign for remembering, and bleated again when it recognized the sheep by it. Language is invented!"[23] The fact that Herder insists that the child sees the lamb "as an image" is another way in which the invention of language becomes an interior event; it is also a significant revision of the idea of infancy as a state in which the mind is wholly confined to material, sense impressions and capable of paying attention only to the objects of its immediate external world. Herder's infant mind, by the very act of paying attention to an object in the world, turns that object into an image, a representation of the object, something that can mean the object. Thus while the bleat of the lamb makes its strong, physical impression – "it fell distinctly within him" and "penetrated most deeply" – infant awareness also re-makes the lamb into an image, its bleat into a mark or sign. The creation of this sign, much as it is an act of awareness and recognition, is also, of course, a form of imitation: the infant is not simply repeating the sounds of animals, but, remaking those sounds into mimetic signs, onomatopoeic words. The imitation of sounds and the thinking of words remain entangled.

Infancy thus takes on an indeterminate status in Herder's writings on language. The internal workings of the infant mind hold the secrets of the origin of language and humanity, and yet these origins remain hidden and inscrutable. The infant proves its humanity by imitating the non-human world, originating human language out of the bleats and barks of animals. This is a set of images and associations representing infancy that appear in a variety of other Romantic writings, and they both extend and complicate the relationship between infant origins and the development of language, between humans and animals. Samuel Taylor Coleridge's lyrics of 1798, "The Nightingale" and "Frost at Midnight," are both meditations on language and the non-human world that turn and return to the figure of an infant who, as we have seen, is a form of opaque interiority and hidden mysteries. Coleridge was a critical reader of Herder, but whether directly influenced by his reading or not, these poems share with Herder's writing an interest in infancy and a common set of images and issues used to represent and interrogate the infant state.[24]

THAT STRANGE THING, AN INFANT'S DREAM

"Frost at Midnight" and "The Nightingale" are poems about how man relates to and understands the non-human world around him in so much as they are both poems about the human forms and meanings man places on non-human figures. In "Frost at Midnight," the speaker sees and meditates upon the form of a film in the fireplace grate; in "The Nightingale," the speaker hears and muses on the nightingale. But in both poems, the speaker's infant son is brought into close relationship with these non-human forms and each poem ultimately becomes, in the words of "The Nightingale," a "father's tale," a meditation on what forms and meanings the father can place on his infant son.

The first section of "Frost at Midnight" immediately begs the question: what kind of company is a sleeping infant? Coleridge's speaker emphasizes his solitude but it is solitude of a particular quality:

> The inmates of my cottage, all at rest,
> Have left me to that solitude, which suits
> Abstruser musings: save that at my side

My cradled infant slumbers peacefully.
'Tis calm indeed! so calm, that it disturbs
And vexes meditation with its strange
And extreme silentness.[25]

These lines move us through different qualities of felt solitude: the solitude of being the only one awake in a house where, tucked into their beds, others are sleeping; the solitude of sitting awake with a sleeping infant at one's side; and – by insisting on the presence of sleeping others and, thereby, inviting us to imagine their absence – the solitude of being awake and entirely alone in a house at night. The sleeping others, in short, qualify and shape this speaker's solitude. They are present but unconscious of the speaker, their interior life impenetrable and closed off to his existence and companionship. Their very presence thus heightens his experience of solitude, just as the calm of the night is also heightened and felt as "extreme silentness."

The presence of the infant pushes this quality of solitude to further extremes, because, even when awake, the infant's mind remains inaccessible, his interior life inexpressible. For Coleridge, a sleeping infant only accentuates the mysteries of the infant mind in any state, and he gestures at such mysteries in "The Nightingale" when he describes how his infant son awoke one night "in most distressful mood" and speculates parenthetically that "(some inward pain / Had made up that strange thing, an infant's dream)."[26] With the parentheses closing off the infant's dream from the rest of the line, Coleridge stages the inaccessibility of the infant's mind. An infant's dream is "strange" in the sense that it is unknown or unfamiliar, or perhaps in the sense that it belongs to some other place. But when reading these two poems together, it is also tempting to think of the "stranger" in "A Frost at Midnight," the customary name for the film at the grate which, Coleridge tells us in a footnote, is supposed to "portend the arrival of some absent friend."[27] The uncanny play between friend and stranger, the familiar and the unfamiliar that animates this folkloric tradition is important to both of Coleridge's poems; the strangeness of the infant's dream is thus that of something once known but long forgotten and estranged. In "A Frost at Midnight," this strangeness is located both in the sleeping infant at his side and dispersed throughout the world around him: "Sea, hill, and wood, / This populous village! Sea, and hill, and wood / With all the numberless goings on of life / Inaudible as dreams."[28] The night is filled with beings, existences, consciousnesses, all mute, unspeaking and unheard, abundantly present yet fully inaccessible to the speaker.

In "Frost at Midnight," the speaker reacts to the "extreme silentness" and palpable solitude by turning the film in the grate into a companion. Describing the film as the "sole unquiet thing" in the room besides himself, Coleridge imagines a sympathy between them: "Methinks, its motion in this hush of nature / Gives it dim sympathies with me who live, / Making it a companionable form." But his acute self-consciousness about this conceit, signaled by the heavily poeticized "methinks," quickly becomes itself the central preoccupation of these lines, as Coleridge describes the film and his attention to it: "Whose puny flaps and freaks the idling Spirit / By its own moods interprets, every where / Echo or mirror seeking of itself, / And makes a toy of Thought."[29] Coleridge idly imagines the film as a "companionable form" and then mildly chastises himself for the facile imaginative gesture of seeing something only through his own mood and or as a reflection of his own self. This is exactly the fault of the "night-wandering man" in 'The Nightingale' who misinterprets the nightingale's song as melancholic based on his own misery:

> But some night-wandering man, whose heart was pierced
> With the remembrance of a grievous wrong,
> Or slow distemper, or neglected love,
> (And so, poor wretch! Filled all things with himself,
> And made all gentle sounds tell back the tale
> Of his own sorrow).[30]

With parentheses again signaling an interiority closed off to the outside world – here the solipsism of a "poor wretch" who makes the bird's song "tell back the tale / Of his own sorrow" – these lines ultimately suggest that personification of the natural world, making the non-human world tell back a human tale, entails a fundamental misapprehension of non-human, inarticulate beings, and one with significant consequences. The misnamed "melancholy strain" of the nightingale becomes a major poetic tradition, as "many a poet echoes the conceit," spending his time "building up the rhyme" (and perpetuating the tradition of the melancholy nightingale) rather than "surrendering his whole spirit" to the natural world.

But how can one understand such inarticulate beings otherwise, especially when one's apprehension is ultimately articulated in language? The animation of a film in the fireplace grate and the expressive sounds of a nightingale's song both invite and impede linguistic interpretation. Coleridge challenges the idea of the nightingale's melancholy song but he makes the same mistake of "fill[ing] all things with himself" when he insists that the bird's song is joyful. "'Tis the merry Nightingale," he proclaims, launching into the most explicit personification of the bird in the poem:

> that crowds, and hurries, and precipitates
> With fast thick warble his delicious notes,
> As he were fearful that an April night
> Would be too short for him to utter forth
> His love-chant, and disburthen his full soul
> Of all its music."[31]

At this point in "The Nightingale," one realizes that this poem is less about "surrendering" the human self to the experience of the non-human, natural world, than about creating an alternative literary tradition of the joyful nightingale to counter that of the melancholic nightingale. "My Friend, and thou, our Sister," the speaker apostrophizes, "we have learnt / A different lore," well aware that this lore of the "merry Nightingale," like that of the "night-wandering man," also involves filling the bird's song with human emotion and significance.

At this point in our discussion we need to ask why "The Nightingale" turns to the infant in its concluding section. Why does this poem about the human forms and meanings man places on non-human figures and the literary lore man creates about the natural world become a "father's tale" about his infant son? Both "The Nightingale" and "Frost at Midnight" conclude with a turn to the infant figure, and they do so, on the one hand, because the child is understood as the inheritor of a new natural lore and as the object of his father's pedagogical attentions. The final lines of both poems suggest just this, as the father hopes his infant son, in "Frost at Midnight," will learn that "all seasons shall be sweet" and, in "The Nightingale," will learn to "associate joy" with the night. "Frost at Midnight," is indeed explicitly a poem about education, one that describes the miseries of Coleridge's own traditional, urban schooling where he was "pent 'mid cloisters dim, / And saw nought lovely but the sky and stars" and imagines the very different education his son will have "wander[ing] like a breeze / By lakes and sandy shores."[32]

On the other hand, Coleridge also takes considerable pains to associate the infant with the non-human natural world that humans so readily misapprehend and misinterpret. This is particularly the case in "The Nightingale" where the baby, who wakes in the middle of the night because of his strange, unknown inner life of dreams, has eyes that "swam with undropped tears" and "glitter in the yellow moon-beam" just as the nightingales have "bright, bright eyes ... eyes both bright and full" that "glisten" in the "moon-lit bushes" of the grove. Both bird and baby also respond to the sight of the moon, altering their songs and cries: the nightingales pause in their singing when the moon is lost behind a cloud and then, when it emerges, "these wakeful birds / Have all burst forth in choral minstrelsy," while the baby, at the sight of the moon, "hushed at once, / Suspends his sobs, and laughs most silently."[33]

With these close associations between bird and baby, the central preoccupations of "The Nightingale" – the human significance man mistakenly but perhaps inevitably places on non-human figures, the lore man creates to explain those creatures in the natural world that he cannot fully know or understand – envelops the figure of the infant. Can one personify a human infant? In turning to the infant at the conclusion of each of these poems, Coleridge raises this question, one that both insists on the strange, nonhuman qualities of the infant and wonders about the significance and emotion the adult speaker places on this figure. These poems become fathers' tales because ultimately they interrogate the meanings and uses to which the father puts his infant son, whether imagining an education and childhood for his son that satisfies the failures and longings of his own, or imagining his child's pure and joyful existence in the natural world as an alternative to his own estrangements. As with both the film and the nightingale, Coleridge fills the child with himself, making the infant figure tell back his own tale, at the same time that he is acutely self-critical and uneasy about these imaginative acts of perceiving and understanding his infant son in his own image.

The infant's *infans* or inarticulate state is, of course, the precondition to this interpretive conundrum. Like the song of the nightingale, the infant's cries both require and bewilder adult, human linguistic interpretation. In fact, they do more. In these two lyrics, the inarticulate state of infancy becomes an original mystery, one that, in turn, originates human culture as efforts are made to understand, imagine and interpret that unknowable and inaccessible *infans* state. There is one significant moment of pause in "The Frost at Midnight" which momentarily halts these strong acts of interpretation and misinterpretation, the moment when the speaker turns and acknowledges the sleeping infant at his side:

> Dear Babe, that sleepest cradled by my side,
> Whose gentle breathings, heard in this deep calm,
> Fill up the interspersed vacancies
> And momentary pauses of the thought![34]

Significantly, the breathings of the baby are heard only in the "pauses of the thought" – much like the drops of the eaves are heard only in the "trances of the blast" – suggesting that the baby is recognized, acknowledged and named like Herder's lamb – "Ah, you are the breathing one" – only in the lull of articulate thought and not in the imaginative and interpretive flights of a father's fancy, no matter how well intentioned they may be. The speaker of this poem, self-described as uncomfortable and vexed by silence and calm, rushes forward, however, to construct his lore of the natural child and a natural education, and the inarticulate breathing one is lost in the father's attempts to redress his own childhood sorrows.

TALKING TO ANIMALS

The tradition of locating the origin of language in the sounds, expressions and gestures of the body – what Condillac calls a "language of action" and Herder calls a "language of sensation" – gives language natural, animal origins and potentially gives animals the capacity for language. "If we wish to call these immediate sounds of sensation 'language,'" Herder comments, after describing the sounds and gestures of savages and children, "then I certainly do find their origin very natural." That natural origin, he adds, is "clearly animal."[35] Whether or not animals could be credited with the ability to speak and to reason; whether or not their capacity for expressive sounds and gestures should be called "language" and understood as the origins of human language; and whether or not humans first learned language by imitating or conversing with animals are all recurring points of debate in eighteenth-century discussions of the origin of language.

For Herder, while this animal language of sensation may not be the origin of human language, the natural or animal elements of language, nevertheless, persist in human language and culture in the mouths of children in the "babbling vocabulary of the wet-nurse's quarters" and in the mouths of adults in the form of poetry. Poetry and, as we shall see, literature more widely, works by employing the sounds and expressions of a natural or original language, thereby returning its audience to a state of primitive, childhood or animal sensation. For Herder, poetry is the "natural language of all creatures poetized by the understanding into sounds, into images of action, of passion, and of living effect!"[36] The extent to which Herder understands poetry as a pan-animal or cross-species language – the "natural language of all creatures" – and language more generally as something shared by humans and animals can be seen in his subsequent discussion of the idea that "the first language of the human species was song," an idea we have seen closely associated with that of poetry as man's first, original language. The "tradition of antiquity," Herder remarks, assigns the origins of language to song and poetry, and "many good, musical people have believed that human beings could well have learned this song from the birds."[37]

Many writers in this tradition of conjectural histories on the origin of language did, indeed, speculate that man learned language by imitating the songs and musical tones of birds and other animals. Monboddo, for example, theorized that men were led to the discovery of articulation "by the imitation of the articulate sounds of other animals."[38] Insisting that some animals, particularly birds such as the cuckoo, cochatoo and crow, "utter sounds that may be called truly articulate," Monboddo offers this conjectural account of the origin of language:

Now if it be true, as I suppose, that the first variation of inarticulate cries was by difference of tone, and that in this way the method of communication by sound was first enlarged, and something like a musical language formed by the imitation of birds, there is nothing more natural than to suppose, and indeed I think it must necessarily have happened, that they would carry the imitation of the birds still farther; and, finding that the difference of musical tones did not vary and distinguish their natural cries sufficiently for the purpose of speech, they added to those cries the further variety of articulation, which they would likewise learn from the birds; and so would form a language.[39]

What supports this account of man imitating birds to form a language is Monboddo's faith in the Aristotelian tenet that man is "the most imitative of all animals." He cites the common wisdom that "men learned at first to build from the swallow ... from the spider to weave; and from the birds to sing" and concludes, "in short ... that we resemble very much an American or West-India bird that I have heard of, called the *Mock-bird*, which has no tune of its own, but imitates the notes of any other bird: For we seem to set out in life without any original stock of our own, or any natural talent besides that faculty of imitation, which nature has bestowed upon us in so high a degree."[40]

To this idea of man with no tune or talent of his own, originally and naturally mute, Herder objects most strenuously, as well as to the larger idea of man learning language by imitating birds. The latter is, Herder observes, "a lot to swallow!":

But to set forth the newly created human being, with his driving motives, with his needs, with his strong sensations, with his almost blindly preoccupied attention, and finally with his primitive throat, so that he might ape the nightingale, and from the nightingale sing himself a language, is – however many histories of music and poetry it may be asserted in – unintelligible to me.[41]

"In the chain of beings," Herder insists, "each thing has its voice and a language in accordance with its voice." If the first human language was song, therefore, "it was song which was as natural to the human being, as appropriate to his organs and natural drives, as the nightingale's song was natural to the nightingale."[42] To imagine the human inventing language for himself by imitating the nightingale – "a creature which is, so to speak, a hovering lung" – is to imagine a monster: "a human nightingale in a cave or in the game forest."[43]

Herder's disagreement with those who posit the imitation of bird song as the origins of language does not, however, prevent him from making frequent comparisons between primitive languages and animal sounds, nor from crediting the ancient myth that men were once able to speak with the animals. The early languages of sensation are thoroughly naturalized in Herder's rhetoric, capable of "rushing with the whirlwind, of resounding in the battle, of raging with the sea, of roaring with the river, of cracking with the collapsing rock, and of speaking with the animals."[44] Easterners "have not entirely left behind bird language," Herder reports, and "an Arab living in the desert can easily learn to distinguish several kinds of animal cry."[45] When the examples of primitive language are closer to home, Herder is less enthusiastic about its animal qualities, as can be seen in his speech "On the Education of Students in Language and Speech":

When we come into the world we are of course able to scream and cry, but not to talk or speak; we emit only animal sounds. These animal sounds remain with some people and races throughout their entire lives. One has only to stand at a distance from which the sound of the voice and accent can be heard without the meaning of the words being conveyed: in some people one will hear the turkey, the goose, the duck; in many speakers it will be the peacock, the bittern; in pretentious dandies it will be the canary; it will be anything but the human voice.... Youths who have acquired this unpleasant dialect of merely animal sounds, whether they come from the cities or the country, should make every effort in school to acquire a human, natural speech possessed of character and soul and to rid themselves of their peasant or shrieking back-alley dialects. They should leave off the barking and yelping, the clucking and cawing, the swallowing and dragging together of words and syllables and speak human rather than animal language.[46]

Friedrich Kittler, who quotes this passage in his discussion of the normalization and purification of speech in Germany in the late eighteenth century, points out that in Herder's program of school reform, dialects are not fully human but are instead "relegated to the animal realm." Herder's complaints about the animal sounds of German dialects echo a refrain one finds throughout writings on the origin of language. John Brown's *Dissertation on the Rise, Union and Power, the Progressions, Separations, and Corruptions of Poetry and Music*, which Herder cites as a main proponent of the theory that man learned language by imitating bird song, describes the language of savages in similarly animalist terms: "their *Voice* is thrown out in *Howls* and *Roarings*: Their *Language* is like the *Gabbling of Geese*."[47] Likewise, Monboddo describes the Huron language as "little better than animal cries from the throat, of different tones, a little broken and divided by some guttural consonants."[48]

There is, of course, another tradition of representing the relationship between man and animal through the language they share, and that is the sentimental literary tradition where scenes of humans and animals in sympathetic communication recur frequently enough to warrant their identification as a major topos of Romantic and sentimental literary culture. As Jonathan Lamb has suggested, "the sentimental novel set itself the task of reconciling the interests of things, animals, and humans."[49] While sentimental culture has been credited with extending the capacity to feel to both animals and things, thus extending the sphere in which human sympathy and identification could operate, the movement of feeling and sympathy across species boundaries often produces troubling encounters: animals who can talk and reason threaten human identity, and acts of sympathetic identification too quickly take on elements of appropriation and possession.[50] Virginie in the midst of her bird colony, which Paul creates by transplanting bird nests from the neighboring forest and where Virginie feeds the wild birds as if they were her own "brood of chickens," is a figure of child-like simplicity and natural fellowship with the birds. But here, as throughout Bernardin de St. Pierre's novel, *Paul et Virginie*, the colonial basis of this human and non-human exchange is barely submerged.[51]

Christian Isobel Johnstone recycles this sentimental bird scene, as well as, perhaps, the famous anecdote of the starling in Laurence Sterne's *A Sentimental Journey*, for her national tale, *Clan-Albin*. Johnstone's young hero Norman first encounters the heroine Monimia in the High-land forests where Monimia is frolicking with her pet bird. Overhearing Monimia's "lisping endearments of baby language" and first supposing that she is conversing with a child, Norman soon discovers that her unseen companion is a tame bird "which she was teaching to sing."

Norman is charmed by the "innocence, simplicity, and warmth of early youth discovered in her fondling expressions" and in the "pretty childishness in the idea of carrying a bird into the words." Bird and girl imitate each other's songs, while Norman loses his heart and can only envy the bird who receives all of Monimia's kisses and caresses.[52] A stock scene of sentimentality – Matthew Lewis has already exploded such a scene into its more pornographic variety in *The Monk*, when Ambrosio spies on Antonia sharing her bath with a pet bird[53] – Johnstone makes evident the extent to which the associations and charges of this scene include the idea that the origins of language lie in the imitation of bird song. Monimia's "baby language" and childishness, and the fact that bird and girl are teaching each other to sing, moving in and out of words and tones, all reinforce the idea that they share a natural language. Monboddo's account of the origin of language in the imitation of bird song is as important to this passage as that of Sterne's starling who repeats "I can't get out" in a voice that Yorick at first mistakes for that of a child. Norman is peeping not simply at a scene of Edenic and erotic play, but at the primal scene of the invention of language. As with Herder's version of a child imitating animal sounds, the invention and imitation of language are entangled.

In sentimental and Romantic poetry, as well as in the novel, scenes of humans and animals communicating through a shared language reinforce the notion of the natural origins and development of language, while also restaging the complex questions about human identity and language raised by such a notion. William Hayley's 1805 volume, *Ballads Founded on Anecdotes Relating to Animals*, with engravings by William Blake, is a particularly interesting example of how Romantic-period texts represent and meditate on the question of animal language. The first stanza of the first ballad, "The Dog," signals the paradox of the mute yet expressive animal that animates the volume as a whole: "Of all the speechless friends of man / The faithful dog I deem / Deserving from the human clan / The tenderest esteem."[54] By repeatedly reminding his readers that Fido is both "speechless" and yet also able to understand and keep faith with his mistress, Lucy, Hayley makes the issue of animal language central to this ballad. Fido may be speechless, but, the ballad insists, he understands his mistress's every sentiment and command, even those which bid Fido to follow her lover, Edward, to India:

> Lucy, who thro' her tears descried
>   His sympathetic air,
> "Go! With him, Fido!" fondly cried,
>   "And make his life thy care!"

> The dog her order understood
> Or seem'd to understand,
> It was his glory to make good
> Affection's kind command.[55]

The poem asserts Fido's understanding of Lucy's command, but then immediately qualifies it – "Or seem'd to understand" – making the question of just how and how much a dog can understand a question that the ballad means for us to consider. The qualification also reminds us of what we can never fully know about a creature whose mental life is inaccessible and unspoken, perhaps making us doubt Lucy's discernment, through her tears, of his "sympathetic air."

Where Lucy either imagines or perceives Fido's "sympathetic air," Edward, unfortunately, does neither, and Fido will sacrifice his own life to save him from the jaws of a crocodile when Edward fails to understand his warnings not to swim one day. The ballad makes speechless Fido's capacity to communicate central to its climatic scene:

> But once, when Edward had begun
> To cast his clothes aside,
> Round him his dog would anxious run,
> And much to check him tried.

> So much, that had dumb Fido said
> "Avoid the stream to day!"
> Those words could scarce have plainer made
> What duty wish'd to say.[56]

Dumb or *infans*, Fido's gestures and sounds, the ballad insists, nevertheless constitute a plain and expressive language. Hayley, however, translates that language of gesture into words, spelling out Fido's sounds and actions as if he were worried that some of his readers shared Edward's dull sensibility. Such acts of translation between animal language and human language, between the language of gesture and the language of words, occur repeatedly in these ballads, on the one hand reinforcing the volume's central idea that humans and animals have a shared language and, on the other hand, suggesting that some humans may need the supplementary assistance of words to understand fully this expressive, animal language.

Fido's ultimate gesture of jumping into the crocodile's yawning jaws, an action performed with "silent tongue," is his most eloquent and effective. Indeed it is Edward who "shriek(s)" and cries when Fido jumps to his death, suddenly but belatedly capable of his own expressive language of sound and gesture. Edward leaves India and returns home to marry Lucy, and the poem concludes with yet more acts of translation, as Edward hopes for a "friendly bard" who will sing the animal's deeds, and a sculptor carves a marble statue of the dog to memorialize and celebrate his silent, faithful act. That statue is given pride of place in Lucy's chamber where its presence "enhanc'd their nuptial bliss" and founds their future happiness. But even as the ballad pays tribute to Fido's animal language, that language is ultimately translated and silenced by both the ballad and the statue. The extent to which the poem's words or the statue's silent form retain or employ that original, expressive language remains a question.

If "The Dog" takes its moral from man's failure to understand animal language, "The Panther" dramatizes successful communication between man and beast to meditate on what constitutes effective and expressive language. As if to evoke the savage scenes typically conjectured in histories of the origin of language, this ballad is set in the forests of "Afric's shore" and describes the traveler Caelius, a Roman, and his encounter with a panther. Immediately questioning distinctions between animals and humans, the ballad begins with an apostrophe to "Maternal love," praising its ability to "humanize the beast of prey! / And make the savage mild"; it is soon clear, by the uncharacteristically gentle behavior of the panther, that she is the mother of the poem.[57] When the panther tries to lead Caelius into the forest with imploring looks and fawning gestures, the Roman, unlike Edward, is quickly able to understand the panther and pledge his assistance. The ballad explains his ready sympathy with a meditation on language and sensibility: "How little is the want of speech, / When kindness rules the heart; / Gesture will then all lessons teach, / That language can impart!"[58] If Hayley here insists that gestural language is fully sufficient to the expression of feeling, he asserts the superiority of gesture to word when Caelius rescues the panther's cubs from a hunter's trap:

> Too faint is language to describe,
> 　　The Panther's grateful glee,
> Contemplating her little tribe
> 　　From deadly bondage free.
>
> By gesture, that with meaning glows,
> 　　All eloquence above,
> She largely, on her friend, bestows,
> 　　Protection, thanks and love![59]

Gesture is an eloquent language of feeling, more powerful than words in communicating sentiment; thus the ballad offers an understanding about the body's capacity to express affect through sounds, looks and actions that is central to sentimental culture and discourse more widely. Hayley's animal ballads insist that a wide range of feelings, as well as the language that best expresses them, are shared by man and animal. Indeed, the volume as a whole repeatedly humanizes animals and animalizes humans in the service of breaking down distinctions between man and the rest of animal creation, suggesting a relationship between humans and animals based not on categorical difference but on a continuum of feeling and sensibility.

BECOMING HUMAN

The preface to Hayley's volume announces that it is "intended for young readers," suggesting that, in addition to the literature of sentimentality, there is, perhaps, another literary context relevant to this book of ballads: children's story books and reading primers. With their focus on the alphabet and the art of reading, children's primers explicitly extend the question of language into the realm of literacy and its various basic components: the recognition, ordering and combination of letters to produce meaningful units that can be read.[60] Children's primers expose the alphabetical basis of literature, reminding us that literature is materially and literally a function of letters. The question of who has language thus becomes not just a question of who can speak (or otherwise express themselves), but a question about who is literate, who can read.

Children's literature frequently features animals, as if to assert the close connections between children and animals assumed by the larger culture. Romantic-period reading primers are filled with animals who talk, children who treat animals unkindly and learn the error of their ways, and children who learn their place in the world through repeated reference and comparison to animals. These didactic texts are, of course, meant to teach the child to read, but they often seem equally concerned about teaching their young audience just what they have in common with animals and, equally important, what they do not. In their lessons, primers emphasize the differences between children and animals in order to teach children what it is to be fully human and to chart a developmental path from animal to human for the child to follow. Their reading lessons thus stage critical moments in the child's process of learning to be human.

Anna Barbauld's primer, *Mrs. Barbauld's Lessons for Children*, a volume particularly "adapted to the comprehension of a child two to three years old," features animals in every lesson and instructs the child on the characteristics of animals and children:

> Grass grows in the fields.
> Cows eat grass, and sheep eat grass, and horses eat grass.
> Little boys do not eat grass.
> No, they eat bread and milk.

> Squirrels crack nuts.
> Kittens are playful.
> Old cats do not play.
> Mice nibble cheese.
> Monkeys are very comical.
> You are very comical sometimes.[61]

Little boys may not eat grass like cows and horses, but they can be comical like monkeys. A secondary, yet explicit aim of many of these reading exercises is to demonstrate the advantages humans have over animals, but the "little boy" has a rather tenuous relationship to humanity, appearing as he does repeatedly on these lists of animals. Thus a list of what each animal eats – "Little Birds eat seeds and fruits. / Partridges eat corn. / Wolves devour sheep. / Blackbirds peck cherries. / The Otter eats fish" – ends with the statement: "Men eat every thing, corn, and fruit, and mutton, and fish, and eggs, and milk, and chickens."[62] Such statements about what "men eat" only potentially include little boys who have just been told, in fact, that they eat bread and milk instead of grass.

Little boys who *may* grow into men will be superior to animals not only in appetite but also in language. In this volume, unlike so many other children's texts, Barbauld insists that animals cannot talk but little boys can. Thus a lesson that begins with an admonishment to little Charles not to torment the cat ends by asking Charles to notice Puss's linguistic limitations:

> Where is puss?
> Puss is under the table.
> You cannot catch puss.
> Do not pull her by the tail.
> You hurt her. Stroke poor puss
> You stroke her the wrong way.
> This is the right way.
> But, puss, why did you kill the rabbit?
> You must catch mice.
> You must not kill rabbits.
> Well, what do you say?
> Did you kill the rabbit?

Puss, why do you not
Speak? Puss cannot speak.[63]

Puss cannot speak, although this does not stop the mother of the text from questioning her much as she questions her little boy. The book thus suggests differences between Charles and Puss even as it positions both of them as objects of the mother's lessons.

Barbauld's lessons about the boy's superiority to the family's pets are most pointed when she is urging young Charles to learn to read. This scene evokes what Patricia Crain has identified as a recurring image in primers, that of a child trying but failing to teach an animal his letters.[64] Barbauld's lesson is worth quoting in full:

What a clever thing, Charles, it is to read! A little while ago, you know, you could only read little words, and you were forced to spell them c a t, cat, d o g, dog. Now you can read pretty stories, and I am going to write you some.

Do you know why you are better than puss? Puss can play as well as you; and puss can drink milk, and lie upon the carpet: and she can run as fast as you, and faster too, a great deal; and she can climb trees better, and she can catch mice, which you cannot do. But can puss talk? No. Can puss read? No. Then that is the reason why you are better than puss … because you can talk and read.

Can Pierrot, your dog, read? No. Will you teach him? Take the pin and point to the words. No, he will not learn. I never saw a little dog or cat learn to read. But little boys can learn. If you do not learn, Charles, you are not good for half as much as a puss. You had better learn your lesson.[65]

Charles is "better" than Puss and Pierrot because he can talk and is now learning to read, although Barbauld makes it clear that the boy is, at most, only making progress toward this better state. In fact, Puss can do a number of things better than the boy, and if Charles does not learn to read, he is "not good for half as much as a puss." The boy's growing ability to read not only confirms his superiority to cat and dog, it also exercises a type of mastery over them, as Charles not only reads, but reads the words "cat" and "dog," breaking these "little words" into their component sounds and letters as needed. Here reading, even more than talking, distinguishes boy from animal and proves his eventual share in man's superior human state.

Barbauld reinforces the idea that reading makes the man in the final lesson of the volume, which takes the form of a dialogue between mother and son over the picture of a horse:

See! I have brought you a picture, what is it a picture of?
It is a picture of a horse.

Is it *like* a horse?

O yes, very like. How well he holds his head. What a fine mane. How he
stretches out his legs. He is galloping along very fast indeed.

What is this word that is written under?

That is *Horse* too.

Is that *like* a horse?

I do not know. I do not quite understand the question, it *means* horse.[66]

The boy can recognize and admire the picture of the horse, and he can
also recognize and read the word "horse." More importantly, he can
understand that the picture of a horse and the word "horse" represent a
horse very differently, the picture being "like" a horse and the word
"meaning" horse. The lesson, a rather remarkable one for a three-year-
old child, continues to emphasize this distinction between different
systems of representation:

If you were to shew [the word "horse"] to a Frenchman that had not learned
English, would he know that it means horse?

No, not till he was told.

If you were to ask him what word means Horse, what would he say?

He would say *Cheval.*

But if you were to shew him this picture, would he know what it is?

Yes, directly.

Or an Italian, or a Spaniard, or a German?

Yes, any body would know it directly, without being told.

If you were to take this picture and cut it in pieces, what would you have?

I should have the head in one piece, and the legs in another, and the body in
another.

And the legs would be like legs, would they not, and the body like a body? Yes.

But if you were to take the *word* horse, and cut it in pieces, what would you have?

I should have the letters h, and o, and r, and s, and e.

Would those letters be the legs and head?

No, they would mean nothing.[67]

Frenchman, Italian, Spaniard and German all have different words for
horse and would need to be told what the English word "horse" means,
but all know the picture of a horse "directly, without being told."
Distinguishing between what one knows with and without being told,
the mother teaches the child that words are learned and have no obvious
or natural connection to the thing they represent. Indeed, broken up into
its component parts, the word "horse" loses meaning all together, as these
letters, in themselves, "mean nothing." Mimetic, pictorial representation,
on the other hand, has immediate and obvious connections to the thing
represented, and the picture of the horse seems to have integrity much like

the original in that it can be divided into parts and still retain its identity. This is a lesson about the arbitrary and conventional quality of words, but it is also a lesson about how letters are made meaningful. Letters, these things the child is learning to put together and take apart, have reference only to each other as they form words; they are made meaningful only through the process of reading.[68]

Running throughout this lesson about letters, words, language and reading is another lesson about the superiority the boy may gain over animals and other creatures. This idea is strongly suggested when the boy is invited to imagine cutting the picture of the horse into its parts and dismantling the word "horse" so that it means nothing. But the point becomes even more explicit in the conclusion of the lesson:

Could you have known that the word horse means a horse before you were told?

No, I remember learning to read it, I did not know it before.

But you would always have known the *picture* of a horse; your little cousin that cannot read at all, and can hardly speak, knows that, and tries to neigh when he sees it. Nay, animals will know a picture if it is very well done; there is a story of a man that painted a bunch of grapes so very well that the birds came and pecked at it; but do you think you could have taught a bird to read?

No, indeed.

Well, then, you see that the *picture* of a horse is really *like* a horse, but the *word* is not. The word only means horse, because people chose to make it so; any other letters would have done as well. If they had chosen that RAB should mean horse, it would have meant horse, but nobody could make the picture of an eagle to be the picture of a horse, because a picture must be *like* the thing it is a picture of.

Words are arbitrary marks of our ideas, but you cannot understand that sentence yet, I have tried to explain the *thing*.[69]

Babies and birds can recognize pictures, but they cannot read letters. While this places baby and bird at the same intellectual level, a level Charles has surpassed by learning to read, it is, perhaps, the baby's response to the picture that is most interesting here. Charles' little cousin, who cannot read and can barely speak, recognizes the picture of the horse and "tries to neigh when he sees it." The imitation of the picture inspires the imitation of the baby. By mimicking animal sounds, the baby recapitulates the conjectured origins of language and makes explicit that these mimetic sounds and pictures are a more primitive form of language and representation. Charles, on the other hand, has entered the arbitrary realm of letters, words and reading, although not fully, as the final statement of the lesson makes clear. Charles cannot yet understand the "sentence" of the lesson, the alphabetical and syntactical statement of an abstract idea, so the mother has "tried to explain the *thing*" with a picture of a horse and the word "horse," both of which he can hold in his hands and even cut up into parts. Using things to show that words have no real reference to things, she accommodates her lesson to Charles' intermediate stage between the baby and bird's world of imitated things and the human world of letters and words.

Barbauld thus suggests that Charles is on his way to becoming more fully human by learning to read. Neither birds nor babies can speak or read, she insists, and her text maintains a strict division between those who can and cannot speak and read, even as she depicts humans moving from one side of that dividing line to the other through the process of learning the lessons in her book. Other books for children are much more playful and flexible about who can and cannot speak. Sarah Trimmer's *Fabulous Histories, Designed for the Instruction of Children, Respecting their Treatment of Animals* begins by describing a little boy and his sister who both have a great fondness for animals and who "used often to express a wish that their birds, cats, dogs, &etc. could *talk*, that they might hold conversations with them."[70] Their mother responds to this wish by inventing a family of robins who can talk and by telling them the various histories of their adventures. The stories are introduced, however, with the caution that they should not be understood as "containing the real conversations of birds (for that it is impossible we should ever understand)."[71]

The text thus begins on a note of ambivalence about talking animals, and that ambivalence continues into one of its better-known episodes, an adult discussion about a "learned pig" staged for the edification of a young girl. Trimmer's learned pig has a historical antecedent: in the summer of 1784, a learned pig toured provincial fairs with such success that he was brought to Sadler's Wells in London in the winter of 1785. This pig certainly made an impression on the writers and intellectuals of the period, as it is mentioned in various writings by James Boswell, Robert Southey, William Cowper, Mary Wollstonecraft, William Darton, Joseph Strutt, William Wordsworth and Samuel Taylor Coleridge; referenced in periodicals of the day, such as *The Public Advertiser*, *The Gentleman's Magazine* and the *New Review*; and made the subject of numerous cartoons and prints by the likes of Thomas Rowlandson, Samuel Collings and Bowles & Carver.[72] Trimmer's discussion repeats the major points of debate circulating in these contemporary texts about the learned pig and reveals the extent to which letters, words and reading become critical reference points in distinguishing the categories of human and animal.

A woman representing the well-established Cartesian position on animals introduces the topic of the learned pig: "I have ... been for a long time accustomed to consider animals as mere machines, ... but the sight of the learned pig, which has lately been shewn in London, has deranged these ideas, and I know not what to think."[73] What is remarkable, and remarkably unsettling, about the learned pig is then related:

> The creature was shown for a sight in a room provided for the purpose, where a number of people assembled to view his performances. Two alphabets of large letters on card paper were placed on the floor; one of the company was then desired to propose a word which he wished the pig to spell: this the keeper repeated to the pig, which picked out every letter successively with his snout, and collected them together til the word was completed.[74]

The pig, in fact, performs a number of tricks, including picking out the numbers for the time of day after closely examining a watch. But it is the pig's literacy that inspires the most interest in the young girl and her mother: "and do you think, mamma," the girl asks, "that the pig knows the letters, and can really spell words?" This is the mother's reply:

> I think it possible, my dear, for the pig to be taught to know the letters one from the other, and that his keeper has some private sign, by which he directs him to each that are wanted; but that he has an idea of *spelling* I can never believe; nor are animals capable of attaining human sciences, because for these human faculties are requisite; and no art of man can *change* the nature of any thing, though he may be able to improve that nature to a certain degree, or at least to call forth to view powers which would be hidden from us, because they would only be exerted in the intercourse of animals with each other.[75]

Recognizing letters is a type of learned skill, one slightly more complex than that performed by Barbauld's bird and baby who can recognize pictures without being told. But this, the mother insists, is not the same as spelling, and despite all reports to the contrary, the mother insists that the pig does not understand how to combine letters to form words, nor how to read those words. The learned pig may spell out words on the cue of his keeper, but he does not have the "idea of *spelling*," which here is compared to other human arts and sciences as being beyond the natural capacities of animals. Like Herder's parrot and starling, the pig can spell a word but cannot think a word.

In his discussion of German civil service and education in these years, Friedrich Kittler has described the establishment of an identity between "being human" and "being alphabetized," and we certainly see these children's primers in Britain laying a similar foundation for human identity and subjectivity.[76] As childhood is alphabetized and as literature becomes a matter of letters and reading, literacy becomes a significant developmental moment in the life of the child, a stage of life that is increasingly represented as a process of becoming fully human. Yet, even as Trimmer's model mother insists that spelling is categorically and exclusively a human activity, the text leaves open the possibility that animals are also capable of remarkable "improvement" and imbued with powers often hidden from human knowledge. Thus a gentleman participating in the discussion insists that brutes have "some portion of intellect, which is even capable of improvement to a certain degree," and speculates that "familiar intercourse with rational creatures" leads to the remarkable improvements and sagacity that domestic animals have been known attain.

Development, it seems, is not limited to the human world, and interaction between humans and animals moves *both* humans and animals along a shared developmental continuum. Nevertheless, the company also concludes that the question of how to understand animals and their abilities is one that can never be fully answered: "if we puzzle our minds for ever on the subject ... we shall never be able fully to comprehend the capacities and feelings of creatures so different from ourselves."[77] Even as these children's primers chart a path for becoming human, they return to assertions of categorical distinction and inscrutable difference between the human and the other. The mysteries of the *animal* mind, its unknown capacities and feelings, persist and, in fact, increasingly envelop the origins of *human* development.

READING AND RECAPITULATION

A notion of infancy as the developmental origin of language and literature thus works to bring infants and infant language into the larger field of literary culture at the same time that it establishes the unspeaking, *infans* state of infancy as the original mystery of culture and communication. The infantile account of poetry we have outlined in the previous chapter and the developmental history of language and literary forms that it assumes – one that understands the stages and styles of language and literature to unfold as mental and psychological stages develop – leads not only to an increasing interest in infancy and infant language acquisition, but also to ways of understanding how one literary genre develops into another and how literary culture more widely should be organized and experienced. Developmental accounts of literature's past thus construct, in turn, developmental accounts of literature's present: ordering its varieties of aesthetic experiences, suggesting how, and even in what order, one should encounter its different literary forms, crafting a national literary culture with the capacity to influence and account for every stage of the individual life, from infancy to old age.

Thus Robert Chambers describes the songs and ballads of the nursery as those that "breathed of a time when society was in its simplest elements."[78] For Chambers, this description of simple society is also a description of childhood; the childhood of the individual and the childhood of the nation thereby come together in the nursery through the singing of ballads and telling of traditional stories. The Scottish child of the "old nursery system":

> might be said to go through in a single life all the stages of a national progress. We began under a superintendence which might be said intellectually to represent the Gothic age; and gradually, as we waxed in years, and went to school and college, we advanced through the fourteenth and sixteenth centuries; finally coming down to the present age, when we adventured into public life. By the extinction of the old nursery system, some part of this knowledge is lost.[79]

Writing in 1826 when the nursery has been "revolutionised," Chambers regrets the lost knowledge of the nation's primitive past, knowledge that every child used to learn through the ballads and tales of his nursemaid. The idea that one goes through "in a single life all the stages of a national progress" is a fantasy of recapitulation that makes national history available to the experience of every individual, or, at least *lost* to each individual only as the earliest memories of childhood are lost. Changes in nursery culture aggravate the ironic fact that the nation's "old natural literature" may present itself as alien and unintelligible to the nation's modern, adult subjects.[80] Here the figure of the child represents the way in which such primitive poetry might remain part of the lived, albeit dimly remembered, experience of the modern, refined nation. Indeed, the recuperative form of the child has precisely this capacity to harness even what is lost, forgotten, or never fully understood to the construction and conservation of a national literary culture.

Hartley Coleridge's essay, "A Nursery Lecture by an Old Bachelor," demonstrates the degree to which that "strange and affecting analogy between childhood, as it still appears, and what we conceive of man, in the simple days of yore" had become the standard organizing principle of literary culture by the mid-nineteenth century.[81] Coleridge puts the words just quoted in the mouth of a "whimsical old bachelor acquaintance" whose rhapsodies on the "extreme antiquity" of nursery rhymes and children's games culminates in the recitation of Wordsworth's popular lines: "The child is Father of the Man, / And I could wish my days to be / Bound each to each by natural piety." Commenting sardonically that "my friend had talked himself quite serious, for he was running into blank verse," Coleridge nevertheless adds his concurring opinion that "the world's infancy is something more than a figure of speech": "there is an analogy between the growth of the individual mind, and the development of the public soul in communities." Coleridge here produces what has become at this point a cultural cliché – the analogy between individual development and social, cultural history – as the serious proposition that adds substance to his friend's rhetorical flights; he also demonstrates again the extent to which Wordsworth's famous lines are understood to represent in shorthand a cultural and historical theory. His subsequent outline of literary cultural history moves from infancy, to the "boyhood of nations," to "amorous, romantic youth" (which he describes as the age of poetry), to the "busy, calculating manhood of society" ("the age of the Aristotles, Horaces, Boileaus, and Popes"), and finally to the old age of "men and nations," each with its own particular literary style and interest. The analogy between individual development and cultural history is so "strange and affecting," as his bachelor friend testifies, because of the cultural nostalgia it enables: "When I see a numerous small family at play, my mind sinks back, through dream and vision, to the world's infancy. In the life, the innocence, the simple bliss before me, I hail a something that is not changed."[82] It is this rather simple nostalgia that Coleridge puts in the mouth of his friend and then legitimates with the historical, cultural theory that supports such sentimental flights.

Development and recapitulation in literary culture thus work together to promise continuity with what has been lost, as well as to organize and give value to literary reading and writing in the present. The idea that the individual recapitulates a national literary history in the course of his mental development, education and reading offers a variety of institutional frames and strategies for constructing and consuming a national literature. Walter Scott's *Tales of a Grandfather*, for example, presents its stories of Scottish history both in chronological order as well as in increasing levels of difficulty. As Katie Trumpener points out: "young readers are meant to mature developmentally alongside Scotland itself."[83] We might find another example in the growing trend of producing adaptations of Chaucer's texts for children over the course of the nine-teenth century. Chaucer was commonly considered the "Father of English Poetry," at the same time that he was understood as having lived and written, in Dryden's words, "in the Infancy of our Poetry."[84] His tales, along with other early classics, were thus considered peculiarly suited to children because they are (this time in the words of a nineteenth-century American educator) "nearer to children and the childhood of the race."[85] Chaucer comes to embody for English literature the cultural theory of Wordsworth's famous line: he is the child who is the father of the tradition.

This historical developmental account of literature also plays a signifi-cant role in defining the cultural work of different genres and forms. When John Stuart Mill turns to the question of "What is Poetry?" in his 1833 essay, he continues the tradition of defining poetry as the representa-tion of feeling, a tradition he traces back *to* Wordsworth but one more accurately traced back *through* Wordsworth to Enlightenment conjectural writings on the origin of language. To make his case for poetry as particularly engaged with human emotion, Mill reproduces the standard history of literary forms and then transforms that history into a hierarch-ical scheme that privileges poetry and censures the novel. Opposing an interest in feeling to an interest in incident, Mill asks: "at what age is the passion for a story, for almost any kind of story, merely as a story, the most intense?" His answer: "In childhood."[86] His next question: "in what stage of the progress of society, again, is storytelling most valued, and the storyteller in greatest request and honor?" His answer: "In a rude state like that of the Tartars and Arabs at this day, and of almost all nations in the earliest ages." The only poetry that is appreciated in these early stages takes the form of "ballads" which are "mostly narrative – that is, essen-tially stories – and derive their principal interest from the incidents." According to Mill and the tradition upon which he draws, the narrative poetry of ballads is of the "lowest and most elementary kind": "the feelings depicted, or rather indicated, are the simplest our nature has; such joys and griefs as the immediate pressure of some outward event excites in rude minds, which live wholly immersed in outward things."[87]

With his sense of childhood and the earliest ages of all nations as developmental stages particularly susceptible to the "immediate pressure of some outward event" and "wholly immersed in outward things," Mill clearly relies on the cultural paradigm of infancy and a stadial history of literary forms. But he does so not to valorize primitive poetry, but rather to rescue poetry from the primitive and the popular and to claim it for an elite and refined few. When he turns his attention away from "childhood, and from the childhood of society, to the grown-up men and women of this most grown-up and unchildlike age," he finds that primitive appetite for narrative poetry in those adults who have the "shallowest and emptiest" minds, those who are "perpetually engaged in hunting for excitement from without" and those who are "addicted to novel-reading." "The most idle and frivolous persons take a natural delight in fictitious narrative," Mill concludes, because "the excitement it affords is of the kind which comes from without."[88] With their attention on "outward things," readers of novels are stuck in an infant stage. By contrast, the "minds and hearts of greatest depth and elevation," those who possess the "vigor of . . . intellectual powers" and a "depth of . . . sensibilities" take the "greatest delight in poetry" which, for Mill, is no longer merely the language of passion and imagination, but the "delineation of the deeper and more secret workings of human emotion."[89] In Mill's essay we see poetry's identification with feeling realigning itself with introspection, solitude and meditation. The qualities and values of Romanticism's developmental literary culture help animate a rhetoric of "surface" and "depth," of outward pressures and inward resources; a poetics of "deep feeling" and introspection coheres as a way of warding off the shallow, popular, frivolous and merely sensational.[90]

Mill uses the developmental paradigm to reassert poetry's privileged position in the hierarchy of literary culture, condemning the novel by comparing it to primitive literary forms such as the ballad. Earlier writers used this same comparison to defend novels and to justify attention to this proliferating, popular form. Hugh Blair devotes a chapter of *Lectures on Rhetoric and Poetry* to "Fictitious History," that "species of composition in prose, which comprehends a very numerous, though, in general, a very insignificant class of writings, known by the name of Romances and Novels." Blair justifies his attention to such "insignificant" writings by quoting Andrew Fletcher on national ballads: "Mr. Fletcher of Salton, in one of his Tracts, quotes it as the saying of a wise man, that give him the making of all the ballads of a nation, he would allow any one that pleased to make their laws."[91] Novels, Blair suggests, have replaced ballads in shaping "the morals and taste of a nation." Anna Letitia Barbauld concludes the introductory essay to her edition of *The British Novelists* (1810) by echoing this point almost verbatim:

Some perhaps may think that too much importance has been already given to a subject so frivolous, but a discriminating taste is no where more called for than with regard to a species of books which every body reads. It was said by Fletcher of Saltoun, "Let me make the ballads of a nation, and I care not who makes the laws." Might it not be said with as much propriety, Let me make the novels of a country, and let who will make the systems?[92]

The "ballads of a nation" stand as a privileged site of "popular literature" for the Romantics: they establish the popular as primitive, original, representative of the people and the tastes of the nation. Novels, on the other hand, evoke the more troubling aspects of the popular, that of an alienated, artificial and mass culture. By replacing ballads with novels as the current "national" form, Blair and Barbauld make strong claims for both the authenticity and significance of the novel. It becomes the literary form that most directly reflects and influences the manners of the current stage of society.[93]

The ballad, nevertheless, retains its privilege as the original national literary form and becomes that which children should experience first. Educational theories throughout the nineteenth century and well into the twentieth century advanced the recapitulative model: the idea that children should learn to talk and read by repeating the process of language invention and then by reading the most primitive and original literary forms first. As Steve Newman has described for the American context, beginning children's literary education with the ballad allowed them to "participate vicariously in the mental growth of our ancestors."[94] Katharine Lee Bates' *Ballad Book* and J. Rose Colby's *Literature and Life in School* both make the old British ballads critical for the early education of American children. As Bates declares, ballads belong to "the youth of our literature, to the youth of our English race, and hence appeal with especial fascination to the youth of the human heart."[95]

RETURNS AND REVIVALS

The promise and possibility of return to earlier stages and earlier literary forms either through the children in their midst or in rare moments of adult life was a central preoccupation of British Romanticism long before it took institutional shape in educational theory and curriculum. A developmental literary history offered the Romantic period an understanding of the contemporary literary field as one comprised of anachronistic or "survivor" forms, such as the ballad, as well as new and modern forms that reflected the current age but made connections to primitive forms, such as the novel. This is an understanding of modern literary

culture that often includes popular literary forms by "historicizing" them –
by seeing them as products of an older or more primitive stage – and that
thereby presents a conservative or retentive ideal of contemporary culture
as working to retain and to situate properly in the present all previous
literary forms and cultural stages. This Romantic cultural ideal is one
reason for the growing popularity of the novel in these years and the
particular dominance of Walter Scott's *Waverley* formula. With an apparatus of footnotes and prefaces as important as the narrative itself, and the
insertion of other literary forms – ballads, songs, tales, poems – into the
prose of the tale, Scott's historical romance seems to include all the literary
forms of the culture from the most primitive to the most scholarly. In
Scott's hands the novel becomes historical not simply in its subject matter
or its retrospective calibration of "sixty years since," but in its use of
various literary forms and genres to frame each other and to stage a
national literary history.

The "Romantic" period is, of course, typically characterized as one of
"revival" or "return," its Romance more accurately described as a
"Romance revival."[96] This is also Francis Jeffrey's diagnosis of the
poetry of his day in his 1814 review of Byron's *Corsair* and *Bride of Abydos*.
His understanding of the "general history of poetry" is recognizably
stadial with an emphasis on the repetition of the developmental cycle.
"We are now coming round to a taste and tone of composition, more
nearly akin to that which distinguished the beginning of its progress,"
he announces, before describing the poetry and passions of the "rude
ages" and the gradual refinements of sentiment and style as civilization
advances in an historical narrative unchanged from the earlier Scottish
Enlightenment histories. That history leads up to "the age to which we are
now arrived," one of return, revival, imitation and descent:

The feats of chivalry, and the loves of romance, are revived with more than their
primitive wildness and ardour. For the sake of the natural feeling they contain,
the incidents and diction of the old vulgar ballads are once more imitated and
surpassed; and poetry does not disdain, in pursuit of her new idol of strong
emotion, to descend to the very lowest conditions of society, and to stir up the
most revolting dregs of utter wretchedness and depravity.[97]

The Romance revival of his age has clearly been a mixed success, in
Jeffrey's opinion. This is an age in search of "strong and natural emotions," and these are more safely and successfully found, Jeffrey proclaims,
in the historical past than in the exotic parts of the present-day globe,
although Southey, Scott, Byron, Moore and Campbell all trade in tales of
geographical and historical distance.

Byron's particular success, according to Jeffrey, lies not in the authenticity of his revival but in the deliberate anachronisms and inaccuracies of his imitations and returns:

Although the necessity of finding beings capable of strong passions, thus occasions the revival, in a late stage of civilization, of the characters and adventures which animated the poetry of rude ages, it must not be thought that they are made to act and feel, on this resurrection, exactly as they did in their first natural presentation.[98]

Primitive poetry, Jeffrey reminds his reader, dwells on the "result" rather than the "delineation of strong passions," on the "events which they produce, rather than the energy that produces them." In the poetic returns of a refined age, the "passion itself must now be pourtrayed – and all its fearful workings displayed in detail before us"; for Jeffrey's is an age interested in the "portraitures of the interior of human nature."[99] Jeffrey understands and describes that central subject of Romantic poetry, the interior self, as a literary form produced by a refined age and a particular historical cultural stage.

"Our modern poets" thus succeed in their project of return and revival, Jeffrey insists, because of the "radically incongruous" quality of their verse: "they have lent their knights and squires of the fifteenth century the deep reflection and considerate delicacy of the nineteenth, – and combined the desperate and reckless valour of a Buccaneer or Corsair of any age, with the refined gallantry and sentimental generosity of an English gentleman of the present day."[100] This is poetry with a foot in two different historical states, bringing together "things that never did exist together in any period of society." This is poetry keenly historical and brazenly anti-historical at the same time.

Jeffrey's critical appraisal of contemporary poetry both extends and troubles any discussion of historical and cultural immediacy as a key condition of strong and vigorous poetry. Jeffrey's praise of an historical poetry that, nevertheless, represents things that "never did exist together in any period of society" allows for a more flexible relationship between poet and period, style and stage. Other critics were less flexible. Thomas Love Peacock's *The Four Ages of Poetry*, the essay which inspired Shelley's *Defence*, parodies the classical ages of history: "Poetry, like the world," the essay begins, "may be said to have four ages, but in a different order: the first age of poetry being the age of iron; the second, of gold; the third, of silver; and the fourth, of brass." Peacock's notions of primitive societies, his description of their literature, social customs and "manners," and his account of how they develop into more civilized forms, are recognizable, if satirical, versions of stadial history. Here, once again, primitive man is a poet: "the savage indeed lisps in numbers," writes Peacock, "and all rude and uncivilized people express themselves in the manner which we call poetical."[101]

The problem for Peacock is not the lisping savage at the origins of poetry and human society, but the modern age's disingenuous return to these crude origins. The brass age of poetry according to Peacock rejects the "polish and learning" of the previous, highly civilized age and takes a "retrograde stride to the barbarisms and crude traditions" of the earliest age. What Jeffrey calls a "revival in a late stage of civilization" Peacock labels the "second childhood of poetry," one which the Lake Poets in particular (a "herd of desperate imitators") have made into a "dotage." Here is only one of Peacock's attacks on Wordsworth:

The descriptive poetry of the present day has been called by its cultivators a return to nature. Nothing is more impertinent than this pretension. Poetry cannot travel out of the regions of its birth, the uncultivated lands of semi-civilized men. Mr. Wordsworth, the great leader of the returners to nature, cannot describe a scene under his own eyes without putting into it the shadow of a Danish boy or the living ghost of Lucy Gray, or some similar phantastical parturition of the moods of his own mind.[102]

For Peacock, any "return to nature" in a civilized age is impossible and can only be sham aesthetic or pretension. By insisting that "poetry cannot travel out of the regions of its birth," he draws on the historicist under-standing of literature as tied to and representative of its own historical and social stage. To write "natural" poetry in a modern age of artifice and refinement is to "compose a modern–antique compound of frippery and barbarism, in which the puling sentimentality of the present time is grafted on the misrepresented ruggedness of the past into a heterogeneous congeries of unamalgamating manners."[103] "Natural" poetry written in an "artificial" age is simply an unnatural hybrid.

But Peacock's critique of Wordsworth also aims more specifically at the images and ghosts of children – the "Danish boy," the "living ghost of Lucy Gray," and other "parturitions" – that populate his "natural poetry." Here Peacock faults Wordsworth not only for attempting an inauthentic, retrograde return to poetry's origins, but also for using the figure of a child to signal that return. For Peacock these figures of children betray Wordsworth's poetry as in a "second childhood" rather than in a first or original state. Peacock has great fun in using the major images of original poetry against the poets of his own belated, imitative age. "While the historian and the philosopher are advancing in, and accelerating, the progress of knowledge," he writes, "the poet is wallowing in the rubbish of departed ignorance, and raking up the ashes of dead savages to find gewgaws and rattles for the grown babies of the age."[104] The child's rattle may once have been an appropriate image for the work of poetry in the world: "poetry was the mental rattle that awakened the attention of intellect in the infancy of civil society." But no longer: "for the maturity of mind to make a serious business of the playthings of its childhood, is as absurd as for a full-grown man to rub his gums with coral, and cry to be charmed to sleep by the jingle of silver bells."[105]

In Peacock's essay, the figures of savage and child come together not as analogies but as wildly mixed metaphors and "heterogeneous congeries." Peacock uses the dominant cultural rhetoric of his day, but rejects its promise of return. In his "lisping savages" and "grown babies" he suggests that something is acutely awry in the way that men and babies are brought together. Romantic poetry's "return to nature" instead involves a puerile infantilization of literary culture.[106] Hartley Coleridge likewise concludes his literary cultural history with a description of the "present state of Britain" as that stage "when men and nations begin to review their days, and finding little to approve in the short-sighted wisdom of latter times, recur, with something of a tender piety, or it may be with a fond idolatry, even to the green and childish issue of their nonage." Coleridge concludes with this judgment on his current literary age:

Such, methinks, is the present state of Britain; and our national taste may best be typified by an old man reading again the fairy tales that delighted his childhood, the amorous stories that engaged his youth, the first plays he had seen, the poems he had first got by heart; striving to recall the age of hope by spells of memory, and loving best the things he has known the longest.[107]

In this image of the old man reading childhood tales and reciting the poems "known the longest," we have a return to primitive poetry that lays no claim to its strength and vigor, but rather resigns itself to a national literary culture characterized by acts of recollection and re-reading, one in which man can recall and re-experience the various stages and representative literary forms of his life.

Coleridge's image recasts the figure of return and revival away from the act of writing toward the experience of reading and re-reading. Indeed, the promise of a return to childhood and a revival of childish memories and emotions becomes a powerful account of how one experiences literature in its reading and reception, as opposed to what the poet achieves in his writing and invention. The extent to which primitive poetry, its imitations and revivals, remains compelling in a modern age depends upon its capacity to revive early memories and return its readers to their first childhood experiences of literature. Herder frames this question within the context of a colonial encounter, another dominant topos for staging modern man's relationship to the primitive, noting that "everywhere Europeans – despite their cultivation [*Bildung*], and miscultivation! – have been strongly moved by the primitive moans of savages."[108] What is it about these primitive sounds, Herder asks, that remains so emotionally moving and so persuasive? It is in answer to this question that he evokes a scene of childhood and the earliest *sounds* of literature:

These words, this sound, the turning point of this horrifying ballad, etc. penetrated our souls in our childhood when we heard them for the first time together with who knows what army of associations of horror, of festivity, of fright, of fear, of joy. The word resounds, and like a throng of ghosts they suddenly all rise from the grave of the soul in their obscure majesty; they obscure the pure, clear concept of the word which could only be grasped without them. The word is gone and the sound of sensation resounds. Obscure feeling overwhelms us; [even] the careless person is horrified and trembles – not about thoughts, but about syllables, about sounds of childhood, and it was the magical power of the orator, of the poet, to make us children once again. No careful thought, no pondering, but this mere law of nature was the fundamental cause: "*The pitch of sensation should transpose the sympathetic creature into the same pitch!*"[109]

What ends as a theory of the sympathetic capacity of pitch and sound to move emotion from one person to another begins as a theory of how literature returns us to childhood through the work of association, memory and sound. Indeed Herder's return to childhood is represented primarily as a return to sound: "the word is gone and the sound of sensation resounds." This trick of turning words back into sounds, particularly into the "sounds of childhood," (as we shall see in our discussion of "prattle" in Chapter 4) becomes an important capacity of literary texts in the Romantic period and a key way in which literature is understood to revive a primitive state and return one to childhood.

Such returns can even explain the troubling popularity of the new novels. In 1773, Anna Letitia Aikin (later Barbauld) and her brother John Aikin published an essay "On the Pleasure Derived from Objects of Terror" (usually attributed to Anna) along with "Sir Bertrand, A Fragment," a short Gothic tale exemplifying the ideas of the essay (usually attributed to John). In the previous twenty years, Edmund Burke, David Hume and Adam Smith had all published discussions of tragedy and sympathy, analyzing the ways in which spectacles of suffering and calamity inspired social affections and, paradoxically, feelings of pleasure.[110] In 1765 Horace Walpole had published *The Castle of Otranto*. The Gothic romances of Clara Reeve and Ann Radcliffe were still five to fifteen years in the future. The Aikins' essay and fragment thus stand as early, even prophetic, accounts of the appeals of terror and the pleasures of fear.

In her essay, Aiken, in fact, rejects the moral account of the uneasy delights of terror described most influentially for the Gothic novel by Edmund Burke. "I am convinced we have a degree of delight, and that no small one, in the real misfortunes and pains of others," Burke wrote in *A Philosophical Enquiry into the Origin of our Ideas of the Sublime and Beautiful*. This is the case, he advances, so that we will not shun the sight of pain and suffering but will instead respond with sympathy: "as our Creator has designed we should be united by the bond of sympathy, he has strengthened that bond by a proportionable delight; and there most where our sympathy is most wanted, in the distresses of others."[111] This may indeed be the case, Aikin acknowledges, in social interactions where "the reflex sense of self-approbation attending virtuous sympathy" produces the most "exquisite and refined pleasure" in attending and responding to a "scene of misery." But this explanation cannot begin to account for the ever-multiplying experiences of terror and distress offered by Aikin's contemporary literary culture: "the apparent delight with which we dwell upon objects of pure terror, where our moral feelings are not in the least concerned, and no passion seems to be excited but the depressing one of fear, is a paradox of the heart, much more difficult of solution."[112]

Aikin is thinking here about "tales of ghosts and goblins," reports of "murders, earthquakes, fires, shipwrecks, and all the most terrible disasters attending human life," tragedy, that "most favorite work of fiction," the "old Gothic romance and the Eastern tale," and the most recent addition to this cultural buffet of terror, the modern novel. Here she wonders if "pleasure" and "delight" are even operable terms, contemplating instead the paradox of narrative desire: "the pain of suspense, and the irresistible desire of satisfying curiosity, when once raised, will account for our eagerness to go quite through an adventure, though we suffer actual pain during the whole course of it." In reading a Gothic tale, Aikin claims, "we rather chuse to suffer the smart pang of a violent emotion than the uneasy craving of an unsatisfied desire." The modern novel, whether suspenseful, terrifying or tedious, works by producing this "uneasy craving":

This is the impulse which renders the poorest and most insipid narrative interesting when once we get fairly into it; and I have frequently felt it with regard to our modern novels, which, if lying on my table, and taken up in an idle hour, have led me through the most tedious and disgusting pages, while, like Pistol eating his leek, I have swallowed and execrated to the end. And it will not only force us through dullness, but through actual torture – through the relation of a Damien's execution or an inquisitor's act of faith.[113]

Less an experience of pleasure designed to produce social cohesion and moral virtue than an experience of compulsion and punishment, Aikin's description suggests that reading the modern novel is an experience of forced ingestion.[114]

Indeed, she extends this sense of narrative compulsion and ingestion in an image significant to our topic here. Aikin compares herself taking up a modern novel in an idle hour to children listening to ghost stories:

When children, therefore, listen with pale and mute attention to the frightful stories of apparitions, we are not, perhaps, to imagine that they are in a state of enjoyment, any more than the poor bird which is dropping into the mouth of the rattlesnake – they are chained by the ears, and fascinated by curiosity.[115]

Aikin juxtaposes these two images of narrative consumption and suggests some interesting inversions and relationships between them. The scene of silent reading in an idle hour is compared to a scene of oral story-telling in which the children are "chained by the ears" rather than the eyes. The forced ingestion of the modern novel in which Aikin "swallowed and execrated to the end" appears here as the bewitched sacrifice of the bird who cannot help but feed itself to the rattlesnake. "Chained by the ears, and fascinated by curiosity," the children are equally compelled to take in the frightful story to its very end, but they also risk being swallowed up by the mouth of the tale. The forced compulsions of the modern novel that are, at least to some extent, self-inflicted, become in this scene of childhood less voluntary and more imposed: their attention is "pale and mute." Indeed, by the 1770s, the practice of disciplining children by terrifying them with stories of ghosts and goblins was widely discussed and criticized as producing a lasting debilitating impression on their character and impairing their rational faculties.[116]

What is significant about Aiken's turn from the modern novel to the children's story, from the scene of novel-reading to the scene of an early oral and aural literary experience, is that she uses the childhood scene to explain the adult's reading experience. She traces the workings of the modern novel back to early, infantile experiences of stories and tales. The

infant's first experiences of literature are particularly useful in accounting
for the paradoxical pleasures of popular literary forms, here the modern
novel and the Gothic tale. Aiken will go on to describe that strange mix of
novelty and familiarity that characterizes the reading of popular narrative,
especially as it coheres into a set of recognizable conventions and well-
worn formulas. Reading a Gothic romance which trades on "strange and
unexpected events" and the wonders of supernatural incidents, nevertheless, offers a "pleasure already experienced." No matter how unexpected a
particular turn of events may be, we always "know before-hand what to
expect"; the thrill of the unexpected itself becomes expected and familiar.
As Aiken does here, eighteenth and nineteenth century writers grappling
with the popular novel's contradictory thrills of both the new and the
familiar – the extent to which they work by exploiting a knowing, yet not-
fully-knowing reader – will repeatedly turn to the figure of the child who
asks to hear the same story over and over – "tell it again, tell it just the
same" – enjoying repetition as much as, if not more than, novelty.[117] The
child's repetitive, conservative and yet fascinated engagement with simple,
early literary forms – songs, ballads, nursery tales – becomes a model for
how adults enjoy and experience modern popular literary forms.

The idea that infantile experiences might offer explanations for adult
literary pleasures is not, however, limited to discussions of novels and
popular, formulaic literature. A developmental and historical sense of
language and literary forms makes the state of infancy relevant to all
literary forms and experiences. Aikin's turn to the image of children in her
essay on Gothic romance is part of a larger aesthetic discussion that locates
the origins of artistic expression and experience in infancy. Thus in *An
Inquiry into the Human Mind*, Thomas Reid proclaims: "the fine arts of
the musician, the painter, the actor, and the orator, so far as they are
expressive . . . are nothing else but the language of nature, which we
brought into world with us."[118] Significantly, he does not here include
written literature as one of the "expressive arts" because, in his opinion,
writing and artificial language have moved so far away from their natural
embodied origins as to have lost their expressive power and vitality.
"Writing is less expressive than reading," Reid notes, "and reading less
expressive than speaking without a book." Eloquence is the noblest of fine
arts for Reid, and it is best when it unites the "proper and natural
modulations, force, and variations of the voice," the "language of the eyes
and features," as well as the "force of action" or gesture.[119] These are the
"natural signs" or "natural language" of infancy – that which "we brought
into the world with us" – and Reid's prescription for renovating the fine

arts is precisely to return man to that state of infancy: "Abolish the use of articulate sounds and writing among mankind for a century, and every man would be a painter, an actor, and an orator."[120] A return to infancy and to the expressive, sonorous and embodied qualities of early language is both the experience offered by the fine arts and the secret to their rejuvenation.

This aesthetic theory of a return to infancy thus works in both directions: a return to infancy can revive modern literature, and vital, expressive art forms can return one to childhood. The cultural recapitulation imagined by a developmental history of literature holds open the possibility of becoming a child again. Rather than dismissing this promise as merely sentimental or nostalgic, we must instead unpack the cultural theory that animates such sentiment and that shapes a specifically literary formation of nostalgia and a literary version of childhood. The Romantics understood literature as having a history that could be recuperated in the life of the individual, and they made childhood central to defining what literature was, what experiences it could offer, and what cultural work it could do.

RHETORICAL EXPRESSIVENESS: FROM PRINT CULTURE TO MEDIA THEORY

Reid's emphasis on the expressive qualities of the various arts suggests that we may benefit by expanding the context in which we understand the developmental histories of language and literature and their translation into contemporary Romantic literary culture. The idea that language could achieve the expressive qualities of music, could return, in fact, to an original state in which it "speaks as much by its sounds as by its words" is, in fact, a central preoccupation of both Enlightenment philosophy and sentimental culture, especially as interest grew in the expressive qualities of language or the capacity of language to communicate emotion.

The standard Enlightenment history of language and literature supports an expanded idea of literary culture, one that includes non-semantic and non-written expressions. Historical and comparative discussions of primitive language as a mixture of word, sound and gesture provided a framework for understanding even the most refined or advanced languages of modern Europe as mixed media. Language was increasingly understood as a diverse system of communication comprised of artificial and natural signs, articulate and inarticulate sounds, markers with conventionally established meaning, and gestures with instinctually and naturally given meaning. Attention to these various elements heightened awareness of the various social functions of language. Words (and writing) were valued for perspicuity and precision, for clear expression directed toward the intellect and understanding. Gesture, tone, sound (and speech), on the other hand, were championed for their persuasive power and emotional expressiveness. "It is by natural signs chiefly," Thomas Reid insists, "that we give force and energy to language; and the less language has of them, it is the less expressive and persuasive."[121] The articulate and inarticulate sounds of language were understood to do very different work and to have very different effects. "Artificial signs signify, but they do not express," Reid explains, rehearsing well-established differences between the semantic, sonic and gestural elements of language: "they speak to the understanding, as algebraical characters, but the passions, the affections, and the will, hear them not."[122] The "sounds of sensation" – Herder's term for the "Ah's" and "Oh's!" of language – are meant "to sound, but not to depict"; they move the emotions, but do not address the intellect.[123]

Eighteenth-century interest in the rhetorical expressiveness of language thus converged on the difference between how natural and artificial signs convey meaning. Natural signs – the modulations of sound, gesture and feature – were understood to offer an immediate and direct expression of feeling, while artificial signs or articulate sounds were understood to carry meaning through acts of signification and representation. Importantly, the immediacy of expression attributed to natural signs is as much a function of reception and comprehension as it is of utterance. That is to say, vocal sounds and facial expressions are expressive largely because they are easily and immediately understood by another.[124] Reid's example of how these natural signs work is that of an infant responding to the expressions of a countenance and a child responding to music: "An infant may be put into a fright by an angry countenance, and soothed again by smiles and blandishments. A child that has a good musical ear, may be put to sleep or to dance, may be made merry or sorrowful, by the modulation of musical sounds."[125] The emphasis here is on the emotion these natural signs provoke; full expression involves *moving another*. John Stuart Mill's famous distinction between poetry – "poetry is feeling expressing itself to itself in moments of solitude" – and eloquence – "eloquence is feeling pouring itself out to other minds, courting their sympathy, or endeavoring to ... move them to passion" – assumes a difference, even an opposition, between expression and eloquence, between the articulation of feeling and the sympathetic movement of another. This distinction,

which had a significant subsequent influence on the tradition and reception of Romantic lyric poetry and expressive poetics, would not have
made sense to these earlier Enlightenment writers who had a much more
functional understanding of language.[126]

Rhetorical expressivism and naturalist accounts of language, in fact, put
their faith in and build their theories upon a notion of sympathy and the
work of social cohesion that sympathy performs. Indeed these linguistic
traditions are major components of the period's larger theorization of
sympathy, of how it works to bind people into social groups and how it
installs social and affective ties at the center of individual subjectivity.
Thus when Hugh Blair describes "tones, looks, and gestures" as the
"natural interpreters of the sentiments of the mind," he immediately
emphasizes the work of sympathy in making these signs clear and legible.
The signs of the body, he elaborates, "remove ambiguities," "enforce
impressions" and, most significantly, "operate on us by means of
sympathy which is one of the most powerful instruments of persuasion."[127] Bernard Lamy's *Rhetoric or the Art of Speaking*, which went
through fifteen, ever-expanding French editions in the early decades of
the eighteenth century and remained an influential text throughout the
century (serving, for example, as an important source for Rousseau's
discussion of tone, accent and sound in his *Essay on the Origin of
Languages*), named that "wonderful sympathy" which allows human
beings to communicate – both to express and to share – passions: thus
"a person with an expression of sadness on his face causes sadness, just as a
sign of joy makes those who notice it share in the joy."[128]

It is significant that Lamy's early theorization of sympathy together with
the expressive qualities of bodily signs occurs in a text on rhetoric or "the
art of speaking." Of course, both Adam Smith and Hugh Blair narrate their
histories of language and develop their accounts of the origin of language in
lectures on rhetoric and *belles lettres*, texts which might be equally at home
on a shelf with Thomas Sheridan's *A Course of Lectures on Elocution:
Together with Two Dissertations on Language*, as with Monboddo's *Of the
Origin and Progress of Language*. When Smith champions the musicality of
the English language or Blair draws attention to sympathy as a "powerful
instrument of persuasion," they signal their engagement with contemporary interest in elocution, oratory and acting, as well as their awareness of
the politics of language. In the case of Smith and Blair, lecturing on
English literature in Scottish halls packed with students eager to master
standard English pronunciation and to rid their speech of "Scotticisms,"
the teaching of rhetoric and the study of English literature (which

included a conjectural history of the origin of language) were offered
together as complementary pursuits; the "classics" of English literature
acquired that status in Scotland within a rhetorical study of language,
serving largely as models for proper and admirable articulation, expression
and composition. Robert Crawford has described the rise of "English
studies" in Scottish universities in the eighteenth century as actively
involving the "suppression of native tradition in a process of cultural
conversion that was thought of as a move from the barbarous Scottish to
the polite British."[129] Histories of primitive language were told in the
service of moving a population through that history, from one linguistic
stage to another.

That a naturalist account of language unfolds within a course of
lectures arguably involved in the suppression of native tradition is just
one of the contradictions and paradoxes we bump into when we expand
the context in which we understand these conjectural histories of original
and primitive language. The fact that the "natural" and "original" qualities of language are so often detailed in texts devoted to teaching what
language can be "rendered capable of" with practice and advanced art is
another. Texts on elocution and rhetoric played a central role in translating the historical discussion of primitive language as a mixture of words,
sounds and gestures into an awareness of the rhetorically expressive
capacities of modern languages. They also place Enlightenment conjectural histories of language and literature in the wider context of
sentimental culture and its fascination with the body's capacity to display
and perform feeling and sentiment.

Tracts and treatises on eloquence and effective oratory dissected the
body's "pathognomic signs" in order to reproduce them in a range of
linguistic performances. Their interest in the natural signs of the body is
primarily an interest "in the body's capacity *to move,*" as Paul Goring has
written, an attention to the body's "complex, multi-layered system of
signing" which was understood as natural, "but at the same time was open
to being manipulated and performed."[130] Indeed, what is most paradoxical about this tradition of linguistic writing is that it relied on and
celebrated the "natural language" of the body theorized in the conjectural
and developmental accounts of original language, at the same time that it
offered prescriptions and instructions for producing and performing that
language.[131] That paradox points to a problem that elocutionary and
rhetorical treatises circle around throughout the century-long effort to
reform oratory and regenerate public speaking: the body proves to have a
tenuous hold on any "natural" or "original" state, and its gestural

expressions can be unstable in how and what they mean. Acting and oratory have changing styles and trends; what is considered a sincere bodily language in one decade or a polite vocabulary of gesture in one context, is improper and immoderate in another time and place.[132]

Another way of understanding and relating the mixed and various modes of language in this period can be approached directly through its historical framework. As an historically representative institution, language was understood to reflect the progress of societies as they advanced and became more complex and refined, a progress, as we have seen, analogous to and often represented as individual and mental development. Without the impulsion of its own "historicity" proper, the change and evolution of language reflects other developments: historical, mental, cultural.[133] In his *Inquiry into the Life and Writings of Homer*, for example, Thomas Blackwell notes the "mighty Distance" between primitive man's "Starting-place of *Ignorance* and *Wonder*" and the modern "Condition of a wise experience'd Man, whom few things surprize; who is acquainted with the Fates of Nations." He insists that language documents these differences of historical and cultural stages: "*Language* is tinctured in proportion, and bears the Marks of the intermediate Stages" or "receive(s) the Impression of each" age.[134] Language was thus also understood as an historically layered institution, carrying its past within it and bearing the marks and impressions of its different stages. Language, comprised of words, sounds, gestures, speech and writing, thus became a cultural site of anachronistic juxtaposition, an element of social life capable of sudden returns and atavistic eruptions.

Despite the unstable and changing status of bodily signs, linking the "natural" elements of language to an original past continued to have broad appeal to a wide range of Enlightenment and Romantic writers. We need, however, to bring into focus the historical associations animating their interest in the "natural language" of the body. To emphasize and employ the embodied aspects of language became a way to bring the past into the present, to claim the natural and original elements within what was otherwise viewed as an artificial and highly refined social institution. Thus Herder acknowledges that "our artificial language may have displaced the language of nature," but the "most violent moment of sensation ... still reassumes its right, and immediately resounds in its mother tongue through emphases." While civilized and polite social life has generally "dammed, dried out, and drained off the flood and sea of the passions," sudden "impetuous storms" of feeling announce themselves in *sounds*, not words.[135] These eruptions of sound, passion and

gesture – the "language of nature" or the "mother tongue" – are understood as violent reassertions of a primitive condition and a return to
original language. But this is no unqualified embrace of voice over script,
speech over writing. Herder is very clear that the linguistic function of
these passionate sounds is limited. They will not make clear whether a cry
is "forced forth by fear or by pain," whether a "soft 'Ah' presses itself to
the breast of the beloved woman with a kiss or with a tear." This language
of sound and sensation does "not exist in order to determine all these sorts
of distinctions."[136]

Likewise, Adam Smith, in his discussion of sympathy in *The Theory of
Moral Sentiments*, describes the cries and gestures that communicate
strong emotion, but insists that many of the most intense passions –
anger, grief, joy, pain – require explanations of cause and situation in
order for sympathy to operate fully:

General lamentations, which express nothing but the anguish of the sufferer,
create rather a curiosity to inquire into his situation, along with some disposition
to sympathize with him, than any actual sympathy that is very sensible. The first
question which we ask is, What has befallen you? Till this be answered, though
we are uneasy both from the vague idea of his misfortune, and still more from
torturing ourselves with conjectures about what it may be, yet our fellow-feeling
is not very considerable.[137]

The cries and bodily contortions which are the body's natural language
here require additional information in order for their full sympathetic
expression and communication to be achieved. We can read the additional exchange of information through words and narrative as a supplement to the natural signs of the body; but they also work to translate one
language into another, to facilitate communication between individuals
who are separated by passion into two separate socio-historical stages. The
sympathy of Smith's enlightened eighteenth-century man requires a more
precise account than the strong but vague emotional expression this
sufferer first offers.

Despite this notion of a polite society peppered with primitive out-
bursts and historical–linguistic regressions, the lament that the progress of
civilization entails a general loss of natural passion and natural language is
a common one. Reid depicts the various artificial and natural elements of
language as engaged in a struggle for dominance, with the artificial clearly
victorious. The "perfection of artificial language" causes the "corruption
of the natural," Reid complains. Words replace sounds, writing replaces
speaking, and the result is a language of diminished vitality and

expression. "Is it not a pity," Reid asks, sounding a key-note of eighteenth-century rhetorical expressivism, "that the refinements of a civilized life, instead of supplying the defects of natural language, should root it out, and plant in its stead dull and lifeless articulations of unmeaning sounds, or the scrawling of insignificant characters?"[138] Rousseau offers the same narrative of linguistic development in his *Essay on the Origin of Languages*:

In proportion as needs increase, as affairs become entangled, as enlightenment extends, language changes character; it becomes more precise and less passionate; it substitutes ideas for feelings, it no longer speaks to the heart but to reason. As a result, accent is extinguished, articulation extends, language becomes more exact and clearer, but more drawn out, more muted, and colder.[139]

"This progress appears completely natural to me," Rousseau concludes, although, like Reid, this "progress" sounds more like a process of loss. In fact, these accounts of how language evolves to match and meet the needs of social development detail both what is gained and lost in the process. Relying on an historical rhetoric of priority, progress, loss and gain, such discussions of language also emphasize the general functionality of language, as well as the various functions and diverse elements within language.

It is thus within an expanded cultural context – one that includes the "elocutionary movement," the turn to rhetorical expressivism, conjectural histories and philosophical accounts of the origin of language, and sentimentality's interest in emotion and its bodily signs – that we must understand the period's recurring privileging of speech over writing. Rousseau's proclamation that writing is only a "substitute," and a poor one at that, for speech, is the most famous, if not the most representative statement of a larger cultural movement to valorize the spoken over the written word.[140] Attention to all the various ways that language and speech consist of more than just words, as we have seen, supported the idea of speech's superiority in terms of vitality, expressiveness and power. Hugh Blair expresses the consensus of the period in his lecture on the "Rise and Progress of Language and of Writing" when he states that "spoken language has a great superiority over written language, in point of energy or force."[141] But heightened interest in what Paul Goring calls "the bodily production and broadcast of words" must be set against the undeniable rise of print culture, the increasing levels of literacy and the remarkable proliferation of writing, texts and varieties of publications that characterize the second half of the eighteenth century. Writing, as Clifford

Siskin has demonstrated, was the new and burgeoning technology; championing speech and its "natural" origins was, in many ways, a rearguard defense or nostalgic screen against the threat of the new.[142]

On the other hand, the widespread emphasis on the bodily and "natural" elements of language also suggests that we must rethink our understanding of print culture and the character of its dominance in these years.[143] From the bodily symptoms of emotion incessantly detailed in sentimental novels, to the popularity of theatrical performance and dramatic celebrities; from the debate about the quality of oratory in the Anglican church, to the recovery and collection of oral ballads; from the gestures and accents of original language, to the "plainer and more emphatic speech" of experimental poetry, Enlightenment and Romantic literary culture is, in fact, fascinated with what is *not* print, with what is *not* written. When they do turn to the question of print forms and writing, it is often to reflect on how writing and textuality relate to, represent, influence, incorporate or alter speech, orality and bodily language. Many genres of the period present themselves as historically layered texts, trying to bring more primitive linguistic forms into modern prose, the conventions of writing and the printed page. The sentimental novel which relies on the episodic spectacles of bodily emotion, the ballad collections which frame ancient oral poetry with elaborate scholarly headnotes and footnotes, or the national tale which anthologizes native verse throughout its prose narrative – all these Romantic genres involve a complex staging of what were understood to be historical relationships between speech and writing, between primitive and advanced stages, between natural and artificial languages. These texts should be seen as attempts to make "print" something more than just "writing" and "silent reading," something more like a multi-media technology. The history of language and the awareness of all the ways language works before and beyond the use of words is, in Hans Aarsleff's words, a media theory for the times.

What emerges in these years is, in fact, a literary culture increasingly invested in containing and accounting for the entire range of literary forms and linguistic performances, from the first songs and stories of the nursery to the most erudite scholarly treatise. Gestures, tones, sounds, facial expressions, songs, novels, narrative poetry, lyric poems, footnotes, prefaces; all are considered, attended to, reviewed and included in Romantic literary culture. The developmental account of early language and its origin in infancy gave the Romantics a framework for attending to, including and organizing the range of natural and artificial signs, native and refined literary forms. Developmental narratives offer both history and hierarchy, and the hierarchies of Enlightenment and Romantic literary culture arguably persist. When Niklas Luhmann begins *Art as a Social System* with the pronouncement that "we are still spellbound by a tradition that arranged psychological faculties hierarchically, relegating 'sensuousness' – that is, perception – to a lower position in comparison to higher, reflective functions of reason and understanding," he points to the tradition under discussion here.[144] Of course, the habit of elevating mind over body extends much farther back than the eighteenth century. Nevertheless, the writers we have just surveyed can be credited with solidifying a modern cultural tradition that maps psychological and historical-developmental narratives onto the hierarchies that structure literary culture in the modern period.

PART II

Prattle and trifles

CHAPTER 4

Retentive ears and prattling mouths

Popular antiquarianism and childhood memory

Iona and Peter Opie's landmark mid-twentieth-century study *The Lore and Language of Schoolchildren* begins by confirming what many adults have long suspected: that we are completely irrelevant. "The scraps of lore which children learn from each other are at once more real, more immediately serviceable, and more vastly entertaining to them than anything which they learn from grown-ups."[1] That children learn more from each other than they do from adults, that they have their own, entirely separate and largely foreign, culture and language, is a central, defining assumption of the Opies' anthropological study. "The folklorist and anthropologist," the Opies write, "can, without travelling a mile from his door, examine a thriving unselfconscious culture ... which is as unnoticed by the sophisticated world, and quite as little affected by it, as the culture of some dwindling aboriginal tribe living out its helpless existence in the hinterland of a native reserve."[2] Children and adults necessarily interact – there are teachers, parents, anthropologists and collectors in these pages – but exchanges between children and adults in this text are cross-cultural, requiring efforts of translation and interpretation, punctuated by, what we might call, the "gentle shocks of mild surprise" when a seemingly shared language falls into silence or flashes with unfamiliarity.

Take, for example, this anecdote in the Opies' chapter on "Parody and Impropriety." After describing parody as the "most refined form of jeering" and one which gives "an intelligent child a way of showing independence without having to rebel"; after reminding us that is always dangerous to confuse children with angels, the Opies, nevertheless, insist that "a child may be never more innocent than when repeating a rude rhyme."[3] They then give this example of a "rude rhyme" recorded by a "valued Swansea contributor":

I'm a man that came from Scotland
Shooting peas up a Nannie goat's bottom,
I'm the man that came from Scotland
Shooting peas away.[4]

"These remarkable words," writes the Swansea contributor, "are sung to the tune of 'Men of Harlech,'" the unofficial national anthem of Wales. The contributor goes on to describe a "school Coronation Tea" of 1937 in which the children were entertained by a "local concert party," their orchestra playing "current popular numbers" which the children sang:

One item was a medley of national tunes beginning with "Men of Harlech." Immediately the whole audience of 450 – dear little girls aged five years to eleven years – broke into these words. I was sitting on the hall floor among them: there was not a smirk on any child's face. They were blissfully unconscious of what they were singing and merely making joyful noise. The pianist nearly fell off his stool in astonishment. He knew that this tune also concluded the medley, and sure enough when he played it the chorus broke out again.[5]

There is much to indulge the literary and cultural critic in this song and scene: the Welsh children drawing on national stereotypes and rivalries to evoke the "man from Scotland"; the abject. feminized figure of the "Nannie goat"; all of this brought into – perhaps to subvert? – the national song of Wales, itself an anti-Saxon anthem in interesting relationship to the Coronation Tea at which it is sung. Of course, one may also suspect that, in this case, the "most refined form of jeering" has let its standards slip a bit, and merely given these little girls a chance to say the word "bottom" at a school event.

Significantly, the Swansea contributor disclaims this entire spectrum of subversion to mere naughtiness, insisting that "there was not a smirk on any child's face." All 450 "dear little girls" were "blissfully unconscious of what they were singing and merely making joyful noise." There could be a strong sense of the uncanny here, much like what Rousseau describes in *Emile* upon hearing a child speak words the child does not understand: "the things a child says are not to him what they are to us."[6] Words suddenly speak the child, and the child's interior life of intellect and intention recedes into greater obscurity, replaced by an odd, unsettling linguistic performance. How do we understand the child's relationship to words he says but does not fully know?

In this scene, however, the children's capacity to turn language into "noise" is less uncanny than it is funny, even blithe. The children "broke into these words," breaking sound apart from sense and allowing "joyful noise" to float free of crude semantics. The charm and appeal of this scene lie in the possibility these children offer of an original innocence persisting within the refined and all-too-knowing form of parody, with all its over-determined institutional and cultural frames. As the Opies conclude: "just as one child can be unaware of what he is saying, so can innocence bless a crowd."[7]

The scene of the child who knows not what she sings is of central importance to the literary culture that takes shape in Britain over the long nineteenth century. The Opies' twentieth-century children's folklore collection is a direct legacy of that literary culture. Here and throughout *The Lore and Language of Schoolchildren*, their task is to accommodate the trivial chants and crude songs of children to the overarching framework of a national literary culture – present here in that Coronation Tea – whose health they hope to prove and promote. It is Romantic work; in other words, work first given shape and urgency in those key years of cultural transformation we know as the Romantic period when the emergence of a national and vernacular literary tradition required new ways to value and describe the crude, the trivial, the scandalous, the childish – in other words, the "popular."

Bringing the "popular" into national literary culture was a central and complex concern of British Romanticism. Literary scholars have tracked it through the tight maneuvers of Wordsworth's "Preface" to the *Lyrical Ballads* with the "language really used by men" on the one side and the "deluges of idle and extravagant stories" on the other. They have also detected an anxiety about popular literature in the period's ambivalent presentation of the novel, as in the case of Anna Barbauld who introduces her collection *The British Novelists* with the rueful acknowledgement that the novel "has a better chance of giving pleasure than of commanding respect."[8] This chapter and the next will describe how Romantic writers used a rhetoric of childhood to grapple with popular literature. The larger topic and terrain of these chapters is Romantic antiquarianism and its absorption of "the popular" into a history of literature and theory of culture that privileged the primitive, native and vernacular. As we shift our focus from the rhetorical history of Shelley's analogy into an investigation of what we will call the "prattle" and "trifles" of Romantic literature, we will continue to uncover the many ways that a developmental literary culture, one that begins in and includes the infant origins of language, shapes how the Romantics defined, valued and organized literature.

These chapters will also track antiquarian sensibility into the discipline of folklore studies. With its close but complex ties to Scottish

Enlightenment historicism, antiquarian practice of the eighteenth and early nineteenth centuries is often cited as one of the disciplinary origins of modern anthropology and sociology. Folklore shares these same intellectual and aesthetic roots, and current practitioners confess that "folklore is a 'romantic' undertaking, still not divorced from its antiquarian origins in the early 1800s."[9] These chapters will thus move between Romantic texts – the collections of oral ballads, nursery rhymes, traditional tales, local superstitions and pastimes that defined popular antiquarianism in the late eighteenth century, in addition to many other poetical and prose writings on children, childhood and education – and the nineteenth- and twentieth-century texts of children's folklore which are Romanticism's legacy. Tracing these lines of influence, we will uncover a remarkably resilient notion of literary culture that uses the figures and rhetoric of childhood to define and negotiate the popular.

Of course, by the mid-twentieth century when the Opies published both *The Lore and Language of Schoolchildren* and *The Oxford Dictionary of Nursery Rhymes*, children's folklore was its own distinct field of inquiry and scholarship. Indeed, within that field, the Opies take great pains to distinguish between nursery culture, on the one hand, and children's culture, on the other. Unlike the lullabies and pat-a-cakes of infancy, the rhymes and songs of the schoolyard are sanctioned neither by Mother Goose nor by any other maternal figure: "while a nursery rhyme passes from a mother or other adult to the small child on her knee, the school rhyme circulates simply from child to child, usually outside the home, and beyond the influence of the family circle."[10] Cadence, subject matter, transmission are all completely different; most significantly, the songs of schoolchildren thrive in the happy knowledge that "adults know nothing about them."[11] Partaking enthusiastically in the romance of childhood's discrete and autonomous realm, the Opies repeatedly insist that the culture of schoolchildren is distinct and separate from that of adults. The Opies' schoolchild leaves the home each day and enters another world, much like Milton's Adam and Eve left Eden: "When a child steps out of his home to go to school, whether he lives in a remote hamlet or in one of the backstreets of a great city, he is on his own, and looking after himself. The day ahead looms large and endless in front of him."[12] *The Lore and Language of Schoolchildren* thus offers its adult readers a glimpse of a culture whose language, customs and codes of behavior are otherwise inaccessible and foreign.

There is no doubt that this romance of childhood as a separate world has its origins in the Romantic period; one only need read *Emile*'s opening gambit – "Childhood is unknown" – to find early traces of this notion.[13] But in the Romantic period, the lines separating nursery lore from other forms of popular literature were much less clearly drawn. Oral ballads, songs sung to children, stories told to infants and "rustics" all overlapped, with traditional songs appearing in both ballad and nursery collections. Ballad scholars such as Joseph Ritson and Robert Chambers also produced important nursery collections. Unlike the Opies in the *Lore and Language of Schoolchildren*, Romantic writers were most interested in precisely those songs sanctioned by Mother Goose and other maternal figures. Women who worked as nurses and mothers were the most common ballad singers in eighteenth-century Scotland and the most significant source of traditional ballads for antiquarian collectors. The image of the old woman singing or telling a story to children gathered around her embodies antiquarian interest in the transmission and continuity of what they called Britain's "native" or "natural" literature.

Indeed, the image of a woman singing to a child circulates in a variety of Romantic discourses and writings and, as many critics have argued, is central to the articulation of cultural categories such as "literature" and "poetry."[14] A major Romantic icon, the image of woman and child, as Friedrich Kittler has suggested, locates the origins of language and poetry in the voice of the mother.[15] In our study of this recurring trope, however, the figure of maternity will more often be that of a nurse than a mother, and the significant charge of the image will as often rest on the figure of the child as much as on that of the woman. Indeed, this classic image of the "mother's mouth" will more accurately be described as one of the "child's ear" once we uncover the Romantic interest in audition and memory that animates these figures. One major task of this chapter, therefore, will be to reframe the dyad of woman and child in order to focus attention on the figure of the child and the Romantic period's investment in how the child hears, retains and reproduces the ballads, rhymes, tales and other forms of language it hears.

An idea of the child's nature – and, more specifically, its mind and memory – as particularly conservative and retentive emerges in the Romantic period in a range of writings, from Rousseau's description of the impenetrable but impressionable child's brain and the Edgeworths' critique of rote memorization, to antiquarian interest in the "tenacious memory" of ballad-singer Anna Gordon Brown. Building on a notion of infancy as an exceptionally impressionable state, these writers describe the child's memory as particularly and exactly retentive, insistently repeating and reproducing exterior forms, and yet doing so as unknowing and innocent play. This idea of the child's mind and memory plays a critical role in the emergence of a national and vernacular Romantic literary culture that can accommodate varieties of popular literature, from the childish to the sensational.

The construction of a vernacular and national literary history and culture must take the literary lives of children into account. Drawing on the rhetoric of infancy and childhood so central to Scottish Enlightenment historicism, Romantic antiquarianism transformed that rhetoric into a critical tool for the larger project of bringing popular literature into a national tradition: central to their recovery of the old oral ballads and other popular literary forms was an evocation of childhood and a sense of childhood's major role in the preservation and transmission of traditional literary culture. Thus to turn from *The Lore and Language of Schoolchildren* to Romantic-era texts is not to lose the company of children or the pleasure of childish things. What is, in fact, most "Romantic" about the Opies' mid-twentieth-century collection is the way they use the form of the child who is "unaware of what he is saying," the child who does not fully understand what she is singing, to negotiate the relationship between crude rhyme and national literary culture. This child and the work she does to produce, reproduce, and remember literary forms is a Romantic antiquarian figure.

ANTIQUARIAN NOSTALGIA: "REMEMBERED FROM CHILDHOOD"

Antiquarianism has recently re-emerged as a major field of Romantic studies, the antiquarian literary "collection" as an important genre of the period. Working within this genre to collect, print and preserve the ballads, songs, stories and traditions of the past, antiquarian writers developed a number of scholarly and literary conventions that we now recognize as exemplifying Enlightenment and Romantic literary values and influencing scholarly practice well into the twentieth century.[16] The protocols for citing and authenticating different versions and sources, the practice of reprinting primitive or unfinished texts in their original, incomplete form (rather than touching up or finishing them), the historical headnotes and scholarly footnotes often far longer than the original text – these are just a few examples of the conventions and practices that gradually consolidated themselves in the antiquarian collections of these years.

To these conventions, I propose that we add another: the often-repeated phrase "remembered from childhood." Sometimes used to describe the source's relationship to a ballad or tale, variations of this verbal gesture – "learned as a child," "remembered from childhood," "often heard sung in my childhood" – are also deployed to establish the antiquarian editor's own childhood relationship to balladry and folklore. Indeed, the Romantic antiquarian's manuscripts and precise transcriptions are so often supplemented by the aura of personal memory, his historical commentary so frequently punctuated by recollections of his own childhood, that we must see these gestures not simply as sentimental indulgences, but as an important element of the scholarly practice and authenticating apparatus taking shape in these collections.

In the introductory essays customary for the ballad collections, for example, the editor often recalls his original childhood attachment to popular poetry before detailing his adult scholarly practice, claiming for that practice a refinement and credibility based largely on the absence of those first emotional charges. Both the child's original ardor and the adult's subsequent stolidity work together to provide authenticity and authority for the antiquarian project. Thus Walter Scott dates his love of ballads to the "earliest period of [his] existence"; William Aytoun dedicates his collection to his "dearest mother" and describes Scottish ballads as "the firstlings of my memory"; Robert Jamieson recalls being a "lover of poetry from his childhood," naturally "fond of popular ballads and songs."[17] Chambers displays characteristic nostalgia when he confesses that:

I must own that I cannot help looking back with the greatest satisfaction to the numberless merry lays and *capriccios* of all kinds, which the simple honest women of our native country used to sing and enact with such untiring patience, and so much success, beside the evening fire in old times. ... There was no philosophy about these gentle dames.... It never occurred to them that children were anything but children – "bairns are just bairns," my old nurse would say.[18]

Here reminiscence blurs cultural and individual childhoods, reaching backward toward a state of simple equivalencies where "bairns are just bairns" and tapping into the ontogenetic cultural paradigm that we have scrutinized in earlier pages. Chambers wants a simple correspondence between personal and collective memory, as a later rhetorical question betrays: "What man of middle age, or above it, does not remember the tales of drollery and wonder which used to be told by the fireside, in cottage and in nursery, by the old women, time out of mind the vehicles for such traditions?"[19]

A practice that makes memory a significant part of its history, antiquarian historicism has been described as "affectionating" or sentimental, part of a larger trend in Romantic history writing to represent the past as lived or felt experience, to "personalize" history by giving it the narrative arc and affect of sentimental fiction.[20] It is also, of course, nostalgic, but in invoking this term we need to follow Richard Maxwell's rigorous account of antiquarianism as a "nostalgic sociology," understanding nostalgia as a tool of historical and cultural practice and not merely the sentiment or affect that confuses practice.[21] In "On the Uses and Disadvantages of History for Life," Nietzsche describes the sentiment with which the antiquarian approaches history as "love," "loyalty" and "piety." These sentimental charges, this desire "to preserve for those who shall come into existence after him the conditions under which he himself came into existence," enable the antiquarian to forge a particular relationship to the history he studies and writes:

> The history of his city becomes for him the history of himself; he reads its walls, its towered gate, its rules and regulations, its holidays, like an illuminated diary of his youth and in all this he finds again himself, his force, his industry, his joy, his judgment, his folly and vices. Here we lived, he says to himself, for here we are living; and here we shall live, for we are tough and not to be ruined overnight. Thus with the aid of this "we" he looks beyond his own individual transitory existence and feels himself to be the spirit of his house, his race, his city. Sometimes he even greets the soul of his nation across long dark centuries of confusion as his own soul.[22]

History is a type of autobiography for Nietzsche's antiquarian: more specifically, it is "an illuminated diary of his youth," an image suggesting that childhood is the most significant chapter of modern autobiography, and lending, as Maxwell notes, the sensibility of a "scrubbed and idealized adolescence" to an antiquarian practice more traditionally associated with age.[23] The antiquarian does indeed make strange bids at eternal youth. The nostalgia that Nietzsche ascribes to antiquarian history allows the personal and the collective to come together in the same backward glance. In this passage, nostalgia works largely through and as affect: the antiquarian "*feels* himself to be the spirit of his house, his race, his city." The nostalgic collapse of historical scales into each other creates nested historical narratives of person, village, region, culture and nation, each of which is *felt* to replicate, exemplify, and fold into the others. Antiquarian nostalgia becomes a nascent sociology, a method for theorizing and studying human history and culture, when evidence from one narrative (individual autobiography, for example) is taken as evidence for another (national history), when "remembered from childhood" stands as evidence for the "infancy of poetry." The nostalgia that animates antiquarian historicism thus draws on the cultural and historical paradigm we have seen in Enlightenment history more widely: that of the analogy between the individual life and human history.

This is the practice encoded in the antiquarian editor's repeated verbal gestures of "I remember in my childhood." It is also the practice embodied in the frequently evoked figures of mother and child. The fact that oral literature was traditionally sung to children and remembered from childhood makes the "old women" who care for children – the nurses, mothers, grandmothers, aunts and domestic servants – the vehicles of oral tradition. The notes in Scott's *Minstrelsy of the Scottish Border*, for example, list their sources as "taken from the recitation of an old woman, residing near Kirkhill"; "communicated to the Editor by Mr. Hamilton, Music-seller, Edinburgh, with whose mother it had been a favourite"; "from the recitation of an old woman, long in the service of the Arbuthnot family"; often "from the recitation of a lady, nearly related to the editor"; or simply "from the memory of an old woman."[24] Charles Kirkpatrick Sharpe is also typical in proclaiming that his ballads have been "mostly gathered from the mouths of nurses, wet and dry, singing to their babes and sucklings."[25] In Katie Trumpener's words, the nurse becomes an important "bardic" figure for Romantic antiquarianism and Romantic literature more generally, particularly in Scotland and Ireland. This figure of the bardic nurse is one that both extends and complicates the maternal figure and its naturalization of poetry.[26]

GATHERED FROM THE MOUTHS OF NURSES, WET AND DRY

Whether cited as the oral source of a particular ballad – "from the recitation of an old woman" – or evoked as an icon of orality – "gathered from the mouths of nurses, wet and dry" – the old singing woman appears so often in the scholarly apparatus of antiquarian collections that Maureen McLane has rightly described Romantic balladeering as an example of "traffic in women."[27] Antiquarians circulate and reproduce this figure in order to claim authenticity for their ballad texts, but exactly how the old singing woman validates the masculine, textual praxis of antiquarianism remains problematic. James Hogg famously remembers (or invents) this encounter between Walter Scott and his mother:

My mother chaunted the ballad of Old Maitlan' to him, with which he was highly delighted, and asked her if she thought it ever had been in print? And her answer was, "O na, na, sir, it never was printed i' the world, for my brothers an' me learned it an' many mae frae auld Andrew Moor, and he learned it frae auld

Baby Mettlin, wha was housekeeper to the first laird of Tushilaw. She was said to hae been another nor a gude ane, an' there are many queer stories about hersel', but O, she had been a grand singer o' auld songs an ballads."

"The first laird of Tushilaw, Margaret?" said he, "then that must be a very old story indeed?"

"Ay, it is that, sir! It is an auld story! But mair nor that, excepting George Warton an' James Stewart, there war never ane o' my sangs prentit till ye prentit them yoursel', an' ye hae spoilt them awthegither. They were made for singing an' no for reading; but ye hae broken the charm now, an' they'll never be sung mair."[28]

This passage is an excellent example of how orality and evocations of "pastness" work together in antiquarian representations of popular ballads and songs. Here the relationship of antiquarian textual practice to oral tradition is staged as a scene of anthropological or ethnographic encounter between collector and source. Hogg thus sets this scene on the border between orality and literacy, opposing singing to printing, learning by reading to learning by hearing. The songs were "made for singing an' no for reading," Mrs. Hogg famously insists; by printing them, antiquarians have "broken the charm now, and they'll never be sung mair." Orality becomes something altogether "spoilt" by the technologies of literacy: reading, writing and printing. The scene thus insists on the pure orality of the ballads, but in doing so, places the popular ballad in the past and imagines its disappearance in the present.

Scott here seems relatively unconcerned by Mrs. Hogg's charges of broken charms and spoiled traditions. He is eager to know if "Old Maitlan" has ever been in print and, in the title and heading to the ballad as printed in the *Minstrelsy*, will happily proclaim the antiquary's coup: "Never Before Published." This is a claim made all the more significant by the ballad's pretensions to "very high antiquity" and the fact that it has been "preserved by tradition." "Old Maitlan," again according to Scott's headnote in the *Minstrelsy*, is "perhaps, the most authentic instance of a long and very old poem, exclusively thus preserved."[29] Here authenticity becomes a factor of both the ballad's age and the purity of its oral transmission. The old woman who learned her ballads as a child, as Scott writes, from a "blind man, who died at the advanced age of ninety, and is said to have been possessed of much traditionary knowledge," is an important authenticating figure both in her own right and as part of a scene of ongoing transmission, that unbroken "charm" or chain of singing. Ultimately, however, "Old Maitlan" is the "most authentic" precisely because it was "never before published." And this is a curious standard of authenticity to proclaim and establish in print and in the act of publication. In the Hogg and Scott texts surrounding "Old Maitlan" we see how antiquarian practice – its standards of authenticity, its representation of orality and tradition – values what it understands itself to put at risk, and uses the figure of the old woman to establish the ballad as a "very old story indeed."[30]

Numerous antiquarian collections use pictorial images of old women singing to children as the frontispiece or as illustrations to their collections of popular literature. These graphic and verbal images of woman and child lend the collections an original, verifying scene of oral transmission that the texts locate in the past of "never mair," a time prior to printing and publication. Marked as historical by the textual and scholarly conventions of the antiquarian collection, the orality of the ballads also becomes something that can be "remembered from childhood," and here the image of woman and child reveals its close ties to the evocations of childhood memories that also recur in these collections. The figure of the old woman dates the ballad, establishing both singer and song as historical relics. But the old age of the woman also dates the long ago of her *childhood*, for antiquarian collectors, as we will see, always emphasize that old women singers learned their ballads as children and keep them perfectly preserved in memory until old age. Additionally, the figure of the child allows the antiquarian to represent his own childhood at the foot of his nurse, to gesture, as Chambers does, toward a personal and communal memory, for "what man of middle age, or above it, does not remember?" Thus in this image of woman and child, antiquarianism crafts precise connections between the "never mair" of orality and the work of personal memory, constructing a past that is both historical and remembered, both cultural and personal.

For the antiquarian editor, in fact, the recuperative form of the child becomes even more important than that of the old woman, for it is the child who represents both the collector's original experience of the ballads and the nation's earliest literary culture, the child who facilitates the exchanges of personal memory and collective history that give this scene its full significance. But the figures of old women, nurses and children recur in a number of Romantic antiquarian-inflected texts, including Scott's *Waverley* novels or Blake's *Songs of Innocence and Experience*, and they always signal the nostalgic sociology underlying their representations of history and culture. In *The Minstrel*, James Beattie writes what might be called an antiquarian progress narrative, tracing "the progress of a Poetical Genius, born in a rude age" in a narrative poem that maps the

development of an individual into a poet onto the history of literature and
the emergence of "poetry." Without autobiographical charges, *The Minstrel* nevertheless anticipates the exchanges between personal memory and
cultural history, between autobiography and anthropology, that are so
critical to Wordsworth's *Prelude*. Both poems use the scene of the matron
or "ancient dame" telling stories and chanting ballads to children as a key
moment or crucial stage in the history of poetry. Listening to the matron's
ballad, Beattie's minstrel child feels a nascent poetic appreciation: "Much
he the tale admired, but more the tuneful art." [31]

Like Beattie, Romantic antiquarians use the image of woman and child
as a scene of authentic cultural transmission, emphasizing how, and for
how many years, the song has been sung, rather than what the song is. But
images of old women or nurses singing or telling tales to children circulate
more widely in Romantic writing, and there is another discourse of nurses
and children that instead emphasizes the "tale" over the "tuneful art." In
the long and much discussed tradition (typically traced from Locke,
through Rousseau, to the Edgeworths) of critiquing and enumerating
the dangers to children posed by nurses and servants, it is precisely the
acculturative work of nurses that is most at issue. Locke sounds the
keynote when he warns of the servant's tendency "to awe Children, and
keep them in subjection, by telling them of *Raw-Head* and *Bloody
Bones*."[32] The problem with nurses is precisely the stories they tell and
the ballads they sing; thus the image embraced by antiquarians as authenticating their literary relics is an image condemned by many educators and
philosophers of the period.

"THE VILLAGE-MATRON . . . SUSPENDS THE
INFANT-AUDIENCE WITH HER TALES"

In *Some Thoughts Concerning Education*, perhaps the most influential
treatise on childhood and education throughout the eighteenth century,
Locke warned that the old ballads and tales are often bloody, superstitious, filled with violence and "strange Visions" and prone to make
children "afraid of their Shadows and Darkness all their Lives after."[33] In
Practical Education, Maria and R. L. Edgeworth extend this point,
insisting that "the ideas of apparitions, and winding sheets, and sable
shrouds, should be unknown to children." The larger culture of poetry is
part of the problem for the Edgeworths. "In the following poetic description of the beldame telling dreadful stories to her infant audience," they
write, introducing a passage from Akenside's *The Pleasures of Imagination*,

"we hear only of the pleasures of the imagination, we do not recollect how dearly these pleasures must be purchased by their votaries." They then quote Akenside's scene in full:

> Hence, finally, by night
> The village-matron, round the blazing hearth,
> Suspends the infant-audience with her tales,
> Breathing astonishment! Of witching rhymes,
> And evil spirits; of the death-bed call
> Of him who rob'd the widow, and devour'd
> The orphan's portion; of unquiet souls
> Risen from the grave to ease the heavy guilt
> Of deeds in life conceal'd; of shapes that walk
> At dead of night, and clank their chains, and wave
> The torch of hell around the murderer's bed.
> At every solemn pause the croud recoil
> Gazing each other speechless, and congeal'd
> With shivering sighs: till eager for the event,
> Around the Beldame all erect they hang,
> Each trembling hear with grateful terrors quell'd.[34]

For Akenside, as for Beattie and Wordsworth, this scene of the "village-matron" or "Beldame" telling stories to children is a primal scene of imaginative and literary pleasures. It is the same for Anna Letitia Barbauld, who brings out and introduces the 1795 edition of Akenside's poem (thereby making the poem available to and appreciated by so many Romantic writers, Coleridge and Wordsworth included). As we have seen, Barbauld (then Aiken) attributes the appeal of Gothic romance, Eastern tales, Shakespeare's ghosts, and Milton's sublime images not, in fact, to pleasure at all, but to the compulsions of narrative and dramatic suspense, a compulsion she images in the figures of children: "when children, therefore, listen with pale and mute attention to the frightful stories of apparitions, we are not, perhaps, to imagine that they are in a state of enjoyment, any more than the poor bird which is dropping into the mouth of the rattlesnake – they are chained by the ears, and fascinated by curiosity." Literature which works through sublimity, suspense and fear, according to Barbauld, returns us to a state of childhood listening when we were first "chained by the ears."[35]

The Edgeworths share Barbauld's and Akenside's interest in the "infant audience" of this scene, in what and how the children hear. But they quote this iconographic passage in order to circumvent its fascination. "No prudent mother will ever imitate this eloquent village matron, nor will she permit any beldame in the nursery to conjure up these sublime shapes, and to quell the hearts of her children with these grateful terrors," they assert confidently.[36] They go on to relate one further instance of traditional tales told to the young:

We were once present when a group of speechless children sat listening to the story of Blue-beard, "breathing astonishment." A gentleman who saw the charm beginning to operate, resolved to counteract its dangerous influence. Just at the critical moment, when the fatal key drops from the trembling hands of the imprudent wife, the gentleman interrupted the awful pause of silence that ensued, and requested permission to relate the remainder of the story. Tragi-comedy does not offend the taste of young, so much as old critics; the transition from grave to gay was happily managed. Blue-beard's wife afforded much diversion, and lost all sympathy the moment she was represented as a curious, tattling, timid, ridiculous woman. The terrors of Blue-beard himself subsided when he was properly introduced to the company; and the denouement of the piece was managed much to the entertainment of the audience; the catastrophe, instead of freezing their young blood, produced general laughter.[37]

Quoting Akenside's verse once again, the Edgeworths announce this prose account as a rewriting of poetry's primal scene. We might be struck by the many similarities between the Edgeworths' Blue-beard scene and Hogg's scene of his mother chanting "Old Maitlan" to Walter Scott. Both scenes share an anthropological frame as stories of fieldwork and cross-cultural encounter. Both stage an oral recitation heard or observed by a "gentle-man" from the world of print and publication; and both scenes meditate on the relationship between oral song or story and the gentleman author who threatens to break the "charm" of tradition. Both scenes, in other words, represent the relationship of modern Enlightenment literary prac-tice to traditional and primitive literature through the scene of a gentle-man interrogating or interrupting an oral performance.

Unburdened by nostalgia, the Edgeworths are clearly less troubled than Scott by their radical transformation of a traditional tale: their gentleman notices "the charm beginning to operate" and deliberately intervenes to "counteract its dangerous influence," translating terror and tragedy into didactic comedy. Scott and the Edgeworths can be seen as standing on opposite sides of what is often described as a debate between imaginative and rationalist defenses of children's literature in the Romantic period, with the one side defending traditional fairytales and other popular lore, and the other side attacking it for promoting superstition and other primitive terrors. The Edgeworths (with Locke and Rousseau before them, Sarah Trimmer and M. M. Sherwood at their side) represent the philosophical changes "revolutionising" the nursery that Chambers complains of in his *Popular Rhymes of Scotland*. The "*realism* and right-down earnest" now demanded by "superiors of the nursery," he insists, are "too exclusively addressed to the intellect" and overlook the fact that "there is such a thing as imagination, or a sense of fun, in the human mind."[38] Chambers, Scott and other antiquarian champions of popular, traditional lore, admit that the old nurse's songs and tales often impress children's minds with "superstitious terrors," but, as we shall see, they find a way to translate the content of traditional tales and ballads into the sounds of "light gabble and jocund song."[39]

The debate about superstition and imaginative terror that circulates around the image of nurse and child is not, however, only a debate about good parenting, early education and the appropriate literature for children. Romantic writers use the image of the old woman singing to a child to debate the values and risks of popular literature, to situate that literature in a native or domestic setting, and to articulate the place of early literary forms within the larger national culture and in relation to their own literary practice. From Addison's influential praise of "Chevy Chase" and "Two Children in the Wood" as examples of the "Songs and Fables that are come from Father to Son" and serve as a "national poetry," to Barbauld's figure of a mother teaching her son to read – "Come to mamma. Sit in mamma's lap. Now read your book" – the image of parent and child, especially of mother and child, makes the forms and technologies of national literary culture part of familial interaction and exchange, what one generation passes down to the next. But because this image so often employs surrogate or foster figures in the British context – the "gentle dames," "old women," "nurses," "village-matrons" and "beldames" – its work of "naturalizing" national literature must be carefully scrutinized. The image of the nurse and child always exposes the cultural life of the nursery: the class differences, regional particularities and troubled lines of continuity between primitive and modern literatures. It is precisely these lines – between oral and written, natural and cultural, original and reproduction – that so interest Romantic antiquarians. While we might see their nostalgic deployment of this image as designed to give national literary culture pre-cultural and natural origins, we must also see the work it does to place all literary forms – even the very "firstlings" of childhood memory – on the national, cultural map.

The image of the nurse and child as an image of British national literature is surprisingly resilient. One finds tribute paid to the authority of the "old British Nurses" in the very earliest collection of nursery rhymes, *Mother Goose's Melody*, where the mock-scholarly preface warns its reader not to "speak irreverently of this antient maternity, as they may be considered as the great grandmothers of science and knowledge."[40] And one finds the bardic status of the nurse evoked well into the twentieth century whenever the tenacity and homely comforts of oral tradition are defended. Here is Vita Sackville-West on the perseverance of nursery culture despite its bibliographical neglect:

Oblivion! no, that is not the right word. The Old British Nurse had a better chance of survival in her own voice than in the print of the so joyfully destructible page. She was too solidly ensconced before the nursery fire to be dependent on so ephemeral a thing as a mere book. Like Homer, she had the retentive ears of an audience that could not read; it could only listen. Like Homer, tradition and legend backed her; she told many lies, and her audience drank them in – drank them in with the suppertime glass of milk, sitting on the flannelled lap rocking them backwards and forwards in the drowsy moment between bath and bed. She was the interpreter of the nursery poet made vocal; her murmuring voice was more durable than the printed word. Oblivion is not for her. That which she recited with infinite patience, repeated, murmured, chanted, crooned, was remembered from generation to generation; remembered, and was passed on.[41]

With its Homeric rhetoric, its interest in the relationship between print and oral cultures, and its embodiment of tradition in the figure of the old nurse, this image announces itself as a direct legacy of Romantic antiquarianism. In reproducing the image here, it costs Sackville-West nothing to admit that the "Old British Nurse" "told many lies"; the magic of the nursery and the power of this scene lie not in the nurse's story, but in the act, even the atmosphere, of its telling. Like Beattie's young minstrel, we are meant to admire "much the tale" but "more the tuneful art." Such an image locates authentic, enduring national culture not in an official story or heroic history – these things are fictions backed by "tradition and legend" – but in an authentic scene of oral transmission. The "lies" of Sackville-West's nurse are what we will see Robert Chambers identify as the "trifles" of the nursery: insignificant in themselves, significant in the fact that they are "repeated, murmured, chanted, crooned" and "remembered from generation to generation."

The importance of the nurse as an image of traditional, national literary culture is readily apparent, if surprisingly complex. But what if we now shift our focus more exclusively to the "retentive ears" and prattling mouths of the children? We have already seen the way the figure of the child in this nursery image animates acts of personal and collective memory and serves a central tool of antiquarianism's nostalgic sociology. Our discussion of Akenside's "village matron" has also asked us to think about the "infant-audience," listening as if "chained by the ears." In Sackville-West's rendering of this mythic scene, the power of the image is located not only in the mouth of the nurse, but also in the figures of the pre-literate children who do not read the nurse's tales, do not really even listen to them, but ingest them in a twilight, half-asleep state of rhythmic repetition – "drank them in with the suppertime glass of milk, sitting on the flannelled lap rocking them backwards and forwards in the drowsy moment between bath and bed." Ears and mouths strangely transmogrify in this passage. In fact, the significance of this iconographic scene of woman and child is as much a function of the child's early, unmediated listening as it is of the nurse's authoritative singing. Romantic antiquarians and the folklorists who follow are invested in the scene not only because of the woman's figure of orality and maternity, but also because of the figure of the child and their particular understanding of how the child hears, remembers and reproduces language it may not fully understand. This image of oral literature contains, in fact, ideas of the child's relationship to language, ideas as well of audition, memory and rote repetition, all of which make its claims to originality and orality much more complex.

PRATTLE: THE NOISE OF THE NURSERY

"Children hear speech from their birth," writes Jean-Jacques Rousseau in *Emile*. In pointing out this simple fact, Rousseau gave the Romantics a cultural conundrum both vexed and productive. In the first few chapters of this book, we focused on the analogy between child and savage, between the life of the individual and the course of human history, and how the emergence of this analogy as a new cultural paradigm enabled innovative ways of thinking about literature and history. Assumed to have a parallel relationship to language and primitive literary forms, both child and savage were used by Enlightenment and Romantic writers to stage a developmental account of the origins and progress of language. But, of course, there are some crucial differences between a child's acquisition of language and a savage's invention of language. The fact that children hear speech from their birth, long before they, themselves, can understand or articulate what they hear, is, in fact, the central distinction between the child, on the one hand, and the savages in that imagined scene of original language, on the other hand, who, it is always emphasized, have "never been taught to speak" and have been "bred up remote from the societies of men."[42] Children hear the sounds of language – significantly, *they hear language as sound* – before they hear and understand the words of language.

Historical comparisons between child and savage often ignore this difference, but one also finds Romantic writers acknowledging and grappling with the child's early pre-linguistic life and the questions it raises. Thus Rousseau continues:

> Children hear speech from their birth. They are spoken to not only before they understand what is said to them, but before they can reproduce the voices they hear. Their still dull organs lend themselves only little by little to imitation of the sounds dictated to them, and it is not even sure that these sounds at first carry to their ears as distinctly as to ours.[43]

Words are sounds that the child cannot understand and cannot even imitate and thus, for Rousseau, are "sounds dictated to them." His question about whether or not the child even hears the sounds "as distinctly" as an adult is, in fact, a question about whether or not the child hears the sounds of speech as words. Modern linguists describe how fluent speakers of a language "hallucinate" the divisions between words when listening to speech because they know and relate to the language through the unit of the word. Without knowledge of words – without comprehension of the language – speech is perceived as sound undifferentiated into particular semantic units: the beginnings and ends of words register neither orally or aurally without that knowledge.[44]

In *Emile*, Rousseau insists that the child's relationship to speech he does not understand should be taken into account when addressing issues of early childcare. The child will hear speech as sound, understanding only its tones and accents. Rousseau thus approves of the nurse who entertains her charge with "songs and very gay and varied accents." But there is also a danger that she might make him "constantly giddy with a multitude of useless words of which he understands nothing other than the tone she gives them." Rousseau's advice on how to talk to an infant follows Enlightenment thinking about how language develops: "I would want the first articulations which he is made to hear to be rare, easy, distinct, often repeated, and that the words they express relate only to objects of the senses which can in the first place be shown to the child."[45] This is a recapitulative model where language acquisition and childhood education follow and reiterate the steps of language's origins and development.

For Rousseau the quantity and quality of speech in the nursery has high stakes and leads directly to the worst habits of advanced, overly refined social life. "The unfortunate facility we have for dazzling people with words we do not understand," he admonishes, "begins earlier than is thought. The schoolboy listens in class to the verbiage of his teacher as he listened in swaddling clothes to the prattle of his nurse."[46] "Prattle" is a favorite Romantic word associated with children and their linguistic life; "prattle" is idle, insignificant or meaningless talk, childish chatter, or the inarticulate sounds that make up the talk of young children. One finds prattle in the mouths of women and children throughout Romantic literature. Sentimental fiction abounds with children, "little prattlers," who utter "artless remarks" in the "unformed accents of childhood."[47] An undisguised antipathy to children – especially "their noise and prattle and monkey tricks" – is a quick and easy way to establish the corrupt, overly refined sensibilities of a character.[48] Anna Letitia Barbauld immediately establishes the "childish treble" and childish matter of her mock-epic "Washing-Day" by calling down the "domestic Muse" to sing "In slip-shod measure loosely prattling on / Of farm or orchard, pleasant curds and cream, / Or drowning flies, or shoe lost in the mire / By little whimpering boy, with rueful face."[49] The "artless prattle" that "evens hours beguile" evokes everyday familial discourse and the iconic domestic scene of parents and children gathered around the fire at the end of the day.[50]

Prattle is not, however, always or even usually communal, shared between children and adults. The "pretty prattle" of a young child at play by herself also suggests the imaginative invention, self-sufficiency and expressive physicality of this being. Shelley's child "at play by itself" who will "express its delight by its voice and motions" leads directly to William Newell's figure of the "inventive child" found in his late nineteenth-century folklore collection *Games and Songs of American Children*. Here he describes a young girl playing next to (significantly, not with) her mother in the park, "incessantly prattling to herself" and "flitting like a bird." "Listen to her monologue, flowing incessantly and musically as the bubbling of a spring," Newell advises, and "you will find a perpetual romance unfolding itself in her mind."[51] The "perpetual romance" of the child's mind, in fact, signals the persistent romantic traces in this child figure.

The prattling, self-sufficient, ever-delighted child is often put forward as the quintessential or ideal Romantic child, a figure for the autonomous and self-engendering Romantic imagination or self.[52] The "gay prattle of infant tongues" can thus serve as an original model, ideal version or inspiration for poetry or poetic production.[53] Keats, in describing his notion of that "delicious diligent indolence" that leads to reflection and poetic conception, suggests that, while "a doze upon a sofa" or a "nap upon clover" cannot hinder this mental voyage, the "prattle of a child gives it wings."[54] Wordsworth's poem "Characteristics, of a Child Three Years Old" describes an infant who is "loving" and "tractable, though wild." For this "happy Creature," "herself / Is all sufficient" and "solitude to her / Is blithe society." The fact that she "fills the air / With gladness and involuntary songs," with the joy and sounds of prattle, is no small part of her blithe solitude and her appeal to the adult poet.[55] This is Herder's "sensitive being which can enclose none of its lively sensations within itself" and who, "without volition and intention, has to express each of them in sound."[56]

This figure of expressive sound, vocalizing involuntarily and without regard for or interest in others, is not wholly an ideal, however, poetic or otherwise. When placed back into comparison with the savage as paired figures of original language, this self-sufficient child potentially takes language out of the sympathetic and affective economy in which we have seen it imagined. The savage who feels hunger or love and expresses his desire in early words and gestures represents language as communicative and social; the words and gestures generated acquire meaning and significance within a sympathetic exchange with another. His desire or idea precedes its articulation and communication. The prattle of a child who simply sounds forth, who expresses physical and emotional sensation in gesture, tone and word in solitude and with no animating interest in another, unmoors language from its social stays.

Thus when Rousseau directs us to go to the nursery to hear original and natural language, he describes the tones and gestures of the infant and nurse as the vocalizations and gestures of the savages were typically imagined. But he adds this curious description of the infant's face:

To the language of the voice is joined that of gesture, no less energetic. This gesture is not in children's weak hands; it is on their visages. It is surprising how much expression these ill-formed faces already have. Their features change from one instant to the next with an inconceivable rapidity. You see a smile, desire, fright come into being and pass away like so many flashes of lightning. Each time you believe you are seeing a different visage. Their facial muscles are certainly more mobile than ours. On the other hand, their dull eyes say almost nothing. Such should be the character of the signs they give at an age when one has only bodily needs.[57]

Here is another description of early language as a "mixture of words and actions" but the confidence that bodily movements – here, facial expressions – are the "natural interpreters of the sentiments of the mind" and a language that makes the interior exterior, visible and present, is strikingly absent. The capacity for expression in the child's face is related to its otherwise "ill-formed" physical state; the "inconceivable rapidity" with which the "features change" – and change to such an extent as to present an entirely "different visage" – all lend an uncanny fluidity and malleability to the child's body. The face, usually that part of the body that manifests or means unique identity, is here overly "mobile" and in constant movement.

The "dull eyes" that say nothing thus confirm what the expressive face that says too many different things suggests: that there is no inside to the child, that the sentiments displayed on the body are not felt, intended or expressive of a "mind" or inner self in the way they might be in the adult body. Elsewhere, Rousseau will make clear that the infant has no identity. It is only after infancy that "the life of the individual begins ... that memory extends the sentiment of identity to all the moments of his existence [and] he becomes truly one, the same, and consequently capable of happiness or unhappiness."[58] Here in his description of an infant's gestural language, he matches the lack of an individual and fully formed self with a mobile, fluid and multiple body. More significantly, he uses the child to call the entire premise of "natural language" into question. At an age or stage of infancy "when one has only bodily needs," the "character of signs" does not move along that mimetic trajectory where surface leads to depths and outsides express insides. Instead, these signs stay on the surface of the body, moving through and unfolding too many unfelt, unanchored emotions. Here the body of the infant challenges ideas of man's natural state and original language that are otherwise upheld by a notion of infancy and origins.

The figure of the prattling child thus inspires bewilderment and anxiety as often as it inspires joy and assurance. This is the reaction of father to child that Coleridge describes at the end of *Christabel* when, in the Conclusion to Part II, he meditates on parental rage with this figure:

> A little child, a limber elf,
> Singing, dancing to itself,
> A fairy thing with red round cheeks,
> That always finds, and never seeks,
> Makes such a vision to the sight
> As fills a father's eyes with light;

And pleasures flow in so thick and fast
Upon his heart, that he at last
Must needs express his love's excess
With words of unmeant bitterness.[59]

This is a classic Romantic figure of the prattling child voicing a seemingly self-referential and self-sufficient speech. Here this vision of autonomy, of delight without cause, of unmotivated expression causes the father to burst forth in words of "rage and pain." Coleridge explains the father's sudden anger as an overflow of "love's excess," and he links the unexpected veer from love to fury with the emotional and expressive habits of the "world" in which this father rears and watches his little child. She may seem a "fairy thing," but Coleridge takes care to place this unsentimental scene of parenting in the world and to demonstrate how that world inflects and infects it. "And what, if in a world of sin," he wonders, "Such giddiness of heart and brain / Comes seldom save from rage and pain, / So talks as it's most used to do." Associating such excessive emotion with the "rage and pain" that typically produce it, the father finds himself "talking as it's most used to do," reproducing, in other words, the expressions and words of the culture. The fact that he responds to this figure by reproducing "unmeant words" also suggests that part of what is so troubling about this child may be the "unmeant words" of her prattle.

In "To H. C., Six Years Old," Wordsworth hints that the relationship of a child to his prattling words might indeed be more complicated: "O Thou! whose fancies from afar are brought; / Who of thy words dost make a mock apparel, / And fittest to unutterable thought / The breeze-like motion and the self-born carol."[60] The child makes his words a "mock apparel"; thus the extent to which they are his own words – "thy words," according to the opening apostrophe of the poem – remains a question. In contrast, it is his "breeze-like motion" and "self-born carol" that the child "fittest to unutterable thought," suggesting that the child's unknown and foreign thoughts – those "fancies from afar" – will not "fit" into words and are better expressed in the sounds and gestures of a language of action.

The "mock apparel" of words here, however, raises a host of questions about children's prattle and their use of words that send us back to Rousseau's anxiety about the modern facility for "dazzling people with words we do not understand." Wordsworth famously echoes Rousseau's concerns in Book V of *The Prelude* when he describes a mock child – "no child, / But a dwarf man" – who "can string you names of districts, cities, towns, / The whole world over" while "his teachers stare"; or even more famously in the *Ode* where the "six years' Darling of a pigmy size" can "fit his tongue / To dialogues of business, love, or strife."[61] These are unnatural children, but central to their characterization as such is a troubling relationship to the words which they produce and pronounce with ease but which, Wordsworth suspects, mean nothing to them. Wordsworth suspects as much and is concerned by it to a large degree because both Locke and Rousseau before him insist on this phenomenon and make it central to Romantic debates about education and theories about childhood memory and mental capacities. "With our babbling education," Rousseau insists, "we produce only babblers."[62]

At the heart of this anxiety about children babbling words they do not fully understand or properly intend is an anxiety about the relationship between individual agency and the forms of language and culture. Here again the figure of the child raises questions that the historical and linguistic analogy between savage and child otherwise minimizes. Children learning the words of their parents (and thus the linguistic habits and customs of their national culture) and savages inventing the first words have, of course, a very different relationship to language. The process embodied in the figure of the child, when not imagined as originary, is acknowledged as one of education and inheritance, a scene in which the child must match his desire or idea to a word that already exists. The process embodied in the figure of the savage is one of invention and communication, a scene in which the savage must formulate a sound or gesture to express his desire or idea. The child's words are given to him by others; the savage's words are his own. The savage's language moves the interior life of thought, desire and intention out into the external world; the child's language takes the forms of the cultural and social world into the interior life of the mind and memory. In this way, the figure of the child learning language often reminds the Romantics that words and other cultural forms can precede and even produce individual desires, needs and ideas. The child who speaks words he does not fully understand or mean is thus a figure that forces Romantic writers to confront the shaping, determinative influence history, language and culture have on the individual. Their acknowledgment of this influence and their strategies for bringing the child into the realm of cultural production and reproduction are central to the theories of national culture and history that emerge in these years.

The Romantic notion of children's prattle thus has a variety of associations and contexts, but our focus here is particularly on the ways in which the insignificance or meaninglessness of children's speech and language is imagined, worried about or put to use. By "insignificant speech" I mean not merely a description of content or an evaluation of what the child has to say, but the ways in which language in the mouths and minds of children splits sense from sound, takes words and turns them back into noise or sounds, or hears words as sounds. For Romantic antiquarians, poets, novelists, essayists and theorists, the child, for better or worse, exposes the non-semantic values of speech and language and the ways in which sound and meaning do not always coincide or cooperate. In Romantic writing, one repeatedly encounters the figure of a child who has "more words than ideas," who "can say more things than he can think," and who does not fully understand what he says, sings or repeats. In educational treatises and essays, the child's facility for retaining sounds and images without the corresponding idea or adequate thought makes him a figure of consternation and anxiety, raising the cultural stakes, for example, in the debate about the use of rote memorization in schools. In antiquarian collections of old ballads and tales, however, this figure of uncomprehending retention and reproduction promises both national cultural continuity as well as the possibility of innocence persisting amidst the scandal, vulgarity and violence of popular literature. Romantic antiquarianism and the discipline of folklore celebrate and privilege the child's relationship to insignificant and meaningless language and literary forms.

ROTE MEMORY AND THE RETENTIVE MIND

In *Practical Education*, Maria and R. L. Edgeworth condemn the beldame in the nursery who conjures up sublime shapes, and they criticize the practice of rote memorization in children's education. Both pronouncements are part of their larger critique of poetry and its pernicious effects on the child's mind.[63] Their chapter on "Memory and invention" opposes "retentive" or rote memory – that which "retains the greatest number of ideas for the longest time" – to "recollective" or "rational" memory – appreciated more by those who "value not so much the number, as the selection of facts; not so much the mass, or even the antiquity, of accumulated treasure, as the power of producing current specie for immediate use."[64] A strong recollective memory aids "invention" and is clearly preferred by the self-described "practical" Edgeworths (who, in this chapter, offer Benjamin Franklin as a role model for up-and-coming Enlightenment children). Retentive memory, on the other hand, they associate with unthinking and unoriginal cultural reproduction, with figurative antiquarians (those who value both the "mass" and the "antiquity" of "accumulated treasure") and, strikingly, with a more primitive cultural moment before printing and books:

At the revival of literature in Europe, before the discovery of the art of printing, it was scarcely possible to make any progress in the literature of the age, without possessing a retentive memory. A man who had read a few manuscripts, and could repeat them, was a wonder, and a treasure: he could travel from place to place, and live by his learning; he was a circulating library to a nation, and the more books he could carry in his head the better.[65]

Here the Edgeworths dramatically display the ways in which the "literate mind" can only imagine oral culture through the images and vehicles of their literate world: the oral sage reads, repeats and becomes a "circulating library to a nation," carrying "books" in his head. The art of printing and the spread of literacy has "lowered the value" of retentive memory, according to the Edgeworths, and rendered it culturally obsolete. In good Protestant fashion, they insist, "It is better to refer to the book itself, than to the man who has read the book."[66]

If here the Edgeworths associate the value of retentive memory with the rote repetition of manuscripts, elsewhere they link it to the oral traditions of poetry and song. "Repetition is found to fix words, and sometimes ideas, strongly in the mind," they point out: "the words of the burthen of a song, which we have frequently heard, are easily and long remembered."[67] Significantly, words *and only sometimes ideas* are fixed in the mind, for with rote memorization and repetition, words function more as sounds than semantically charged signs:

When we want to get any thing by rote, we repeat it over and over again, till the sounds seem to follow one another habitually, and then we say we have them perfectly by rote. The regular recurrence of sounds, at stated intervals, much aids us. In poetry, the rhymes, the cadence, the alliteration, the peculiar structure of the poet's lines, assist us. All these are mechanical helps to the memory.[68]

Rote memory transforms words into their more "mechanical" aspects of sound and rhythm. For the Edgeworths, this is largely why it works against the promotion of what they call "rational memory": "whilst we repeat, we exclude all thought from the mind, we form a habit of saying certain sounds in a certain order." Repeating blocks thinking; the sound of words drowns out their semantic values.

The Edgeworths devote so much attention to rote memorization in *Practical Education* not only because it is a common – and, in their opinion, harmful – schoolroom exercise, but also because they believe children's minds are naturally and peculiarly retentive in ways too easily

exploited by such practices. Following Locke and Rousseau, they note that
children learn words first as sounds, only later as ideas or meanings, and
they evoke that common image of the "prattling vivacious child pour[ing]
forth a multiplicity of words without understanding their meaning."[69]
Children appear to learn words that they, in fact, only "retain" and repeat.
Rousseau describes the child's mind in these terms: "Their brain, smooth
and polished, returns like a mirror, the objects presented to it. But
nothing remains; nothing penetrates. The child retains the words; the
ideas are reflected off of him."[70] Note that this smooth, impenetrable
child's brain does, in fact, receive some impressions: images, but not ideas;
words, but not their meanings. According to Rousseau, children "retain
sounds, figures, sensations, ideas rarely, the connections between ideas
more rarely."[71]

Rote memorization is thus such a tempting tool for the educator
because it plays to children's "apparent facility at learning" which,
according to Rousseau, is no learning at all and can instead be "the cause
of children's ruin." The meaningless prattle of the bright young child
organizes itself easily into meaningless rote recitation, especially when that
child wants to charm parents too easily "pleased with the mere sound of
words of high import from infantine lips."[72] Poetry is particularly risky in
this regard. In both *Practical Education* and in R. L. Edgeworth's *Poetry
Explained for the Use of Young People*, the Edgeworths warn that "children
seldom understand the poetry, which they early learn by rote, and that
thus instead of forming a poetic taste, they acquire the habit of repeating
words to which they affix no distinct ideas, or of admiring melodious
sounds which are to them destitute of meaning."[73] Edgeworth speculates
that the "want of originality of thought" and the "perpetual sameness of
expression" which plagues "the world of literature" is due to these early
exercises of rote memorization. Children, the Edgeworths argue, should
"never be praised for merely remembering exactly" what they have heard
or read; instead "they should be praised for selecting with good sense what
is worth their attention, and for applying what they remember to useful
purposes." In rhetoric that anticipates later twentieth-century pedagogical
practice, the Edgeworths encourage parents and teachers to "let [the
children] speak in words of their own."[74]

Rote memorization performs the possible meaninglessness of words, as
children recite what means nothing to them and as words become mere
"melodious sounds." The Edgeworths (along with Rousseau and
Barbauld) stress simple vocabularies for children so that they might attach
fixed, concrete meanings to the words they hear and read. The goal is not

only for children to understand what they hear, but to mean what they say. Not everyone was convinced, however. Taking aim at this pedagogical philosophy, Robert Southey writes: "Oh! what blockheads are those wise persons who think it necessary that a child should comprehend everything it reads!"[75] In one of his short essays penned by the "Doctor," Southey represents the debate about rote memorization and children's relationship to language as a dialogue between his "Doctor" and an overeducated blue-stocking who has been "carried from lecture to lecture, like a student who is being crammed at a Scotch university" and who has a shelf-full of books "composed for the laudable purpose of enabling children to understand everything." "What sir," the lady demands, "are we to make our children learn things by rote like parrots, and fill their heads with words to which they cannot attach any significance?" In response, the Doctor reminds the woman that she is a mother and, as such, should use "the proper and natural language of the nursery," one which communicates more by sound and tone than meaning. "When children are beginning to speak," Southey reminds her, "they do not and cannot affix any meaning to half the words which they hear; yet they learn their mother tongue."[76] Southey stresses the sonic, spoken and inherited aspects of language to suggest that words are not exclusively pedagogical or even chiefly semantic in function. Children can read and repeat words they do not understand without causing Southey much alarm because they are reproducing the "mother tongue." The image of the child whose head is crammed with words he cannot fully understand becomes, for poets and antiquarians, an image of cultural transmission and continuity.

The uneven and peculiar quality of the child's memory – retaining sounds, images, words, but not ideas or fixed meanings – is something often noticed and discussed in a variety of Romantic writing, most extensively and influentially in Wordsworth's *Prelude*, as we shall see in Chapter 6. In a notebook entry, Coleridge also notices what children can easily remember and what they seem perpetually to forget:

Important Distinction between the Memory, or reminiscent Faculty, of Sensations – which young Children seem to possess in so small a degree from their perpetual Desire of having a Tale repeated, & the Memory or words & images which the very same young Child manifestly possess in an unusual degree – even to sealing wax accuracy of retention & representation. – Idiots probably the same/perhaps defective in both; but in the latter less so. – [77]

Here Coleridge returns us to the nursery and to that central paradox of children's stories in particular, and of popular, formulaic literature more generally: the desire to hear or read the same story over and over which one already knows word for word, turn for turn. Significantly the child's mind in this passage takes on impressions of words and images with "sealing wax accuracy of retention & representation," a textual image that suggests not only perfect reproduction but closure and safe keeping. The child becomes a missive, a communication sent into the future, with the stories and songs of the past impressed and inscribed on its brain.

These Romantic-era ideas of the child's mind and memory, and the child's relationship to literature imagined as a result, persist well into the nineteenth and twentieth centuries, informing both literary and folklore studies. In *Games and Songs of American Children*, William Newell sets forth a cultural paradox that he locates in the figure of the child, one that comes directly out of these earlier Romantic debates and one that continues to shape the discipline of children's folklore today: the child as paradoxically both "inventive" and "conservative." Newell celebrates the inventive child at play, "incessantly prattling to herself" in a language at least partly of her own invention, and "flitting like a bird" with a "perpetual romance unfolding itself in her mind."[78] But this romantic figure does not distract him from the fact that most of the games and rhymes this child will play "have existed in many countries, with formulas which have passed from generation to generation."[79] For Newell, the stability of children's lore over centuries is at least partly attributable to the way in which individual children experience tradition.[80] Here the child's conservative nature becomes important: "No deputy is so literal, no nurse so Rhadamanthine, as one child left in charge of another. The same precision appears in the conduct of sports. The formulas of play are as Scripture, of which no jot or tittle is to be repealed. Even the inconsequent rhymes of the nursery must be recited in the form in which they first became familiar."[81]

Precision and exact repetition characterize children's play and culture for Newell. Vita Sackville-West also assures us that, listening in at the door to the nursery, we would hear not only the narrative of the nurse, but the clamour of the children saying, "Tell it again, tell it just the same." Like Newell, Sackville-West insists on the conservative nature of children: "Children do not welcome novelty; like the unsophisticated adult in matters of art, they like what they know. Innovations disturb them; variation meets with disapproval."[82] It is this child, the small tyrant of tradition, that is repeatedly set against the prattling, playful, bird-like child of invention. As the Opies conclude: "the unromantic truth is that children do not 'go on inventing games out of their heads all the time.'"

Invention and preservation rarely go together; if the nursery is culturally conservative, it is largely because the child is "every bit as conservative as was George VI with his lifelong preference for the hymns he sang in the choir at Dartmouth."[83]

THE CASE OF ANNA GORDON BROWN

The conservative child whose mind is permanently inscribed with the songs, ballads, tales and traditions of a vernacular culture and who insists on their exact repetition and reproduction is a figure of childhood that popular, literary antiquarians develop in the Romantic period. We have an excellent example of the importance of childhood memory to Romantic antiquarianism in the lore surrounding Anna Gordon's (Mrs. Brown of Falkland) ballad-singing career. In turning to this figure, we are also returning to the iconic figures of mother and child so important to Romantic literary culture. While most critical discussion has concentrated on the maternal figure of this pair – whether mother, grandmother or nurse – our attention will continue to fall on the figure of the child and how these ideas of the child's retentive mind and memory animate antiquarian interest in this scene.

Anna Gordon's importance to the British ballad archive is legendary and her recognition longstanding. David Buchan, in *The Ballad and the Folk*, describes her ballads as the "oldest extant corpus (repertoire of one singer) in Anglo-Scottish balladry."[84] In *The English and Scottish Popular Ballads*, Francis James Child proclaims that "No Scottish ballads are superior in kind to those recited in the last century by Mrs. Brown, of Falkland."[85] And in 1801, Walter Scott describes Brown as "an ingenious lady, to whose taste and memory the world is indebted." Scott credits Alexander Tytler's transcriptions of Brown's ballads as a significant source for his *Minstrelsy*, and he quotes Tytler's account of how Mrs. Brown learned her ballads in his introduction to the collection:

An aunt of my children, Mrs. Farquhar, now dead . . . a good old woman, who spent the best part of her life among flocks and herds, resided in her latter days in the town of Aberdeen. She was possest of a most tenacious memory, which retained all the songs she had heard from nurses and countrywomen in that sequestered part of the country. Being maternally fond of my children, when young, she had them much about her, and delighted them with her songs, and tales of chivalry. My youngest daughter, Mrs. Brown, at Falkland, is blest with a memory as good as her aunt, and has almost the whole of her songs by heart.[86]

Here are the familiar figures of "good old woman," "nurses and country-women," all "maternally fond" and singing to children. Tytler's account, however, insists on that dimension of generation and reiteration in what is often treated as a static image. The transmission of ballads from "nurses and countrywomen" to child, and then, when that child is herself an old woman and aunt, to a new generation of children, establishes oral tradition as an ongoing and repeated series of exchanges between old women and children.

But it is the fact that both the old aunt and Mrs. Brown learned their ballads as children and remembered them from childhood that establishes both the age and authenticity of these ballads.[87] Although the written transcriptions of Gordon's ballads date from 1783 and 1800, the ballads themselves can be dated from "before 1759" because they were all learned before she was ten or twelve years old.[88] Robert Jamieson, who used Mrs. Brown's ballads in his *Popular Ballads and Songs*, defends their authenticity simply by noting that she "learnt most of them before she was twelve years old, from old women and maid-servants; what she once learnt, she never forgot."[89] This claim is not absolutely unique to Gordon. Jamieson, for example, also describes a "lady in Aberbrothick" who had "when a child, learnt the ballad from an elderly maid-servant, and probably had not repeated it for a dozen years before I had the good fortune to be introduced to her; it may be depended upon, that every line was recited to me as nearly as possible in the exact form in which she learnt it."[90]

Gordon, herself, emphasizes that "she learned them all when a child," and indeed the memory of the ballads is woven into her memories of childhood. She writes to Tytler:

You judge rightly in supposing that I should take pleasure in recalling those scenes of infancy & childhood which the recollection of those old songs brings back to my mind, it is indeed what Ossian call[s] the joy of grief, the memory of joys past pleasant, but mournful to the soul – but enough of this prattle . . .[91]

Recalling old ballads is like remembering childhood; even writing about them returns Brown to the "prattle" of infancy. "Prattle," as we have seen, signals the separation of words from their meanings, the functioning of words as sounds. Here we can see the extent to which the figure of the old woman – imaged in the antiquarian frontispiece or evoked in the oft repeated citation "from the memory of an old woman" – always overlays the figure of a child. The figure of the old singing woman is, in fact, meant to embody the associations, memories and sounds of childhood.

This image points to all the complexities of childhood audition, retention and reproduction.

Buchan insists that Anna Gordon was not "unduly precocious" in learning her ballads at such a young age and in remembering them so long. For Buchan, early learning and remarkable feats of memory characterize the "woman's tradition" of eighteenth-century Scotland; he lists a number of "very old women" who learned their ballads in "infancy," preserving them in their memory for seventy years or more.[92] Brown's contemporary ballad scholars were more impressed. Of central importance in the discussion (which at times became a debate) about her exceptionally "tenacious" memory is the fact that Gordon never saw any of her ballads in print or in writing. As Robert Anderson reports to Thomas Percy:

It is remarkable that Mrs. Brown ... never saw any of the ballads she has transmitted here, either in print or MS., but learned them all, when a child, by hearing them sung by her mother and an old maid-servant who had been long in the family, and does not recollect to have heard any of them either sung or said by any one but herself since she was about ten years.[93]

Brown's ballads exist apart from any others she might read or even hear; the purity of their form a function of how separate they are from any current time and context. Anna Gordon's level of education and rank make the purity and distinct form of her oral ballads all the more remarkable. Buchan describes her case as a "paradox": "the woman who preserved the finest representatives of the old oral tradition, the tradition of the nonliterate rural folk, was herself an educated woman, daughter of a Professor and wife of a minister."[94]

In Brown's own words describing how she has "lately, by rummaging in a by-corner of my memory, found some Aberdeenshire ballads which totally escaped me before" and in her repeated insistence that she "never saw any of [the ballads] either in print or Manuscript but have kept them entirely from hearing them sung when a child," we begin to see the full importance of childhood, particularly of the child's hearing and memory, to Romantic antiquarianism.[95] Brown's "by-corners" of memory become preserves of childhood and orality marooned in an adult mind and a textual world. The antiquarians describe Brown as an exceptional "depository" of Scottish oral poetry, her memory a "hoard" of old ballads, her mind neatly divided between the oral culture of her childhood and the print culture of her educated adult life.[96] But childhood is not simply associated with orality in this discourse. Childhood represents a privileged oral and *aural* state, one in which what one hears passes unmediated into memory, and what one remembers persists intact and protected. The persistence of childhood memory, its pure preservation within the adult mind, in this way holds the promise of renewed access to a past oral culture. The image of the old woman singing to a child lends authenticity to the ballad collections from both the child's original incorruptible hearing and the woman's access to the childhood "by-corners" of her mind.

Antiquarian interest in Anna Gordon's memory reveals a romance of the child's mind that becomes central to ballad scholarship and children's folklore studies as they develop in the nineteenth and twentieth centuries. This version of childhood memory certainly shows its antiquarian colors. Ballads imagined to be imprinted or impressed on the child's memory and then preserved in dedicated parts of the adult mind have the quality of a "fixed text" and, as such, seriously misrepresent the creative and re-creative dynamics of oral tradition. Writing in the wake of Albert Lord's *The Singer of Tales*, Buchan chastises the "literate mind" which understands the "process of traditional oral transmission" as "merely a process of memorization by rote."[97] Yet Buchan reproduces the Romantic antiquarian map of Gordon's neatly divided mind:

> Mrs. Brown, then, learned her ballad-stories and the old re-creative technique of composition at an early age, retained the ballad-stories in her mind by a purely auditory process without any recourse to writing, and kept them mentally distinct and separate from written material. It is as if she possessed a bicameral mind, the one part literature and the other oral, the one part capable of writing letters, and the other capable of composing ballads orally.[98]

Buchan might have added: the one part adult, the other part child; and indeed he speculates that "it is possible, though, given her father's profession, not entirely probable, that Anna Gordon learned her ballad-stories and method of composition before she learned to read and write."[99] According to Buchan, Gordon learned stories and a "method of composition" in childhood, rather than the exact words of a set of ballads; but it is no less important to him that she learned what she learned in childhood, and that this oral/aural childhood realm persisted, unassimilated and apart, into adulthood. The pure preservation of the child's mind is important to how antiquarians and folklorists situate popular ballads in literary culture and in the literary life of the mind. Scott describes his own relationship to the popular ballad "Hardiknute" in terms similar to those used to describe Gordon and other singers: "I was taught Hardiknute by heart before I could read the ballad myself. It was the first poem I ever learnt – the last I shall ever forget."[100] We should not let the sentimentality of Scott's claim distract us from the cultural theory such literary reminiscences advance: what is first heard is remembered to the last.

The figure of the old singing woman and the antiquarian's characteristic gesture of "I remember from childhood" work together to point to the figure of a child and signal antiquarian investment in a rhetoric and notion of childhood both individually and collectively conceived. We have been tracing an idea of the child's mind and memory as particularly retentive – retaining sounds, forms and images, but not ideas, meanings and semantic content – as well as an idea of the child's specific relationship to language – her insignificant or prattling speech, her capacity to turn words into sounds – both of which emerge alongside and support antiquarian cultural theory and literary practice. In the next chapter we will specify that theory and practice still further, examining antiquarian ideas of the nursery as a cultural space, their strategies for bringing nursery literature into the larger literary field and their strikingly ahistorical historicist sensibility. In their efforts to accommodate popular literature within a larger national literary culture, Romantic antiquarians also bring children and the child-like into Britain's literary life, giving the child who knows not what she sings an important cultural and historical role.

CHAPTER 5

One child's trifle is another man's relic

Popular antiquarianism and childhood formalism

In a 1787 letter, Walter Scott attributes his poetical pursuits to his life-long love of "ballads and other romantic poems," poems which he has "read or heard" from the "earliest period of [his] existence" as a "favourite, and sometimes as an exclusive gratification."[1] It would seem, however, that not all of Scott's beloved ballads provided gratification exclusively, for he recalls a scene much like those Akenside, Aiken and the Edgeworths describe and debate:

I remember in my childhood when staying at Bath for my health with a kind aunt of mine, there was an Irish servant in the house where we lodged, and she once sung me two ballads which made a great impression on me at the time. One filled me with horror. It was about a mason who because he had not been paid for work he had done for a certain nobleman, when that lord was absent, conveyed himself into the castle with the assistance of a treacherous nurse and murdered the lady and her children with circumstances of great barbarity.[2]

The ballad Scott describes here is *Lamkin*, one of the many Scottish ballads that contain an account of infanticide. In most versions of this ballad, a "false nurse" helps Lamkin achieve his revenge. Together, the nurse and the mason fatally wound the infant son so that its cries will bring the mother down the stairs to meet her own death. When the nobleman returns at the end of the ballad, he rights these wrongs by hanging, burning or boiling Lamkin and the nurse to death.

The ballad takes its name from Lamkin's revenge, but the figure of the nurse is the most horrifying, precisely because she uses the forms and practices of her traditional role to kill her charge rather than care for him. In most versions of the ballad, it is she who tells Lamkin to "Stab the babe to the heart wi a silver bokin" and encourages him to kill her mistress. In at least one version, the mother calls down to the nurse to comfort the crying child, saying "There is a silver bolt lies on the chest-head; / Give it to the baby, give it sweet milk and bread." The next stanza describes what the nurse does instead: "She rammed the silver bolt up the baby's nose / Till the blood it came trinkling down the baby's fine clothes."[3]

But the perversion of the nurse's care is most clearly seen in the ballad's central image of Lamkin and the nurse around the cradle: "Then Lamkin he rocked, and the fause nourice sang, / Til frae ilkae bore o the cradle the red blood out sprang." As the nurse sings to the dying child, she mocks her usual practice of singing to amuse and comfort, and the ballad itself becomes implicated in her crimes. Indeed, in these lines the ballad effectively recreates the scene of its own production, suggesting troubling connections between the "fause nourice" and the nurse commonly singing the ballad, between the child in the cradle and the child listening to the ballad's tale. This self-reflective moment, in which the gruesome contents of the ballad spill over into the context of its singing, suggests something potentially horrifying about the traditional forms of ballad singing more generally, about who sings to whom and to what end. The ballad threatens the child who is hearing it sung with an excessive violence that implicates his own nurse; perhaps this is why *Lamkin* made such a "great impression" of horror on Scott in his early childhood.[4]

Scott does not include *Lamkin* in his *Minstrelsy of the Scottish Border*, but not out of any residual squeamishness about the barbarity of the tale. He includes two other infanticide ballads, one of which also features a "fause nourice" and which reminds Scott of a third that he "often heard sung in my childhood." Furthermore, he discusses *Lady Anne*, the fragment of *The Cruel Mother*, and *The Queen's Marie* with no apologies for their sordid content, no acknowledgment or expression of horror whatsoever. In publishing these ballads of child murder, Scott reproduces what was standard fare in ballad revival collections: tales of familial violence in all its possible manifestations, as well as stories of illicit, incestuous affairs and illegitimate children. Ballads of infanticide and child murder, in which mothers and nurses murder their children, often without hesitation or remorse, form a significant share of these tales. They place representations of motherhood and nursing in front of Romantic readers that directly challenge the period's investment in the maternal nature of women, the acculturative role of mothers and nurses, and the idea of a native and national literature passed down from one generation to the next as naturally and as tenderly as a woman normatively cares for a child.

Child murder is a particularly troubling crime for Romantic literary culture; this is, paradoxically, one reason why it was such a popular literary theme in these years.[5] From ballads, old and new, to sentimental novels and prose essays, the scene of infanticide is a significant Romantic topos. Critics usually emphasize the crisis of maternity and female sexuality that such scenes exhibit and explore and, indeed, Romantic representations of infanticide tend to focus on the subjectivity and situation of the woman, perhaps because infants are so resistant to literary representation and impervious to adult inquiry. But infants and the state of infancy, as we have seen, carry larger cultural and historical significations, and child murder stages not only a crisis of maternity, but also a crisis for the period's cultural investments in infancy, childhood and the role children play in cultural production and reproduction. Accompanying the notion of the child's mind and memory as particularly and exactly retentive – insistently repeating and reproducing exterior forms, and yet doing so as unknowing and innocent play – is the idea of childhood and the nursery as a privileged site of cultural memory and preservation. Violence in the nursery, committed by women on the bodies of children, thus threatens an important idea of national literary culture and the innocent autonomy the individual can retain as a cultural subject.

In the previous chapter we traced an idea of the child's mind and memory at the heart of a theory of literary culture articulated first by Romantic antiquarians and continued in literary and folklore studies throughout the nineteenth century. In this chapter we will continue to move between popular antiquarian and folklore texts, between collections of ballads and collections of nursery rhymes, to specify further the theory and practice of literature and the rhetoric of infancy and childhood that emerged in Romantic antiquarian discourse. We will examine antiquarians' complex relationship to Enlightenment historicism, their transformation of "trifles" into "relics," their excessive scholarly apparatus, and their strategies for coping with the scandalous content of popular literature. We will see that the figure of the child and an idea of the child's mind and memory remain critical to a literary theory and practice we will call antiquarian formalism.

The importance of childhood memory and childish "trifles" to Romantic literary culture will thus help us address the question raised by Scott's reflections on *Lamkin* and other infanticide ballads: how do popular antiquarian collections of the Romantic period accommodate the scandalous content of their ballads within the nationalist frame of their project? In antiquarian discourse, the "ancient ballads," "reliques" and "primitive poetry" contained in these collections constitute an "inheritance of Ancient National Minstrelsy"; their rescue and preservation is a "bounden duty on all true and patriotic Scotsmen."[6] Yet the stories these ballads tell are often far from being the "celebration of the acts of Kings, and the warlike deeds of Heroes" that antiquarians such as Peter Buchan claimed them to be.[7] This poetry clearly straddles the fault lines of "popular" literature: both original, primitive and "of the people," at the same time that it is sensational, "vulgar" and exploiting "mass appeal." Most significantly, there is a sharp contradiction between the tales of the ballads, particularly those considered "romantic ballads," and the national value they are made to bear; tales of family violence challenge visions of national continuity, strength or historical perseverance.[8]

Ballad collectors dealt with these challenges in different ways. Infrequently, they offered brief apologies for the subject matter, as Scott does in his introduction to "The Bonny Hynd," a ballad about sibling incest. Slightly more often, the antiquarian firmly assigned the violence and perversion of the ballad's story to the primitive period of its production, as if such things as incest or infanticide no longer occurred or appealed to readers in a "more refined age."[9] But most frequently, the scandalous contents go unnoticed altogether. Scott and his fellow antiquarians simply fail to comment on such material beyond noting different versions, historical accuracies or anachronisms.

The lack of comment on the ballads' sensational stories is less a sign of antiquarian tolerance than it is a strategy for coping with the contradictions and embarrassments created when "popular" literature is re-defined as a "national treasure." Antiquarian collectors manage their difficult content, I will argue, by producing a reading practice that disregards content and privileges form as a vehicle of national cultural transmission. The impressive scholarly apparatus that the ballad revival bequeaths to British literature is, we will see, a way of *not* reading or responding to the contents of popular literature, whether trivial or scandalous; it thus models how a "refined" editor and reader might appreciate popular poetry while still maintaining a proper, critical distance. It also models how the nation can maintain a proper historical distance from the violence of the primitive past while still claiming cultural continuity with that past.

A central strategy, however, is embodied in the figure of the child, who by virtue of a peculiarly retentive and selectively resistant mind and memory, becomes the ideal formalist. Antiquarians construct a strange oral/aural/textual image of the child's mind and memory, re-imagining the child's original, powerful attachment to the ballads – which Scott recalls and cites as the origin of his adult poetic pursuits – as less of an unmediated response to their contents than a pure channeling and retention of their form. The Romantic antiquarian child has a stadial, layered mind in which the poems, stories and other "trifles" of the nation's cultural past remain deeply preserved.

An "antiquarian of popular culture" is today an oxymoron, but in the late eighteenth century and throughout the nineteenth century, literary antiquarians were widely and enthusiastically engaged in defining and defending the "popular." Thomas Percy's *Reliques of Ancient English Poetry*, John Brand's *Popular Antiquities of Great Britain*, Francis Grose's *Classical Dictionary of the Vulgar Tongue* and *Provincial Dictionary*, Joseph Ritson's *Select Collection of English Song* and *Scottish Song in Two Volumes*, Walter Scott's *Minstrelsey of the Scottish Border*, Robert Jamieson's *Popular Ballads and Songs*, Robert Chambers' *Popular Rhymes of Scotland*, James Halliwell's *Nursery Rhymes of England*, and Francis James Child's *The English and Scottish Popular Ballads* are only a few examples of the most influential antiquarian collections of literature, language and custom, many of which included introductory essays with such titles as "Remarks on Popular Poetry," "On the Oral Tradition of Poetry" and "A Historical Essay on the Origin and Progress of National Song." Central to the literary antiquarianism of the Romantic period was the ballad; indeed so pervasive was the interest in ballad recovery, collection and imitation that scholars have often pointed to a "ballad revival" as a crucial component of Romantic literary culture.[10] But "popular literature" in antiquarian discourse also included the songs, rhymes, tales, games and chants of the nursery and kitchen, field and street, private home and public house. All were understood as participating in the customs, superstitions, dialects and local traditions of what we now call "popular culture."[11]

Often ridiculed in the eighteenth century for their dry-as-dust cataloguing of obscure sources, versions, etymologies or histories – always with an eye to the most minute and trivial of details – antiquaries nevertheless developed an aesthetic of literary culture that privileged "authenticity" over literary "refinement"; that read a literary text as representative of a particular historical and cultural moment or as vitally tied to a local or regional tradition; and that valued the literature and lore of the "people" or "folk" as the most expressive of native or national culture.[12] This is, of course, an aesthetic that we recognize as central to British Romanticism more generally, a broad outline of how, in Susan Manning's words, "the significance of antiquarian activities reaches right into the quiddity of Romantic writing."[13] Romantic antiquarianism is not only where we find our own current interest in historical analysis, local detail and material culture mirrored back to us, but also where we can trace the formation of vernacular and national literary culture for the modern, post-Enlightenment age.[14]

In particular, attention to the literary antiquarianism of the period will give us insight into why Romantic accommodations of popular literature involved such strange dating schemes. The cultural logic that enthusiastically conflates the "popular" with the "primitive" is the same that produces the "antiquarian of popular culture." Antiquarian practice developed and elaborated this logic through the course of the eighteenth and nineteenth centuries, systematically dating the popular literature they studied in a distant, disappearing past. If today the study of popular culture is the study of the contemporary, immediate and ephemeral, then it was the study of the ancient, original and enduring.[15] The popular was, simply put, a thing of the past.

The historicizing sensibility of literary antiquarians is part of a larger turn to history and historical explanation that characterizes Romantic writing and culture more generally.[16] Recent discussions of antiquarianism, however, tend to locate it on the margins of that trend, or at least on the margins of our current understanding of that trend. With their recovery, collection and accumulation of objects and relics, antiquaries can be seen as supplying the archive and material evidence for Enlightenment philosophical history, and as exemplifying its empiric–scientific foundations. But those same practices of collection and accumulation too easily pursued for their own sake, and the temptation to convert objects into relics of singular and peculiar value, can also be seen as resisting the synthesizing and universalizing work of theoretical history, and indeed, as resisting narrative drive itself.[17] Indeed, antiquarianism's determination to fix textual and material objects to local sites and traditions of origin is matched only by its reverence for precisely those "relics" and "survivors" that slip free of context to circulate out of time and place. The result is a practice that seems to collapse the poles of "historicism" and "formalism" that literary scholars, for the most part, continue to oppose. Stressing the ancient origins of a popular rhyme at the same time as they celebrated its survival in the nursery (as we shall see them doing), literary antiquarians viewed contemporary cultural forms as overlaid with historical charge and value, creating synchronic hierarchies within vernacular literary culture that replicated diachronic histories of literary progress.

The other way of understanding the strange dating schemes of popular antiquarianism is to note that representing the popular as historically primitive or ancient was also a way of writing it out of existence. Here the work of representation and writing collude. In the case of the popular ballad, for example, antiquarians routinely ignored the street ballads and broadsides of their own day in order to elevate the oldest, original versions of "ancient balladry" that they ascribed to a vanished class of minstrels and bards. This involved minimizing the extent to which ballads circulated in written form and, as the romance of orality took greater hold, increasingly representing the ballad as a pure, embodied oral form.[18] It also involved the invention and evocation of an oral culture prior to (both superceded by and lost to) the antiquarian's own print culture and textual enterprise, thus representing and effecting through writing the passing away of oral tradition. Whether or not the antiquarian practice of transforming oral tradition into written artifacts or fixed texts did more to damage that tradition than to preserve it remains a question of some debate today.[19] What is important for our purposes here is that we understand the antiquarian habit of historicizing popular literature as central to a larger cultural fascination with orality, as part of a sustained effort to investigate the "oral-literate conjunction" that characterizes Romantic literary culture.[20]

Richard Maxwell has described the early *Waverley* novels (themselves so thoroughly and complexly antiquarian in form and sensibility) as "experiments intended to gauge the pastness of the past," which keeps creeping up on, slipping into the present.[21] Maxwell reminds us that antiquarian historicism is as much a theory of the present as of the past, an insight into their cultural practice that, I believe, Scott and his fellow antiquarians shared and explicitly embraced. Working, we might say, to gauge and preserve the pastness in the present, their representations of past literary forms and literary histories were always at the same time accounts of their current cultural field. Nowhere is this more evident than in their treatment of popular literature and, more particularly, in the rhetoric of childhood they use to represent and value popular literary forms.

FROM TRIFLE TO RELIC

Historicizing the popular is, of course, a way of interpreting and valuing literary forms that remains very much with us today. In the Romantic period, as now, the serious study of popular literature required justification and defense. "Antiquing" the ballad or the nursery rhyme removes it to a sufficient distance as to make it a suitable object of study for the proper, refined poet scholar of the eighteenth century.[22] But even at that distance, it required defense, and Romantic antiquarians were usually unprepared to champion the literary merits of these poems. Indeed, they habitually introduced their collections of oral ballads, traditional songs, popular customs and nursery lore with an apology for the triviality of the rhymes, tales, riddles and rituals they gathered. They are "vulgar rites," "trifles" and "trivial verses," and they are of dubious literary and cultural value.[23]

In his "Introductory Remarks on Popular Poetry" in the *Minstrelsy of the Scottish Border*, for example, Walter Scott insists that the old ballads have little literary or poetic merit. While there may be "passages in which the rude minstrel rises into sublimity or melts into pathos," they "occur seldom," and so Scott enumerates exactly how and why popular ballads display "tenuity of thought and poverty of expression," "loose and trivial composition," "sameness and crudity."[24] Thomas Percy referred to the ballads printed in his *Reliques of Ancient English Poetry* as a "strange collection of trash."[25] Almost a century later, James O. Halliwell, the preeminent nineteenth-century collector of nursery rhymes, states: "it is difficult to impress on the public mind the importance of a subject apparently in the last degree trifling and insignificant, or to induce an opinion that the jingles and simple narratives of a garrulous nurse can possess a worth beyond the circle of their own immediate influence."[26]

"Trifles" or "trifling" are terms that recur often in antiquarian discourse, both in their own introductions and apologies, as well as in the critical barbs thrown at them so often in this period. Antiquarian researches are "excessively insignificant," one of the "most fatiguing and least amiable species of trifling," according to an *Edinburgh Review* critic.[27] This is a charge that Scott's fictional antiquary, Oldbuck, tries turning to their credit: "If you want an affair of consequence properly managed, put it into the hands of an antiquary; for, as they are eternally exercising their genius and research upon trifles, it is impossible they can be baffled in affairs of importance."[28] Popular rhymes or tales, fragments of nonsensical verse or sonically driven chants are almost always presented as "trifles," a word which, in this context, confesses their frivolity and insignificance and injects an interesting rhetoric of play into the scholarly pursuits of antiquarians. "Trifle" and "trifling" must therefore take their place next to "prattle" as central terms in the infantilization of Romantic literary culture, in the ways in which Romantic writers engage with and appropriate what is considered childish and infantile. Like "prattle," "trifle" has interesting ways of representing insignificance. A "trifle" is a matter of little value or importance, a thing of little intrinsic value; it is also a toy or trinket. For Romantic antiquarians, literary trifles take on material status as objects and forms that can be rescued, collected, even repaired.

Thus one child's trifle is another man's relic. In his influential collection, *Popular Rhymes of Scotland*, Robert Chambers demonstrates precisely how to transform a trifle into a relic, thereby consolidating a formula for advancing the importance of popular literature that will influence literary and folklore studies for the next century. Cautioning his reader "not to expect here anything profound, or sublime, or elegant, or affecting," he offers instead the following encouragement:

> But if he can so far upon occasion undo his mature man, as to enter again into the almost meaningless frolics of children – if to him the absence of high-wrought literary grace is compensated by a simplicity coming direct from nature – if to him there be a poetry in the very consideration that such a thing, though a trifle, was perhaps the same trifle to many human beings like himself hundreds of years ago, and has, times without number, been trolled or chanted by hearts light as his own, long since resolved into dust – then it is possible that he may find something in this volume which he will consider worthy of his attention.[29]

These rhymes have no "high-wrought literary" value, Chambers admits, or, more accurately, insists. On the one hand, Chambers counters a high literary aesthetic by suggesting an alternative one of "simplicity coming direct from nature." In this, he follows a well-established rhetoric (typically traced through Addison and Wordsworth) of admiring the old British ballads for their simple, natural, native graces.

On the other hand, Chambers embraces the insignificance of his material and asks the reader to do the same. His reader must "undo his mature man," become a child, and "enter again into the almost meaningless frolics of children." For Chambers, the child-like reader is important precisely for his or her ability to appreciate the "almost meaningless." Indeed the "trifles" of his collection, he advises, are meaning*ful* only because they constitute a continuous form of meaninglessness through hundreds of years of national history; it is the "same trifle" sung "to many human beings like himself hundreds of years ago." Here, the sameness of the trifle produces the "likeness" of the human beings across so many years; what the trifle is means nothing, that it has stayed relatively the same and produced the same cultural effect gives it significance.

Chambers locates the value of the popular rhyme not in its literary qualities – its rhymes, images, wit or narrative acuity – but in the historical endurance and cultural continuity it represents and effects. By stressing the age and endurance of even the most "trivial" of rhymes, Chambers turns our attention away from the content or literary value of the rhyme toward the perseverance of its form. His invitation to read like a child thus implies an evaluation of traditional popular literature that empties it of what we typically call "content" and emphasizes the continuity of what we might call its cultural "form," its shape as a vehicle of cultural transmission.

THE OLD AGE OF CHILDISH VERSE

Chambers thus shapes and participates in the rather odd but prevalent convention of introducing verses for the very young by stressing their extreme age and antiquity. Halliwell – who considered his *Nursery Rhymes and Nursery Tales of England* a complement to Chambers' *Popular Rhymes of Scotland* as together containing "nearly all that is worth preserving of what may be called the natural literature of Great Britain" – proclaims the "immense age" of the nursery rhyme.[30] Alice Bertha Gomme, who published the extremely influential *Traditional Games of England, Scotland and Ireland* in the 1890s, values the games and chants of children as "some of the oldest historical documents belonging to our race."[31] Henry Bett, rather extravagantly, introduces his *Nursery Rhymes and Tales* with notices of "incredible" and "extreme" antiquity, as well as "traces of their origin in prehistoric times."[32]

Animating interest in the old age of childish verse is a vivid sense of cultural paradox. "It seems strange that such childish trifles should be amongst the most ancient things of the world," Henry Bett writes; "but it is difficult to exaggerate the extreme tenacity of tradition in little things."[33] The extreme tenacity of tradition in little things – whether in the "childish trifle" or in the child, itself – becomes a founding principle of folklore studies as it develops out of Romantic antiquarian collections. We might trace it from John Brand's insistence in 1795 that "tradition has in no instance so clearly evinced her faithfulness as in the transmittal of vulgar rites and popular opinions," to the Opies' rationale of 1951 that "these trivial verses have endured where newer and more ambitious compositions have become dated and forgotten. They have endured often for nine or ten generations, sometimes for considerably more, and scarcely altered in their journey."[34] "Like the savage," the Opies proclaim, "children are respecters, even venerators, of custom."[35] Cultural continuity quickly becomes a romance of filial allegiance, as Edward Rimbault says of his "old vernacular rhymes of the English Nursery": they have been "traditionally preserved by the people – a people who have ever clung with peculiar fondness to the old customs of their forefathers, and cherished with feelings of delight the rude saws and rhymes of their childhood."[36] Proving the age and antiquity of childhood's trivial verses proves the age and continuity of traditional, native British culture. The more trivial, frivolous and insignificant, the more traditional, ancient and unchanged.

Childhood thus becomes the place where traditional, oral culture thrives in an otherwise modern world, and the nursery becomes a site of cultural memory, a repository for old literary forms and ancient fragments. This construction of childhood as the locus of cultural memory is central to a larger theory of literary and cultural transmission that significantly shapes the development and practice of literary and folklore studies. As the nineteenth-century American folklorist William Newell insists, popular lore does not originate with the peasants, folklore is not necessarily of the folk. "The tradition, on the contrary, invariably came from above, from the intelligent class. If ... usages seem rustic, it is only because the country retained what the city forgot." In his study on *The Games and Songs of American Children*, he extends this theory into the nursery: the country retains what the city forgets; the nursery retains what the country forgets. For Newell, an American folklorist very interested in tracing continuity between American and English culture, it is also important that "the New World has preserved what the Old World has forgotten; and the amusements of children to-day picture to us the dances which delighted the court as well as the people of the Old England before the settlement of the New."[37] Thus children's rhymes and rounds have great "historical interest" for they "preserve for us some picture of the conduct of the ballads, dances, and games which were once the amusement of the palace as of the hamlet."[38]

This theory of cultural transmission locates original invention in the upper, educated or intelligent classes and follows their compositions down to uneducated adults and eventually to the nursery of children. We can find a prototype for this cultural theory in the antiquarian idealization of the minstrels as the original "authors" of the old ballads, a notion advanced by Percy in the introduction to his *Reliques of Ancient English Poetry* and soon after criticized by Joseph Ritson as, in Marilyn Butler's words, "a cheat, or a form of theft, to suppose that culture belonged to the upper orders and merely trickled down to the people, if it reached them at all."[39] But this theory of folk literature was also current well into the twentieth century, repeatedly used to justify the study of this seemingly trivial literary lore. Introducing their *Dictionary of Nursery Rhymes*, Iona and Peter Opie testify: "We believe that if all the authors were known, many more of these 'unconsidered trifles' would be found to be of distinguished birth, a birth commensurate with their long and influential lives."[40] They quote with approval G. K. Chesterton's claim that "so simple a line from the nursery as 'Over the hills and far away' is one of the most beautiful in all English poetry," but then qualify his claim: "Chesterton would have been more exact if he had said 'preserved by the nursery' rather than coming 'from the nursery.' Indeed, the farther one goes back into the history of the rhymes, the farther one finds oneself being led from the cot-side."[41]

Nursery rhymes are thus valued precisely to the extent that they are not of the nursery, but instead represent or provide a window into adult culture of the past. The nursery becomes a place of preservation rather than invention, making its songs and stories both out of place and out of time. "It can be safely stated that the overwhelming majority of nursery rhymes were not in the first place composed for children," the Opies insist, adding: "we can say almost without hesitation that, of those pieces which date from before 1800, the only true nursery rhymes (i.e. rhymes composed especially for the nursery) are the rhyming alphabets, the infant amusements (verses which accompany a game), and the lullabies. Even the riddles were in the first place designed for adult perplexity."[42] For the Opies, the nursery is an echo chamber of other times and places:

[The nursery rhymes] are fragments of ballads or of folk songs ("One misty moisty morning" and "Old woman, old woman, shall we go a-shearing?"). They are remnants of ancient custom and ritual ("Ladybird, ladybird," and "We'll go to the wood"), and may hold the last echoes of long-forgotten evil ("Where have you been all day?" and "London Bridge"). Some are memories of street cry and mummers' play ("Young lambs to sell! young lambs to sell!" and "On Christmas night I turned the spit"). One at least ("Jack Sprat") has long been proverbial. Others ("If wishes were horses," and "A man of words") are based on proverbs.[43]

Here the Opies describe nursery lore as a patchwork of culture, and in doing so, they employ a distinctly antiquarian sensibility. We see this not only in the terms used to describe the rhymes – "survivals," "fragments," "remnants," "echoes," "memories" and "legacy" – but also in the fragmented form they themselves give the poems in this passage punctuated with bits and scraps of rhymes.

Of course nursery rhymes that are "survivals" of an "adult code of joviality" quickly reveal themselves as "strikingly unsuitable for those of tender years." The passage continues:

One ("Matthew, Mark, Luke, and John") is a prayer of Popish days, another ("Go to bed, Tom") was a barrack room refrain. They have come out of taverns and mug houses ("Nose, nose, jolly red nose" still flaunts the nature of its early environment). They are the legacy of war and rebellion ("At the siege of Belle Isle" and "What is the rhyme for porringer?"). They have poked fun at religious practices ("Good morning, Father Francis") and laughed at the rulers of the day ("William and Mary, George and Anne"). They were the diversions of the scholarly, the erudite, and the wits (as Dr. Wallis on a "Twister," Dr. Johnson on a "Turnip seller," and Tom Brown on "Dr. Fell").[44]

The nursery becomes a hodge-podge repository of the forms and traditions from other cultural spaces, many of them (taverns, battlefields, barrack rooms) deeply incongruous with the nursery itself. For the Opies, it is important that the nursery can collect and preserve bits of the barroom and the battlefield while preserving its own innocence, just as children can repeat "rude rhymes" and yet remain "blissfully unconscious of what they [are] singing."

The study of nursery and children's lore in the present thus becomes a way of studying adult culture in the past. Historicizing the nursery rhyme, however, betrays strikingly anti-historicist motives. By tracing these rhymes and tales to a distant and markedly different time and place, antiquarians remove them from their current context, insisting on their value as literary or cultural forms circulating out of their proper time and place. The historical treatment of literary forms practiced by antiquarians and folklorists must thus be understood as strongly formalist in sensibility. Nineteenth- and twentieth-century children's folklore studies continued to practice Romantic antiquarian dating schemes, making the popular "trifles" of the present into antiquarian "relics" of the past. In fact, the powerful myth of childhood as a window into the past and as the preserver of older customs and literary forms – as the place, in short, where modernity remembers the primitive – drove the theory of what children's lore is and why it should be studied throughout much of the twentieth century.

There is, of course, a fantasy of recuperation powerfully at work here, the notion that the child inhabits and moves through earlier cultural and historical stages, making the primitive part of modernity's lived experience. Antiquarians who describe the popular ballad as representing the "infancy of the art of poetry," or value the "early poetry of every nation" as forming a "chapter in the history of the childhood of society," use this rhetoric of infancy and childhood to enable and reinforce these acts of comparison and exchange between individual and nation, the cultural present and the historical past.[45] Thus, as we have seen, Robert Chambers describes the Scottish child of the "old nursery system" as going "through in a single life all the stages of a national progress" by hearing and learning the old songs and ballads in his infancy.[46]

By describing nursery rhymes and traditional ballads as ancient and of the past, antiquarianism places popular literature on the present vernacular cultural map. A mythology of childhood and nursery cultures as the last preserves of otherwise lost and forgotten literary forms plays a significant role in giving value to the otherwise "meaningless" tales and hums of infancy and the everyday. But the calibrations of individual development to national progress offered by Blair, Chambers and others, and the understanding of literary cultural hierarchies *through and as* a developmental history of literary forms, produce antiquarian investment in a childhood both individually and culturally conceived. Primitive, trivial and popular literature is given a place in both the past and the present, and the figures of child and nursery facilitate movement between them.

NOTES AND OCCASIONAL DISSERTATIONS

I have argued that Romantic antiquarian dating schemes which transform the "trifle" of the present into the "relic" of the past are both historicist – attempting to situate a literary piece within an original historical context – and formalist – celebrating and valuing those bits of literature that slip free of their historical context and persist into the present. In antiquarian accounts of ballad singers and nursery culture, children are credited with hearing, remembering, reciting and thus reproducing and preserving the oldest, most traditional elements of a national literary culture. But running through this discussion (and that of the preceding chapter) has been the question of what, exactly, the child is hearing and repeating. From the folklorists hearing bits of the bar-room and battlefield innocently sung in the nursery, and the educational philosophers warning of "*Raw-Head* and *Bloody Bones*" terrifying the young, to the child who learns words as sounds free of meaning or fixed significance, the question of how children understand and relate to the cultural forms they preserve and reiterate marks a larger concern about cultural production and reproduction.

The Opies' account of a Coronation tea in which the children inno-cently sang crude parodies of national songs stages the problem of how to accommodate the trivial, vulgar and nonsensical bits of popular poetry to a thriving national literary culture. Repeatedly the "trifles" of the literary antiquarian or folklorist are presented as "meaningless" and "inane" in content, "crude" and "trivial" in composition. As we have seen, these trifles take on value only as they become relics, forcibly extracted from their present context, placed and dated in the past. In the case of the Romantic ballad collections, which will be our focus now, the monotony and inanity of the ballads are less of a problem than their spectacular gore and pervasive immorality. Indeed, nothing categorizes these ballads as "popular" so much as their violent and sexual sensationalism. Gruesome death, bodily dismemberment, incestuous affairs, illegitimate children murdered by their mothers or nurses – all of this is standard fare in the ballad revival collections. Despite Scott's particular memory of horror, *Lamkin* is more representative than it is extreme. This sensationalist fare posed problems not only for the proper scholarly posture of the antiquarian collectors, but also for the nationalist framework of their project, a cultural agenda that was particularly explicit in the Scottish collections.

How then did the antiquarians of the Romantic period accommodate the scandalous content of their ballads to the nationalist frame of their project? How did they articulate a "national literature" that could include popular literature both trivial and sensational? Standard editorial practice, in fact, changed a good deal over the course of the period as these questions were debated. Both Percy and Scott, for example, often cleaned up and "improved" the old ballads, a practice that involved filling in missing lines, creating an ideal composite version from many competing versions, or replacing crude references and images with more "refined" lines of their own manufacture.[47] By the 1820s, however, when William Motherwell was collecting, the practice of "piecing and patching up [a ballad's] imperfections, polishing its asperities, correcting its mistakes, embellishing its naked details, purging it of impurities, and of trimming it from top to toe with tailor-like fastidiousness" was out of favor and like to "breed a sickly loathing in the mind of every conscientious antiquary." These "pernicious and disingenuous practices," according to Motherwell, "lay the broad axe to the root of everything like authenticity in oral song."[48] Indeed, the difference between Percy's collection of the 1760s and Motherwell's collection of the 1820s would suggest that the major achievement of British Romanticism was the ascendancy of "authenticity" as a preeminent literary category.[49]

Authenticity, as Susan Stewart has argued, becomes a literary value when literature is given an "external history," when its significance is located not in intrinsic qualities but in its capacity to represent and express an extrinsic, original moment.[50] The popular rhymes and ballads of Romantic antiquarianism, with their trivial content or insignificant literary worth, are thus valued not only for age and endurance, but also as representations of the primitive culture thought to have produced them. Antiquarian editors typically produced an excessive number of headnotes, footnotes and introductory essays all commenting on the language and stories of the ballads and seemingly testifying to the collector's interest in the original historical context of the ballads. Scott's *Minstrelsy of the Scottish Border* exemplifies the scholarly excess of the ballad revival. Its three introductory essays and lengthy "Notes and Occasional Dissertations" introducing the individual ballads – including, for example, the eighty-two page introduction to the "Tale of Tamlane," itself only fourteen pages in length – demonstrate Scott's self-proclaimed interest in contributing "to the history of my native country; the peculiar features of whose manners and character are daily melting and dissolving into those her sister and ally."[51] Scott's attention to the details of the ballads would seem to signal his own level of interest in their contents as well as the degree and kind of attention he expects from his readers. But his interest in the "history of my native country" is, in fact, not that of an historian; it is that of a nationalist antiquarian whose sense of the past is both that which is in danger of being lost and that which is capable of being rescued and recovered. The antiquarian, in other words, is less interested in history than in history's artifacts and "remains," less interested in the past than in the "antique," the object collected and preserved from the past. Ultimately the ballads are important to Scott less as historical records than as antiques, objects or cultural forms that have survived the course of history, more or, hopefully, less altered in the process.[52]

Scott, in other words, is interested in the content of the ballads in order to prove their form as a vehicle of national cultural transmission. This explains both the excess and arbitrariness of his scholarly commentary: these notes are produced for reasons beyond what the content of the ballads demands. The effect in the *Minstrelsy* is that of a rather arbitrary accumulation of stories, facts and definitions, one that does not explain or illuminate the ballads so much as call attention to its own supplementary information, a scholarly apparatus that accompanies Scott's mixed attitude of praise and denigration toward the ballads themselves. If there are "grand and serious beauties" in the ballads, he comments, they "occurred but rarely to the old minstrels; and, in order to find them, it became necessary to struggle through long passages of monotony, languor, and inanity."[53] Scott's ballads often sound like Chambers' rhymes, inane and "almost meaningless."

What most plagues the poetic merit of these ballads according to Scott is the "joint-stock" of rhymes and phrases that the "ballad-maker" uses, "thereby greatly facilitating his own task, and at the same time degrading his art by his slovenly use of over-scutched phrases." Even worse, "ballad-mongers" use these stock lines to spare themselves the "labour of actual composition."[54] Clearly Scott is running up against the ways in which popular literature – first oral tradition, then a commercial, print-culture of "ballad-mongering" – refuses to conform to a high poetic ideal of individual inspiration and composition. The stability of what characterizes "good poetry," however, should not be assumed; Scott's discussion reveals that the categories of both "refined" and "popular" poetry are in the process of being defined against each other. Here the collective and commercial qualities of the popular ballad reaffirm the importance of originality and compositional effort to "good poetry."

Scott's discussion of the popular ballad's poetic shortcomings is most striking for the extent to which he defines the problems of "over-scutched phrases" and "dull and tedious iteration" as products of the ballad's formal charge. The repetition of words and phrases simply aids transmission, as Scott writes: "If a message is to be delivered, the poet seizes the opportunity of saving himself a little trouble, by using exactly the same words in which it was originally couched, to secure its being transmitted to the person for whose ear it was intended."[55] Indeed, when the exact words or "over-scutched phrases" are *not* used, the integrity of the ballad tradition is threatened. Scott describes the course of "innumerable instances of transmission" *not* as a vital oral tradition, but as a possible threat to the "authenticity" of the ballad. He asks us to consider that over the "long course of centuries," the ballads "have been transmitted through the medium of one ignorant reciter to another, each discarding whatever original words or expressions time or fashion had, in his opinion, rendered obsolete, and substituting anachronisms by expressions taken from the customs of his own time." The trouble with these ignorant reciters in Scott's opinion, however, is that they are not ignorant enough. He continues:

And here it may be remarked, that the desire of the reciter to be intelligible, however natural and laudable, has been one of the greatest causes of the deterioration of ancient poetry. The minstrel who endeavoured to recite with fidelity the words of the author, might indeed fall into errors of sound and sense, and substitute corruptions for words he did not understand. But the exercise of a slight degree of ingenuity on the part of a skilful critic could often, in that case, revive and restore the original meaning; while the corrupted words became, in such cases, a warrant for the authenticity of the whole poem.[56]

The desire "to be intelligible," to have the ballad mean something to its audience, results in the "deterioration" of the poetry. In other words, an interest in content threatens the ballad's integrity as a vehicle or form of transmission. Far better for the minstrel to recite something he cannot understand, learning the sounds of words rather than the meaning of words. The "errors of sound and sense" that may result are then not only easily repaired, they are also "warrant" for the ballad's age and authenticity.

In Scott's description of oral tradition, the content and form of the ballad are opposed to and work against one another. The preservation of the ballad's form requires either repetitive, degraded content or a total lack of attention to content. In the *Minstrelsy*, this representation of oral transmission leads to an aesthetic evaluation of popular literature that encourages a particular reading practice. Scott insists that the ballads have little poetic merit or significant meaning and suggests that their value instead lies in their ability to serve as a vehicle back to the "childhood of society." The "moral philosopher," the "historian of an individual nation," and the "admirers of poetry as an art" should be interested in these ballads not because of their content, but because of their capacity for what we now call cultural transmission, their formal ability to shape and carry a continuous, national culture. Since this quality only becomes evident through the scholarly apparatus that frames each ballad, Scott's notes and introductions produce a reading practice that makes their own erudite commentary central to the proper appreciation of popular literature.

Disregarding the content of the literature they collect is, in fact, a characteristic gesture of antiquarian practice. In this way, Scott's "Introductory Remarks on Popular Poetry" exemplifies Pierre Bourdieu's account of how an aesthete approaches popular art. "Whenever he appropriates one of the objects of popular taste," Bourdieu writes, the aesthete "introduces a distance, a gap – the measure of his distant distinction . . . by displacing the interest from the 'content', characters, plot etc., to the form, to the specifically artistic effects which are only appreciated relationally, through a comparison with other works which is incompatible with immersion in the singularity of the work immediately given."[57] Here Bourdieu uses "form" in the sense of "artistic effects" and not in the

cultural and antiquarian sense of "artifact" or "vehicle." But his description of the way in which the aesthete resists "immersion in the singularity
of the work immediately given" perfectly describes Scott's editorial practice in the *Minstrelsy*, allowing us to see his excessive production of notes
and commentary as, in fact, resistance to immersion in an individual
ballad.

Like Scott, Bourdieu's aesthete aims to appreciate a work "'independ-
ently of its content,'" and does so by a tendency to "bracket off the
nature and function of the object represented and to exclude any 'naïve'
reaction – horror at the horrible, desire for the desirable, pious reverence
for the sacred ... in order to concentrate solely upon the mode of
representation, the style, perceived and appreciated by comparison to
other styles."[58] The aesthete's formal knowledge and reading practice
establish his class status and its cultural capital. Bourdieu's analysis of
the aesthetic disposition is useful for our discussion of Scott's antiquarianism because it suggests that Scott's denigration or disregard of the ballads'
contents is precisely what establishes his proper, scholarly and refined
response to this popular literature.

Romantic antiquarianism is well aware that the appeal of "popular"
ballads to the "people" is their sensational contents. In the introduction to
his collection, *Minstrelsy Ancient and Modern*, William Motherwell points
out that many ballads present "domestick Tragedies" and attributes this to
the "appetite in the vulgar mind for true incident" which, he continues,
remains evident today in the popularity of "miserable rhymes, hawked
about the streets, and palmed off as the poetick effusions of notorious
criminals under sentence of death."[59] Motherwell follows Scott's example
of paying little notice to the contents of the ballads that he publishes, but
he does discuss the problems created by editors who do not follow this
practice of disregard. The "Ancient Minstrel," according to Motherwell,
does not hesitate to "call a spade a spade," and "the Modern affects to
shudder at the grossness and vulgarity of antiquity," stigmatizing the
"Muse of Antiquity as being rather 'high kilted.'"[60] This obviously clichéd
way of distinguishing oneself from the vulgar content of popular literature
is both misguided and hypocritical, according to Motherwell:

In truth, it is by such impertinent and pernicious labors [of re-appareling the
"high-kilted" Muse in a "trailing gown"] that the obscenities of early writers
become disgustingly obtruded on the publick eye. Had they been allowed to pass
uncommented on, they would never have called a blush to the innocent cheek, or
in the unaffectedly pure mind have wakened one unhallowed thought.... In
their bitter wrath and in their lachrymose exclamations against the licentiousness

of ancient song ... these well-meaning individuals not unfrequently manifest a lurking affection for their task, and a perfect acquaintance with its subject, seldom to be found in conjunction with that unspotted purity and extraordinary refinement and maiden-like delicacy which they profess.[61]

Editorial attention of any kind to the sensational content of the ballads becomes, in this passage, evidence of a "lurking affection" for that content, a desire no different than the vulgar mind's unending appetite for shocking incident. Motherwell, like Scott before him and antiquarianism more generally, would rather demonstrate how *not* to respond to the content of popular ballads, how to let their scandals "pass uncommented on." His aim is instead to produce a reading practice that can appreciate popular literature without participating in popular response.

The result is, once again, exemplary formal attention: discussion of style at the level of variations, corrections, "authenticity," and an interest in the details of the tale only as they can be traced back to a geographical or historical origin. Here we can return to the ballad of infanticide with which we began the chapter; for Motherwell's formal reading practice has its best example in the notes to his version of *Lamkin*, entitled *Lambert Linkin*. His introduction to the ballad lists and assesses its other published versions; suggests that his version establishes the correct "name and nickname of the revengeful builder"; and confesses that discovering the exact location of the castle in question has proven as difficult as fixing the "topography of Troy." The stabbing of the infant and beheading of the mother, the nurse's suggestion to Lamkin that "ye'll be laird o' the Castle, / And I'll be ladye," Lamkin's eventual hanging and the nurse's burning, are never mentioned in Motherwell's commentary on the poem. Indeed, Motherwell's one footnote to the ballad would seem to exemplify a determination *not* to acknowledge the content of the tale. To the lines describing the central scene of the ballad – "Belinkin he rocked / And the fause nurse she sang, / Till a' the tores o' the cradle / We' the red blude down ran" – Motherwell attaches this note:

Tores. The projection or knobs at the corners of old fashioned cradles, and the ornamental balls commonly found surmounting the backs of old chairs. Dr. Jamieson does not seem to have had a precise notion of this word. *Vide* IV. Vol. of his Dictionary, *voce Tore*.[62]

Calling attention to the structure, style or *form* of the cradle, Motherwell ignores its contents, even as those contents overflow the form of the cradle. The difficulty of these lines for Motherwell, the anxiety perhaps provoking the pedantry of this footnote, is that they, in fact, dismantle the original, authenticating scene of the ballad, that of the woman singing to the child, and undermine Motherwell's own formal practice to the extent that it relies on the smooth and repeated transmission of ballads from woman to child, from woman to child again.

In this way, the ballad or tale of child murder is not simply another instance of the sensational violence that characterizes the traditional ballads but a crime that causes the antiquarian collector particular anxiety. The horrors of *Lamkin* felt by Scott as a child do not seem to trouble the adult collectors, although one might read their careful lack of attention to the details of the ballads' gory infanticides as attempts to suppress the circulation of sensational affect around their adult, scholarly texts. Likewise their insistence that the crime of infanticide is a symptom of a more violent and primitive past and is, therefore, less relevant and less interesting to their more refined, contemporary audience is an attempt to relegate and contain the horror of infanticide to the cultural past. The childish response of horror to the infanticide ballad can be safely recalled on both the personal and cultural levels because childhood works as a container for such affective responses to literature.

But the scene of infanticide, especially as it is evoked in *Lamkin*, carries some adult and, in fact, some peculiarly antiquarian horrors of its own that are not so easily contained. Indeed, a ballad such as *Lamkin* dismantles a key image of antiquarian literary theory, that of the mother or nurse and child, threatening notions of cultural transmission and the natural continuities of national literature. If collectors such as Scott and Motherwell repeatedly insist that the content and the form of the traditional ballads are opposed to each other and must be held apart by the discerning editor, the infanticide ballad insists that its story cannot be cordoned off from its formal charges. In the ballad of child murder, content directly threatens form, as the mother or nurse who should sing and care for the child instead harms the child, violently cutting short the course of cultural transmission and reproduction that the figures of mother and child embody. The harm to the infant deals a blow to antiquarian formalism and, as we shall see, to their hope for innocence and individual autonomy persisting within the cultural field.

MEN AT WORK, CHILDREN AT PLAY

The formalism of these ballad collections works not simply to model the appropriate, detached relationship to the sensationalism of popular literature, nor simply to establish and reinforce the differences between popular and refined literatures. It is also motivated by the desire to claim a continuous national culture which is as free as possible from the familial and various other "border" conflicts that these ballads otherwise insist upon. Reviving the literature of the past and describing it as "national" always risks reviving the conflicts, prejudices and violence of that past. Scott and his fellow antiquarians manage this risk largely through their formal appreciation of the ballads and the scholarly apparatus it generates. Their reading and editorial practice, by what it revives and what it resists, enacts what we might call a formal nationalism, one that defines the nation around the continuity of cultural forms, rather than in the stories, characteristics and creeds that these forms express.[63]

Chambers, who is, in fact, less invested in the antiquity of the ballads than many of his fellow antiquarians, provides an example of this formal understanding of the ballads even at a moment when he questions the exact degree of continuity they represent. "It would be absurd to contend, that these compositions have existed in their present shape for a great length of time," he insists. "All that can be said in favour of their antiquity, is, that they are the last *shape* or *form* into which the stories which amused our earliest ancestors have been resolved" (his emphasis).[64] In order to claim that the stories of the ballads are properly assigned to a distant past, rather than to the present, Chambers must, of course, ignore the reports of familial violence, supernatural occurrence and base crime that made up the popular culture of his own day and any other. In order to state the antiquarian commonplace that these stories "have the appearance of having been conceived in the very cradle of human nature" and are "only such simple and familiar incidents as take place in a rude state of society," he must reject the possibility that these stories continue to be repeated because they continue to be, in some way, topical. Placing these stories at an historical arm's length, Chambers turns to the "shape" or "form" of the ballads as that which, always changing and evolving, nevertheless establishes a line of continuity between "us" and "our earliest ancestors."

The formal nationalism of the antiquarians and its favorite form, the ballad, thus conceive of nation and literature quite differently than that literary form usually associated with the nation, the epic. The move from epic to ballad as the privileged form of national literature involves a number of adjustments in how the nation is imagined: scenes of domestic women and children on knees replace those of courtly bards and royal audience; the work of transcription replaces that of translation; primitive origins replace heroic foundations. While the antiquarians often claim the legacy of Homeric bards and heroic minstrelsy in the prose introductions to their collections, the ballads necessitate a radically different relationship to the national past than that proffered by the epic. Rather than relating the modern nation through elegy and reverence to an idealized version of itself projected back into an absolute and inaccessible past, the ballad equates personal and national nostalgia and makes longing and loss its central affective orientations toward an equally inaccessible past.[65] For the ballad, the nation is located not in a particular past or official story, but in an authentic scene of oral transmission. To put it crudely: the epic imagines a nation of strong content and kings; the ballad imagines a nation of unchanging form and children.

The formal practice of the ballad revival therefore embraces the child as its ultimate formalist. Able, according to Chambers, to enjoy "meaningless frolics," children are also able to approach the all too meaningful as meaningless, hearing, even learning by rote, ballads they do not fully comprehend. In the child's mind and mouth, the most violent ballad or vulgar song can become, in the words of that valued Swansea contributor, "joyful noise." The child, equipped with the incorruptible hearing and memory that we saw attributed to Mrs. Brown thus becomes Scott's desired "ignorant" reciter, the ignorance cleansed of vulgarity and translated into the idealized form of childhood innocence. Not fully understanding the ballad's story, the child learns its words more by sound than by sense; what the child learns, she never forgets. This ideal child is thus able to "recite with fidelity the words of the author," producing something more like a "fixed text" of the written world than a re-creative ballad of the oral. Penny Fielding has described the paradox troubling Scott's *Minstrelsy* as his investment in both orality's purity of origins as well as its impurity of transmission.[66] The figure of the child acquires its significance for Scott and his fellow antiquarians by resolving this paradox, by inhabiting a pure oral, pre-literate state and, at the same time, enacting a pure transmission. The ideal child represents what Scott wants the form of the ballad to be, but what he must always lament it is not: a fixed text in oral form, an embodied text.

The child's formalism not only promises a pure, formal transmission; it also represents the fantasy of cultural innocence persisting within the forms and practices of cultural knowledge. Antiquarian and folklore collections of children's lore and literature repeatedly give us the figure of a child, nurse or mother who does not fully comprehend what she sings. The nurse needs to provide comfort or discipline, but unknowingly inhabits and perpetuates a vast cultural heritage: "The British Nurse in her ignorance may have found [nursery rhymes] convenient to her hand, but she little knew, poor woman, on what funds of mythology and literature she was drawing."[67] Children may have a "touching faith in the novelty of their oral acquisitions," proclaiming their original invention; but the child cracks his jokes and verbal pranks "little thinking that he is flogging a joke his father and his grandfather knew" or is "perpetuating an illusion which has passed from brow to brow since Shakespeare's time."[68] On the one hand, such comments establish the superior, knowing status of the scholar and collector who can pity the poor woman or child for their impoverished sense of cultural history. On the other hand, and particularly in the case of the child, this lack of full knowledge and agency becomes a playful innocence and becomes, for the collector, a fantasy of cultural innocence persisting within the forms and practices of cultural knowledge.

Understanding childhood as an oral, original state places the child on the cusp of the cultural world; the definitive object of acculturation, she is not yet fully a cultural subject, not yet fully subjected. The child who knows not what she sings represents an illusory, because imaginary, relationship to culture in which one can play with and participate in cultural forms without being subjected to their power. Bourdieu's aesthete is again relevant to our discussion because, significantly, Bourdieu compares him to a child:

To be able to play the games of culture with the playful seriousness which Plato demanded, a seriousness without the spirit of seriousness, one has to belong to the ranks of those who have been able, not necessarily to make their whole existence a sort of children's game, as artists do, but at least to maintain for a long time, sometimes a whole lifetime a child's relation to the world. (All children start life as baby bourgeois, in a relation of magical power over others and, through them, over the world, but they grow out of it sooner or later.)[69]

The aesthete's detachment from economic urgency here becomes a child's relation of "magical power" over others and the world. The child has "magical power" over the world to the extent that all its stories, songs, pictures, images are equally available and suitable for games and play, all are equally meaningful and meaningless. The adult aesthete retains this magical power in his belief that "beautiful" art can be made "from objects socially designated as meaningless ... or as ugly and repulsive ... or as misplaced."[70] But this belief that all objects are equally meaningful and meaningless, all equally suitable for artistic production, relies on a firm sense that these objects are fundamentally not related to or determinative of one's self. The "baby bourgeois" who never grows up maintains a confidence in his detachment from cultural objects, in his power to play with, interpret and evaluate cultural forms without in any way being a part or product of those forms.

Bourdieu's "baby bourgeois" helps us understand one more connection between the antiquarian and the child, as well as to understand what is perhaps at stake for the antiquarian when a child is killed in a ballad or tale: the child represents a relation to culture that the antiquarian would have for himself, particularly as he revives the scandalous stories of popular ballads. In dwelling on the childhood of Mrs. Brown, or in recalling his own early love of ballads, the antiquarian is less interested in differentiating between his adult, scholarly practice and the child's naïve enthusiasm, than he is in connecting his own formal practice to a playful, original formalism. Chambers' invitation to approach traditional, oral literature as a child, to "undo [one's] mature man, as to enter again into the almost meaningless frolics of children," implies that antiquarian pursuits and childish games share a delicate, even paradoxical, cultural negotiation: their meaningless frolics make them national, bring them into culture, at the same time that they manifest an original innocence or enduring autonomy within the national, cultural field.

CHILDREN'S DARKER DOINGS

We have seen this romance of innocence surviving the most crude, violent, partisan or scandalous cultural forms in Iona and Peter Opie's account of the Swansea girls singing a bawdy parody of the Welsh national anthem at a 1937 school Coronation tea. Their gloss on this scene – "just as one child can be unaware of what he is saying, so can innocence bless a crowd" – reads like a benediction of popular literature in the antiquarian style.[71] Here at the conclusion of this chapter, we can return to the Opies' influential mid-twentieth-century account of children's folklore to see their elaboration of antiquarian formalism, their version of the child's playful, formalist relationship to popular culture. The map of the child's mind offered by the Opies in *The Lore and Language of Schoolchildren* is also a literary cultural map and one that draws on antiquarian formalism for its ideas and aesthetics.

The paradox of the child's inventive yet conservative relationship to cultural material, as we have seen, has shaped the study of children's folklore and become one of the central "mysteries" in its theory of cultural invention and transmission. In *The Lore and Language of Schoolchildren*, Iona and Peter Opie approach this mystery from several different angles.

They present children as "tradition's warmest friends" whose "basic lore and language seems scarcely to alter from generation to generation." Yet this claim argues against the more widespread fear that "standardized education, mass entertainment, and national periodical literature have already subverted local traditions and characteristics," and in the 1950s, the Opies must acknowledge the influence of film and television on children's lore.[72] In doing so, they often appear to contradict themselves. After lamenting, for example, that "even among Scottish children the name Charlie now conjures up the picture of a doleful clown, rather than a bonnie prince," the Opies offer this confident assessment of children's traditional life:

But popular as "film star" rhymes undoubtedly are, it is worth remembering that they do not comprise more than 3 per cent of the oral rhymes collected. When one contemplates the amount of money, and talent, and publicity which is expended on the cinema, radio, and T.V., and the amount of time some children give to these entertainments, it is perhaps remarkable how little the new arts have affected child lore. Indeed, one cannot help gaining the impression that by and large the cinema and T.V. only have superficial effects on schoolchildren.[73]

The popular culture of cinema and television has only "superficial effects" on the culture of children, representing only the latest in a series of topical, contemporary influences. When describing the lore of "1945–1958," for example, the Opies comment that the children's "post-war scene" was notable for "pre-fabs, spivs, the Festival of Britain, flying saucers, the ascent of Everest, the Coronation, Teddy Boys, and a wave of particularly unsavoury murders." Each of these, they note, "left some impression on the child lore of Britain." But they add this caution: "Not that we must fall into the error of supposing that the young had suddenly become creative. Children merely, as the old proverb has it, 'pick up words as pigeons peas, and utter them again as God shall please.'"[74] As they catalogue the various "topical rhymes" of 1930 to 1958 (under such headings as "The Second World War," "Charlie Chaplin," "Popeye" and "Dog Film Stars") and simultaneously insist that children are *not* creative, the Opies seem to suggest that children reproduce (even channel) the culture around them with little inventive agency of their own.

To the paradox of the inventive yet conservative child, we should thus add that of Rousseau's impressionable yet impenetrable child, for the Opies insist that despite the wave of current names and events that wash through children's rhymes, there is a deeper, less accessible cultural channel. That is, they cope with the contradictions in their theory of children and children's lore by layering the cultural life of the child:

Two distinct streams of oral lore flow into the unending river of schoolchild chant and chatter, and these two streams are as different from each other as slang and dialect. The slangy superficial lore of comic songs, jokes, catch phrases, fashionable adjectives, slick nicknames, and crazes, in short that noise which is usually the first that is encountered in playground and street, spreads everywhere but, generally speaking is transitory. The dialectal lore flows more quietly but deeper; it is the language of the children's darker doings: playing truant, giving warning, sneaking, swearing, snivelling, tormenting and fighting. It belongs to all time, but is limited in locality.[75]

It is important to note that the child's "deeper" dialectal lore is taken out of time – here it "belongs to all time" and later it "is so time-worn indeed that it cannot be dated" – while simultaneously put firmly in place – it is "limited in locality" and thus some terms can be "shown to have belonged to their present localities not merely for the past two or three generations, but for centuries."[76] The Opies thus participate in that trick of historical and cultural intersection that assigns certain geographical points (the regional, the local, the rural) historical values of an earlier, more primitive period.

What is also important here is the way in which the figure of the child and the culture of childhood can accommodate different time/place intersections of history and culture. Indeed the Opies encode the various elements of children's culture as superficial and current, or deep and traditional, locating them in the historical geography of the child's mental and social life. For example, the language and rituals children use to "regulate their relationships with each other" – what the Opies term the child's "code of oral legislation" – are both regional or dialectal, and permanent, traditional and primitive. The "juvenile language of significant terms and formulas" whereby the schoolchild "conducts his business with his fellows" is a "legacy of the days when the nation itself was younger and more primitive" and is usually "of barbarian simplicity."[77] After describing the ritual of "bets" – two boys lick thumbs and press them together to seal a wager or promise truth – the Opies comment: "so it is that an ancient manner of securing a wager or bargain – for countless generations an accepted token in Scottish life – lives on and retains its significance in the seclusion of children's playgrounds."[78] Of particular interest to the Opies is the child's "truce term," the word he uses to gain "immediate but temporary relief" to which "there is now no exact equivalent in adult speech."[79] These terms vary widely from region to region (the Opies suggest that Britain has "nine main truce-term territories"), yet they are usually the oldest terms in the children's language ("a medieval knight offered his opponent 'barlay,' and children today in the north-west seek respite with the same cry").

"Two apparently conflicting emotions are active in schoolchild language: respect for tradition and desire for fun," the Opies suggest, and again they map tradition onto dialect and fun onto innovative and current slang. Money must be particularly of the moment as it is most susceptible to slang terms: "brass, lolly, tin, dough, mazuma, moolah, dosh (common), sploosh, bees and honey, and champagne coupons." Words of honour, as we might expect, are more stable, traditional and dialectal. But so are the names for birds and animals: "blackie (blackbird), barker or growler (dog), moggy (cat), drummer (snipe), horse-stinger (dragonfly), Joey (owl), Scribbly Jack (yellowhammer), spuggy (sparrow), and stiggy (starling)."[80] Children express approval in fashionable, ever-changing terms (is their assent superficial?): "topping," "ripping," "super," "wizard" "smashing." But "terms of disapproval, on the other hand, scarcely alter from generation to generation," suggesting what any parent often feels, that the child's "no" is spoken with the force and conviction of the ages.

This theory of the layered child as only superficially engaged with her contemporary cultural context and more deeply and permanently participating in traditional, ancient lore allows the Opies to reconcile the inventive, fun-loving, slang-slinging child with the conservative, formulaic, dialect- and tradition-bound child. It also gives them a literary theory of how the rhymes and chants of children can be both topical and traditional. Topical rhymes, they admit, have an immediate value to the student of oral lore because they betray the era to which they belong. Or do they? As they document the King of France, Napoleon, the Boers and Kaiser Bill marching up to the top of the hill and marching down again, they suggest that the most topical rhyme may only have "the trappings of a particular period." Current names and new words are put into the old, reliable rhyme or form. What Scott observed with dismay as the deterioration of ancient verse, the Opies are able to celebrate, valuing both the innovation and the conservation at work in traditional lore. "Topical rhymes," they conclude "can have as deep roots as any other kind of oral verse."[81] This is a formal analysis of children's chants that can be traced from the Romantic antiquarians through Alice Bertha Gomme's collection *The Traditional Games of England, Scotland, and Ireland* where she admits that "there is, probably, not one game in the same condition, especially as regards words, as it was fifty or a hundred years ago; but

I consider the 'form' or 'method' would remain practically the same even if the words get materially altered."[82] Gomme's formal analysis allows her, as it does the Opies, to find a long historical tradition in even the most topical games, rhymes and chants of children.

Underlying this notion of the formal continuities present in children's lore and the formalism of the child's acts of cultural reproduction is what we might call a notion of the child's stadial mind, one which follows from the idea of the child's stadial development. Chambers elaborated a central cultural fantasy when he described the growth and development of the individual as repeating the stages of cultural progress. The child who begins his life in the old Scottish nursery "might be said to go through in a single life all the stages of a national progress," from the "Gothic age" of the nursery through to the "present age" of adulthood.[83] Nineteenth-century social science develops this notion into a formula whereby children can be equated with "savages," children's games and rhymes compared to the rituals of "primitives" all over the world. By the time the Opies describe their children as little savages, this stadial theory has also met up with psychology's depth analysis and the idea that the individual never leaves behind those early stages of childhood, but instead carries them in the unconscious depths of the mind. The diachronic narrative of the child's development now becomes a synchronic layering of the child's mind; history is remapped onto mental geography. Thus the Opies can insist that even when a child seems most modern, there are deeper, older cultural claims manifested. "Outwardly the children in the back streets and around the housing estate appear to belong to the twentieth century, but ancient apprehensions, even if only half believed in, continue to infiltrate their minds." Ultimately the Opies' children do not exist in the contemporary moment, no matter how much the current slang peppers their speech. We should not be surprised: "it must, after all, be borne in mind that the children here under observation are only at the stage of mental development sometimes ascribed to a savage tribe, whom anthropologists are not at all surprised to find dominated by superstition."[84]

The child thus becomes a critical figure of mediation between individual and collective memory, individual and cultural development, the present and the past. Equated mentally and socially with the "savage," the child is the primitive in our midst, a figure of an earlier cultural stage and one who carries past literary forms into the present and future. As such, the child carries the promise that each adult once had the child's unmediated access to a primitive culture and, perhaps even more important, an original or innocent relationship to culture. Bourdieu's aesthete and artist make their lives into "a sort of children's game," maintaining a magical power over others and the world. Bourdieu's "baby bourgeois" thus also helps us see the extent to which a rhetoric of child's play and of childish innocence underpins our sense of culture and cultural agency. In her collection of nursery rhymes, Vita Sackville-West extends the unconscious qualities of nursery culture into that of high-art poetry. Her nursery rhymes are "tiny, unconscious works of art within their own limitations; very young sisters of their grown-up brother, Poetry, but of the same parentage as he." They are related because:

in all 'pure' poetry there is an element which eludes definition; loose and unscientific terms flap vaguely round it. The very expression I have just employed, 'pure' poetry, is one of them, and perhaps 'magic' is the most overworked of all. No critic can tell you how this 'magic' may be attained … it is only the poet who can bring off the conjuring trick, and even the poet does not know how he does it. The writing of pure poetry is a chancy affair.[85]

The poet "does not know how he does it" much like the child does not what she sings. The mystery or magic of poetry resembles the mystery of child's play which, according to Newell, is "a sacred mystery, at which their elders can only obtain glances by stealth through the crevice of the curtain."[86] Describing child's play as a "sacred mystery" reveals the significance it is made to bear: the mystery of child's play is the mystery of culture itself: of invention within conservation, of blissful innocence and unconscious transmission, of semantics turned back into sound.

CHAPTER 6

The layers and forms of the child's mind

Scott, Wordsworth and antiquarianism

The second half of this study may be described as having traced the cultural implications and literary elaborations of John Locke's simple statement from the opening of *Some Thoughts Concerning Education*: "the little, and almost insensible Impressions on our tender Infancies, have very important and lasting Consequences."[1] Locke's idea about the importance of impressions made on the infant mind became a central feature in eighteenth-century theories of the mind. But it also served as a cornerstone of the new literary culture taking shape over the course of the century, providing a way to theorize the relationship of the individual to his historical and cultural environment and, therefore, a way to historicize language and literature. Thus, as we have seen, Thomas Blackwell argues influentially about the importance of Homer's childhood in shaping his "genius" as a poet; thus Romantic ballad collectors date the ballads of Anna Gordon Brown from her childhood years and value their unchanging, pristine form; thus the affective and sociological charge of the antiquarian's refrain "remembered from childhood."

An increasingly vernacular literary culture organized on national lines must necessarily account for childhood and the first things of the child's literary life. The infantilization of literary culture that we have tracked in these pages involved not only bringing childhood and childish things into the literary field, but understanding all aspects of literary culture through a developmental narrative that begins in an infancy both individually and culturally conceived. The ontological or recapitulative cultural paradigm that dominates literary culture in this period gives the child a critical mediating role between individual memory and development on the one hand, and cultural history on the other. For the Romantic antiquarians, childhood is a site of cultural memory, a notion that becomes a guiding principle of literary and folklore studies generally, and children's literature and folklore specifically, in the nineteenth and early twentieth centuries. Within these emerging theories of how children remember and how they reproduce traditional literature, we have identified two major theories about the child's mind and memory. The first is the idea of the child's mind as stadial, as having depths and layers that replicate the stages of cultural history. The second is the idea of the child's memory as formal, as permanently imprinted by various forms and images – physical shapes, aural sounds, even literary forms – but flexible in the meanings, content and significance that it attaches to those forms.

In this concluding chapter I want to follow these ideas about the child's mind and memory into the somewhat wider world of Romantic literature, into texts not typically understood as directly tied to the antiquarian project, but which, I believe, are significantly influenced by antiquarian ideas about childhood and popular literature. As such, these are texts that offer important elaborations of what we have called an infantile account of literature, one that makes the state of infancy the historical and genetic origin of language and literature. The similarities between Walter Scott's Waverley novels and Romantic antiquarian collections are, of course, easy to spot, as Scott layers the narratives of his novels with ballads and footnotes and sends his heroes into the wilds of Scotland with a hearty appreciation for the romance of national songs and native lore. We will turn to *Guy Mannering* to uncover the idea of the child's stadial memory at the crux of the novel's plot and to examine the complex intersection of individual and collective memory that animates this story of the lost heir's happy homecoming.

Finally we will turn to William Wordsworth's *The Prelude* and the literary genre of childhood memory that he works out in this autobiographical poem, the "spot of time." Wordsworth's interest in the mind and memory of childhood is deeply formal – "forms" are a recurring element of the major "spots of time" – and the formalism of the Wordsworthian child needs to be understood in relation to antiquarian formalism and antiquarian ideas of childhood. Scott's Waverley novels are an explicit elaboration of his own antiquarian pursuits and the larger nationalist, vernacular project that is the context of his literary career. We can also draw direct lines of influence from Romantic antiquarianism to the *Lyrical Ballads* where Wordsworth and Coleridge emphasize the influence of Thomas Percy's *Reliques of Ancient English Poetry* and David Herd's *Ancient and Modern Scottish Songs*. Indeed we will see that the antiquarian ballad collections give the *Lyrical Ballads* not only a traditional literary form for Wordsworth to imitate and renovate, but a strategy for managing his relationship to popular literature and its sensationalist content.

But Romantic antiquarianism, with its particular interest in form under-pinning its historicist sensibility and its close attention to childhood, is also an important intellectual and aesthetic context for Wordsworth's autobio-graphical poetry of childhood where he grapples with the task of bringing the accidental, random and trivial memories of childhood into poetry and into a narrative of the self. In his spots of time, Wordsworth develops what we might call a *poetics of the trifle*, a way of valuing the insignificant that is deeply indebted to the formalism of the Romantic antiquarianism.

HARRY BERTRAM'S HOMECOMING

In his second novel, *Guy Mannering; or, The Astrologer*, Walter Scott makes the notion of the child's stadial mind central to the plot of homecoming and cultural inheritance. In turning to this major Romantic text, we look not for early anticipations of a later cultural theory, but for the romance narrative that made this version of childhood popular and compelling and thus available to reinforce the theoretical emergence of anthropology and psychology over the course of the nineteenth century. Scott's novel makes it clear that the idea of the child as primitive, while it may seem to alienate and banish the child to another, foreign cultural space, also works as a romance of cultural homecoming and full belonging. Scott is fascinated with childhood memory and with the question of what the adult mind retains from childhood. The idea of childhood as recapitulating in the individual life the stages of cultural development is particularly important to the plotting of his novels as well as to how he encodes various cultural forms (the ballad, the nurse, the second sight vision) within the prose medium of the novel.

In *Guy Mannering*, Scott turns to the standard plot of the lost child restored and subjects it to that question of childhood so important to Romantic antiquarianism: what can we remember and preserve of a childhood both individually and culturally imagined? The novel gets its title from the name of a character that epitomizes Scott's Waverley-hero formula: Guy Mannering, a young English gentleman travelling in Scotland. In the opening pages of this novel, Mannering loses his way and seeks shelter at Ellangowan, the estate of a "second-rate" Laird, Godfrey Bertram, whose wife gives birth to their first son, Harry Bertram, the very night of Mannering's arrival. Mannering finds a variety of companions waiting up with the Laird for the birth of the heir: an awkward, eccentric cleric and tutor, Dominie Sampson and an old gypsy woman, Meg Merrilies. Indeed the estate of Ellangowan is at the center of a traditional yet uneasily mixed society of landed gentry, gypsy tribes and foreign smugglers who work the coast of Scotland. Mannering is charmed by the ancient ruins of the estate and the traditional songs and charms of Meg Merrilies, if repulsed by the character of the smuggler captain, Dirk Hattaraick, and he returns to England with dreams of a Scottish retirement, disappearing from the narrative for five chapters and twenty-two years.

Our English hero will not be the only character temporarily lost to this narrative of disappearing figures. The narrative next jumps ahead to the approaching fifth birthday of Harry Bertram, the heir of Ellangowan. Harry is "already a little wanderer" – a term meant to convey his familiarity and close attachment to his home: "he was well acquainted with every patch of lea ground and dingle around Ellangowan, and could tell in his broken language upon what *baulks* grew the bonniest flowers." One of the "hardiest and most lively children," Harry spends his days "clambering about the ruins of the old castle" and making excursions "as far as the gypsy hamlet."[2] Of course, Harry is a favorite of Meg Merrilies, whose "ancient attachment" to the Bertram family has otherwise been "repelled and checked" by the Laird's new persecutions of the gypsies. Meg does not extend her resentment of the father to the son; indeed her love of the family finds in the son an "object on which it could yet repose and expand itself." In the midst of clearings and curses, the gypsy nurse finds in the child an acceptable object of attachment. She "often contrived to way-lay him in his walks, sing him a gypsy song, give him a ride upon her jack-ass, and thrust into his pocket a piece of gingerbread or a red-cheeked apple." When the child was ill, "she lay all night below the window, chaunting a rhyme which she believed sovereign as a febrifuge, and could neither be prevailed upon to enter the house, nor to leave the station she had chosen, till she was informed that the crisis was over."[3]

Raised in the Laird's house as heir, Harry spends his childhood wandering the woods and ruins, nursed from the threshold and border spaces of his world by this figure of an ancient, other maternity. It is Meg who both saves Harry's life and claims him for that other world when he wanders too far from the Laird's center and is inadvertently entangled in a violent encounter between Hattaraick's gang of smugglers and Frank Kennedy, an ambitious customs officer. The young child witnesses the murder of Kennedy and is therefore almost murdered himself. Meg persuades Hattaraick and his band of smugglers to kidnap the boy rather than kill him, and this time it is Harry's turn to disappear from the pages of the novel.

The plot centered around this child hinges on the fact that young Harry was, as one character puts it, "old enough to tell what he had seen." When Bertram comes back to Scotland as a young man, the plot hinges on the question of whether and when Harry will remember and tell what he knows. Bertram returns to Scotland as Captain V. Brown of the British Army in India, a young man who knows nothing about his true identity and childhood except that he is of Scottish descent. He is again a "wanderer," reminding us of his childhood state, but now a "harassed wanderer," and the term is meant to convey not his intimate knowledge of his birth-place, but his unconscious alienation from it. Scott is staging the return of the child, but this child does not fully know that he is home.

Scott exploits the unwitting state of his hero by repeatedly putting him into conversations and situations with Meg Merrilies whom he cannot, at first, remember and who raises "some internal, probably capricious, association of feelings, to which he had no clew."[4] Brown is mystified by his own reactions to this exotic figure: "he was surprised to find that he could not look upon this singular figure without some emotion," and wonders, "Have I dreamed of such a figure? ... or does this wild and singular-looking woman recal to my recollection some of the strange figures I have seen in an Indian pagoda?"[5] Brown's (Bertram's) time in India gives Scott the rationale for making the now familiar jump from a memory of the distant past to a memory of a distant place; the child's earliest memories take on the exotic, primitive elements of an Indian scene. The adult can only wonder if the strange "association of feelings" he experiences is triggered by memories of his own childhood or memories of an earlier age.

Brown's (Bertram's) feelings about the Scottish landscape are only slightly easier to understand, as he describes in a letter to a friend:

Of the Scottish hills, though born among them, as I have always been assured, I have but an indistinct recollection. Indeed my memory rather dwells upon the blank which my youthful mind experienced in gazing on the levels of the isle of Zealand than on any thing which preceded that feeling. But I am confident, from that sensation, that hills and rocks had been familiar to me at an early period, and that though now only remembered by contrast, and by the blank which I felt while gazing round for them in vain, they must have made an indelible impression on my infant imagination. I remember when we first mounted that celebrated pass in the Mysore country, while most of the others felt only awe and astonishment at the height and grandeur of the scenery, I rather shared your feelings and those of Cameron, whose admiration of these wild rocks was blended with familiar love, derived from an early association. Despite my Dutch education, a blue hill to me is as a friend, and a roaring torrent like the sound of a domestic song that has soothed my infancy.[6]

Brown (Bertram) builds his conviction of native attachment to the hills of Scotland not out of any positive emotional charge or specific recollections, but out of the "blank" he experienced amidst the flat Dutch landscape of his youth. From that sensation of blankness, he surmises that "hills and rocks had been familiar to me at an early period" and must have made an "indelible impression on my infant imagination." We will encounter this notion of the impression that the forms of nature – the hills and rocks of a landscape – can make on the child's mind in Wordsworth's *Prelude*. For Scott's hero, an Indian landscape once again figures prominently in the retrieval of his childhood memories. Brown claims affinity to his Swiss and Scottish friends who react to the Indian mountains with traces of "early association" and "familiar love." By the end of the passage, what is *not* felt by Brown (Bertram) and *is* felt by others somehow adds up to Brown's positive attachment to the hills of Scotland.

In such passages Scott suggests that the adult's attachment to a "native" landscape is felt because of (not in spite of) a lack of clear and specific recollections and a confusion as to whether or not the associations of memory and emotion are specific to the individual's childhood or rather to a collective memory of something actually experienced by others. The natural forms of landscape are impressed on the child's mind and associated with a complex network of culture and kinship. Brown (Bertram) thus re-describes the hill as a "friend" and the torrent of a waterfall as "the sound of a domestic song that has soothed my infancy." Nature is given to the child as cultural inheritance, and cultural forms, such as the song of a nurse, acquire natural status. Yet Scott insists that one's emotional attachment to the landscape of home is not a product of clear connection and direct inheritance, but rather of mysterious and unknown associations. As Brown (Bertram) finally approaches the coastline of Ellangowan (still without knowing its connection to him), Scott speculates "perhaps some early associations retaining their effect long after the cause was forgotten, mingled in the feelings of pleasure with which he regarded the scene before him." But he also questions: "who can presume to analyse that inexplicable feeling which binds the person born of a mountainous country to his native hills?"[7]

Who can presume? Wordsworth for one. Harry Bertram for another. As Brown enters the ruined castle of Ellangowan, Scott now names him Bertram "(whom, since he has set foot upon the property of his fathers, we shall hereafter call by his father's name of Bertram)."[8] The scene continues as one in which Bertram, the "harassed wanderer," repeatedly identifies himself correctly but unconsciously. Studying the carved escutcheon on an archway, he muses: "and the powerful barons who owned this blazonry . . . does their posterity continue to possess the lands which they had laboured to fortify so strongly? Or are they *wanderers*, ignorant perhaps even of the fame or power of their forefather."[9] Wandering becomes wondering, as Harry asks himself:

Why is it that some scenes awaken thoughts, which belong as it were to dreams of early and shadowy recollection, such as my old Bramin Moonshie would have ascribed to a state of previous existence? Is it the visions of our sleep that float confusedly in our memory, and are recalled by the appearance of such real objects as in any respect correspond to the phantoms they presented to our imagination? How often we find ourselves in society which we have never before met, and yet feel impressed with a mysterious and ill-defined consciousness, that neither the scene, the speakers, nor the subject are entirely new; nay, feel as if we could anticipate that part of the conversation which has not yet taken place! It is even so with me while I gaze upon that ruin; nor can I divest myself of the idea, that these massive towers and that dark gateway, retiring through its deep vaulted and ribbed arches, and dimly lighted by the court-yard beyond, are not entirely strange to me. Can it be that they have been familiar to me in infancy?[10]

The brain has uncanny dreams, at once familiar and strange, and Bertram associates them once again with both the exotic figures of India and the depths of infancy. This soliloquy of Bertram's describes a "mysterious and ill-defined consciousness," one shadowed and confused by the dream-like associations and memories of childhood, sleep and previous existences. The inclusive "we" of this passage extends this mysterious consciousness into that of adult consciousness generally; and while these wondering wanderings within his own mind do not provide Harry Bertram with any psychological character proper or individual to himself, they are asking the questions about both childhood and consciousness that will produce psychology and the pscyhological subject. The suspense of this scene is not, "does he remember?" but rather, "when and how will his memories be made conscious and communicable?" This is a drama of recovered memory premised on the faith that the adult mind somehow, somewhere always remembers its childhood state. Even Glossin (the current and illegal owner of Ellangowan) who appears on the scene and immediately recognizes Bertram as the image of his father, is confident that Harry will soon recall who and where he is, if he has not already. Glossin is "on the one hand eager to learn what local recollections young Bertram had retained of the scenes of his infancy, and, on the other, compelled to be extremely cautious in his replies, lest he should awaken or assist by some name, phrase, or anecdote, the slumbering train of association."[11]

This drama of childhood memories and mysterious consciousness allows Scott to showcase his antiquarian sensibilities as he weaves both antique text and traditional song into Bertram's layers of recollections. Deciphering the "half-defaced motto" on the carved arms without knowing that he is reading his own family motto, Bertram again marvels:

It is odd the tricks which our memory plays us; the remnants of an old prophecy, or song, or rhyme, of some kind or other, return to my recollection upon hearing that motto – stay – it is a strange jangle of sounds:

> The dark shall be light,
> And the wrong made right,
> When Bertram's right and Betram's might
> Shall meet on ——

I cannot remember the last line – on some particular height – *height* is the rhyme, I am sure; but I cannot hit upon the preceding word.[12]

What begins as an act of reading and translation becomes, through conversation with Glossin, an act of speaking and hearing. Bertram speaks the family motto aloud and it is upon "hearing" it that the old song or rhyme returns to recollection. On the one hand, this perfectly recreates the antiquarian practice of blending textual deciphering and personal memory to produce an "old song" that "returns" to "re-collection." On the other hand, Scott is very precisely locating Bertram's memories in the primitive stages of childhood, translating text back into speech, words back into sounds. It is significant, therefore, that Bertram remembers the old prophecy as a "strange jangle of sounds" and, as he tries to reconstruct the last line, recalls the "rhyme" but not the words or meaning of the line that will land him on that rhyme. Bertram is remembering the song of his childhood as a child remembers, as sound and rhyme rather than words with meaning.

This scene is thus meant to contrast with one of the earliest scenes in the novel where Guy Mannering overhears Meg Merrilies singing one of her traditional gypsy songs. Mannering is the antiquarian with no personal recollection or childhood associations to ground his practice of collection and transcription. Walking the grounds of Ellangowan on his first morning there, he comes across Meg in the old castle ruins:

Equipt in a habit which mixed the national dress of the Scottish common people with something of an eastern costume, she spun a thread, drawn from wool of three different colours, black, white, and grey, by assistance of those ancient implements of housewifery now almost banished from the land, the distaff and spindle. As she spun, she sung what seemed to be a charm. Mannering, after in vain attempting to make himself master of the exact words of her song, afterwards attempted the following paraphrase of what, from a few intelligible phrases he concluded was its purport:

> Twist ye, twine ye! even so
> Mingle shades of joy and woe,
> Hope and fear, and peace and strife,
> In the thread of human life.
>
> While the mystic twist is spinning,
> And the infant's life beginning,
> Dimly seen through twilight bending,
> Lo, what varied shapes attending!
>
> Passions wild, and follies vain,
> Pleasures soon exchanged for pain;
> Doubt, and jealousy, and fear,
> In the magic dance appear.
>
> Now they wax, and now they dwindle,
> Whirling with the whirling spindle.
> Twist ye, twine ye! even so,
> Mingle human bliss and woe.

Ere our translator, or rather our free imitator, had arranged these stanzas in his head, and while he was yet hunting out a rhyme for *spindle*, the task of the sybil was accomplished, or her wool was expended.[13]

Although Scott is sympathetic to his position, Mannering will not be a reliable vehicle for the preservation of this song; unable "to make himself master of the exact words of her song," he resorts to paraphrase and free imitation where the child would resort to sound and rhyme. Indeed in this impressive on-the-spot free translation, Mannering has trouble only with a rhyme, in precise contrast to Bertram who remembers by rhyme. Scott is deliberately unclear about exactly when Mannering composes his version of Meg's song. He "afterwards attempted the following paraphrase" – suggesting a later exercise, perhaps for a letter or diary – but he is already busy "hunting out a rhyme for *spindle*" when Meg finishes her task, suggesting that Mannering is composing his free translation as he listens to Meg sing. The antiquarian distance implied in the later exercise is made part of how Mannering first hears and responds to the song.

In this scene with Mannering, Scott imports the "gypsy song" into his narrative but frames it awkwardly, improbably, as if to emphasize the mediation that such imports require both in the narrative and in the response of the English tourist. In the scene of Bertram's return to Ellangowan, Scott again emphasizes the mediating frames that incorporate a ballad into his narrative and allow Bertram to hear a ballad. But Bertram has a significantly different relationship to the song he overhears than does Mannering. After sounding out the old family rhyme, Bertram continues to recall bits of old songs, "dragged on as it were by the current of his own associations."[14] "There are other rhymes connected with these early recollections," he tells Glossin, and wonders if "there is any song current in this part of the world, respecting a daughter of the King of the Isle of Man eloping with a Scottish knight?"[15] When Glossin insists that he is the "worst person in the world to consult upon legendary antiquities," Bertram continues: "I could sing such a ballad ... from one end to another when I was boy." Bertram's conversation with Glossin turns back to soliloquy as he dwells further on "the embarrassing state of his own feelings and recollections," trying to remember a particular ballad. This is how Scott's stages the recovery of the ballad:

"I used to sing all that song over from beginning to end – I have forgot it all now – but I remember the tune well, though I cannot guess what should at present so strongly recall it to my memory."

He took his flageolet from his pocket, and played a simple melody. Apparently the tune awoke the corresponding associations of a damsel, who at a fine spring about half way down the descent, and which had once supplied the castle with water, was engaged in bleaching linen. She immediately took up the song:

"Are these the links of Firth, she said,
Or are they the crooks of Dee,
Or the bonnie woods of Warroch-head
That I so fain would see?"

"By heaven," said Bertram, "it is the very ballad! I must learn these words from the girl."

"Confusion!" thought Glossin, "if I cannot put a stop to this, all will be out. O the devil take all ballads, ballad-makers, and ballad-singers, and that d – d jade too, to set up her pipe!"[16]

Again Bertram remembers the song from his childhood as sound, here as melody, rather than as words, a fact that signals his original, child-like relationship to the ballad.

Scott's antiquarian project promises the individual an authentic, lived connection to ancestral, primitive cultural forms. In this scene the ballad enters crucially to signal that the value of childhood memories is not yet wholly individual and interiorized, but rather will be played out for its national significance across different cultural forms and stages. When Bertram plays the melody and a rural "damsel" suddenly materializes to echo the tune and give back the missing words, we are in the grips of high cultural Romance where one's childhood memories are returned to one as part of the landscape and cultural surroundings. As it is for the antiquarian editors, to recover a ballad is for Bertram to recover a lost and forgotten childhood. The magic of the scene is that the individual childhood and the childhood of culture (the primitive forms of the ballad, the flute, the rural woman) are so perfectly united.

Scott maps the depths of the individual mind and memory onto a literary history that we have seen as central to stadial theory, with the more primitive cultural forms, such as the ballad, demonstrating a more primitive relationship to language based on sound, melody, rhyme and repetition. As the ballad gives shape to Bertram's childhood memories, that childhood becomes both personal and collective. This is why it is so important that he hear the ballad completed outside himself, that he understand his reaction to a mountainous landscape by seeing it in a friend. His interior depths are also outside him in the larger cultural history of Scotland. The same drama occurs in the eventual establishment of Bertram's identity. When his family and friends corroborate his increasingly clear childhood memories and claim him as their "*Enfant trouvé*," only Pleydell, the Edinburgh lawyer, expresses the need for proof that Bertram is, indeed, the heir of Ellangowan returned. Legal proof, he insists, requires more than childhood memories: "Mr Bertram's recollections are his own recollections merely, and therefore not evidence in his own favour."[17] This idea that Bertram's childhood memories are "his own recollections merely" is not upheld by any other character or the events of the narrative. While the law will assemble a number of different testimonies and evidences to establish that Bertram is indeed the rightful owner of Ellangowan, the crucial scene of recognition that establishes Bertram's identity is staged as a tableau of collective assent. Significantly, it is also the scene of Meg Merrilies' death, and it is on her deathbed that Meg calls out to the "group of tenants and peasants" gathered around: "'Look at him . . . all that ever saw his father or his grandfather, and bear witness if he is not their living image.'" The crowd responds with "popular feeling" and shouts of "'Bertram for ever!'" and Meg dies murmuring "he's owned! – he's owned! – I lived but for this."[18] Bertram's identity, like his childhood memories, is given back to him from the people around him in a collective act of popular expression.

Young Harry was kidnapped because he was "old enough to tell what he had seen." But ultimately what he remembers and is able to tell does not help convict Hattaraick and Glossin. This is not, however, because his memories are indistinct. They are distinct in some ways and confused in others, and Scott is very interested and precise in exactly how clarity and confusion come together in childhood memories, in what and how Bertram remembers these key childhood scenes. Bertram has a "strong recollection, perhaps more deeply impressed upon me by subsequent hard usage, that I was during my early childhood the object of much solicitude and affection." He also has strong "impressions" of the murder and kidnapping, although here Bertram admits what no lawyer likes to hear: that "though the terrible outlines of that day are strongly impressed upon my memory, yet somehow the very terror which fixed them there has in a great measure confounded and confused the details."[19] Bertram's description of his own memory is quite Lockean: the "outlines" of the day are "strongly impressed" and "fixed" upon the mind and memory like lines imprinted on a page or inscribed in a tablet. Yet the details are confused. Indeed the strong imprint of memory, and the strong feeling of terror which fixes its form on the brain, enables a kind of forgetting to join up with remembering.

LYRICAL (ABOUT) BALLADS

Wordsworth shares Scott's interest in childhood memory, but to understand the extent to which Wordsworth's understanding of the child's mind is inflected by antiquarian ideas, we should first turn to the *Lyrical Ballads* and its more general engagement with antiquarian practice. The poems and prose notes of the *Lyrical Ballads* are important texts in uncovering just what Wordsworth learned from antiquarian literary culture because of their explicit connection to antiquarian collections, the questions they pose about popular poetry and their interest in traditional forms. Indeed, the relation of the *Lyrical Ballads* to the popular poetry of its day has been a question under discussion since Wordsworth, himself, first made it one. When the volume appeared in 1798, it included a short "Advertisement" instructing its readers to consider these poems as "experiments" and advising that those "accustomed to the gaudiness and inane phraseology of many modern writers" will "perhaps frequently have to struggle with feelings of strangeness and aukwardness." "Readers of superior judgment," the advertisement suggests, will judge the volume on the "style" of the poems, and they may disapprove of the poems' low, overly familiar and undignified expressions. But those conversant with "our elder writers" will have fewer complaints. Wordsworth does not name these "elder writers" in the 1798 "Advertisement," but a description of "The Rime of the Ancient Mariner" as written in imitation of the style and spirit of the "elder poets" suggests that Wordsworth might have had the popular poetry of the ballad tradition in mind.[20]

With the second edition of the *Lyrical Ballads* in 1800, Wordsworth is at even greater pains to establish the "experimental" or innovative quality of his poems. A "Preface" is needed, he writes, to introduce poems "so materially different from those, upon which general approbation is at present bestowed"; and he famously rails against the "craving for extraordinary incident" and the "degrading thirst after outrageous stimulation" that characterize national life and literary taste. "The invaluable works of our elder writers," Wordsworth fumes – and now these "elder writers" are specifically named Shakespeare and Milton – "are driven into neglect by frantic novels, sickly and stupid German tragedies, and deluges of idle and extravagant stories in verse."[21] In the 1800 "Preface," Wordsworth makes a claim for the originality and difference of his verse by describing the sensational quality of *other* poetry and by attacking the sensibility of popular literature that his poems resist and work to reform. His poems are not and will not be popular, Wordsworth insists. And indeed the title page of the 1800 edition includes a Latin epigraph that practically dares the reader to like the poems: "How utterly unsuited to your taste!"[22]

Perhaps Wordsworth protests too much? We know, for example, that his ballads were neither as radically different nor as misunderstood and unappreciated as he insists. As Robert Mayo commented some time ago, when read alongside the magazine poetry of the day, what is truly surprising about the *Lyrical Ballads* is not their departure from popular traditions, but rather their "intense fulfillment of an already stale convention," a wonderful description of how Wordsworth's poems relate to popular poetry that we still have not fully understood and explored.[23] What is intensely conventional about the *Lyrical Ballads* is also, in fact, what is most sensationally intense: the mad, infanticidal mothers, lost children, vagrants, idiots, old rustics, criminals and abandoned women of Wordsworth's and Coleridge's poems are the stock characters of the very same "frantic novels" and "extravagant stories in verse" that Wordsworth condemns so energetically in his "Preface."[24] The "Preface" is needed, it seems, not to introduce radically different poems to the reading public but to assert the strangeness of the poems in the face of their apparent familiarity. As Karen Swann has persuasively argued, the 1800 "Preface" works as a "defense against the poet's more licentious and exploitative generic practices of 1798," a defense characterized mainly by an attempt to draw firm lines of distinction between popular and serious poetry.[25]

Perhaps the act of naming those endangered "elder writers" as Shakespeare and Milton in 1800 is part of Wordsworth's effort to solidify and specify the difference between high and low art: the cultural affiliation of the ballad tradition's unnamed "elder poets" becomes too ambiguous and risky.

Indeed, the ballad haunts Wordsworth's efforts in the "Preface" to distance himself from popular, sensational literature.[26] Valued as the simple, unaffected and natural poetry of our elder writers (or their modern imitators), old and new ballads filled magazines and volumes in the last decades of the eighteenth century, popular not in the least because of their sensational, eventful, often violent contents.[27] Ballads thus expose the fault line in our idea of "the popular" as both, in Karen Swann's words once again, "a lost authentic culture" and "an inauthentic and alienated mass culture symptomatic of cultural decline."[28] The *Lyrical Ballads*, and Wordsworth's "Preface" in particular, contribute significantly to this contradictory notion of the popular, but this uneasy yoking of authenticity and suspect sensationalism was first a product of antiquarian literary sensibility and the larger British ballad revival. There are many reasons why Wordsworth and Coleridge turn to the ballad form in 1798. From Thomas Percy's *Reliques of Ancient English Poetry* and David Herd's *Ancient and Modern Scottish Songs*, to name only two collections that he knew well, Wordsworth inherits a sense of the ballad as a native, original poetic form, the form privileged to carry and create national continuity and character.[29] But the antiquarian ballad collections of England and Scotland, as we have seen, also offer a formal strategy for coping with the contradictions, embarrassments and anxieties created when "popular" literature is redefined as a "national treasure," when a literature of sensational content is made to bear national and high cultural value. The *Lyrical Ballads* participate in the development of this formal practice; reading the volume within the context of Romantic antiquarianism allows its complex relationship to popular literature to come more fully into view.

An awareness of how the *Lyrical Ballads* reproduces the antiquarian formalism of the ballad collections, for example, should certainly inflect our understanding of Wordsworth's insistence in the "Preface" that these poems are distinguished from the "popular Poetry of the day" by the fact that "the feeling therein developed gives importance to the action and situation, and not the action and situation to the feeling."[30] On the one hand a statement of Wordsworth's commitment to the idea that the "human mind is capable of excitement without the application of gross and violent stimulants," this statement also directs his readers' attention away from action and situation, or content of the poems, toward feeling, which takes on quite formal properties in the *Lyrical Ballads*. Seeing this statement within the discourse of antiquarian formalism, in fact, allows us to see our own critical practice as in a continuum with that tradition and to begin to describe more clearly how the ballad persists in unsettling this formal practice.

For this privileging of feeling over action – the hallmark of the "lyrical ballads" and precisely what makes them *lyrical* – produces ballads that often refuse to be ballads. Wordsworth's demotion of action and situation is present not only in the prose discussions surrounding the ballads, but in the poems themselves, and even in those ballads featuring the kinds of characters and figures of the most traditional, seemingly plot-driven tales. In "Hart-Leap Well," for example, the ballad narrator declares: "The moving accident is not my trade, / To curl the blood I have no ready arts; / 'Tis my delight, alone in summer shade, / To pipe a simple song to thinking hearts."[31] In "Simon Lee, The Old Huntsman," Wordsworth promises at least some degree of eventfulness with the subtitle "with an incident in which he was concerned" and with the ballad stanza itself. But here the narrator delights in thwarting these expectations:

> My gentle reader, I perceive
> How patiently you've waited,
> And I'm afraid that you expect
> Some tale will be related.
>
> O reader! had you in your mind
> Such stores as silent thought can bring,
> O gentle reader! you would find
> A tale in every thing.
> What more I have to say is short,
> I hope you'll kindly take it;
> It is no tale; but should you think,
> Perhaps a tale you'll make it.[32]

Here and in many of the other poems in the volume, Wordsworth writes ballads that insist they are not ballads. He takes a poetic form traditionally defined as narrative, popularly conceived as eventful and sensational, and he drains its narrative action and even its level of feeling to the most minimal level.

Critics have followed Wordsworth's lead and pointed to the ballads' lack of clear action or events, pointed, in fact, to their lack of real content, as what makes these ballads not only lyrical, but also original, serious poetry of high cultural value. Thus critical discussion of the *Lyrical Ballads* has long debated the degrees of "tradition" and "experiment" in these poems, often understanding those terms as an opposition of content and form. Wordsworth gets his figures and scenes from the popular ballad tradition of his day, but his poems take on high literary value because of their formal experiments and, more precisely, because of the ways in which those formal innovations work to undermine, minimize or elide the contents of the poetry. As Mary Jacobus remarks, "his achievement is to adapt the ballad to portraying precisely those states and feelings least susceptible to narrative presentation."[33] Indeed, the extent to which Wordsworth strips his ballads of content can be understood as one of his greatest accomplishments and what establishes his poetry as a major advent of modernity.

Are the *Lyrical Ballads* a poetry divested of content? Or do they instead enact a complex antiquarian practice of historicizing their content in favor of a more formal reading? Perhaps turning to the example of one ballad will help clarify these questions and suggest some answers. In "The Thorn," Wordsworth makes his debts to the ballad tradition most explicit. The poem takes its landscape of woman, thorn tree, pool and mound from such old Scottish ballads as "The Cruel Mother," from a tradition in which the thorn tree is commonly associated with the misery of child murder. Another important source for the poem is Gottfried Burger's infanticide ballad, translated by William Taylor for the British periodicals as "The Lass of Fair Wone."[34] This popular ballad was, itself, an imitation of the old Scottish ballads, and Wordsworth's borrowings from Taylor's English translation of Burger's German imitation of old Scottish ballads is a wonderful example of how Wordsworth's access to the old, native ballads is entangled in the foreign, current and popular.

In "The Thorn," Wordsworth does not simply narrate the tale of Martha Ray, her love for Stephen Hill, his abandonment of her, her pregnancy, infanticide and madness. Wordsworth instead presents this traditional, sensational and intensely conventional story through the character of a narrator who does not or cannot know exactly what happened at the spot that Martha Ray, and now the narrator himself, obsessively haunt. The narrator's lament, "I cannot tell, I wish I could," "I cannot tell but some will say," is almost as repetitive as Martha Ray's "O misery, o misery." He relates the local lore surrounding this mysterious woman, repeating what "Old Farmer Simpson did maintain" and what "some will say," but it is lore that he cannot fully accommodate himself to or credit, as he repeatedly insists "I cannot tell how this may be." His function as a narrator, along with the ballad's narrative form, thus winds down as the ballad proceeds and he cannot or will not tell the tale.[35]

Indeed, this narrator has been troubling readers since his first appearance in 1798, and the poem received so much criticism that Wordsworth, in good antiquarian fashion, added an extensive note to the ballad for the 1800 edition. This note, also in good antiquarian fashion, directs the reader's attention away from the sensational content of the ballad toward the formal presentation of that content which is, here, the narrative style of the poem's speaker, whom Wordsworth now describes as someone like a retired sea captain, a man with "little to do" who thus becomes "credulous," "talkative" and "prone to superstition." Wordsworth declares that he selected such a character in order "to exhibit some of the general laws by which superstition acts upon the mind." "The Thorn" is not an infanticide ballad, Wordsworth insists, but a poem to "shew the manner in which such [superstitious] men cleave to the same ideas."[36] As Stephen Parrish once put it, if we fully credit Wordsworth's note to "The Thorn," the poem "becomes not a poem about a woman but a poem about a man (and a tree); not a tale of horror but a psychological study; not a ballad but a dramatic monologue." Indeed Parrish argued influentially that "the point of the poem may very well be that its central 'event' has no existence outside of the narrator's imagination – that there is no Martha Ray sitting in a scarlet cloak behind a crag on the mountain top."[37]

Redirecting readerly attention away from the body of a woman toward the mind of a man, Wordsworth's note to "The Thorn" models an antiquarian approach for his readers: he would have them relate to the poem as antiquarians related to the old ballads they collected, historicizing the sensationalist stories and paying attention only to the form that conveys such stories. As Wordsworth describes the narrator's adhesive mind, his attachment to and repetition of words, his fear and his feeling, superstition itself takes on formal qualities and becomes a kind of style. It is this superstitious style – the very repetitions, stutterings and uncertainties that so many considered the faults of the poem – that should be the reader's object of interest and analysis. We should not be frustrated with the narrator's tortured desire to know and not to know what Martha Ray did to her child, to tell and not to tell what happened at that spot; such frustration would only reveal our own desire to know what happened, our own craving for "extraordinary incident." The task Wordsworth sets for his privileged readers is to analyze the desires and cravings of the narrator, not to indulge their own.

With the construction of this narrator and the addition of the note to "The Thorn," Wordsworth effectively distances himself and his reader from what are, in fact, the rather sensational contents of this ballad. This is a strategy that is, indeed, an innovative re-working of a traditional ballad, but one that must be seen as borrowing and extending the formal practice of Enlightenment and Romantic antiquarian ballad collections. This formal practice enables a poem such as "The Thorn" to have sensational contents and disavow them at the same time. Thus Wordsworth does not write a poetry divested of content as much as he writes a poetry that both desires and disowns its own content, or in other words, a poetry not coterminous but in relation to its own content.

Of course all poetry crafts a relationship to its own content. To understand what is at work in a poem like "The Thorn," we must go further and note the specifically *historical* relationships between content and form embedded in the structure of Wordsworth's ballad. For the structure of "The Thorn" assumes and presents the stadial history of language and literature that was the dominant cultural narrative of Wordworth's day. Alan Bewell, who first linked "The Thorn" and other early Wordsworth poems to the anthropological encounters of Enlightenment histories, reads Martha Ray's moans as a representation of the origin of language in sound and feeling, and the question and response form of the poem as meant to approximate primitive poetry. "The Thorn," according to Bewell, is "an experimental primitive ballad aimed at dramatizing the primitive origins of poetry."[38] Bewell turns to ancient Hebrew poetry as the model of primitive poetry informing "The Thorn," but one can just as easily compare the narrator's struggles to understand and make sense of Martha Ray's inarticulate cries and sounds to Coleridge's struggles with the song of the nightingale or the cries of the infant, both of which produce language and lore in an attempt to grapple with the inarticulate origins of language.[39] Martha Ray, like Coleridge's bird and baby, is an inarticulate being – *infans*, or capable only of sound and cries – and the poem stages the generation of story, tradition and lore that arises out of the attempt to interpret and know the infant origins of self and culture.

In "The Thorn," however, the generation of primitive language and lore is arguably located not in the narrator, but in the community whose collective wisdom about Martha Ray the narrator repeatedly evokes in his stuttering, hesitant attempt to tell the tale of the infanticidal woman. Indeed, I would argue that reading this speaker's narration as an imitation of primitive poetry does not adequately account for the problematic belatedness of the narrator and his inability to tell the tale of the ballad. The primitive ballads that Wordsworth knew from Percy's *Reliques* and Herd's *Ancient and Modern Scottish Songs* are driven by narrative and sensational or historical events; unlike the first-person narrator of "The Thorn," their third-person omniscient or folk narrator has no trouble telling a story. The creation of this hesitant and uncertain narrator not only shifts the focus of the poem away from the sensational story of Martha Ray to the psychological workings of the narrator's mind, it also stages a belated relationship to primitive culture and the origins of language and literature.

This is surely what Wordsworth dramatizes in the figure of his sea captain narrator who "has retired to some village or country town of which he was not a native," who has arrived too late to know what happened to Martha Ray and who cannot fully trust what the locals tell him.[40] Belated, without a local context or native knowledge, the narrator's relationship to the figure and story of Martha Ray represents the Romantic ballad revival's relationship to an old ballad tradition that it imagines and recreates for itself. The belatedness of the poem's speaker is critically important to the type of story he can produce; not present when the events occurred, not having passed his childhood in the community whose stories he relates, this narrator does not have that privileged historical distance to the events he describes that, we recall, Blackwell points to as the source of Homer's genius and critical to the vigor of primitive poetry.[41] Wordsworth means the narrator's speech to be less an example of primitive poetry, than a belated attempt to access and return to primitive origins. Indeed, with his telescope, his measurements of the pond and mound, and his emphasis on personal observation, Wordsworth's narrator is an Enlightenment figure, superstitious in spite of his scientific and empiricist habits.

The layers of "The Thorn" – Martha Ray, the rural community, the narrator and, finally, the author and reader implied by the poem's note – stage a stadial history of language and literature (similar in many ways to those described by both Jeffrey and Peacock)[42] that includes the primordial origins of language, the collective lore of a primitive community, a belated attempt to return to and understand those primitive origins and early lore and, finally, an antiquarian formalist assessment of the superstitious conditions that produce both primitive poetry and its belated revivals. Wordsworth's early poetry is indeed an anthropological poetry, as Bewell observed, in that it pays as much attention to the observer as to what he observes;[43] but it is also a particularly antiquarian poetry, one that presents different literary historical stages, frames the relationship between those different stages, and models the proper modern relation to primitive origins. Wordsworth's *Lyrical Ballads* could thus be described as lyrical or reflective about the ballad form itself, as well as the literary tradition the ballad represents in 1798. "The Thorn" becomes not simply a poem that reframes the sensationalistic and conventional story of illegitimate pregnancy and infanticide that it borrows from the old ballads, but rather a poem that frames and, to some extent, interrogates the larger literary culture of the ballad revival and its construction of native, national literature.

Wordsworth the antiquarian thus locates the primitive sources of his ballads in an inaccessible past as something to be desired but also guarded against. "The Thorn," in particular, also dramatizes the gendering of poetic form and content at work in antiquarian formalism. As we have seen, antiquarian collections of ballads frequently cite the "recitation of an old woman" or the "mouths of nurses" as the oral source of their written transcriptions;[44] so, too, in "The Thorn" does Wordsworth make Martha Ray and her inarticulate cries of misery the source of the ballad. The questions debated throughout Enlightenment discussions on the origins of language – does language have deictic origins and come into being to name objects in the world? or does it have expressive origins in man's metaphoric and imaginative transformations of the material world? – animate Martha Ray's close connection to the features of her particular plot of ground: the thorn, the pond and the hill of moss. Her ties to a place that becomes both the source and the product of her lament rewrite the origins of language and literature into a scene haunted by both past origins and present obsessions.

Such present obsessions, as evidenced by the narrator of the poem, are not Martha Ray's alone. As Karen Swann acutely observes, the "limited yet endlessly modifiable stories of maternal suffering and criminality" that prove so fascinating in the Romantic period make the maternal woman a favorite cultural preoccupation; Martha Ray's power "derives not from her buried crimes but from her extraordinary cultural currency."[45] Much of that currency adheres in the central position given to the maternal figure in Romantic constructions of a national culture, language and literary tradition. The maternal figure, whether mother, grandmother or nurse, becomes the oral source of language and literature, as well as the carrier of cultural inheritance. The maternal voice thus offers an embodied and natural origin to a native and national literary tradition, and the process of education and acculturation is naturalized and brought into the intimate sphere of family and home.[46]

As an infanticidal mother, Martha Ray already challenges the myth of the woman as an embodiment of culture's natural origins, but this figure unsettles these notions of maternity and culture still further. The narrator understands her voice and figure as part of the natural world and describes her as such, even mistaking her for a natural form. Caught out in a storm and thinking he sees a "jutting crag" that might offer shelter, the narrator instead runs straight into Martha Ray:

> And, as I am a man,
> Instead of jutting crag, I found
> A woman seated on the ground.
>
> I did not speak – I saw her face,
> Her face it was enough for me;
> I turned about and heard her cry,
> "O misery! O misery!"[47]

This is the moment that is arguably the origin of the narrator's obsession with Martha Ray, the moment when he becomes, in Swann's words, "not so much a producer but a product of impassionated signs," and the moment that signals the extent of the poem's interest in the problem of the subject's relationship to a culture that determines him.[48] What is so unsettling about this moment for the narrator is not that he has mistaken a woman for a rock, but that his mistake is challenged. Martha Ray resists identification with a natural form and turns a human face back on the narrator's gaze, a gaze given to him by a larger culture that insists on such connections between woman, language and nature. Thus while Wordsworth suggests that his poem is about "the general laws by which superstition acts upon the mind," we suspect its concerns are larger.[49] As Swann notes, "what Wordsworth comes to call the laws by which superstition acts on the mind are the laws governing the subject's relation to received cultural materials."[50]

"The Thorn" thus reveals itself as a meditation on the literary and cultural forms generated by the expressive body of a woman and her primal connection to a particular plot of ground. The narrator's *misrecognition* of Martha Ray stages the poem's *recognition* of the ballad revival's problematic identification of the origins of language and literature with the figure of woman and the forms of the natural world. This is not, however, an insight that we find carried throughout Wordsworth's poetry. In *The Prelude*, for example, we will find the voice of the nurse blended with the sounds of the river Derwent to represent the child's original relationship to language as sound and to evoke a primitive cultural orality.

In turning to *The Prelude*, we take our understanding of Wordsworth's more general antiquarian practice into his influential account of the child's mind and his transformation of childhood memory into a poetic resource.

THE INDEPENDENT LIFE OF FORMS

Harry Bertram, as both a child wandering among the hills and woods and as an adult fascinated with retrieving and analyzing his memories of childhood, has much in common with the child and adult figure of William Wordsworth that emerges in *The Prelude*. Not the least striking similarity is their shared childhood experience of witnessing the violent death of an adult, although the murder of Kennedy and the drowning of James Jackson are very different events indeed. Wordsworth's scene is one of hush and waiting:

>   – I chanced to cross
> One of those open fields which, shaped like ears,
> Make green peninsulas on Esthwaite's lake.
> Twilight was coming on, yet through the gloom
> I saw distinctly on the opposite shore,
> Beneath a tree and close by the lake side,
> A heap of garments, as if left by one
> Who there was bathing. Half an hour I watched
> And no one owned them; meanwhile the calm lake
> Grew dark with all the shadows on its breast,
> And now and then a leaping fish disturbed
> The breathless stillness. The succeeding day
> There came a company, and in their boat
> Sounded with iron hooks, and with long poles.
> At length the dead man, 'mid that beauteous scene
> Of trees and hills and water, bolt upright
> Rose with his ghastly face.[51]

In addition to an intense interest in childhood memory and its cultural work, Scott and Wordsworth share certain antiquarian assumptions about how and what the child remembers, emphasizing the distinct visions and impressions that the child's mind retains in fixed forms. We begin to see this above in Wordsworth's emphasis on the shapes that he "saw distinctly" and recalls in very simple terms: fields like ears, the heap of clothes, trees, hills, water.

The Drowned Man episode is famously moved and reframed when Wordsworth lengthened and revised the 1799 two-part *Prelude* into the thirteen-book poem of 1805. The 1799 text is single-mindedly devoted to childhood memories which Wordsworth names and theorizes as "spots of time." In this earlier poem, the Drowned Man episode immediately precedes the articulation of that theory: "There are in our existence spots of time / Which with distinct preeminence retain / A fructifying virtue." In the 1805 poem, the Drowned Man passage occurs in the fifth book entitled "Books" and devoted to Wordsworth's ideas on education and his childhood relationship to books and reading. While the scene or memory of this episode remains largely intact, the frame (or the uses to which it is put) is altered. The 1799 passage concludes with these lines:

> I might advert
> To numerous accidents in flood or field,
> Quarry or moor, or 'mid the winter snows,
> Distresses and disasters, tragic facts
> Of rural history, that impressed my mind
> With images to which in following years
> Far other feelings were attached – with forms
> That yet exist with independent life,
> And, like their archetypes, know no decay.[52]

There are a number of elements in this passage that are important for our discussion here. I want to begin by pointing out how Wordsworth positions himself and this memory within local lore and history. With the evocation of the "tragic facts of rural history" heard in childhood, Wordsworth takes pains to establish the ideal childhood relationship he had to the stories he now relates as an adult poet. Like Blackwell's account of Homer's poetic genius, Wordsworth's *Prelude* asserts that when and where Wordsworth was a child shapes what poetry he writes as a man, and, indeed, his aptitude to write poetry at all.[53] Of course, in Wordsworth's attention to how these accidents and tragic facts "impressed my mind / With images" that "know no decay," we should hear an echo of Locke's insight that "the little, and almost insensible Impressions on our tender Infancies, have very important and lasting Consequences." But Wordsworth's understanding of how "rural history," the events and lore of a particular place and group, has impressed his mind also echoes Blackwell's historicist insistence that "*Young Minds* are apt to receive such strong Impressions from the Circumstances of the Country where they are born and bred, that they contract a mutual kind of Likeness to those Circumstances, and bear the Marks of the Course of Life thro' which they have passed."[54]

Such an understanding of the degree to which the poet is shaped by his historical and cultural position – more specifically, by the period and place where he finds himself as a child – also informs other passages in *The Prelude*. For example, it is surely behind Wordsworth's account of his lifelong affection for shepherds, a class of people and a style of existence to which he pays tribute in Book VIII of the 1805 *Prelude*. Just as Blackwell carefully calibrates Homer's historical relationship to the manners and culture he describes – at a sufficient, yet not too distant remove – Wordsworth carefully describes the particular cultural moment in which he finds himself observing and living among the shepherds of the Lake District. The shepherds of his childhood are not, he makes clear, those of Shakespeare's comedies or Spenser's pastoral romances. Wordsworth has only "heard" what Spenser "perhaps had seen"; of May-Pole dances and annual festivals, Wordsworth has simply heard the tales "from those who yet remember'd." Such pastoral customs are things of the past by the time Wordsworth is alive, as he comments in lines that evoke the nostalgic sociology of antiquarianism:

> This, alas,
> Was but a dream; the times had scatter'd all
> These lighter graces, and the rural ways
> And manners which it was my chance to see
> In childhood were severe and unadorn'd,
> The unluxuriant produce of a life
> Intent on little but substantial needs,
> Yet beautiful, and beauty that was felt.[55]

Wordsworth's awareness of the "rural ways / And manners which it was my chance to see / In childhood" positions both himself and the shepherds in an anthropological and historical frame. As in the Drowned Man episode of 1799, he again relates that the "images of danger and distress" and the "tales" and "tragedies of former times" took "deepest hold of me": "Man suffering among awful Powers and Forms: / Of this I heard and saw enough to make / The imagination restless."[56] Wordsworth's account of shepherds at this point in the 1805 *Prelude* serves the larger theme of Book VIII, "Love of Nature leading to love of Mankind," and much of what he describes here is how his childhood encounters with the figure of the shepherd – those moments in his childhood wanderings when suddenly "His Form hath flash'd upon me" – lead to his later love for and delight in the "human form." But significantly he establishes this aspect of his adult poetic sensibility by detailing the striking sights, forms and images impressed on his child mind, evoking early days "When but a half-hour's roam through such a place / Would leave behind a dance of images / That shall break in upon [a child's] sleep for weeks."[57]

Wordsworth thus presents himself as a privileged poet by placing himself as a child in a specific historical and cultural relationship to the customs and manners of the Lake District of a particular period. Just like a ballad singer who stores her songs in her mind since childhood, thus offering access to an earlier cultural moment in her singing, Wordsworth carries in his mind the forms and images of what he saw and heard as a child, and they become the forms and images of a poetry rooted in an earlier age. Indeed, the account in Book VIII of his early affection for shepherds introduces a particular story that Wordsworth brings into his poem with the gesture of an antiquarian editor, locating the tale in a past time that is simultaneously his own individual childhood and a cultural childhood. Wordsworth recalls that there were many tales and "tragedies of former times" which "in my walks / I carried with me among crags and woods / And mountains"; and "of these may here be told / One, as recorded by my Household Dame." The "Matron's Tale," which follows, a story of a shepherd and his son, was originally written for the poem *Michael*, another oral tale "not unfit . . . for the fire-side."[58] In moving the story to this section of *The Prelude*, Wordsworth explicitly connects the growth of his mind as a poet, the central topic of *The Prelude*, to the oral, popular literature recorded and preserved by the antiquarian collections of the day, suggesting that he can somehow serve as both bard, singing the songs and reproducing the forms of a particular culture on which he has a privileged vantage point, and antiquarian collector, recording and introducing the old tales "remembered from childhood."

We have long recognized that Wordsworth builds a sense of himself as a chosen poet in *The Prelude* by returning to his memories of early childhood. But we have not yet fully situated that turn to childhood in the antiquarian discourse that informs it. The continuities between childhood and adulthood so important to Wordsworth's sense of himself and his poetry are not simply individual and psychological. They are equally historical (concerning the individual's relationship to his circumstances and environment) and stadial (concerning the individual's relationship to and recapitulation of the stages of cultural development). Like Scott, Wordsworth understands the child to progress through the stages of cultural history and he layers these stages in his text. For Wordsworth, to imagine or describe the workings of a young child's mind and memory is also to conjecture the primitive origins of language, the rise of early literary forms, and the structures of continuity and repetition at work in national literary culture. Wordsworth, I believe, engages fully with this antiquarian vision of childhood and with the form of the child as mediating between individual and cultural memory and history.

We can track Wordsworth's awareness and correlation of the stages of cultural and individual development in his revisions to the Drowned Man episode when he moves the passage to Book V, "Books," in the 1805 *Prelude*. Placed within a discussion of "what I owed to books in early life," the concluding lines of the later Drowned Man episode do not evoke the oral lore of "rural history" but instead acknowledge that the dead man was a "spectre shape – / Of terror even," and then offer the following assurance:

> And yet no vulgar fear,
> Young as I was, a Child not nine years old,
> Possessed me, for my inner eye had seen
> Such sights before among the shining streams
> Of Fairy Land, the Forests of Romance –
> Thence came a spirit, hallowing what I saw
> With decoration and ideal grace,
> A dignity, a smoothness, like the works
> Of Grecian Art and purest poetry.[59]

These lines admit, only to deny, the affective charge that, as Harry Bertram knew, fixes the forms and images of the child's memory. They also move this episode into a different stage of the child's cultural life. While the 1799 text is one of traditional lore and rural history, in 1805 only the unclaimed garments tell a "plain tale." Wordsworth's narrative is now one of "Grecian art and purest poetry" and of romance, particularly those found in his "little, yellow canvass-cover'd Book" of Arabian tales which he immediately goes on to describe as his "precious treasure." In moving from the stories and tales the child *hears* to those he *reads* (perhaps even in a language learned only in elite schools), Wordsworth moves from a description of early childhood memory where forms move into and impress the mind of the child without the child's full understanding, to a description of later childhood memories where the child is able to use other aesthetic forms and experiences to understand and organize what he encounters.[60] Book V treats a later stage of the child's literary development and, thus, the episode is reframed to fit that later stage.[61]

In turning his attention to books and the particular experience of reading, Wordsworth expresses regret that he does not say more about primitive literary forms, the first things of his literary life. In fact, he says quite a lot. Recalling the "deep entrancement" he experienced "when I have held a volume in my hand," he links the powerful experience of childhood reading to even earlier literary experiences: the "thoughtless melodies" heard first in his "lisping time of Infancy" and later in his "prattling Childhood," and the "simply-fashion'd tale" that "did bewitch me then, and soothes me now."[62] Wordsworth embodies the absorption of the child's earliest literary experiences in the image of a child's face: "The trickling tear / Upon the cheek of listening Infancy / Tells it, and the insuperable look / That drinks as if it never could be full." The child's hungry, engrossed look – one that conflates listening with ingesting, as we have seen in other antiquarian accounts of oral literature – registers the compulsive power of an oral tale; we can recall Aikin's children who "are chained by the ears, and fascinated by curiosity."[63] The image also evokes the developmental idea of literary culture that understands literary genres as developing out of the primitive infant forms and later literature as working to return its readers to earlier, child-like states of emotional absorption. Thus Wordsworth's tribute to the "Powers" of books includes "the low and wren-like warblings, made / For Cottagers and Spinners at the wheel . . . ballad-tunes, / Food for the hungry ears of little Ones, / And of old Men who have surviv'd their joy."[64] More significantly, his fond memorial of that "little, yellow canvass-cover'd Book," *The Arabian Nights*, connects the experience of reading these romance legends back to the first appetites of childhood:

> adventures endless, spun
> By the dismantled Warrior in old age,
> Out of the bowels of those very thoughts
> In which his youth did first extravagate,
> These spread like day, and something in the shape
> Of these, will live till man shall be no more.
> Dumb yearnings, hidden appetites are ours,
> And they must have their food; our childhood sits,
> Our simple childhood sits upon a throne
> That hath more power than all the elements.[65]

In connecting both the writing and reading of adventure stories back to the "dumb yearnings" and "hidden appetites" of childhood, Wordsworth offers an anthropological account of the human need for narrative, and, once again, makes infantile literary experience the source of adult literary pleasure and production. The "power" of childhood is here the power to shape literary culture and experience.

Wordsworth concludes Book V by describing how his infant "cravings for the marvellous" in tales, ballads and romances eventually subsided, replaced by a love for "words in tuneful order," words he began to find "sweet / For their own sakes, a passion and a power."[66] Book V stands as an anthropological autobiography of his early literary life, one that demonstrates how he, in his own individual history, has recapitulated the stages of literary and cultural history. We began our discussion of the antiquarian sensibility at work in *The Prelude* with the Drowned Man episode of the 1799 *Prelude* and have seen two important antiquarian elements exemplified in this passage. We have discussed how the earlier version of this "spot of time" positions Wordsworth as a poet with a privileged historical relationship to a particular culture, and we have tracked how the revisions to these lines and their new location in Book V of the 1805 *Prelude* reveal Wordsworth's stadial understanding of the child's literary life and development. We now need to return to the original 1799 Drowned Man passage, this time to attend to its interest in the "forms" that inhabit the child's mind, as well as to begin to build our understanding of the antiquarian formalism that shapes Wordsworth's understanding of the child's mind and memory.

As we have seen, the Drowned Man episode in the 1799 *Prelude* concludes with a set of lines that do not appear in later versions of *The Prelude*:

> I might advert
> To numerous accidents in flood or field,
> Quarry or moor, or 'mid the winter snows,
> Distresses and disasters, tragic facts
> Of rural history, that impressed my mind
> With images to which in following years
> Far other feelings were attached – with forms
> That yet exist with independent life,
> And, like their archetypes, know no decay.[67]

The fact that these lines disappear from *The Prelude* when the Drowned Man episode is revised makes them no less fundamental to Wordsworth's conception of what, in the 1799 version, he immediately goes on to name and describe as "spots of time," his major theorization of the child's mind and memory. In these lines, Wordsworth extends Locke's theory of the lasting impressions made on the child's mind in important and characteristically antiquarian ways, addressing exactly how these impressions continue to operate in the life of the mind. The images are lasting and unchanging – they "know no decay" – but Wordsworth adds a critical insight: that the significance and emotional charge of these images change over time. They are permanent, but they are also flexible in the meanings assigned to them. In addition, Wordsworth adds another important term: what is impressed on the child's mind are "images," but they are also "forms," and he ascribes an "independent life" to the forms here and throughout his "spots of time."

"Form" – the word or term – appears repeatedly in the "spots of time" passages and throughout *The Prelude*. With its range of meanings extending from the most material aspects of configuration, shape and physical appearance to the more immaterial aspects of image, representation or essential type, "form" is a useful term for Wordsworth in charting (and sometimes collapsing) distinctions between the exterior world and interior life. We recognize "form" as a key term for describing the external world in *The Prelude*. The "beauteous" or "lovely" "forms of Nature" are frequently repeated phrases, and Wordsworth is particularly interested in how these natural forms acquire charges of significance and emotion in childhood.[68] Describing a process of metonymic association, he recalls how "the beauteous forms / Of Nature were collaterally attach'd / To every scheme of holiday delight, / And every boyish sport."[69] But to emphasize the distinct shape of these forms, Wordsworth often turns to listing their basic types, as when he again credits nature for "haunting" him in the midst of his "boyish sports," impressing the "characters" of his childhood emotions on the "caves and trees, upon the woods and hills" and on "all forms," thus making "the surface of the universal earth / With triumph, and delight, and hope, and fear / Work like a sea."[70] "Form" takes up its meanings of "shape," "outline" or "figure" in these cases, as when Wordsworth describes "the mountain's outline and its steady form" or, as we have seen, when he describes how the "Form" of the shepherd "flash'd upon me."[71]

But Wordsworth also uses "form" to describe how the external world works on, impresses or, somehow, simply moves into the child's mind and memory. The "tragic facts of rural history" in the original Drowned Man passage above *impress* the mind with "images" and "forms," making their mark, leaving a print or impression on the brain, remaining "in their substantial lineaments / Depicted on the brain."[72] Elsewhere – as in the "Boy of Winander" passage where the "visible scene / Would enter unawares into his mind" – external forms simply move inward as if to bypass any acts of perception, cognition or representation. Their life in the mind can thus remain vaguely external and even alien, as in those wonderful concluding lines to the boat-stealing episode: "But huge and mighty Forms that do not live / Like living men mov'd slowly through my mind / By day and were the trouble of my dreams."[73] The child's mind is impressed, inhabited, even crowded by "forms" both lovely and awful, familiar and unfamiliar, forms that often acquire a greater material presence in the mind than they had in the world. At one point Wordsworth writes "Those lovely forms / Had also left less space within my mind."[74] Forms become the population of the child's mind; his project in the first books being to "trace" how "Nature ... peopled first / My mind with forms or beautiful or grand."[75]

Forms make their medium visible or manifest, but in the case of Wordsworth's "spots of time," the medium of these forms that "exist with independent life" remains a question. Cognitive linguists such as Stephen Pinker might call these visual images of an inner eye the forms of a "silent medium of the brain – a language of thought, a 'mentalese'" translated with difficulty into poetic language.[76] But Wordsworth places these mental forms within a network of various and differentiated media, and so it would be more correct to say that the forms of his memory make the mind visible as multiple media which Wordsworth understands as related in stages of both individual and cultural development.

Thus the creative tension in *The Prelude* between flow and fix, between fluidity and fixed forms. We know this tension in the first book of the 1805 *Prelude* as the hope of the "glad preamble" which understands the freedom to wander "enfranchis'd and at large" as a freedom to "fix my habitation where I will," a translation of movement or flow into fixed location that is also Wordsworth's poetic ambition: "to fix in a visible home / Some portion of those phantoms of conceit / That had been floating loose about so long."[77] These phantoms floating loose are, perhaps, unassembled images or fragments of poetry, but the image here suggests that they may also be those "forms" fixed or impressed on the child's mind and still moving in the adult mind with independent life, the forms that once "ma[de] the imagination restless" and are now counted as among the resources of the poet: "nor am I naked in external things / Forms, images; nor numerous other aids / Of less regard, though won perhaps with toil / And needful to build up a Poet's praise."[78] These forms, alternately fixed and moving, have themselves taken shape against other differentiated movements and flows; and here we should recall the Lockean rhetoric of imprint or impression that Wordsworth employs to characterize the permanence of these forms as the permanence of writing and inscription. They are meant to give a fixed and textual shape to what is otherwise characterized as the sounds and scenes of aural and visual flow.

Indeed as the murmurs of the river Derwent blend with his nurse's song and together send a "voice" that "flow'd along [the child's] dreams," Wordsworth takes one of the central images of Romantic orality, the nurse, and characterizes original language as sound not yet perceived as speech.[79] Once again the child's development follows the progress of literary culture and history, moving from a more fluid and evanescent orality into the more fixed and permanent forms of writing. Yet this primitive orality of the nurse's song has, for Wordsworth, something prior, which is the murmur of sound undifferentiated into words. In the blend of the murmuring river and the nurse's song, Wordsworth dramatizes what Stephen Pinker might describe as the brain's ability to flip between hearing something as sound and hearing something as speech. Pinker reminds us that words in speech are not the same as words on a page; in perceiving speech we hallucinate the boundaries between words, fixing form on what is also seamless, undifferentiated sound.[80] Underneath or alongside our perception of speech is unperceived sound. For Wordsworth hearing speech instead of sound is a developmental moment: in putting the murmuring river together with the Nurse's song, he suggests the infant's initial blurring and gradual distinctions of sound and speech. But the movement from sound to speech is also a cognitive switch that the adult sometimes experiences as well, as in that moment in "Resolution and Independence" when the voice of the leech-gatherer becomes "like a stream / Scarce heard" and the narrator "nor word from word could . . . divide." Here Wordsworth describes the phenomenon of sound fixed and formed into words and then let loose again to flow into an undifferentiated stream. As we saw with the prattle of children, words can turn back into noise, can be drained of semantic significance and returned to a more primal, sonic insignificance.[81]

Wordsworth thus uses the language of form, fix, impression and fluidity to describe the moments in the mind when language forms itself, when images take shape, when the mind is suddenly impressed, invaded or flashed upon with external forms that will have a lasting and permanent, yet simultaneously fluid and changeful life in the mind. But I would also like to draw connections between Wordsworth's understanding of the child's mind and memory and the formalist idea of the child's mind and memory that we have seen emerge in antiquarian discourse. Like the antiquarians, Wordsworth endows the forms of the child's memory with both continuity and flexibility as vehicles or carriers of significance. Thus he ascribes an autonomy to the forms that populate the mind, exploring the particular ways in which, as he writes in the original Drowned Man passage, these forms "exist with independent life."

The sense of the interior life of the child inhabited by exterior, material forms is a significant part of the "independent life" of these forms. Their ability to move through the mind, to trouble the dreams, to rise up unbidden before the mind's eye is another part of that independent life.

But the independence or autonomy of these forms is also an independence from fixed meaning or significance, a freedom from context despite the fact that they are originally produced in a specific spot and specific time. Here we should note how often the "spots of time" record impressive forms and their passage into the mind and memory of the child, but resist assigning any major significance or sometimes even specifying the affect associated with those forms. Many of the "spots of time" from childhood take shape out of what Wordsworth calls "ordinary sight[s]" and arguably trivial events: spinning circles on the ice, rowing a boat out to the middle of a lake and back again. In those episodes in which something undeniably significant or traumatic does occur – the drowning and discovery of James Jackson, for example, or the death of Wordsworth's father – Wordsworth tends to locate that occurrence in the caesura of a line, in a break or gap of his memory. In many episodes, the significant event is imaginary, something that registers only in the mind of the boy and not in the exterior world; in other episodes, the pause or hiatus in what is otherwise happening is, itself, the significant event, as when "pauses of deep silence" mock the skill of the "Boy of Winander." Like this boy, we may often feel a "gentle shock of mild surprise" at the silences of these episodes, at their quiet and deliberate turn away from event, from interpretation, from stating significance.

Often what they turn to is a simple reiteration of the forms. In the Penrith Beacon episode, for example, the boy re-ascends the moor and sees "a naked Pool that lay beneath the hills, / The Beacon on the summit, and more near / A Girl who bore a Pitcher on her head." An "ordinary sight," he acknowledges, but one of "visionary dreariness" that he cannot and does not put into words, resorting instead to listing once again the elemental forms of this memory: "the naked Pool, / the Beacon on the lonely Eminence, / The Woman."[82] In the Christmas-time episode, there are again three significant forms impressed on his memory: "I sate, half shelter'd by a naked wall / Upon my right hand was a single sheep, / A [. . .] hawthorn on my left."[83] Immediately after the death of his father, the child Wordsworth associates "chastisement" with this memory, but the adult Wordsworth sees this emotional exposition as merely "trite reflections of morality." For him, the significance of the memory lies in the "afterwards," not in any particular emotion or meaning associated with the scene but in the simple persistence of the forms in his mind, a persistence he registers by simply repeating the elements of the memory: the "single sheep, and the one blasted tree, / And the bleak music of that old stone wall." In the "spots of time," Wordsworth describes and constructs what we have called a formalism of the child's mind, repeatedly narrating an attention that is fixed on and by forms but that is uninterested in or unable to attach particular or significant meaning to those forms.

For the adult self and the project of the autobiographical poem, the continuity and permanence of the forms becomes more important than the immediacy, importance or stability of their significance or content. After describing the "visionary dreariness" of the Penrith Beacon scene, for example, Wordsworth makes literal the formal persistence and acts of return implicitly at work in all "spots of time" by describing how "Long afterwards [he] roamed about / In daily presence of this very scene," and "Upon the naked pool and dreary crags, / And on the melancholy beacon, fell / The spirit of pleasure and youth's golden gleam."[84] "Feeling comes in aid of feeling," he concludes; the dreariness and melancholy first associated with these forms animates the later joy even as they are submerged. But the flexibility of these forms to acquire new charges of affect and meaning – coupled with their permanent, persistent, working presence in the mind – is critical to Wordsworth's account of mind and memory. Thus to the "indisputable shapes" and forms of his school-boy, Christmas-time vigil – the sheep, the tree and the old stone wall – Wordsworth repeatedly and, he claims, unconsciously returns: "unknown to me / The workings of my spirit thence are brought."[85] In these "spots of time," Wordsworth describes the formal pulls and movements of a mind filled with and fixed by permanent yet often ordinary forms, forms that are capable of carrying a variety of meanings and emotional charges and which are valued for their continued presence rather than their weighty significance.

WORDSWORTH'S POETICS OF THE TRIFLE

In Wordsworth's conception of the child's mind and memory an idea of literary formalism emerges that has much in common with the formalism underpinning popular, national antiquarianism. Animating the antiquarian understanding of literary form, as we have seen, is the larger project of bringing literature's trivial, vulgar and childish things into the larger literary tradition. The forms of literature and culture – the ballad, the tale, the game, the rhyme – come to be understood as historically produced, thus originally connected to a particular historical and cultural moment, as well as formally autonomous, capable of continuing beyond their original context, of shedding inconvenient or irrelevant charges of meaning and affect and acquiring new associations and significances. This antiquarian mixture of historical formalism which elides literary content and values literary form as a vehicle of cultural continuity plays a central role in crafting a national, vernacular literary tradition in the Romantic period. For Wordsworth it plays a central role in crafting a narrative that is simultaneously autobiographical and anthropological: a narrative of individual history characterized by continuity and development that recapitulates the progress and development of cultural history. Like the child constructed in and by antiquarian discourse, Wordsworth's child is the ultimate formalist, and Wordsworth's understanding of how the memories of childhood inhabit the mind of the man is essentially formalist as well. The forms of his mind and memory are valued for their continuity, their continued presence, rather than their high importance or stability of significance. They are forms and images originally tied to a particular time and place, a "spot of time," yet able to slip free of that original context and to have an independent life of unfixed and flexible association. As such, they become a resource for his poetry as well as for his sense of self.

Wordsworth's interest in proving continuity between his childhood and adult self could be said to be the driving concern of *The Prelude*, a poem which takes development as its conceptual paradigm and which sets itself the task of describing the "growth of the poet's mind." That the adult poet grew out of the child, that there are vital, shaping connections between the experiences of the child and the life and poetry of the adult is not something Wordsworth takes for granted, but something that must be questioned, proven and even crafted in this autobiographical poem. Wishing for the "eagerness of infantine desire" in his adult pursuit of duty and truth, Wordsworth is led to wonder about his connection to the days of his childhood:

> A tranquillizing spirit presses now
> On my corporeal frame: so wide appears
> The vacancy between me and those days,
> Which yet have such self-presence in my mind
> That, sometimes, when I think of them, I seem
> Two consciousnesses, conscious of myself
> And of some other Being.[86]

The "vacancy" between his present moment and his childhood days is so great as to create the sense that the child he remembers is "some other Being." Here Wordsworth is also interested in the idea of having or being "two consciousnesses," of having or being two selves, and his childhood "spots of time" could be described as the product of two consciousnesses, describing both the memory of the child and the reflections of the adult. Indeed, the temporal structure built into Romantic antiquarian collections, in which "remembered from childhood" is a critical gesture of authentication and the collector's adult pursuits are always presented in relation to his childhood memories, is closely allied to the temporal structure and divided consciousness of the "spots of time." Wordsworth, however, stages the cultural nostalgia of the antiquarian's turn to child-hood as a possible source of alienation.[87] In fact, what is clear here and in the passage that immediately follows, is that Wordsworth understands the adult self as divided, split or multiple rather than singular and continuous. The ensuing lines work as an extended simile of this idea:

> A grey stone
> Of native rock, left midway in the Square
> Of our small market Village, was the home
> And centre of these joys, and when, return'd
> After long absence, thither I repair'd
> I found that it was split, and gone to build
> A smart Assembly-room.[88]

The singular grey stone is like one of the natural forms of his childhood memories, but upon his attempted return (to origins, to childhood), he finds it "split, and gone."

Indeed the grey stone has more integrity and permanence of form in his mind than it does in the world, and it is this uncanny phenomenon of his interior, mental life that suggests to Wordsworth that there may be some connection and continuity between his child consciousness and his adult consciousness. The days of his childhood have "yet have such self-presence in my mind," he writes, a curious phrase given the extent to which this passage calls his own self-presence into question. But if the stability and singularity of his own self is uncertain, the formal presence and persistence of his childhood memories are not, and it is the "self-presence" in his mind of a rather random, ordinary and even trivial collection of memories that ultimately gives Wordsworth the material with which to forge a sense of continuity between his childhood and adult self.

Continuity between infancy and adulthood, how it is crafted out of the forms and things of the mind and world, are antiquarian preoccupations. Scott puts just such musings in the mouth of Jonathan Oldbuck, the Antiquary, who comments:

It is at such moments as these ... that we feel the changes of time – the same objects are before us – those inanimate things which we have gazed on in wayward infancy and impetuous youth, in anxious and scheming manhood – they are permanent and the same – but when we look upon them in cold unfeeling old age – can we, changed in our temper, our pursuits, our feelings, changed in our form, our limbs, and our strength, can we be ourselves called the same? – or do we not rather look back with a sort of wonder upon our former selves, as beings separate and distinct from what we now are?[89]

Oldbuck's Wordsworthian meditations are explicitly that, Wordsworthian. He goes on to recite two stanzas from Wordsworth's "The Fountain," a poem that he has only heard repeated since, as the narrator tells us, the *Lyrical Ballads* had not yet been published. Those lines again take up the question of the connection between infancy and old age:

> My eyes are dim with childish tears,
>   My heart is idly stirr'd,
> For the same sound is in my ears
>   Which in these days I heard.
>
> Thus fares it still in our decay;
>   And yet the wiser mind
> Mourns less for what times takes away,
>   Than what he leaves behind.[90]

The Antiquary is Scott's novel that is, perhaps, the most explicitly engaged with Wordsworth's poetry. The "Advertisement" to the novel announces its commitment to portraying that "class of society who are the last to feel the influence of that general polish which assimilates to each other the manners of different nations."[91] This is, of course, another attempt to craft continuity and to locate it in the world, and it is a project that Scott pursues in agreement with "Mr. Wordsworth" who, he reminds us, credits the "lower orders" with the "strongest and most powerful language," a language of "antique force and simplicity" which Scott finds peculiarly present in the "peasantry of my own country." In the "Preface" to the *Lyrical Ballads*, which is Scott's point of reference here, Wordsworth in fact credits the "low and rustic" with a "more permanent" language and hopes, by using such a language, to write a "class of Poetry" that is "well adapted to interest mankind permanently."[92] But this is a language of strong feeling, a language of feeling expressed without restraint, that the Antiquary, caught between the passionate youth and "cold unfeeling old age," cannot speak. It is this antiquarian project of locating and crafting continuity from a divided and discontinuous position that Scott identifies with Wordsworth.

Scott's Antiquary unwittingly describes the problems of antiquarianism as a tension between trivial and consequential things: "if you want an affair of consequence properly managed, put it into the hands of an antiquary; for, as they are eternally exercising their genius and research upon trifles, it is impossible they can be baffled in affairs of importance."[93] Of course the assumption underlying the irony at work in this passage is that the antiquary's preoccupation with trifles blocks his perception and understanding of larger, more significant matters. Wordsworth voices a similar concern about those trifles of his mind and memory in a fragment associated with the 1799 *Prelude*:

> That what we see of forms and images
> Which float along our minds, and what we feel
> Of active or recognizable thought,
> Prospectiveness, or intellect, or will,
> Not only is not worthy to be deemed
> Our being, to be prized as what we are,
> But is the very littleness of life.[94]

These lines continue by criticizing that "false secondary power by which / In weakness we create distinctions, then / Believe that all our puny boundaries are things / Which we perceive, and not which we have made," a caution that finds its way into the 1799 *Prelude* where Wordsworth asks, "who shall parcel out / His intellect by geometric rules / Split like a province into round and square?"[95] Such passages signal Wordsworth's privileging of some sort of felt unity – variously glossed as the "One Life," "organic form" or, in Wordsworth's own words "that one interior life / That lives in all things" – over the work of the intellect and even over individual consciousness itself.[96] As Jonathan Wordsworth commented, "this passage is remarkable in its . . . out-and-out rejection of the life of the mind."[97] Indeed, it is remarkable to the extent that this passage takes the "forms and images / Which float along our mind," those forms which fix Wordsworth's attention throughout the "spots of time" and constitute his major resource as a poet, and insists they are not "our being," not "what we are." Here, and, I would argue, even more deliberately throughout the "spots of time," Wordsworth insists that the life of the mind and the life of the self are not the same, and thus that the independent life of these material forms is not to be confused with the independent or autonomous life of the self. Even when Wordsworth credits certain forms and images with a "fructifying" or, later, a "renovating" virtue, he leaves them mysteriously apart from and yet persistently present in the life and narrative of the self. His reticence at assigning these forms of memory specific meaning, heightened significance or fixed emotional value ultimately constructs a deeply impersonal formal structure at the heart of this personal, autobiographical account. Indeed many of the "spots of time" can be understood as Wordsworth's attempt to grapple with the strangeness of sharing one's mind with impersonal forms of uncertain meaning.

That childhood is important to the life of the adult, that the "Child is Father of the Man" is perhaps Wordsworth's most enduring and misunderstood legacy. Today we habitually turn to the events and memories of childhood to explain the adult self, but our tendency is to turn to traumatic memories, to major events, or to features of our upbringing that have been deemed significant and influential: whether or not we were put in daycare, whether or not we were breastfed, whether or not our parents read to us at an early age. Wordsworth models this turn to childhood as an explanation of the adult life, crafting a narrative that explains and explores exactly how his privileged upbringing in and by nature shaped the poet he became. But the most revolutionary aspect of *The Prelude*'s autobiographical project are the "spots of time" which simply describe how the ordinary and insignificant events of childhood somehow, for some reason, persist in the memory of the adult. It is the simple persistence of the trivial – how the forms and images of childhood arise unbidden in the mind, appear suddenly, acquire new meanings and emotional associations – that Wordsworth brings into poetry. His "spots of time" do not bestow significance on the forms of memory as much as they attempt to register their persistent insignificant presence.

Notes

INTRODUCTION

1. "Whether the Present Age Can, or Cannot be Reckoned Among the Ages of Poetical Excellence," 170–171.
2. *Ibid.*, 172.
3. The poems that appeared under the title "Moods of my own Mind" include "To a Butterfly," "My Heart Leaps up when I Behold," "I Wandered Lonely as a Cloud," "The Small Celandine," "The Sparrow's Nest," and "To the Cuckoo," among others. For a thorough account of the creation of this volume see Wordsworth, *Poems in Two Volumes*, 3–39.
4. Byron, "Review of Wordsworth's *Poems in Two Volumes*," 293–295.
5. Jeffrey, "Review of Wordsworth, *Poems, in Two Volumes*," 214–231.
6. Wordsworth, *Lyrical Ballads*, 743. These phrases are taken from the 1802 version of the "Preface."
7. While literary scholars have analyzed the conflict between Jeffrey and Wordsworth and dissected Jeffrey's criticism of Wordsworth's poetry, very little attention has been paid to either the rhetorical or substantive elements of Jeffrey's charge of infantilization.
8. Mintz, *Huck's Raft*, viii.
9. Such statements also reinforce the presumed differences between humanistic and scientific studies: i.e. that history presumes change and difference over time while biology presumes an unchanging or relatively constant organism. To be fair, recent biological, neurological and psychological studies of the child are less interested in an unchanging organism and more invested in an idea of the child's brain and body as always in the process of formation, always under construction.
10. Cunningham, *Children and Childhood*, 1–2; Steward, *The New Child*, 13.
11. Cunningham, *Children and Childhood*, 3.
12. Ariès uses the phrase as the title of a chapter but, as Judith Plotz points out, the phrase is present in eighteenth- and nineteenth-century discussions of childhood. Rousseau describes childhood as an unknown territory and the Victorians commonly refer to the "new continent of childhood" as something to be discovered and explored. See Ariès, *Centuries of Childhood*; Plotz, *Romanticism and the Vocation of Childhood*, 1–5.

13. Heywood, *A History of Childhood*, 19.
14. Cunningham, *Children and Childhood*, 11. For an excellent survey of the historiography of childhood, see Cunningham, 3–16.
15. de Mause, ed., *The History of Childhood*; Stone, *The Family, Sex and Marriage in England*.
16. For critical responses to Ariès and Stone, see Pollock, *Forgotten Children* and Wrightson, *English Society*.
17. Cunningham, 58–59. See also Heywood, *A History of Childhood*, 23–27. In addition to the influence of these intellectuals and their ideas, Cunningham cites increasingly secular attitudes toward children and childhood and the increasing "privacy and comfort of upper- and middle-class family life" as other factors contributing to the century's "move toward a more child-oriented society."
18. Coveney, *Poor Monkey*, ix. For similar claims see Babenroth, *English Childhood*, 299; Plumb, "The New World of Children in Eighteenth-Century England," 64–93; Grylls, *Guardians and Angels*, 35; Pattison, *The Child Figure*, 50; Richardson, *Literature, Education, and Romanticism*, 8–10.
19. Higonnet, *Pictures of Innocence*, 15–30. See also Neumeister, ed., *The Changing Face of Childhood*, and Steward, *The New Child*.
20. Mintz, *Huck's Raft*, 75–93.
21. Higonnet, *Pictures of Innocence*, 9.
22. Ariès, *Centuries of Childhood*, 119.
23. Boas, *The Cult of Childhood*, 31 and 64–65.
24. The child-studies movement of the late nineteenth century plays a significant part in diffusing the ideas of recapitulation. See the work of G. Stanley Hall in the United States, William T. Preyer in Germany, and James Sully in the United Kingdom for key examples of this strain of thinking about childhood.
25. Shelley, *Shelley's Poetry and Prose*, 511.
26. Culler, *The Victorian Mirror of History*, 280. Peter Bowler also points to "a comparison with the life cycle of the individual" as the "most common metaphor used by Victorians in discussing the process of historical development." See Bowler, *The Invention of Progress*, 10.
27. Sully, *Studies of Childhood*, 5.
28. Quoted in Coleman, *Biology in the Nineteenth Century*, 52. For an account of how the new science of biology and psychology impacted the understanding of childhood and the centrality of recapitulation theory to the child-studies movement, see Morss, *The Biologising of Childhood*.
29. Quoted in Bowler, *The Invention of Progress*, 56.
30. *Ibid.*, 37.
31. Iona and Peter Opie, *The Lore and Language of Schoolchildren*, 210.
32. Bewell, *Wordsworth and the Enlightenment*, 58; Locke, *Essay Concerning Human Understanding*, Vol. 1, 61.
33. For discussions of childhood and recapitulation see Steedman, *Strange Dislocations*, and Trumpener, *Bardic Nationalism*.
34. Barbauld, *Selected Poetry and Prose*, 144.

35. Jeffrey, "Review of Wordsworth, *Poems, in Two Volumes*," 214.

36. Kittler, *Discourse Networks*, 25–69.

37. Markidou, "'Bubbles' and Female Verse: A Reading of Anna Laeticia Barbauld's 'Washing Day,'" 24–25.

38. Inchbald, *Nature and Art*, 79.

39. Wordsworth, *Lyrical Ballads*, 746.

40. *Ibid.*, 744 and 739.

1 THE CHILD IS FATHER OF THE MAN

1. Wordsworth, *Poems in Two Volumes*, 206. The line is the seventh line of the nine-line poem, "My Heart Leaps Up." After 1815, Wordsworth used the last three lines of this poem as an epigraph for his "Ode, Intimations of Immortality from Recollections of Early Childhood."

2. See Higonnet, *Pictures of Innocence*; Mintz, *Huck's Raft*; Neumeister, *The Changing Face of Childhood*; Steward, *The New Child*.

3. Plotz, *Romanticism and the Vocation of Childhood*, 13.

4. Steedman, *Strange Dislocations*.

5. Plotz, *Romanticism and the Vocation of Childhood*, 24.

6. Siskin, *Historicity of Romantic Discourse*, 18.

7. Chandler, *England in 1819*, xiv.

8. Davis, *Acts of Union*; Duncan, *Modern Romance* and *Scott's Shadow*; Ferris, *Achievement of Literary Authority*; St. Clair, *Reading Nation*; Trumpener, *Bardic Nationalism*.

9. Hopkins, *Selected Poetry*, 141.

10. Siskin, *Historicity of Romantic Discourse*, 67–147; Chandler, *England in 1819*, 135–140.

11. *Oxford English Dictionary*, 916–917.

12. Meek, *Social Science*, 2.

13. *Ibid.*, 5.

14. *Ibid.*, 5.

15. For the relationship of the "battle of the ancients and the moderns" to Scottish Enlightenment four-stages theory, see Meek, *Social Science*, 26–28.

16. Quoted in Guyer, "C'est nous qui sommes les anciens," 258–259.

17. *Ibid.*, 260–261.

18. Pascal, "Fragment de preface sur le traite du vide," 167–168.

19. Perrault, *Parallele des Anciens et des Modernes*, 188–189.

20. Other writers question the continuities of inheritance and bequest from the ancient period to the present, emphasizing what has been lost along the way rather than the totality of what has been accumulated. See, for example, Temple, "Of Ancient and Modern Learning," in *Miscellaneous Essays*, 38.

21. Fontenelle, *Digression sur les Anciens et les Modernes*, 176.

22. *Ibid.*, 184.

23. As Kathleen Wilson notes, the cultural comparison between ancients and moderns gives way to "a conception of the primitives as the ancients." See Wilson, *The Island Race*, 70.
24. Stewart, "Account of the Life and Writings of Adam Smith," 33.
25. For the debate about the relationship between Locke and Condillac, see Hans Aarsleff's introduction to Condillac's *Essay*. Condillac, *Essay*, v.
26. *Ibid.*, 7.
27. *Ibid.*, 8.
28. *Ibid.*, 69.
29. Aarsleff, *The Study of Language in England*, 14. This is that key development in the understanding of language described by Foucault: the idea that language refers to ideas alone, that it works as a representation of a representation of a thing and never the thing itself. See Foucault, *The Order of Things*, 78–124.
30. Condillac, *Essay*, 6.
31. *Ibid.*, 6.
32. *Ibid.*, 42.
33. *Ibid.*, 113.
34. *Ibid.*, 115.
35. Aarsleff, *Locke to Saussure*, 161.
36. Hume, *Treatise*, 273 and xvi.
37. Stewart, "Account of the Life and Writings of Adam Smith," 34.
38. Condillac, *Essay*, 113.
39. Aarsleff, *Locke to Saussure*, 158.
40. Stewart, "Account of the Life and Writings of Adam Smith," 33.
41. *Ibid.*, 33–34.
42. *Ibid.*, 34.
43. Of course conjectural history is just one genre of historical writing in this period. For a discussion of the variety of historical genres in this period, see Phillips, *Society and Sentiment*.
44. Meek, *Social Science*, 2.
45. John Locke, *Two Treatises*, 301.
46. Lafiteau, *Customs*, Vol. 1, 27.
47. Millar, *Origin of Ranks*, 3–5. Both Ronald Meek and James Chandler use this passage to exemplify the stadial theory of the Scottish Enlightenment. See Meek, *Social Science*, 162–176; and Chandler, *England in 1819*, 128.
48. Alan Bewell has alerted us to the many complexities of this stance and other writers have detailed the complicity of this philosophical tradition in the colonial enterprise. See Bewell, *Wordsworth and the Enlightenment*; Wheeler, *Complexion of Race*; and Wilson, *The Island Race*.
49. Degérando, *Observation of Savage Peoples*, 63.
50. Quoted in Stewart, *William Robertson*, 154.
51. Turgot, "A Philosophical Review of the Successive Advances of the Human Mind," in Meek, *Turgot on Progress, Sociology and Economics*, 42.
52. Fabian, *Time and the Other*, 15–16.

53. Chandler, *England in 1819*, 100.
54. Robertson, *History of America*, Vol. 1, 310.
55. *Ibid.*, Vol. 1, 310.
56. *Ibid.*, Vol. 1, 293.
57. *Ibid.*, Vol. 1, 293.
58. *Ibid.*, Vol. 1, 294.
59. Quoted in Meek, *Social Science*, 149.
60. Chandler, *England in 1819*, 128.
61. Phillips, *Society and Sentiment*, 173.
62. Aarsleff, *From Locke to Saussure*, 159.
63. Bewell, *Wordsworth and the Enlightenment*, 22.
64. Ferguson, *History of Civil Society*, 80.
65. Chandler, *England in 1819*, 108.
66. Ferguson, *History of Civil Society*, 80.
67. To that extent, the universal human nature of Scottish Enlightenment histories is an "embodied universalism." In *British Romanticism and the Science of the Mind*, Alan Richardson argues that this embodied idea of a universal human nature emerges later with Romantic mental science theorists; opposition between the Enlightenment and Romantic periods is reinforced as opposition between universal rational mind and universal embodied human nature. In Scottish Enlightenment histories I find more interest in embodied human nature and thus more continuity between Enlightenment and Romantic writers. See Richardson, *British Romanticism and the Science of the Mind*, 74–75.
68. Ferguson, *History of Civil Society*, 81.
69. *Ibid.*, 1.
70. *Ibid.*, 4–5.
71. Herder, *Philosophical Writings*, 127.
72. *Ibid.*, 141.
73. *Ibid.*, 141.
74. *Ibid.*, 130.
75. *Ibid.*, 131.
76. *Ibid.*, 131.
77. Ferguson, *History of Civil Society*, 208–209.
78. *Ibid.*, 4.
79. *Ibid.*, 6.
80. *Ibid.*, 8.
81. Locke, *Essay Concerning Human Understanding*, Vol. 1, 100–101.
82. These images are not of the child *as* island, which is Judith Plotz's description of the Romantic child: "every child is an island." She quotes Thomas De Quincey's childhood as "a separate world of itself; part of a continent, but also a distinct peninsula." In fact children are almost always stranded in woods, wilds or deserted islands in groups of at least two. The social element of this metaphor is particularly important to Ferguson and Scottish Enlightenment historicism. See Plotz, *Romanticism and the Vocation of Childhood*, 3.

83. Anderson, *Imagined Communities*, 24 and 26.
84. Benjamin, *Illuminations*, 261.
85. Writers throughout the eighteenth century, such as Addison and Wordsworth, praise the native simplicity of this ballad and make it central to the growing valorization of vernacular and national literature. See De Man, "The Rhetoric of Blindness," in *Blindness and Insight*, 134.
86. For a brief discussion of childhood and the nursery as a site of cultural reproduction, see Trumpener, *Bardic Nationalism*, 201–203.
87. For another critique of Benedict Anderson's account of national and novel-istic temporality, see Craig, "Scott's Staging of the Nation," 13–28.
88. Aarsleff, *Locke to Saussure*, 279–280.
89. Bewell, *Wordsworth and the Enlightenment*, 60.
90. Ferguson, *History of Civil Society*, 5.
91. Rousseau, *Discourses*, 132.
92. Quoted in Steedman, *Strange Dislocations*, 61.
93. *Ibid.*, 63.
94. *Ibid.*, 63.
95. *Ibid.*, 75.
96. Siskin, *Historicity of Romantic Discourse*, 39.
97. Steedman, *Strange Dislocations*, 83–84.

2 INFANCY, POETRY AND THE ORIGINS OF LANGUAGE

1. Shelley, *Shelley's Poetry and Prose*, 511 and 535.
2. *Ibid.*, 535.
3. *Ibid.*, 511.
4. *Ibid.*, 511. It is a common remark within Enlightenment discussions of the origin of language that humans seem physically designed to produce a range of complex sounds. In *Vestiges of the Natural History of Creation*, Robert Chambers also uses the image of the Aeolian harp to represent man's physical propensity for language. He notes the "peculiar organization of the larynx, trachea, and mouth" and insists that "such an arrangement of mutually adapted things was as likely to produce sounds as an Eolian harp placed in a draught is to produce tones." See Chambers, *Vestiges*, 312.
5. Shelley, *Shelley's Poetry and Prose*, 511.
6. Hans Aarsleff, *From Locke to Saussure*, 147.
7. Shelley, *Shelley's Poetry and Prose*, 514.
8. *Ibid.*, 514–515.
9. *Ibid.*, 512.
10. Keach, *Shelley's Style*, 7; Wright, *Shelley's Myth of Metaphor*, 24.
11. Shelley, *Shelley's Poetry and Prose*, 512.
12. Keach, *Shelley's Style*, 8.
13. Shelley, *Shelley's Poetry and Prose*, 512.
14. For a discussion of the anthropological foundation of Shelley's *Defence* see McLane, *Romanticism and the Human Sciences*, 32–35.

15. Bewell calls this scene the "primitive encounter topos." See Bewell, *Wordsworth and the Enlightenment*, 59 and 73.
16. Condillac, *Essay*, 113.
17. Smith, "First Formation of Language," 203.
18. *Ibid.*, 204.
19. *Ibid.*, 204.
20. Murray, *History of the European Languages*, 29–30 and 178–179.
21. Herder, *Philosophical Writings*, 63.
22. Cohen, *Sensible Words*, 122.
23. Browne, *Hermes Unmasked*, 99.
24. Bayly, *Introduction to Languages*, 26.
25. Monboddo, *Origin and Progress of Language*, Vol. I, 207.
26. Sharpe, *Two Dissertations*, 3.
27. Chambers, *Vestiges*, 313–314.
28. Monboddo, *Origin and Progress of Language*, Vol. I, 142 and 144.
29. *Ibid.*, 143.
30. Douthwaite, *The Wild Girl*, 23.
31. Pinker, *The Language Instinct*, 20–23.
32. Quoted in and translated by Douthwaite, *The Wild Girl*, 37.
33. Shearer, "Wordsworth and Coleridge Marginalia," 73.
34. Bewell, *Wordsworth and the Enlightenment*, 27–41.
35. Ferguson, *History of Civil Society*, 8.
36. Browne, *Hermes Unmasked*, 27.
37. Locke, *Essay Concerning Human Understanding*, Vol. I, 48–49.
38. *Ibid.*, Vol. I, 61–62.
39. The phrase is Alan Bewell's, *Wordsworth and the Enlightenment*, 58.
40. Monboddo, *Origin and Progress of Language*, Vol. I, 141.
41. Locke, *Essay Concerning Human Understanding*, Vol. I, 206. Hans Aarsleff credits Condillac for taking these connections between thought and language even further.
42. Aarsleff, *From Locke to Saussure*, 108.
43. Locke, *Essay Concerning Human Understanding*, Vol. I, 49 and 61.
44. *Ibid.*, Vol. II, 17.
45. *Ibid.*, Vol. II, 4–5.
46. *Ibid.*, Vol. II, 5.
47. Condillac, *Essay*, 165. This is a theory of metaphor that remains current today in conceptual metaphor theory.
48. Aarsleff, *The Study of Language*, 33.
49. Hume, *Treatise*, 1.
50. The impressions made on a child's mind are understood to be stronger and last longer than those on the adult mind, and to form the habits and associations of the adult. As Locke says in *Some Thoughts Concerning Education*, "the little, and almost insensible Impressions on our tender Infancies, have very important and lasting Consequences." The cultural implications of this notion are explored in the second half of this study. Locke, *Some Thoughts*, 83.

51. Locke, *Essay Concerning Human Understanding*, Vol. i, 61.
52. Sharpe, *Two Dissertations*, 4.
53. Rousseau, *Emile*, 61.
54. *Ibid.*, 62.
55. *Ibid.*, 61.
56. For a discussion of the infantilization of "savages" see Richardson, *Literature, Education and Romanticism*, 160–161.
57. Stewart, *Adam Smith*, 33.
58. Locke, *Essay Concerning Human Understanding*, Vol. ii, 8; see also Cohen, *Sensible Words*, 38.
59. *Ibid.*, Vol. ii, 3.
60. Stewart, "Account of the Life and Writings of Adam Smith," 33.
61. Rousseau, "Essay on the Origin of Languages," 289.
62. Monboddo, *Origin and Progress of Language*, Vol. i, 185.
63. *Ibid.*, Vol. i, 188.
64. Rousseau, *Discourses*, 157.
65. Rousseau, "Essay on the Origin of Languages," 294.
66. *Ibid.*, 295.
67. Rousseau, *Discourses*, 146.
68. Rousseau, *Emile*, 65.
69. Aarsleff argues that Condillac got this term from Léonard des Malpeines' translation of William Warburton's *The Divine Legation of Moses*. See Aarsleff's introduction to Condillac, *Essay*, xxxii–xxxiii.
70. Condillac, *Essay*, 115–116. Rousseau will also insist that passion, as opposed to physical needs, is the origin of language: "if we never had anything but physical needs, we might very well never have spoken." See Rousseau, "Essay on the Origin of Languages," 292.
71. Herder, *Philosophical Writings*, 66.
72. *Ibid.*, 66.
73. Condillac, *Essay*, 116.
74. Reid, *Inquiry into the Human Mind*, 51.
75. *Ibid.*, 50 and 51.
76. Condillac, *Essay*, 116.
77. *Ibid.*, 116–117.
78. Murray, *History of the European Languages*, 29.
79. Monboddo, *Origin and Progress of Language*, Vol. i, 254.
80. Blair, *Lectures on Rhetoric*, Vol. i, 107.
81. Condillac, *Essay*, 120.
82. Rousseau, "Essay on the Origin of Languages," 296.
83. Herder, *Philosophical Writings*, 63–64 and 72.
84. Condillac, *Essay*, 121.
85. Rousseau, "Essay on the Origin of Languages," 296.
86. *Ibid.*, 301 and 303.
87. Adam Smith, *Lectures on Rhetoric*, 15.
88. *Ibid.*, 16.

89. Blair, *Lectures on Rhetoric*, Vol. I, 248.
90. Condillac, *Essay*, 165.
91. *Ibid.*, 166.
92. Blair, *Lectures on Rhetoric*, Vol. I, 279.
93. *Ibid.*, Vol. I, 279.
94. *Ibid.*, Vol. I, 280.
95. *Ibid.*, Vol. I, 283.
96. *Ibid.*, Vol. I, 280.
97. *Ibid.*, Vol. I, 280–281.
98. Condillac, *Essay*, 78.
99. Blackwell, *Life and Writings of Homer*, 42–43.
100. *Ibid.*, 41–42.
101. Herder, *Philosophical Writings*, 64.
102. Rousseau, "Essay on the Origin of Languages," 294.
103. Blair, *Lectures on Rhetoric*, Vol. I, 281.
104. Blair, "Critical Dissertation on Poems of Ossian," 345.
105. *Ibid.*, 346.
106. Wordsworth, *Lyrical Ballads*, 743.
107. Richardson, *British Romanticism and the Science of the Mind*, 81.
108. *Ibid.*, 81 and 84–85.
109. Blackwell, *Life and Writings of Homer*, 38.
110. Blair, *Lectures on Rhetoric*, Vol. II, 314.
111. Smith, *Lectures on Rhetoric and Belles Lettres*, 135.
112. Rousseau, "Essay on the Origin of Languages," 294.
113. Blair, *Lectures on Rhetoric*, Vol. II, 314.
114. Smith, *Lectures on Rhetoric and Belles Lettres*, 34.
115. Blair, *Lectures on Rhetoric*, Vol. II, 314.
116. Smith, *Lectures on Rhetoric and Belles Lettres*, 135.
117. Blair, *Lectures on Rhetoric*, Vol. II, 314.
118. Ferguson, *History of Civil Society*, 172.
119. *Ibid.*, 172.
120. Smith, *Lectures on Rhetoric and Belles Lettres*, 135 and 137.
121. *Ibid.*, 111.
122. *Ibid.*, 111.
123. Blackwell, *Life and Writings of Homer*, 44.
124. *Ibid.*, 13.
125. Blair, *Lectures on Rhetoric*, Vol. I, 115–116.
126. *Ibid.*, Vol. I, 124–125.
127. Murray, *History of the European Languages*, 178.
128. Herder, *Philosophical Writings*, 103–104.
129. Blair, *Lectures on Rhetoric*, Vol. II, 312.
130. For a discussion of metre as definitive of poetry or not, see Enfield, "Is Verse Essential to Poetry?"; and Rowland, "Romantic Poetry and the Romantic Novel," 123.
131. Blair, *Lectures on Rhetoric*, Vol. II, 317.

132. *Ibid.*, Vol. II, 312. See also Wordsworth's discussion of metre as adding pleasure to poetry and the importance of poetry being pleasurable in the 1802 "Preface" to the *Lyrical Ballads*, 752–756.
133. Blair, *Lectures on Rhetoric*, Vol. II, 315.
134. Blackwell, *Life and Writings of Homer*, 34.
135. Sorensen, *Grammar of Empire*, 160.
136. Blackwell, *Life and Writings of Homer*, 35.
137. *Ibid.*, 35.
138. Ferguson, *History of Civil Society*, 166.
139. Burns, *The Canongate Burns*, Vol. I, 3.
140. Blackwell, *Life and Writings of Homer*, 11.
141. Browne, *Hermes Unmasked*, 57.
142. *Ibid.*, 34.
143. *Ibid.*, 65–66.
144. *Ibid.*, 77.
145. *Ibid.*, 81.

3 BECOMING HUMAN

1. Herder, *Philosophical Writings*, 65.
2. For an account of the growing tendency among eighteenth-century intellectuals to credit animals with a language of movement, sound and gesture see Thomas, *Man and the Natural World*, 127–128.
3. *Ibid.*, 32 and 135.
4. Herder, *Philosophical Writings*, 77.
5. Monboddo, *Origin and Progress of Language*, Vol. I, 146.
6. *Ibid.*, Vol. I, 183.
7. As Thomas points out, it is because of such passages that Monboddo is often pointed to as an early theorist of the ideas of evolution. See Thomas, *Man and the Natural World*, 133.
8. For a discussion of literature as defining the human species, see McLane, *Romanticism and the Human Sciences*, 10–42.
9. Herder, *Philosophical Writings*, 81.
10. Reid, *Inquiry Into the Human Mind*, 13.
11. *Ibid.*, 15.
12. Herder, *Philosophical Writings*, 80–81.
13. *Ibid.*, 81.
14. *Ibid.*, 75.
15. *Ibid.*, 81.
16. *Ibid.*, 84.
17. *Ibid.*, 87.
18. *Ibid.*, 85.
19. *Ibid.*, 88.
20. *Ibid.*, 88.
21. *Ibid.*, 99.

22. *Ibid.*, 95.
23. *Ibid.*, 89.
24. For Coleridge's possible reading of Herder, see Richardson, *British Romanticism and the Science of the Mind*, 66; and G. A. Wells, "Man and Nature," 314–315.
25. Coleridge, *Collected Works*, Vol. XVI: 1, 453.
26. *Ibid.*, Vol. XVI: 1, 520.
27. *Ibid.*, Vol. XVI: 1, 454. The note appears only in earlier versions of the poem.
28. *Ibid.*, Vol. XVI: 1, 453.
29. *Ibid.*, Vol. XVI: 1, 454. These lines were revised in later versions of the poem and do not appear in the original 1798 poem.
30. *Ibid.*, Vol. XVI: 1, 517.
31. *Ibid.*, Vol. XVI: 1, 518.
32. *Ibid.*, Vol. XVI: 1, 455–456.
33. *Ibid.*, Vol. XVI: 1, 519–520.
34. *Ibid.*, Vol. XVI: 1, 455.
35. Herder, *Philosophical Writings*, 74.
36. *Ibid.*, 103.
37. *Ibid.*, 103.
38. Monboddo, *Origin and Progress of Language*, Vol. 1, 492.
39. *Ibid.*, Vol. 1, 494.
40. *Ibid.*, Vol. 1, 208–209.
41. Herder, *Philosophical Writings*, 103.
42. *Ibid.*, 104.
43. *Ibid.*, 104.
44. *Ibid.*, 61.
45. *Ibid.*, 61.
46. Quoted in Kittler, *Discourse Networks*, 37.
47. Brown, *Dissertation on Poetry and Music*, 27.
48. Monboddo, *Origin and Progress of Language*, Vol. 1, 479.
49. Lamb, "Modern Metamorphoses," 160.
50. For discussion of the enlarged area in which the sentiments of humanity were allowed to operate, see Thomas, *Man and the Natural World*, 150. For discussion of the more troubled aspects of these cross-species acts of sympathetic identification, see Lamb, "Modern Metamorphoses," 160–166.
51. Saint Pierre, *Paul and Virginia*, 44.
52. Johnstone, *Clan-Albin*, 96–97.
53. Lewis, *The Monk*, 239–240.
54. Hayley, *Ballads Founded on Anecdotes Relating to Animals*, 1.
55. *Ibid.*, 4.
56. *Ibid.*, 7.
57. *Ibid.*, 61.
58. *Ibid.*, 65.
59. *Ibid.*, 68.
60. Crain, *The Story of A*, 84.

61. Barbauld, *Mrs. Barbauld's Lessons*, 8.
62. *Ibid.*, 80–81.
63. *Ibid.*, 5.
64. Crain, *The Story of A*, 103.
65. Barbauld, *Mrs. Barbauld's Lessons*, 70–71.
66. *Ibid.*, 165.
67. *Ibid.*, 166–167.
68. This lesson thus works differently than those in many alphabet primers which typically establish associations between letters and things, letters and images. See Crain, *The Story of A*, 38.
69. Barbauld, *Mrs. Barbauld's Lessons*, 167–168.
70. Trimmer, *Fabulous Histories*, ix–x.
71. *Ibid.*, x.
72. Bentley, "The Freaks of Learning," 91–102.
73. Trimmer, *Fabulous Histories*, 71.
74. *Ibid.*, 75.
75. *Ibid.*, 76.
76. Kittler, *Discourse Networks*, 59–60. Kittler quotes a German primer from 1804 that instructs the child to read and write the sentence: "I call myself a human being."
77. Trimmer, *Fabulous Histories*, 71–72.
78. Chambers, *Popular Rhymes*, 48.
79. *Ibid.*, 12.
80. Ian Duncan discusses this sense of discontinuity haunting the Scottish romance revival through the important figure of the uncanny. See Duncan, *Modern Romance*, 9; and Duncan, "The Upright Corpse," 34–36.
81. H. Coleridge, *Essays and Marginalia*, 306.
82. *Ibid.*, 305.
83. Trumpener, "Tales for Child Readers," 185.
84. Dryden, *Fables Ancient and Modern*; quoted in Knutson, "'Lessons Fairer than Flowers,'" 79.
85. Richmond, *Chaucer as Children's Literature*; quoted in Knutson, "'Lessons Fairer than Flowers,'" 81.
86. Mill, "What is Poetry?" 7.
87. *Ibid.*, 7.
88. *Ibid.*, 7–8.
89. *Ibid.*, 8.
90. Mill follows Wordsworth here, but drops Wordsworth's interest in the ordinary and trivial as cause enough for deep feeling and poetry.
91. Blair, *Lectures on Rhetoric*, Vol. II, 303.
92. Barbauld, *Selected Poetry and Prose*, 416–417.
93. For further discussion of how novels are defined in relation to poetry, see Rowland, "Romantic Poetry and the Romantic Novel," 123–127.
94. Hatfield, *An Experience Curriculum in English*, 47; quoted in Newman, *Ballad Collection*, 209.

95. Bates, *Ballad Book*, iii; quoted in Newman, *Ballad Collection*, 207. For an excellent discussion of the place of ballads in nineteenth-century American educational culture and in the development of New Criticism, see Newman, *Ballad Collection*, 185–228.
96. Duncan, *Modern Romance*, 7.
97. Jeffrey, "Review of *Corsair*," 56.
98. *Ibid.*, 58.
99. *Ibid.*, 58–59.
100. *Ibid.*, 59.
101. Peacock, *The Four Ages of Poetry*, 3 and 4.
102. *Ibid.*, 15.
103. *Ibid.*, 16.
104. *Ibid.*, 15.
105. *Ibid.*, 18.
106. See Byron's and Jeffrey's reviews of Wordsworth's poetry discussed in the Introduction for similar accounts of the infantilization of Romantic poetry.
107. H. Coleridge, *Essays and Marginalia*, 307.
108. Herder, *Philosophical Writings*, 73.
109. *Ibid.*, 74.
110. See Burke, *Philosophical Enquiry*; Smith, *Theory of Moral Sentiments*; Hume, "Of Tragedy."
111. Burke, *Philosophical Enquiry*, 46.
112. Aikin, "On the Pleasure," in *Miscellaneous Pieces*, 119.
113. *Ibid.*, 121.
114. For more on the ingestion imagery associated with early novels, see Ferris, *Achievement of Literary Authority*, 36–44.
115. Aikin, "On the Pleasure," 119.
116. See Chapter 4, pp. 172–175.
117. See Chapter 4, pp. 187–189.
118. Reid, *Inquiry Into the Human Mind*, 53.
119. *Ibid.*, 52.
120. *Ibid.*, 53.
121. *Ibid.*, 52.
122. *Ibid.*, 53.
123. Herder, *Philosophical Writings*, 68.
124. For further discussion on language and physiognomy, see Richardson, *British Romanticism and the Science of the Mind*, 76–77.
125. Reid, *Inquiry Into the Human Mind*, 60.
126. Mill, "What is Poetry?" 12. For Mill's influence on subsequent understandings of Romantic lyric poetry, see Zimmerman, *Romanticism, Lyricism, and History*, 1–37.
127. Blair, *Lectures on Rhetoric*, Vol. 1, 136.
128. Quoted in Aarsleff's introduction to Condillac, *Essay*, xxi.
129. Crawford, *Devolving English Literature*, 22–23. For another excellent account of Scottish linguistic improvement, see Sorensen, *Grammar of Empire*, 138–171.

130. Goring, *Rhetoric of Sensibility*, 42.
131. *Ibid.*, 43.
132. *Ibid.*, 35–39.
133. Foucault, *The Order of Things*, 91.
134. Blackwell, *Life and Writings of Homer*, 43.
135. Herder, *Philosophical Writings*, 66–67.
136. *Ibid.*, 68.
137. Smith, *Theory of Moral Sentiments*, 11–12.
138. Reid, *Inquiry Into the Human Mind*, 52–63.
139. Rousseau, "Essay on the Origin of Languages," 296.
140. *Ibid.*, 334. His full statement is, "Languages are made in order to be spoken, writing serves only as a substitute for speech."
141. Blair, *Lectures on Rhetoric*, Vol. 1, 136.
142. Siskin, *The Work of Writing*, 2–3.
143. For excellent discussions of Romantic-era intersections of writing and speech, textuality and orality, see Fielding, *Writing and Orality*, and McLane, *Balladeering*.
144. Luhmann, *Art as a Social System*, 5.

4 RETENTIVE EARS AND PRATTLING MOUTHS

1. Opie and Opie, *Lore and Language*, 1.
2. *Ibid.*, 1–2.
3. *Ibid.*, 87 and 94.
4. *Ibid.*, 95.
5. *Ibid.*, 95.
6. Rousseau, *Emile*, 106.
7. Opie and Opie, *Lore and Language*, 95.
8. Barbauld, *Selected Poetry and Prose*, 377.
9. Sutton-Smith, *Children's Folklore*, 4.
10. Opie and Opie, *Lore and Language*, 1.
11. *Ibid.*, 1.
12. *Ibid.*, 213.
13. Rousseau, *Emile*, 33.
14. Kittler, *Discourse Networks*, 25–69; Trumpener, *Bardic Nationalism*, 194–200.
15. Kittler, *Discourse Networks*, 24.
16. Trumpener, *Bardic Nationalism*, 3–34; Manning, "Antiquarianism, Balladry, and the Rehabilitation of Romance"; McLane, *Balladeering*.
17. Scott, *Letters of Sir Walter Scott*, 4; Aytoun, *The Ballads of Scotland*, xvii; Jamieson, *Popular Ballads and Songs*, i-ii.
18. Chambers, *Popular Rhymes*, 12.
19. *Ibid.*, 48.
20. Ferris, "Pedantry"; Manning, "Antiquarianism, Balladry, and the Rehabilitation of Romance"; Butler, "Antiquarianism (Popular)"; Phillips, *Society and Sentiment*.

21. Maxwell, "Inundations of Time," 420 and 422–423.
22. Nietzsche, *Untimely Meditations*, 73.
23. Maxwell, "Inundations of Time," 423.
24. Scott, *Minstrelsy of the Scottish Border*, Vol. II, 250, 276; Vol. III: 36, 59, 79.
25. Sharpe, *A Ballad Book*, vi.
26. Trumpener, *Bardic Nationalism*, 211–212.
27. McLane, *Balladeering*, 33.
28. Hogg, *Anecdotes of Scott*, 37–38.
29. Scott, *Minstrelsy of the Scottish Border*, Vol. I, 15.
30. For a more complete discussion of antiquarian citation and dating practices, see McLane, *Balladeering*, 16–84.
31. Beattie, *The Minstrel*, 18.
32. Locke, *Some Thoughts*, 196.
33. *Ibid.*, 196.
34. Akenside, *Pleasures of Imagination*, 24–25. Quoted in Edgeworth and Edgeworth, *Practical Education*, Vol. III, 141.
35. Aikin, "On the Pleasure," in *Miscellaneous Pieces*, 119.
36. Edgeworth and Edgeworth, *Practical Education*, Vol. III, 142.
37. *Ibid.*, Vol. III, 142–143.
38. Chambers, *Popular Rhymes*, 11–12. For best discussion of this debate, see Richardson, *Literature, Education, and Romanticism*, 112–127. See also Darton, *Children's Books in England*; Summerfield, *Fantasy and Reason*; Pickering, *John Locke and Children's Books*.
39. Chambers, *Popular Rhymes*, 11.
40. *Mother Goose's Melody*, x.
41. Sackville-West, *Nursery Rhymes*, 14–15.
42. Smith, *Lectures on Rhetoric and Belles Lettres*, 203.
43. Rousseau, *Emile*, 70.
44. See Pinker, *Language Instinct*, 155. We will return to this notion in our discussion of Wordsworth in Chapter 6.
45. Rousseau, *Emile*, 70.
46. *Ibid.*, 70.
47. Opie, *Adeline Mowbray*, 223.
48. Fenwick, *Secresy*, 50.
49. Barbauld, *Selected Poetry and Prose*, 144.
50. Clare, "The Woodman" in *The Early Poems of John Clare*, 294. See also the "little prattling tongue" and the mother who "stops its ill-timed prattle with a kiss" in Baillie's "A Winter's Day," in *Dramatic and Poetical Works*, 775.
51. Newell, *Games and Songs*, 22. Newell was the first secretary of the American Folklore Society and the first editor of the *Journal of American Folklore*; his book appeared eleven years before Alice Gomme's important British collection of children's folklore, *The Traditional Games of England, Scotland, and Ireland*.
52. See Chapter 1, pp. 25–26.

53. Wordsworth, "Epistle to Sir George Howland Beaumont," in *Shorter Poems*, 91.
54. Keats, "Letter to J. H. Reynolds, 19 February 1818" in *Letters of John Keats*, 65.
55. Wordsworth, *Shorter Poems*, 118. For a discussion of this and other "self-sufficing" children see Plotz, *Romanticism and the Vocation of Childhood*, 78.
56. Herder, *Philosophical Writings*, 66. See Chapter 2, p. 86.
57. Rousseau, *Emile*, 65.
58. *Ibid.*, 78.
59. Coleridge, *Collected Works*, Vol. XVI: 1, 503.
60. Wordsworth, *Poems in Two Volumes*, 100. See Plotz's discussion of Hartley as depicted in writings by both Wordsworth and Coleridge, *Romanticism and the Vocation of Childhood*, 191–251.
61. Wordsworth, *The Thirteen-Book Prelude*, 169 and 170, and *Poems in Two Volumes*, 273 and 274.
62. Rousseau, *Emile*, 180.
63. For a discussion of the Edgeworths' opposition to poetry and rote recitation see Richardson, *Literature, Education, and Romanticism*, 57–58.
64. Edgeworth and Edgeworth, *Practical Education*, Vol. III, 56–57.
65. *Ibid.*, Vol. III, 58–59.
66. *Ibid.*, Vol. III, 60.
67. *Ibid.*, Vol. III, 72.
68. *Ibid.*, Vol. III, 73.
69. *Ibid.*, Vol. I, 98.
70. Rousseau, *Emile*, 107. Locke describes how words in the child's mouth are only "so much insignificant noise." See Locke, *Essay Concerning Human Understanding*, Vol. II, 12.
71. Rousseau, *Emile*, 107.
72. Edgeworth and Edgeworth, *Practical Education*, Vol. I, 104.
73. R. L. Edgeworth, *Poetry Explained*, iii. See also Edgeworth and Edgeworth, *Practical Education*, Vol. II, 154 and 166–167.
74. Edgeworth and Edgeworth, *Practical Education*, Vol. III, 101 and 96.
75. Southey, *The Doctor*, 87.
76. *Ibid.*, 88.
77. Coleridge, *Notebooks*, Vol. I, 1828.
78. Newell, *Games and Songs*, 22.
79. *Ibid.*, 27.
80. Fine, "Children and Their Culture," 180.
81. Newell, *Games and Songs*, 28.
82. Sackville-West, *Nursery Rhymes*, 11.
83. Opie and Opie, *Lore and Language*, 12.
84. Buchan, *The Ballad and the Folk*, 62.
85. Child, *The English and Scottish Popular Ballads*, Vol. I, vii.
86. Scott, *Minstrelsy of the Scottish Border*, Vol. I, cxxxii–cxxxiii.
87. The fact that one can recall a ballad from one's own childhood, or can refer to an individual who recollects a ballad from infancy becomes an important

credential that the antiquarian frequently mentions to establish the age and authenticity of the ballad. See Scott's introduction to "Fause Foodrage" as just one example, *Minstrelsy of the Scottish Border*, Vol. III, 3.

88. Buchan, *The Ballad and the Folk*, 62.
89. Jamieson, *Popular Ballads and Songs*, ix.
90. *Ibid.*, 23. McLane discusses this citation in *Balladeering*, 60–61.
91. Quoted in Buchan, *The Ballad and the Folk*, 64.
92. *Ibid.*, 66.
93. Quoted in Nichols, *Illustrations of the Literary History of the Eighteenth Century*, 89.
94. Buchan, *The Ballad and the Folk*, 64.
95. Quoted in *ibid.*, 66.
96. Quoted in Nichols, *Illustrations of the Literary History of the Eighteenth Century*, 89 and 90.
97. Buchan, *The Ballad and the Folk*, 56.
98. *Ibid.*, 67–68.
99. *Ibid.*, 66.
100. Lockhart, *Memoirs of the Life of Sir Walter Scott*, Vol. I, 83.

5 ONE CHILD'S TRIFLE IS ANOTHER MAN'S RELIC

1. Scott, *The Letters of Sir Walter Scott*, 4.
2. *Ibid.*, 4.
3. Child, *English and Scottish Popular Ballads*, Vol. II, 342.
4. For a discussion of the prominence of violent subject matter in Gaelic lullabies see Hillers, "Dialogue or Monologue?", 34.
5. See McDonagh, *Child Murder and British Culture*, 9.
6. Motherwell, *Minstrelsy Ancient and Modern*, iv; Buchan, *Ancient Ballads and Songs*, iii.
7. Peter Buchan, *Ancient Ballads and Songs*, iii. Susan Stewart identifies the contrast between the revival's emphasis on the ballads' martial qualities and the thematics of the ballads themselves. See Stewart, *Crimes of Writing*, 114–115.
8. Nick Groom discusses the problem posed by the ballad's rude, scandalous and violent contents to Percy's *Reliques of Ancient English Poetry* in *The Making of Percy's* Reliques, 40–60.
9. Scott, *Minstrelsy of the Scottish Border*, Vol. III, 100–101; and, in reference to infanticide, Kinloch, *Ancient Scottish Ballads*, 44.
10. Friedman, *Ballad Revival*, 8. For a contextualization of the ballad revival within the period's larger revival of older poetic forms, see Curran, *Poetic Form and British Romanticism*, 14–28 and 129.
11. Marilyn Butler defines "popular antiquarianism" as the study of British national culture: of English, Welsh, Gaelic and Irish as vernacular languages, and of their oral as well as their written traditions – not merely

literary forms and art, but beliefs, customs, and festivities." See Butler, "Antiquarianism (Popular)," 328.

12. For discussion of antiquarians as comic types and objects of caricature and ridicule, see Ferris, "Pedantry," 280, and Manning, "Antiquarianism, the Scottish Science of Man," 58.

13. Manning, "Antiquarianism, Balladry, and the Rehabilitation of Romance," 45.

14. For more on recent interest in Romantic antiquarianism and its similarities to current historicist practice, see Ferris, "Melancholy, Memory," 90.

15. For the Romantic habit of locating the popular in the past, see Groom, *The Making of Percy's* Reliques, 26, and Stewart, *Crimes of Writing*, 67 and 107.

16. For the most complete and influential account of Romantic historicism, see Chandler, *England in 1819*.

17. Ferris, "Pedantry"; Manning, "Antiquarianism, Balladry, and the Rehabilitation of Romance"; Maxwell, "Inundations of Time."

18. For an account of how ballads circulated in manuscripts and letters and how that textual circulation constructed its oral sources, see McLane, *Balladeering*, 44–83.

19. See Groom, *The Making of Percy's* Reliques, 26–30; Stewart, *Crimes of Writing*, 68 and 121–122; McLane, *Balladeering*, 76–77.

20. The term is McLane's in *Balladeering*, 213–215.

21. Maxwell, "Inundations of Time," 439.

22. Stewart, *Crimes of Writing*, 67.

23. Rimbault, *Nursery Rhymes*, v; Brand, *Observations on the Popular Antiquities*, vii; Halliwell, *Nursery Rhymes and Nursery Tales*, ix; Opie and Opie, *Oxford Dictionary of Nursery Rhymes*, 1.

24. Scott, *Minstrelsy of the Scottish Border*, Vol. I, xii.

25. Quoted in Groom, *The Making of Percy's* Reliques, 40.

26. Halliwell, *Nursery Rhymes and Nursery Tales*, 127.

27. Review of *A Vindication of the Celts, from Ancient Authorities* in the July 1803 issue of the *Edinburgh Review*. Quoted in Ferris, "Pedantry", 275 where she also notes the period's predilection for the term "trifling."

28. Scott, *The Antiquary*, 282. Maxwell quotes this line and defines the term "trifles" as "those tiny clues … from which the ardent investigator attempts to reconstruct the medieval or ancient past." See Maxwell, "Inundations of Time," 452.

29. Chambers, *Popular Rhymes*, vi.

30. Halliwell, *Nursery Rhymes and Nursery Tales*, 128.

31. Gomme, *Traditional Games*, 531.

32. Bett, *Nursery Rhymes and Tales*, 1.

33. *Ibid.*, 2.

34. Brand, *Observations on the Popular Antiquities*, vii; Opie and Opie, *Oxford Dictionary of Nursery Rhymes*, 1.

35. Opie and Opie, *Lore and Language*, 2.

36. Rimbault, *Nursery Rhymes*, v.
37. Newell, *Games and Songs*, 3–4 and 7.
38. *Ibid.*, 10.
39. Butler, "Antiquarianism (Popular)," 332.
40. Opie and Opie, *Oxford Dictionary of Nursery Rhymes*, 3.
41. *Ibid.*, 2 and 3.
42. *Ibid.*, 3 and 4.
43. *Ibid.*, 3–4.
44. *Ibid.*, 4.
45. Scott, *Minstrelsy of the Scottish Border*, Vol. I, ix, x, xi.
46. Chambers, *Popular Rhymes*, 12. See the full passage in Chapter 3, p. 136.
47. Scott's *Minstrelsy* contained a section of imitations and new ballads, suggesting a fluidity between those collected and those created.
48. Motherwell, *Minstrelsy Ancient and Modern*, iv. Joseph Ritson was influential in this shift of sensibility in ballad collection.
49. The nineteenth-century culmination of this literary aesthetic of authenticity in the realm of ballad collection is Francis James Child's five-volume, ten-part *English and Scottish Popular Ballads*, which prints every available version of every known ballad.
50. Stewart, *Crimes of Writing*, 105.
51. Scott, *Minstrelsy of the Scottish Border*, Vol. I, cxxxvii.
52. Penny Fielding notes that the ballads are not "themselves historical" in Scott's understanding, although he does understand the language of the ballads as more "representational than creative." While I agree and am indebted to Fielding's analysis of the *Minstrelsy*, I would like to specify further Scott's interest in the formal qualities of the ballads' language, the difference being between representing history and tradition and carrying them. See Fielding, *Writing and Orality*, 55–56.
53. Scott, *Minstrelsy of the Scottish Border*, Vol. III, xii.
54. *Ibid.*, Vol. I, xiii.
55. *Ibid.*, Vol. I, xiii.
56. *Ibid.*, Vol. I, xvi–xvii.
57. Bourdieu, *Distinction*, 34.
58. *Ibid.*, 53–54.
59. Motherwell, *Minstrelsy Ancient and Modern*, xxvi.
60. *Ibid.*, viii.
61. *Ibid.*, viii.
62. *Ibid.*, 297.
63. Jack Kerkering discusses an instance of what I consider formal nationalism in the *Letters of Malachi Malagrowther*, demonstrating how Scott locates "Scottishness" in such formal qualities as metre, rather than, for instance, in a poem's thematic call-to-arms, in order to accommodate his mixed allegiances to both Scottish nationalism and the British Union. See "'We are Five-and-Forty': Meter and National Identity in Walter Scott," 86.
64. Chambers, *Scottish Ballads*, 4.

65. For a discussion of epic as national form, see Stewart, *Crimes of Writing*, 74–78; Bakhtin, *The Dialogic Imagination*, 13–40; Quint, *Epic and Empire*.
66. Fielding, *Writing and Orality*, 53.
67. Vita Sackville-West, *Nursery Rhymes*, 31.
68. Opie and Opie, *Lore and Language*, 12 and 57.
69. Bourdieu, *Distinction*, 54.
70. *Ibid.*, 35.
71. See Chapter 4, pp. 161–162.
72. Opie and Opie, *Lore and Language*, 2 and 14.
73. *Ibid.*, 109 and 118.
74. *Ibid.*, 104–105.
75. *Ibid.*, 14–15.
76. *Ibid.*, 15.
77. *Ibid.*, 121.
78. *Ibid.*, 129.
79. *Ibid.*, 141–142.
80. *Ibid.*, 154–155.
81. *Ibid.*, 98–99.
82. Gomme, *Traditional Games of England, Scotland, and Ireland*, 460.
83. For full quote, see Chapter 3, p. 136.
84. Opie and Opie, *Language and Lore*, 208 and 210.
85. Sackville-West, *Nursery Rhymes*, 66.
86. Newell, *Games and Songs*, 12.

6 THE LAYERS AND FORMS OF THE CHILD'S MIND

1. John Locke, *Some Thoughts*, 83.
2. Scott, *Guy Mannering*, 40.
3. *Ibid.*, 40.
4. *Ibid.*, 146.
5. *Ibid.*, 123.
6. *Ibid.*, 114.
7. *Ibid.*, 241–242.
8. *Ibid.*, 243.
9. *Ibid.*, 244.
10. *Ibid.*, 244.
11. *Ibid.*, 246.
12. *Ibid.*, 247.
13. *Ibid.*, 23–24.
14. *Ibid.*, 248.
15. *Ibid.*, 247.
16. *Ibid.*, 248.
17. *Ibid.*, 320.
18. *Ibid.*, 337 and 339.
19. *Ibid.*, 307 and 308.

20. William Wordsworth, *Lyrical Ballads*, 738–739.

21. *Ibid.*, 742, 746–747.

22. *Ibid.*, 122, 377.

23. Robert Mayo, "Contemporaneity," 491.

24. Jacobus, *Tradition and Experiment*, 184.

25. Swann, "'Martha's Name,'" 61.

26. For an excellent discussion of how the popular ballad troubles elite literary forms in the eighteenth century, see Newman, *Ballad Collection*.

27. Jacobus, *Tradition and Experiment*, 209; Mayo, "Contemporaneity," 495–496.

28. Swann, "'Martha's Name,'" 76.

29. Parrish, *The Art of the* Lyrical Ballads, 85.

30. Wordsworth, *Lyrical Ballads*, 746.

31. *Ibid.*, 136.

32. *Ibid.*, 67.

33. Jacobus, *Tradition and Experiment*, 233.

34. *Ibid.*, 241–242; and Parrish, *The Art of the* Lyrical Ballads, 86.

35. Wordsworth, *Lyrical Ballads*, 77–85.

36. *Ibid.*, 350–351.

37. Parrish, *The Art of the* Lyrical Ballads, 101 and 100.

38. Bewell, *Wordsworth and the Enlightenment*, 171.

39. See Chapter 3, p. 120.

40. Wordsworth, *Lyrical Ballads*, 350.

41. See Chapter 2, pp. 103–106.

42. See Chapter 3, pp. 140–144.

43. Bewell, *Wordsworth and the Enlightenment*, 34.

44. See Chapter 4, pp. 169–172.

45. Swann, "'Martha's Name,'" 68 and 69.

46. Mother and nurse, in fact, offer very different versions of cultural and literary origins, but these distinctions are beyond the scope of my discussion here. See Trumpener, *Bardic Nationalism*, 193–203.

47. Wordsworth, *Lyrical Ballads*, 83.

48. Swann, "'Martha's Name,'" 66.

49. Wordsworth, *Lyrical Ballads*, 351.

50. Swann, "'Martha's Name,'" 67.

51. Wordsworth, "The Two-Part *Prelude* of 1799" in *The Prelude*, 8.

52. *Ibid.*, 8.

53. See Chapter 2, pp. 103–106.

54. Blackwell, *Life and Writings of Homer*, 11.

55. Wordsworth, *The Thirteen-Book Prelude*, 216.

56. *Ibid.*, 216.

57. *Ibid.*, 215.

58. Wordsworth, *Lyrical Ballads*, 253.

59. Wordsworth, *The Thirteen-Book Prelude*, 173, Book v.

60. Of course, as a number of important readings of the revisions to this passage point out, literary allusions to both Shakespeare and Milton exist in the 1799

version, thus lending the passage a "bookish" quality even before it lands in Book V of the 1805 *Prelude*. The importance of books and literature is made more explicit, however, to signal both the individual and cultural development that Wordsworth understands as having occurred between Part 1 and Book V, as it were, as well as to reinforce their recapitulating relationship to each other. See Goodman, "Making Time for History," 563–577; Peter Manning, "Reading Wordsworth's Revisions," 3–28; Wolfson, "The Illusion of Mastery," 917–935.

61. Thus where Siskin describes the revisions to this episode as producing the effect of continuous individual development or growth, I read the revisions as replicating the period's understanding of historical or stadial development and its analogous relationship to individual development. See Siskin, *Historicity*, 115–124.
62. Wordsworth, *The Thirteen-Book Prelude*, 166.
63. See Chapter 3, p. 147.
64. Wordsworth, *The Thirteen-Book Prelude*, 167.
65. *Ibid.*, 174.
66. *Ibid.*, 176.
67. Wordsworth, "The Two-Part *Prelude* of 1799" in *The Prelude*, 8.
68. Wordsworth, *The Thirteen-Book Prelude*, 122, 124 and 126.
69. *Ibid.*, 126.
70. *Ibid.*, 120.
71. *Ibid.*, 211 and 221.
72. *Ibid.*, 123.
73. *Ibid.*, 117.
74. *Ibid.*, 144.
75. *Ibid.*, 122.
76. Pinker, *Language Instinct*, 61. Coleridge and his account of the creation of "Kubla Khan" is the Romantic poet Pinker turns to for an example of "mentalese."
77. Wordsworth, *The Thirteen-Book Prelude*, 107 and 110.
78. *Ibid.*, 111.
79. *Ibid.*, 113.
80. Pinker, *Language Instinct*, 154–155.
81. See Chapter 4, pp. 183–184.
82. Wordsworth, *The Thirteen-Book Prelude*, 302.
83. *Ibid.*, 303.
84. *Ibid.*, 302.
85. *Ibid.*, 304.
86. *Ibid.*, 125.
87. For discussion of how the "spots of time" suspend the autobiographical self between its felt origins and the knowledge of its subsequent ineffability, see Pfau, *Wordsworth's Profession*, 316.
88. *Ibid.*, 125.
89. Scott, *The Antiquary*, 75.

90. Wordsworth, "The Fountain," quoted in Scott, *The Antiquary*, 75.
91. *Ibid.*, 3.
92. Wordsworth, *Lyrical Ballads*, 744 and 742.
93. Scott, *The Antiquary*, 282.
94. Wordsworth, *The Prelude*, 496.
95. Wordsworth, "The Two-Part *Prelude* of 1799" in *The Prelude*, 19–20.
96. For discussions of this fragment see Wu, *Wordsworth: An Inner Life*, 145–146; Jonathan Wordsworth, "As with the Silence of the Thought," 60–63; Seamus Perry, "Coleridge and Wordsworth: Imagination, Accidence, and Inevitability," 172–175; Pfau, *Wordsworth's Profession*, 324–325.
97. Jonathan Wordsworth, "As with the Silence of the Thought," 60.

Bibliography

PRIMARY SOURCES

Aikin, John and Anna Laetitia. *Miscellaneous Pieces in Prose*. London: Joseph Johnson, 1773.

Akenside, Mark. *The Pleasures of Imagination*. Otley: Woodstock Books, 2000. Reprint of 1795 edition.

Aytoun, William. *The Ballads of Scotland*. Edinburgh: William Blackwood and Sons, 1858.

Baillie, Joanna. *The Dramatic and Poetical Works of Joanna Baillie*. London: Longman, Brown, Green, and Longmans, 1851.

Barbauld, Anna Letitia. *Mrs. Barbauld's Lessons for Children*. New York: C. S. Francis & Co., 18?.

  Selected Poetry and Prose. Ed. William McCarthy and Elizabeth Kraft. Peterborough, Ontario: Broadview, 2002.

Bates, Katharine Lee. *Ballad Book*. Freeport, NY: Books for Libraries Press, 1966.

Bayly, Anselm. *An Introduction to Languages, Literary and Philosophical*. London: John Rivington, 1758.

Beattie, James. *The Minstrel, Or the Progress of Genius*. London: Charles Dilly, 1795.

Bett, Henry. *Nursery Rhymes and Tales: Their Origin and History*. London: Methuen & Co., 1924.

Blackwell, Thomas. *An Inquiry into the Life and Writings of Homer*. London: 1734.

Blair, Hugh. "A Critical Dissertation on the Poems of Ossian, the Son of Fingal." Reprinted in Macpherson, James. *The Poems of Ossian and Related Works*. Ed. Howard Gaskill. Edinburgh University Press, 1996.

  Lectures on Rhetoric and Belles Lettres. Ed. Harold F. Harding. Carbondale, IL: Southern Illinois University Press, 1965.

Brand, John. *Observations on the Popular Antiquities of Great Britain*. Ed. Sir Henry Ellis. New York: AMS Press, 1970.

Brown, John. *A Dissertation on the Rise, Union and Power, the Progressions, Separations, and Corruptions of Poetry and Music*. London: L. Davis, 1763.

Browne, Thomas Gunter. *Hermes Unmasked*. Facsimile of 1795 Edition. Menston: Scolar Press, 1969.

Buchan, Peter. *Ancient Ballads and Songs of the North of Scotland.* Edinburgh:
   W. & D. Laing, 1828.
Burke, Edmund. *A Philosophical Enquiry into the Origin of our Ideas of the Sublime
   and Beautiful.* Ed. James T. Boulton. Notre Dame, IN: University of Notre
   Dame Press, 1986.
Burns, Robert. *The Canongate Burns.* Ed. Andrew Noble. Edinburgh: Canongate
   Books, 2001.
Byron, George Gordon. "Review of Wordsworth's *Poems in Two Volumes,*"
   *Monthly Literary Recreations, or Magazine of General Information and
   Amusement,* XIV (August, 1807). Reprinted in Moore, Thomas. *The
   Works of Lord Byron: With his Letters and Journals, and his Life.* London:
   John Murray, 1832.
Chambers, Robert. *Popular Rhymes of Scotland.* London and Edinburgh: W. & R.
   Chambers, 1870.
   Scottish Ballads. Edinburgh: Ballantine and Co., 1829.
   Vestiges of the Natural History of Creation and other Evolutionary Writings. Ed.
   James Secord. Chicago: University of Chicago Press, 1994.
Child, Francis James. *The English and Scottish Popular Ballads.* New York: Dover, 1965.
Clare, John. *The Early Poems of John Clare: 1804–1822.* Ed. Eric Robinson and
   David Powell. Oxford: Clarendon Press, 1989.
Coleridge, Hartley. *Essays and Marginalia.* London: Edward Moxon, 1851.
Coleridge, Samuel Taylor. *The Collected Works of Samuel Taylor Coleridge.* Ed. J. C. C.
   Mays. Vol. XVI, Part 1. *Poetical Works.* Princeton University Press, 2001.
   The Notebooks of Samuel Taylor Coleridge. Vol. 1. Ed. Kathleen Coburn. New
   York: Pantheon Books, 1957.
Condillac, Etienne Bonnot de. *Essay on the Origin of Human Knowledge.* Ed.
   Hans Aarsleff. Cambridge University Press, 2001.
Degérando, Joseph-Marie. *The Observation of Savage Peoples.* Ed. F. C. T.
   Moore. Berkeley, CA: University of California Press, 1969.
Edgeworth, Maria and R. L. *Practical Education.* New York: Woodstock Books, 1996.
Edgeworth, R. L. *Poetry Explained for the Use of Young People.* London: J. Johnson, 1802.
Enfield, William. "Is Verse Essential to Poetry," *The Monthly Magazine.* London:
   R Phillips (2 July 1796).
Fenwick, Eliza. *Secresy, or The Ruin on the Rock.* Ed. Isobel Grundy.
   Peterborough, Ontario: Broadview Press, 1998.
Ferguson, Adam. *An Essay on the History of Civil Society.* Ed. Duncan Forbes.
   Edinburgh University Press, 1966.
Fontenelle, Bernard Le Bovier de. *Digression sur les Anciens et les Modernes.*
   Reprinted in *The Idea of Progress.* Tr. and ed. Frederick J. Teggart.
   Berkeley, CA: University of California Press, 1949.
Gomme, Alice Bertha. *The Traditional Games of England, Scotland, and Ireland;
   with Tunes, Singing-Rhymes, and Methods of Playing According to the Variants
   Extant and Recorded in Different Parts of the Kingdom.* New York: Dover, 1964.
Halliwell, James Orchard. *Nursery Rhymes and Nursery Tales of England.* London:
   Frederick Warne and Co., 1842.

Hatfield, W. Wilbur. *An Experience Curriculum in English.* New York: D. Appleton, 1935.

Hayley, William. *Ballads Founded on Anecdotes Relating to Animals with Prints Designed and Engraved by William Blake.* London: Richard Phillips, 1805.

Herder, Johann Gottfried von. *Philosophical Writings.* Tr. and ed. Michael N. Forster. Cambridge University Press, 2002.

Hogg, James. *Anecdotes of Scott.* Ed. Jill Rubenstein. Edinburgh University Press, 1999.

Hopkins, Gerard Manley. *Selected Poetry.* Oxford University Press, 1986.

Hume, David. "Of Tragedy," in *Essays Moral, Political and Literary.* Ed. Eugene F. Miller. Indianapolis: Liberty Fund, 1985.

A Treatise of Human Nature. Second edition. Ed. P. H. Nidditch. Oxford: Clarendon Press, 1978.

Inchbald, Elizabeth. *Nature and Art.* Ed. Shawn Lisa Maurer. Peterborough, Ontario: Broadview Press, 2005.

Jamieson, Robert. *Popular Ballads and Songs.* Edinburgh: Constable and Co., 1806.

Jeffrey, Francis. "Review of *Corsair,*" *Edinburgh Review*, 23 (April, 1814). Reprinted in *Byron: The Critical Heritage.* Ed. Andrew Rutherford. London: Routledge and Kegan Paul, 1970.

"Review of Wordsworth, *Poems, in Two Volumes,*" *Edinburgh Review* 11 (October, 1807).

Johnstone, Christian Isobel. *Clan-Albin: A National Tale.* Glasgow: Association for Scottish Literary Studies, 2003.

Keats, John. *Letters of John Keats.* Ed. Robert Gittings. Oxford University Press, 1970.

Kinloch, George. *Ancient Scottish Ballads.* London: Longman, 1827.

Lafiteau, Joseph François. *Customs of the American Indians Compared with the Customs of Primitive Times.* Ed. and tr. William N. Fenton and Elizabeth L. Moore. Toronto: 1974.

Lewis, Matthew. *The Monk.* Peterborough, Ontario: Broadview Press, 2004.

Locke, John. *An Essay Concerning Human Understanding.* Ed. Alexander Campbell Fraser. New York: Dover Publications, 1959.

Some Thoughts Concerning Education. Ed. John W. and Jean S. Yolton. Oxford: Clarendon Press, 1989.

Two Treatises of Government. Cambridge University Press, 1960.

Lockhart, J. G. *Memoirs of the Life of Sir Walter Scott.* Vol. 1. Edinburgh: Robert Cadell, 1837.

Mill, John Stuart. "What is Poetry?" Reprinted in *Essays on Poetry.* Ed. F. Parvin Sharpless. Columbia, SC: University of South Carolina Press, 1976.

Millar, John. *The Origin of the Distinction of Ranks.* Third edition. London: J. Murray, 1781.

Monboddo, James Burnet, Lord. *Of the Origin and Progress of Language.* Edinburgh: J. Balfour, 1774.

Mother Goose's Melody: A Facsimile Reproduction of the Earliest Known Edition. London: A. H. Bullen, 1904.

Motherwell, William. *Minstrelsy Ancient and Modern*. Glasgow: John Wylie, 1827.

Murray, Alexander. *History of the European Languages*. Edinburgh: Constable & Co., 1823.

Newell, William Wells. *Games and Songs of American Children*. New York: Harper & Brothers, 1883.

Nichols, John Bowyer. *Illustrations of the Literary History of the Eighteenth Century*. London: J. B. Nichols and Son, 1848.

Opie, Amelia. *Adeline Mowbray*. Ed. Shelley King and John B. Pierce. Oxford University Press, 1999.

Opie, Iona and Peter. *The Lore and Language of Schoolchildren*. New York: New York Review of Books, 2001.

The Oxford Dictionary of Nursery Rhymes. Oxford University Press, 1997.

Pascal, Blaise. "Fragment de preface sur le traite du vide." Reprinted in *The Idea of Progress*. Tr. and ed. Frederick J. Teggart. Berkeley, CA: University of California Press, 1949.

Peacock, Thomas Love. *Peacock's Four Ages of Poetry*. Ed. H. F. B. Brett-Smith. Oxford: Basil Blackwell, 1921.

Perrault, Charles. *Parallele des Anciens et des Modernes en ce qui regarde les arts et les sciences*. Reprinted in *The Idea of Progress*. Tr. and ed. Frederick J. Teggart. Berkeley, CA: University of California Press, 1949.

Reid, Thomas. *An Inquiry into the Human Mind, on the Principles of Common Sense*. Ed. Derek R. Brookes. University Park, PA: Pennsylvania State University Press, 1997.

Rimbault, Edward F. *Nursery Rhymes, with The Tunes to which They are Still Sung in the Nurseries of England, Obtained Principally from Oral Tradition*. London: Cramer, Beale, & Co. 1846.

Robertson, William. *The History of America*. Eighth edition. London: Cadell and Davies, 1800.

Rousseau, Jean-Jacques. *The Discourses and Other Early Political Writing*. Ed. Victor Gourevitch. Cambridge: Cambridge University Press, 1997.

Emile, or On Education. Tr. and ed. Allan Bloom. New York: Basic Books, 1979.

"Essay on the Origin of Languages in which Melody and Musical Imitation are Treated." *The Collected Writings of Rousseau*. Vol. vii. Tr. and ed. John T. Scott. Hanover, NH: University Press of New England, 1998.

Sackville-West, Vita. *Nursery Rhymes*. London: Michael Joseph, 1950.

Saint Pierre, Bernardin de. *Paul and Virginia*. Tr. Helen Maria Williams. Doylestown, PA: Wildside Press, 1851.

Scott, Walter. *The Antiquary*. Edinburgh University Press, 1995.

Guy Mannering. Ed. P. D. Garside. Edinburgh University Press, 1999.

The Letters of Sir Walter Scott, 1787–1807. Ed. H. J. C. Grierson. London: Constable & Co., 1932.

Minstrelsy of the Scottish Border. Vols. i–iii of *Poetical Works*. Edinburgh: Cadell & Co., 1830.

Sharpe, Charles, Kirkpatrick. *A Ballad Book*. Edinburgh: William Blackwood and Sons, 1823.

Sharpe, Gregory. *Two Dissertations Upon the Origin, Construction, Division, and Relation of Language and Upon the Original Powers of Letters*. London: John Millan, 1751.

Shelley, P. B. *Shelley's Poetry and Prose*. Ed. Donald Reiman and Neil Fraistat. New York: W.W. Norton & Company, 2002.

Smith, Adam. "Considerations Concerning the First Formation of Languages." *Lectures on Rhetoric and Belles Lettres*. Ed. J. C. Bryce. Indianapolis: Liberty Fund, 1985.

Lectures on Rhetoric and Belles Lettres. Indianapolis: Liberty Fund, 1985.

The Theory of Moral Sentiments. Ed. D. D. Raphael and A. L. Macfie. Indianpolis: Liberty Fund, 1982.

Southey, Robert. *The Doctor &c*. New York: Harper & Brothers, 1836.

Stewart, Dugald. "Account of the Life and Writings of Adam Smith." Vol. x of *The Collected Works of Dugald Stewart*. Ed. Sir William Hamilton. Edinburgh: Thomas Constable and Co., 1812.

"Account of the Life and Writings of William Robertson." Vol. x of *The Collected Works of Dugald Stewart*. Ed. Sir William Hamilton. Edinburgh: Thomas Constable and Co., 1812.

Sully, James. *Studies of Childhood*. New York: D. Appleton and Co., 1908.

Temple, Sir William. *Miscellaneous Essays*. Ed. Samuel Holt Monk. Ann Arbor, MI: University of Michigan Press, 1963.

Trimmer, Sarah. *Fabulous Histories, Designed for the Instruction of Children, Respecting their Treatment of Animals*. London: T. Longman, 1791.

"Whether the Present Age Can, or Cannot be Reckoned Among the Ages of Poetical Excellence," *Monthly Literary Recreations, or Magazine of General Information and Amusement*, 15 (September, 1807) 170–171.

Wordsworth, William. *Lyrical Ballads and Other Poems, 1797–1800*. Ed. James Butler and Karen Green. Ithaca, NY: Cornell University Press, 1992.

Poems in Two Volumes, and other Poems, 1800–1807. Ed. Jared Curtis. Ithaca, NY: Cornell University Press, 1983.

The Prelude: 1799, 1805, 1850. Ed. Jonathan Wordsworth, M. H. Abrams, and Stephen Gill. New York: W. W. Norton & Company, 1979.

Shorter Poems: 1807–1820. Ed. Carl H. Ketcham. Ithaca, NY: Cornell University Press, 1989.

The Thirteen-Book Prelude. Ed. Mark L. Reed. Vol 1. Ithaca, NY: Cornell University Press, 1991.

SECONDARY SOURCES

Aarsleff, Hans. *From Locke to Saussure: Essays on the Study of Language and Intellectual History*. Minneapolis: University of Minnesota Press, 1982.

The Study of Language in England, 1780–1860. Minneapolis: University of Minnesota Press, 1983.

Anderson, Benedict. *Imagined Communities: Reflections on the Origin and Spread of Nationalism.* Revised edition. London: Verso, 1991.

Aravamudan, Srinivas. *Tropicopolitans: Colonialism and Agency, 1688–1804.* Durham, NC: Duke University Press, 1999.

Ariès, Philippe. *Centuries of Childhood: A Social History of Family Life.* Tr. Robert Baldick. New York: Vintage Books, 1962.

Babenroth, Charles A. *English Childhood: Wordsworth's Treatment of Childhood in the Light of English Poetry.* New York: Columbia University Press, 1922.

Bakhtin, M. M. *The Dialogic Imagination.* Tr. Caryl Emerson, Michael Holquist. Austin: University of Texas, 1981.

Barker-Benfield, G. J. *The Culture of Sensibility: Sex and Society in Eighteenth-Century Britain.* University of Chicago Press, 1996.

Benjamin, Walter. *Illuminations.* Ed. Hannah Arendt. New York: Schocken Books, 1968.

Bentley, Jr., G.E. "The Freaks of Learning," *Colby Quarterly.* 18. 2 (June, 1982).

Bewell, Alan. *Wordsworth and the Enlightenment: Nature, Man and Society in the Experimental Poetry.* New Haven, CT: Yale University Press, 1989.

Boas, George. *The Cult of Childhood.* London: Warburg Institute at the University of London, 1966.

Bourdieu, Pierre. *Distinction: A Social Critique of the Judgement of Taste.* Tr. Richard Nice. Cambridge, MA: Harvard University Press, 1984.

Bowler, Peter J. *The Invention of Progress: The Victorians and the Past.* Oxford: Basil Blackwell, 1989.

Brissenden, R. F. *Virtue in Distress: Studies in the Novel of Sentiment from Richardson to Sade.* New York: Harper & Row, 1974.

Brown, Laura. *Fables of Modernity: Literature and Culture in the English Eighteenth Century.* Ithaca, NY: Cornell University Press, 2001.

Brown, Mary Ellen. "Old Singing Women and the Canons of Scottish Balladry and Song," in *A History of Scottish Women's Writing.* Ed. Douglas Gifford and Dorothy McMillan. Edinburgh University Press, 1997.

Buchan, David. *The Ballad and the Folk.* East Lothian: Tuckwell Press, 1997.

Butler, Marilyn. "Antiquarianism (Popular)," in *Oxford Companion to the Romantic Age: British Culture 1776–1832.* Ed. Jon Mee, Gillian Russel and Clara Tuite. Oxford University Press, 1999.

Chandler, James. *England in 1819: The Politics of Literary Culture and the Case of Romantic Historicism.* Chicago University Press, 1998.

"Moving Accidents: The Emergence of Sentimental Probability," in *The Age of Cultural Revolutions: Britain and France, 1750–1820.* Ed. Colin Jones and Dror Wahrman. Berkeley: University of California Press, 2002.

Wordsworth's Second Nature: A Study of the Poetry and the Politics. Chicago University Press, 1984.

Clayton, Jay. *Romantic Vision and the Novel.* Cambridge University Press, 1987.

Cohen, Murray. *Sensible Words: Linguistic Practice in England, 1640–1785.* Baltimore: The Johns Hopkins University Press, 1977.

Coleman, William. *Biology in the Nineteenth Century: Problems of Form, Function, and Transformation.* Cambridge University Press, 1977.

Coveney, Peter. *The Image of Childhood: The Individual and Society: A Study of the Theme in English Literature.* Harmondsworth: Penguin Books, 1967. *Poor Monkey: The Child in Literature.* London: Rockliff, 1957.

Craig, Cairns. "Scott's Staging of the Nation," *Studies in Romanticism.* 40. 1 (Spring, 2001).

Crain, Patricia. *The Story of A: The Alphabetization of America from* The New England Primer *to* The Scarlet Letter. Stanford University Press, 2000.

Crawford, Robert. *Devolving English Literature.* Oxford: Clarendon Press, 1992.

Culler, A. Dwight. *The Victorian Mirror of History.* New Haven, CT: Yale University Press, 1985.

Cunningham, Hugh. *Children and Childhood in Western Society Since 1500.* Harlow: Pearson Longman, 2005.

Curran, Stuart. *Poetic Form and British Romanticism.* Oxford University Press, 1986.

Darton, F. J. Harvey. *Children's Books in England: Five Centuries of Social Life.* Rev. Brian Alderson. Cambridge University Press, 1982.

Davis, Leith. *Acts of Union: Scotland and the Literary Negotiation of the British Nation, 1707–1830.* Stanford University Press, 1998.

De Man, Paul. *Blindness and Insight: Essays in the Rhetoric of Contemporary Criticism.* Minneapolis: University of Minnesota Press, 1971.

de Mause, Lloyd, ed. *The History of Childhood.* New York: The Psychohistory Press, 1974.

Derrida, Jacques. *Of Grammatology.* Tr. Gayatri Chakravorty Spivak. Baltimore: The Johns Hopkins University Press, 1974.

Douthwaite, Julia. *The Wild Girl, Natural Man and the Monster: Dangerous Experiments in the Age of Enlightenment.* Chicago University Press, 2002.

Dugaw, Dianne. "'High Change in Change Alley': Popular Ballads and Emergent Capitalism in the Eighteenth Century," *Eighteenth-Century Life,* 22 (May 1998).
"The Popular Marketing of 'Old Ballads': The Ballad Revival and Eighteenth-Century Antiquarianism Reconsidered," *Eighteenth-Century Studies,* 21 (1987).

Duncan, Ian. *Modern Romance and Transformations of the Novel: the Gothic, Scott, Dickens.* Cambridge University Press, 1992.
"The Pathos of Abstraction: Adam Smith, Ossian, and Samuel Johnson," *Scotland and the Borders of Romanticism.* Ed. Leith Davis, Ian Duncan, Janet Sorensen. Cambridge University Press, 2004.
Scott's Shadow: the Novel in Romantic Edinburgh. Princeton University Press, 2007.
"The Upright Corpse: Hogg, National Literature and the Uncanny," *Studies in Hogg and his World* 5 (1994).

Fabian, Johannes. *Time and the Other: How Anthropology Makes its Object.* New York: Columbia University Press, 2002.

Favret, Mary. *Romantic Correspondence: Women, Politics and the Fiction of Letters.* Cambridge University Press, 1993.

"Telling Tales About Genre: Poetry in the Romantic Novel," *Studies in the Novel*, 26. 3 (October, 1994).

Ferris, Ina. *The Achievement of Literary Authority: Gender, History, and the Waverley Novels.* Ithaca: Cornell University Press, 1991.

"Melancholy, Memory, and the 'Narrative Situation' of History in Post-Enlightenment Scotland," in *Scotland and the Borders of Romanticism*. Ed. Leith Davis, Ian Duncan, Janet Sorensen. Cambridge University Press, 2004.

"Pedantry And The Question Of Enlightenment History: The Figure Of The Antiquary In Scott," *European Romantic Review*, 13. 3 (2002).

Festa, Lynn. *Sentimental Figures of Empire in Eighteenth-Century Britain and France.* Baltimore: The Johns Hopkins University Press, 2006.

Fielding, Penny. *Writing and Orality: Nationality, Culture and Nineteenth-Century Scottish Fiction.* Oxford: Clarendon Press, 1996.

Fine, Gary Alan. "Children and Their Culture: Exploring Newell's Paradox," *Western Folklore*, 39.

Foucault, Michel. *The Order of Things: An Archaeology of the Human Sciences.* New York: Vintage Books, 1973.

Friedman, Albert B. *The Ballad Revival: Studies in the Influence of Popular on Sophisticated Poetry.* University of Chicago Press, 1961.

Gagnier, Regenia. *Subjectivities: A History of Self-Representation in Britain, 1832–1920.* Oxford University Press, 1991.

Galbraith, Gretchen R. *Reading Lives: Reconstructing Childhood, Books, and Schools in Britain, 1870–1920.* New York: St. Martin's Press, 1997.

Goodman, Kevis Bea. *Georgic Modernity and British Romanticism: Poetry and the Mediation of History.* Cambridge University Press, 2004.

"Making Time for History: Wordsworth, the New Historicism, and the Apocalyptic Fallacy," *Studies in Romanticism*, 35. 4 (Winter, 1996).

Goring, Paul. *The Rhetoric of Sensibility in Eighteenth Century Culture.* Cambridge University Press, 2005.

Groom, Nick. *The Making of Percy's* Reliques. Oxford: Clarendon Press, 1999.

Grylls, David. *Guardians and Angels: Parents and Children in Nineteenth-Century Literature.* London: Faber and Faber, 1978.

Guyer, Foster E. "C'est nous qui sommes les anciens," *Modern Language Notes*, 36. 5 (May, 1921).

Haughton, Hugh. *The Chatto Book of Nonsense Poetry.* London: Chatto & Windus, 1988.

Heywood, Colin. *A History of Childhood.* Cambridge: Polity Press, 2001.

Higonnet, Anne. *Pictures of Innocence: The History and Crisis of Ideal Childhood.* London: Thames and Hudson Ltd., 1998.

Hillers, Barbara. "Dialogue or Monologue? Lullabies in Scottish Gaelic Tradition," *Litreachas & Eachdraidh/Literature & History: Rannsachadh na Ga\idhlig.* Ed. Michel Byrne *et al.* University of Glasgow, 2006.

Hofkosh, Sonia. *Sexual Politics and the Romantic Author.* Cambridge University Press, 1998.

Jacobus, Mary. *Tradition and Experiment in Wordsworth's Lyrical Ballads* (1798). Oxford: Clarendon Press, 1976.

Jones, Catherine. *Literary Memory: Scott's Waverley Novels and the Psychology of Narrative.* Lewisburg, PA: Bucknell University Press, 2003.

Jones, Chris. *Radical Sensibility: Literature and Ideas in the 1790s.* London: Routledge, 1993.

Keach, William. *Shelley's Style.* New York: Methuen, 1984.

Kerkering, Jack. "'We are Five-and-Forty': Meter and National Identity in Walter Scott," *Studies in Romanticism*, 40. 1 (Spring, 2001).

Kittler, Friedrich A. *Discourse Networks 1800/1900.* Tr. Michael Metteer, with Chris Cullens. Stanford University Press, 1990.

Klancher, Jon P. *The Making of English Reading Audiences, 1790–1832.* Madison: University of Wisconsin Press, 1987.

Knutson, Karla. "'Lessons Fairer than Flowers': Mary Eliza Haweis's Chaucer for Children and Models of Friendship," in *Studies in Medievalism: Defining Neomedievalism(s) II*. Ed. Karl Fugelso. Vol. xx. Cambridge: D. S. Brewer, 2011, 79–97.

Lamb, Jonathan. "Modern Metamorphoses and Disgraceful Tales," *Critical Inquiry*, 28. 1 (Autumn, 2001).

Land, Stephen K. "The Silent Poet: An Aspect of Wordsworth's Semantic Theory," *University of Toronto Quarterly*. 42. 2 (Winter, 1973).

Lane, Harlan. *The Wild Boy of Aveyron.* Cambridge, MA: Harvard University Press, 1976.

Lee, Yoon Sun. *Nationalism and Irony: Burke, Scott, Carlyle.* New York: Oxford University Press, 2004.

Luhmann, Niklas. *Art as a Social System.* Tr. Eva M. Knodt. Stanford University Press, 2000.

Lynch, Deidre. *The Economy of Character: Novels, Market Culture, and the Business of Inner Meaning.* University of Chicago Press, 1998.

Manning, Peter J. "Reading Wordsworth's Revisions," *Studies in Romanticism*, 22 (1983).

Manning, Susan. "Antiquarianism, Balladry, and the Rehabilitation of Romance," in *The Cambridge History of English Romantic Literature.* Ed. James Chandler. Cambridge University Press, 2003.

"Antiquarianism, the Scottish Science of Man, and the Emergence of Modern Disciplinarity," in *Scotland and the Borders of Romanticism.* Ed. Leith Davis, Ian Duncan, Janet Sorensen. Cambridge University Press, 2004.

Markidou, Vassiliki. "'Bubbles' and Female Verse: A Reading of Anna Laeticia Barbauld's 'Washing Day,'" *Critical Survey*, 19.2 (May, 2007).

Maxwell, Richard. "Inundations of Time: A Definition of Scott's Originality," *ELH*, 68 (2001).

Mayo, Robert. "The Contemporaneity of the *Lyrical Ballads*," *PMLA*, 69 (1954), 491.

McDonagh, Josephine. *Child Murder and British Culture, 1720–1900.* Cambridge University Press, 2003.

McLane, Maureen N. *Balladeering, Minstrelsy, and the Making of British Romantic Poetry.* Cambridge University Press, 2008.

Romanticism and the Human Sciences. Cambridge University Press, 2000.

Meek, Ronald L. *Social Science and the Ignoble Savage.* Cambridge University Press, 1976.

Turgot on Progress, Sociology and Economics. Cambridge University Press, 1973.

Mintz, Steven. *Huck's Raft: A History of American Childhood.* Cambridge, MA: Harvard University Press, 2004.

Morss, John R. *The Biologising of Childhood: Developmental Psychology and the Darwinian Myth.* London: Lawrence Erlbaum Associates, 1990.

Neumeister, Mirjam, ed. *The Changing Face of Childhood: British Children's Portraits and their Influence in Europe.* Frankfurt and Cologne: Städel Museum and DuMont Literatur und Kunst Verlag, 2007.

Newman, Steve. *Ballad Collection, Lyric, and the Canon: The Call of the Popular from the Restoration to the New Criticism.* Philadelphia: University of Pennsylvania Press, 2007.

Nietzsche, Friedrich. *Untimely Meditations.* Tr. R. J. Hollingdale. Cambridge University Press, 1983.

Nussbaum, Felicity A. *The Limits of the Human: Fictions of Anomaly, Race, and Gender in the Long Eighteenth Century.* Cambridge University Press, 2003.

Torrid Zones: Maternity, Sexuality, and Empire in Eighteenth-Century English Narratives. Baltimore: The Johns Hopkins University Press, 1995.

Parrish, Stephen Maxfield. *The Art of the Lyrical Ballads.* Cambridge, MA: Harvard University Press, 1973.

Pattison, Robert. *The Child Figure in English Literature.* Athens, GA: University of Georgia Press, 1978.

Paulin, Tom. *The Faber Book of Vernacular Verse.* London: Faber & Faber, 1990.

Perry, Seamus. "Coleridge and Wordsworth: Imagination, Accidence, and Inevitability," in *1800: the New Lyrical Ballads.* Ed. Nicola Trott and Seamus Perry. London: Palgrave, 2001.

Pfau, Thomas. *Wordsworth's Profession: Form, Class, and the Logic of Early Romantic Cultural Production.* Stanford University Press, 1997.

Phillips, Mark Salber. *Society and Sentiment: Genres of Historical Writing in Britain, 1740–1820.* Princeton University Press, 2000.

Picker, John. *Victorian Soundscapes.* Oxford University Press, 2003.

Pickering, Samuel F. *John Locke and Children's Books in Eighteenth-Century England.* Knoxville: University of Tennessee Press, 1981.

Pinch, Adela. *Strange Fits of Passion: Epistemologies of Emotion, Hume to Austen.* Stanford University Press, 1996.

Pinker, Steven. *The Language Instinct: How the Mind Creates Language.* New York: Harper Collins, 1995.

Plotz, Judith. *Romanticism and the Vocation of Childhood.* London: Palgrave, 2001.

Plumb, J. H. "The New World of Children in Eighteenth-Century England," *Past and Present,* 67 (1975).

Pollock, Linda. *Forgotten Children: Parent–Child Relations from 1500 to 1900.* Cambridge University Press, 1983.

Price, Leah. *The Anthology and the Rise of the Novel: From Richardson to George Eliot.* Cambridge University Press, 2000.

Quint, David. *Epic and Empire.* Princeton University Press, 1993.

Richardson, Alan. *British Romanticism and the Science of the Mind.* Cambridge University Press, 2001.

    Literature, Education, and Romanticism: Reading as Social Practice, 1780–1832. Cambridge University Press, 1994.

Richmond, Velma Bourgeois. *Chaucer as Children's Literature: Retellings from the Victorian and Edwardian Eras.* Jefferson, NC: McFarland & Co., 2004.

Rowland, Ann Wierda. "The Childish Origins of Literary Studies," in *Child's Children: Ballad Study and its Legacies.* Ed. Barbara Hillers and Joseph Harris. Wissenschaftlicher Verlag Trier, 2011.

    "'The Fause Nourice Sang': Childhood, Child Murder and the Formalism of the Scottish Ballad Revival," in *Scotland and the Borders of Romanticism.* Ed. Ian Duncan, Leith Davis, Janet Sorensen. Cambridge University Press, 2004.

    "Romantic Poetry and the Romantic Novel," in *The Cambridge Companion to British Romantic Poetry.* Ed. James Chandler and Maureen N. McLane. Cambridge University Press, 2008.

    "Sentimental Fiction," in *The Cambridge Companion to Romantic Fiction.* Ed. Katie Trumpener and Richard Maxwell. Cambridge University Press, 2008.

    "Wordsworth's Children of the Revolution," *Studies in English Literature,* 41 (Autumn, 2001).

Shearer, Edna Aston. "Wordsworth and Coleridge Marginalia in a Copy of Richard Payne Knight's *Analytical Inquiry into the Principles of Taste.*" *Huntington Library Quarterly,* 1 (1937).

Simpson, David. "Is Literary History the History of Everything? The Case for 'Antiquarian' History," *SubStance,* 88 (1999).

Siskin, Clifford. *The Historicity of Romantic Discourse.* Oxford University Press, 1988.

    The Work of Writing: Literature and Social Change in Britain, 1700–1830. Baltimore: The Johns Hopkins University Press, 1998.

Sorensen, Janet. *The Grammar of Empire in Eighteenth-Century British Writing.* Cambridge University Press, 2000.

Spadafora, David. *The Idea of Progress in Eighteenth-Century Britain.* New Haven, CT: Yale University Press, 1990.

St. Clair, William. *The Reading Nation in the Romantic Period.* Cambridge University Press, 2004.

Starr, G. Gabrielle. *Lyric Generations: Poetry and the Novel in the Long Eighteenth Century.* Baltimore: The Johns Hopkins University Press, 2004.

Steedman, Carolyn. *Strange Dislocations: Childhood and the Idea of Human Interiority, 1780–1930.* Cambridge, MA: Harvard University Press, 1995.

Steward, James Christen. *The New Child: British Art and the Origins of Modern Childhood, 1730–1830*. Berkeley, CA: University Art Museum and Pacific Film Archive, 1995.

Stewart, Susan. *Crimes of Writing: Problems in the Containment of Representation*. Durham, NC: Duke University Press, 1994.

   On Longing: Narratives of the Miniature, the Gigantic, the Souvenir, the Collection. Durham: Duke University Press, 1993.

Stone, Lawrence. *The Family, Sex and Marriage in England, 1500–1800*. London: Weidenfeld and Nicolson, 1977.

Summerfield, Geoffrey. *Fantasy and Reason: Children's Literature in the Eighteenth Century*. London: Methuen and Co., 1984.

Sutton-Smith, Brian. *Children's Folklore: A Source Book*. New York: Garland Publishing, 1995.

Swann, Karen. "'Martha's Name,' or The Scandal of 'The Thorn,'" *Dwelling in Possibility: Women Poets and Critics on Poetry*. Ed. Yopie Prins, Maeera Shreiber. Ithaca, NY: Cornell University Press, 1997.

Sweet, Rosemary. "Antiquaries and Antiquities in Eighteenth-Century England," *Eighteenth-Century Studies*, 34. 2 (2001).

Thomas, Keith. *Man and the Natural World: Changing Attitudes in England, 1500–1800*. London: Allen Lane, 1983.

Todd, Janet. *Sensibility: An Introduction*. London: Methuen, 1986.

Tompkins, J. M. S. *The Popular Novel in England: 1770–1800*. Lincoln, NE: University of Nebraska Press, 1961.

Trumpener, Katie. *Bardic Nationalism: The Romantic Novel and the British Empire*. Princeton University Press, 1997.

   "Tales for Child Readers," *Cambridge Companion to Fiction in the Romantic Period*. Ed. Richard Maxwell, Katie Trumpener. Cambridge University Press, 2008.

Vincent, David. "The Decline of the Oral Tradition in Popular Culture," in *Popular Culture and Custom in Nineteenth-Century England*. Ed. Robert D. Storch. London: Croom Helm, 1982.

Wahrman, Dror. *The Making of the Modern Self: Identity and Culture in Eighteenth-Century England*. New Haven, CT: Yale University Press, 2004.

Wells, G. A. "Man and Nature: An Elucidation of Coleridge's Rejection of Herder's Thought," *The Journal of English and Germanic Philology*, 51. 3 (July, 1952).

Wheeler, Roxann. *The Complexion of Race: Categories of Difference in Eighteenth-Century British Culture*. Philadelphia: University of Pennsylvania Press, 2000.

Williams, Ioan. *Sir Walter Scott on Novelists and Fiction*. New York: Barnes & Noble, Inc., 1968.

Williams, Raymond. *The Country and the City*. New York: Oxford University Press, 1973.

Wilson, Kathleen. *The Island Race: Englishness, Empire and Gender in the Eighteenth Century*. London: Routledge, 2003.

Wolfson, Susan J. "The Illusion of Mastery: Wordsworth's Revisions of 'The Drowned Man of Esthwaite,' 1799, 1805, 1850," *PMLA*, 99 (1984).

Wordsworth, Jonathan. "As with the Silence of the Thought," *High Romantic Argument: Essays for M. H. Abrams*. Ed. Lawrence Lipking. Ithaca: Cornell University Press, 1981.

Wright, John. *Shelley's Myth of Metaphor*. Athens, GA: University of Georgia Press, 1970.

Wrightson, Keith. *English Society 1580–1680*. New Brunswick: Rutgers University Press, 2003, 1983.

Wu, Duncan. *Wordsworth: An Inner Life*. Oxford: Blackwell, 2002.

Zimmerman, Sarah. *Romanticism, Lyricism, and History*. Albany: State University of New York Press, 1999.

Index

Aarsleff, Hans, 40, 61, 69, 79, 267
acculturation, 18, 32, 217, 243
Addison, Joseph, 175, 202, 267
Aikin, Anna Laetitia (*see also* Barbauld), 145–148
  "On the Pleasure Derived from Objects of Terror," 145
Aikin, John, 145
Akenside, Mark, 172–174, 194
Alcott, Bronson, 9
America, 9, 35, 43–47, 48, 49–52, 55, 73, 77, 97
analogy, 12, 15, 16, 25, 26, 27, 28–29, 30, 33, 34, 35, 40, 45, 48, 51, 52, 54, 58, 59, 60, 63, 65, 68–69, 71–77, 100–101, 107, 136–137, 163, 169, 177, 183
ancients, 29–34, 37, 91, 264
Anderson, Benedict, 57, 59, 191
animal, 13, 29, 44, 52–54, 55, 62, 63, 81, 84, 86, 109–111, 113–116, 121–135, 221, 271; animal language, 113, 121–128; animal sounds, 115, 123–128, 132
anthropology, 10, 13, 16, 29, 45, 59, 66, 76, 164, 172, 226
antiquarianism, 20–22, 163–164, 176, 177, 189, 191, 196, 198–200, 207–214, 215, 225–226, 232, 233, 235, 237, 239, 241, 259, 278, 279; antiquarian collections, 18, 27, 166, 169–172, 184, 196–197, 198–199, 203, 225, 235, 237, 241, 243, 248, 258; and formalism, 21, 196–198, 199, 214–218, 237, 242–243, 251; and historicism, 167–169, 198–200; and nostalgia, 166–169
antiquity, 30–34, 44, 96, 122, 137, 170, 184–185, 203, 204, 212, 215
Ariès, Philippe, 8, 10, 262
articulate speech, 78, 81, 83–84, 87, 122, 149, 150
artificial language, 83, 87, 148, 153, 154, 156; and signs, 88, 89, 150, 156
audition, 165, 177, 191–192; and the aural, 19, 147, 192, 197, 225, 253
authenticity, 105, 140, 142, 167, 169, 170, 190, 192, 208–211, 237, 278, 280
autobiography, 26, 168, 172, 251, 256–258, 261
Aytoun, William, 167, 275

Babenroth, Charles A., 263
"Babes in the Wood topos," 59, 71
Bacon, Francis, 30, 69
ballad, 3, 4, 21, 102, 111, 125, 126, 128, 136, 138, 139–140, 141, 148, 165, 166, 167, 169–172, 175, 184, 189–193, 194–198, 200–203, 204, 205, 207–214, 215–216, 218, 224, 225, 233, 236, 237, 238, 239, 240, 242, 243, 250, 274, 275, 278, 279, 280; and collection, 5, 156, 167, 192, 208, 214, 237; and orality, 20, 156, 164, 166, 191, 201; popular, 5, 167, 170, 192, 198–203, 213, 218; and preservation, 4, 20, 55, 166, 189, 191–192, 196, 205, 211, 232; and revival, 59, 195, 197, 208, 209, 216, 237, 242–245, 278; and transmission, 20, 165, 166, 169–172, 190, 197, 203, 209–211, 214, 215–218, 223
Barbauld, Anna Letitia, (*see also* Aikin) 16–19, 128–133, 134, 139–140, 163, 173, 175, 179, 186, 263, 273, 275, 276; *The British Novelists*, 139, 163; *Mrs. Barbauld's Lessons for Children*, 128–133; "Washing-Day," 16–19, 179
Barrie, J.M., 110
Bates, Katharine Lee, 140
"Battle of the Ancients and the Moderns," 264
Bayly, Anselm, 74
Beattie, James, 69, 171–172, 173
Benjamin, Walter, 35, 57, 184
Bett, Henry, 203
Bewell, Alan, 62, 76, 241, 242, 265, 268
biogenetic law, 13
biology, 13, 262, 263
birds, 53, 84, 119–120, 122–125, 132–133, 134, 147, 173, 179, 188, 221, 241
Blackwell, Thomas, 4, 69, 91–92, 95–96, 99, 103–107, 153, 224, 242, 247
Blair, Hugh, 4, 69, 76, 80, 88, 89, 90, 91, 93–94, 96, 97, 99–100, 102–103, 139, 151, 155, 207
Blake, William, 125
Boas, George, 10
Boswell, James, 133
Bourdieu, Pierre, 211, 217

298

CAMBRIDGE STUDIES IN ROMANTICISM

General Editor
JAMES CHANDLER, University of Chicago

Made in the USA
Middletown, DE
21 May 2016